Doing Business in Latin America

Doing Business in Latin America integrates practitioners' and scholars' ideas to examine business conducted in Latin America through the lens of international business and globalization. It introduces, discusses, and explains in detail the historical, economic, cultural, political, and technological impacts of globalization and business conduct in Latin American countries. It also considers the contemporary business environment of the area, looking at how current country and regional factors have affected the process of starting and operating businesses. Finally, it examines emerging trends that will impact the future of the region. With its combination of contemporary analysis and historical discussion, this book is a vital tool to all scholars and practitioners with an interest in the current Latin American business environment.

John E. Spillan, is Professor of Business at the University of North Carolina at Pembroke, USA. His research interests center on crisis management, international marketing, entrepreneurship, and international business with a specific interest in Latin America and Eastern Europe. His articles have appeared in several leading journals including the *Journal of Teaching in International Business*, The *Journal of Small Business Strategy*, and the *Journal of Business in Developing Nations*.

Nicholas Virzi is Senior Vice President of the American Chamber of Commerce, as well as a director at the Private Sector Council for Competitiveness in Guatemala. He is a conference speaker for entities active in Latin America, such as the IMF, the United Nations, the Organization of American States, and several universities in the region, where he talks about issues pertaining to trade and competitiveness, business ethics, and growth and political issues.

Mauricio Garita is a Professor at the Universidad Rafael Landivar and Universidad Galileo, Guatemala, specializing in international economy, game theory and micro-economics. He has worked as a consultant in several international organizations, and was the director of economic policy in the Secretariat for Economic Integration for Central America, as well as economic director at the Federation of Industry Chambers of Central America.

Doing Business in Latin America

Challenges and Opportunities

John E. Spillan, Nicholas Virzi, and Mauricio Garita

Routledge
Taylor & Francis Group

NEW YORK AND LONDON

First published 2014
by Routledge
711 Third Avenue, New York, NY 10017

and by Routledge
2 Park Square, Milton Park, Abingdon, Oxon OX14 4RN

Routledge is an imprint of the Taylor & Francis Group, an informa business

Library of Congress Cataloging-in-Publication Data
Spillan, John E.
Doing business in Latin America : challenges and opportunities / John E. Spillan, Nicholas Virzi, Mauricio Garita. — 1 Edition.
pages cm
Includes bibliographical references and index.
1. Latin America—Economic conditions—1945- 2. New business enterprises—Latin America. 3. Corporate culture—Latin America. 4. Marketing—Latin America. I. Title.
HC125.S695 2013
330.98—dc23
2013038259

ISBN: 978–0–415–89598–9
ISBN: 978–0–415–89599–6
ISBN: 978–0–203–08508–0

Typeset in Minion Pro
by Swales & Willis Ltd, Exeter, Devon, UK

Printed and bound in the United States of America by
Edwards Brothers Malloy

Dedication

I dedicate this book to my wife, Martha, who has been there for me every step of our journey over the past three and a half decades. Her unending love and encouragement has pushed me to accomplish higher levels of achievement than I ever thought I could.
John (Jack) E. Spillan PhD 2013

I dedicate this book to my beloved mother, Maria Eugenia Arroyave de Virzi, who passed away as I began this work. RIP.
Nicholas Virzi, 2013

I dedicate this book to my father and mother for believing in me. To my wife for understanding, for supporting me, and for the love. To Jack for the great opportunity and to Nick for encouraging my dreams. Finally to P&M for cheering me up always.
Mauricio Garita PhD, 2013

CONTENTS

PREFACE

Success in today's globalized business environment requires deep knowledge of various areas, and the willingness to engage in commerce across not just geographic areas, but cross-culturally and environmentally as well.

Globalization is here to stay. The globalization process has intensified the need for business professionals to educate themselves in the ways of business in foreign markets. Wherever we go in the world, the principles and practices of business will vary from place to place. With this in mind, this book focuses on doing business in Latin America.

While conventional wisdom dictates that Latin America should be easily accessible and readily understood by Americans living basically right next door, a diligent study of the region would quickly bring to light that business transactions are substantially more complex than simple intuition would suggest. The geographic terrain, the infrastructure, the language, and culture, the political-economic climate all factor into the complexities that must be considered when doing business in Latin America.

The definition of Latin America varies depending on what international organization one consults: the IMF, ECLA C, World Bank, etc.[1] Some organizations include the Caribbean, others do not. Some consider Puerto Rico, others do not. The consensus among all is that the "big three" are the ABC countries—Argentina, Brazil, and Chile—and that Mexico is worthy of particular note. Their economies, business development, and responses to the modern world of commerce have shown impressive results, even during the latest major recessionary period. Independent of their size and geopolitical and economic importance, all of the major countries in the region have made strong advances in their processes of modernization and development. Although the region as a whole has progressed, the process of modernization has not been linear, or even within the region. Various countries lag in the process of development exemplified by Argentina, Brazil, Chile, and Mexico, and even Argentina and Brazil seem to be taking some missteps. The lesser developed countries, or LDCs, continue to struggle with corruption, poverty, drug trafficking, and political instability.

For a plethora of reasons made clear later on in this book, many Latin American countries have not grown or developed as fast as might have been anticipated. Despite improvements, they are not living up to their full economic potential. Having lived, traveled, and studied in Latin America for decades, the authors have seen this first hand, noting progress in certain regions that would have been unimaginable twenty years ago, but also a distinct lack of progress in certain other parts that serves only to bring further to light the disparities that plague the region and frustrate the agent seeking to do business in Latin America.

Perceiving the latent potential through the manifest problems in the region is a valuable insight that this book provides. If one understands the language, knows the culture, and has the multicultural mindset and patience to empathize with different ways of doing business, the profit potential is large. That is what this book is about.

Very few books on Latin America provide the detail and perspective of this book. The authors have lived, worked and conducted business in Latin America, and still do. This allows us to proffer a more authentic perspective. Our version of doing business in Latin America is not just a superficial rehash of other people's trite observations (quite often wrong and misleading). Our integration of scholarly ideas with real-life observations and original case studies constitutes an important value-added attribute of this book.

Although intended for practitioners, this book has great academic merits and value. The facts, case studies, and timely data and analysis presented herein provide a one-stop shop, if you will, for academicians who are new to the study of the region. This would be ideal for MBA students taking a first course on Latin American business, politics, economics, etc. Of course, business people, whether new to the region, or seasoned, who want a different view of the what, why, where, and how of doing business in Latin America will gain the most from this book.

In this book we go in to significant detailed discussions about the geography, economics, culture, and marketing characteristics that exist, and some of the dos and don'ts of doing business in various countries in Latin America. For example, one area that is not evident in other contemporary books about doing business in the region relates to the infrastructure, how difficult it is to move goods from one geographic area to another—for instance, the highlands of Bolivia and Peru or the deteriorating highway structure in Guatemala and other Central American countries. Institutional quality is another neglected variable. Infrastructural obstacles greatly increase the costs of transportation and shipping. Institutional obstacles greatly increase transaction costs, to which we must add the costs of corruption. Truly these country factors have a major impact on the conduct of business in the region. Make no mistake, these neglected, unstudied factors can make or break you if you are doing business in Latin America.

Another significant constraint to doing business in Latin America is the violence associated with the intense drug trafficking that has become a major problem in countries such as Mexico, Guatemala, Honduras, Bolivia, and Colombia. The risk level is without a doubt elevated to alarming levels, but this doesn't mean that you can't do business in these regions. It depends on one's risk tolerance. How to identify, diagnose, and negotiate the risk involved in doing business in these parts of Latin America is one of the things we help you with in this book.

We talk about all of the elements that make business feasible or infeasible in Latin America. In this book, we detail the pros and cons of doing business in the region, with the intent of providing an authentic and timely picture of the real business environment in Latin America. We must admit that the subject matter of this book is constantly evolving, constantly changing. When an enterprise makes the decision to do business in the region, and begins its analysis, and contemplates its potential paths of business development, it will likely have to update its stock of operating knowledge. What we provide is the first light, we point the way. Hopefully, we will be able to provide annual editions that keep the interested business people current and knowledgeable about the extensive opportunities available in Latin American business environment.

In short, there are at least two possible audiences for this book. One is the undergraduate and graduate students who need to understand the contemporary business environment in Latin America. Since this book is written from an integrated academic and practitioner point of view, students can use it for study of a particular country or for use in exploring actual business ventures in a given country.

Practitioners make up the other audience for this book, those interested in exploring the international business background and activities in Latin America, specifically in the seven focal countries.[2] There is a relative dearth of books focused on domestic and international business activity in Latin America. This book would bridge that gap and provide a foundation for a more in-depth understanding of what business opportunities exist in this region, how businesses operate and thrive there, as well as which internal and external factors affect the ability to do business in Latin America.

The book topic is timely. Most universities in the US have departments of Latin American studies. In many business schools there are specific tracks associated with the study of international business and business in Latin America. A comprehensive book in English will bridge important knowledge gaps, which currently exist, inasmuch as many of the best books on Latin American business are in Spanish. This book could be used in a course on international business as a supplement, or could be used as a primary book for the study of Latin American business. Either way, it provides an in-depth discussion of the contemporary business principles, theories and/or practices concerning business activity in Latin American countries.

This book will present case studies on various industries, sourced from private sources, publications such as *The Financial Times* and *The Economist*, international organizations such as the IMF, WEF and CEPAL, financial statements and press conferences from the major multinationals with operations in Latin America, and personal interviews conducted with important business, economic, and political personalities, as well as local press experts.

NOTES

1. The United Nations Economic Commission for Latin America and the Caribbean includes 33 nations. See http://websie.eclac.cl/infest/ajax/cepalstat.asp?carpeta=estadisticas.
2. Argentina, Brazil, Chile, Colombia, Peru, Mexico, Guatemala.

1

INTRODUCTION TO THE LATIN
AMERICAN BUSINESS ENVIRONMENT

OPENING CASE: BUSINESS CASE—OPEN ENGLISH

Open English was established in Caracas, Venezuela in 2006 as an online English learning company. Over time the company expanded its offices to Bogotá, Columbia, Sao Paulo, Brazil, Miami, Florida and Panama City. The business is a multi-million dollars enterprise with an estimated 80,000 users in Latin America.

Andres Moreno, the CEO, originally started the company when he was 25 years old. His first business venture was Optimal English, an English learning academy for international executives. With his experience operating the English learning business in Latin America Mr. Moreno and his classmate, Wilmer Sarmientos, formed a partnership. In 2008, the company had just three employees and targeted a very small market. During their tenure administering the business, Mr. Moreno and Mr. Sarmientos noticed broader business opportunities in other parts of Latin America (Miami Herald, 2012). As such, they developed an online learning system that allows students to tune in from their computers to a live class with native English speakers. The program works by just having an Internet connection anywhere in the world. With this approach a student can continue his/her learning despite travels or other activities that would generally preclude them from attending traditional classroom lectures.

This online learning business strategy focuses on three traits: achievable goals, human interaction and fun. Students can achieve their English speaking goals by improving or expanding their English speaking capabilities; they can advance their human interaction because the classes are live with instructors who are native English speakers; and they can have fun because the classes are dynamic and entertaining (Andres Moreno, 2013). All of these program components have become part of the Company's marketing strategy. By incorporating creativity in their advertising campaigns by using English language comedy that can be understood by persons who speak both English and Spanish, they have livened up the message and attracted a broader client market. Additionally, their advertising campaign has been so popular that their Facebook page has people in Latin America commenting on the advertisements. Presently, the company employs 1,000 people and, as mentioned earlier, serves an estimated 80,000 students in 20 countries. In 2013, they started an expansion to Brazil by using venture funding of $43 million dollars (TC, 2012). In 2012, the company grew 350% in their revenues and was expecting a 300% growth in 2013.

Their aim, apart from Brazil and other Latin American clientele, is the Asian market, with China specifically in mind. They will be using the same model that has helped them develop a $43 million dollar company by focusing on students in the middle class, businesses that need English to achieve their business goals and for other clients that need continuing improvement in their English proficiency.

This opening case provides an overview of a business that started small and took advantage of the opportunities existing in Latin America. Developing smart business strategies, being deliberate in its focus and using hard work gave this business the success it always desired. This case illustrates how people with ideas in the digital age can build a company that can reach all of Latin America. This is just one example of how innovative business people can take advantage of the challenges and opportunities that exist in this land of great potential.

In this chapter the aspects of business trends, combined with examples of popular business ventures, will give an idea of what is currently happening in Latin America and what will happen in the near future. Latin America is now a strategic region for investment and has the capability of expanding and competing with other regions through innovation, product development and localization. This chapter elaborates on the importance of these factors and how they have influenced the economic development of the region.

INTRODUCTION

Latin America is no longer the closed-off mercantilist system it once was, where trade was viewed as a zero-sum game, made up of only winners and losers. The forces of globalization, the exchange of ideas, information, and technology, and the processes of democratic consolidation have served to improve and expand Latin American market systems and thus potential opportunities for business investment in the region.

However, a one-size-fits-all approach to doing business in Latin America will not work. The important changes just mentioned have not occurred uniformly across the Latin American region. Some areas of the Latin American region, indeed, seem bent on a return to the anti-foreign, anti-trade past. The foreign investor seeking to do business in Latin America should be forewarned. Those countries embracing the challenges posed by the globalized economy will provide different business opportunities than those opting for more statist-oriented developmental models. This book will help readers determine which economies are more likely to prosper and thereby offer better business opportunities for the foreseeable future.

Latin America is a region worthy of further consideration by both academics and practitioners. The richness of opportunities is matched by its incredible diversity on many fronts: geography, ethnic, and racial composition; European heritage, religion, historical experience with the US—among many other lines of differentiation. In addition to the Caribbean, the region consists of 19 large, medium, and small countries in Central and South America.[1] It has a combined population of more than 500 million, and three main languages: Spanish, Portuguese, and English. The biggest economies are those of Mexico, Brazil, Colombia, Venezuela, Argentina, Peru, and Chile.

Without any doubt, Latin America represents a huge business potential for venturing entrepreneurs, especially as investment opportunities seem to be souring in the developed world. Investment and business opportunities in Latin America are growing, particularly in those countries that have committed to taking the first steps in developing efficient market systems. Rich in natural resources and with a predominantly young and hard-working population, the region has shown an ability to learn from US businesses, and others around the globe, and to successfully turn new capital investments into wealth and welfare, albeit with mixed success.

The business terrain in Latin America is ready to be worked. In a sharp break from its recent past, Latin America is a region with a predominantly market-oriented education and culture. The business class there is savvy. It speaks the same language and utilizes the same principles and concepts as do American business people and others from around the world. The region has the potential to grow tremendously, given the proper institutional settings. Culturally, Latin America is much closer to the United States than many people realize, and can thus present a much easier path for entry by Americans into its markets than is the case in other developing areas of the world. This is particularly so as the United States becomes more like Latin America, given the surging influence of Hispanics in the United States.

Care should be taken not to overstate the case. Much progress has yet to be made. Despite signal advancements, Latin America can still be characterized as a land of contradictions. For instance, it is rich in resources, but many of its people are poor. Sentiments of opposition to "Yankee imperialism" still abound, but most people want to buy American, and, given the chance, they'd want to be Americans. During the past fifty years, the Latin American population has grown to almost 600 million people (World Bank, 2013). However, GDP per capita growth has not kept pace with population growth.

Even though Latin America has presented a record of stable economic growth over the past decade, the sustainability of this progress is not guaranteed, especially as certain governments begin tinkering with ways to undermine the democratic process and efficient markets. With its incomplete and sub-par infrastructure, along with its political uncertainties, anything can happen to derail progress. Unfortunately for Latin America as a whole, in the past this has always been the case.

But all is not bad news. One of the major advantages of the large, growing population is the immediate access to a potential labor pool that is not only large, but also young. This is important for the future growth and development of the region, as it lowers expectations of future wages in the medium run. Latin America, for the most part, can expect to enjoy a positive demographic boom in the economic sense of the word—more workers, more consumers, more investment and employment opportunities, more democracy and, it is to be hoped, political stability.

It helps to tell the reader where the book is going. The remainder of this chapter is organized around several introductory, contemporary topics that have had a major influence on how business is done in Latin American countries. First, we discuss the geography of the region and how integrated it really is. Then we go on to discuss the various opportunities presented by the multiple phenomena of globalization, the rise of the middle class, the ensuing democratic consolidation, and the spread of markets and democracy throughout the region. After a brief treatment of the opportunities posed by these new phenomena, we move on to a frank discussion of the challenges to business and development still posed by poor infrastructure, cultural difficulties with modernization, social conflict, political uncertainty, and suboptimal institutions. These are very important issues that need to be taken into consideration when doing business in Latin America.

GEOGRAPHY: WHAT AND WHERE IS LATIN AMERICA?

As discussed in the Preface, the region known as Latin America consists of 19 countries of differing size, while the region of Latin America and the Caribbean is considered to have 33 countries, according to the United Nations.[2] Before getting into a detailed substantive discussion of the theoretical and practical concepts and issues of doing business in Latin America, it is important to understand the geography of the area being discussed.

Figure 1.1 presents a map of Latin America (19 countries), from Tierra del Fuego in the southernmost part of the continent in Chile all the way to Mexico on the US border. As one can see, it is a vast landmass. It has both densely concentrated population centers, such as Buenos Aires in Argentina, as well as sparsely populated areas, as in the case of whole regions of Brazil. Brazil, of course, is the largest Latin American country, the fifth largest in the entire world by area and population (Laura, 2010; Rosenberg, 2011). Brazil is also an important member of the BRIC nations, a grouping of emerging economies (Brazil, Russia, India, and China) once considered to be the fastest-growing group of nations in the world. It is noteworthy that, since 2010, Brazil and India have stalled, and many analysts see Mexico as the Latin American country with the strongest potential of growth through trade (Latino.Foxnews.com, 2012).

Latin America's geography makes the region a strategic imperative for growth-oriented enterprises and entrepreneurs. As a region, Latin America is conveniently situated between north and south, providing the most direct conduit for east–west trade. Uniting the world's two largest oceans, the Panama Canal has been perhaps the biggest single boon to east–west commerce in the last century, and now rumors abound about interesting new "land canals" traversing other Central American countries. Other trade-facilitating arrangements, like regional trade agreements, have effectively shortened the geographic distances among Latin American countries, and between the region and the United States and the rest of the world as well.

Figure 1.1 Map of Latin America

SOME OF THE MAJOR THEMES IN LATIN AMERICA

Once explained, the story of doing business in Latin America is relatively easy
to understand. The modern Latin American narrative revolves around the

phenomena of globalization, the rise of the middle class, democratic consolidation, and the spread of markets. As a consequence of the debt crisis of the 1980s, the biggest economies in the region were effectively broke. The Washington Consensus introduced reforms designed to whip inflation and debt, raise the state revenue base, and liberalize markets and trade.

These reforms were, and are, highly unpopular, but much needed. The bottom line is, they worked. Beginning in earnest in the 1990s, Latin America embraced the challenges of participating in a globalized economy. Mexico led the way, signing on to NAFTA with the US and Canada. The region as a whole lowered trade barriers and practiced sounder money policies; this had the effect of facilitating commerce. The economies of the region eventually recovered from the "lost decade" of the 1980s, and trade and foreign direct investment flowed in to the region.

Testimony to the positive effects of trade is that the Latin American middle class has grown substantially, by some 50 million consumers in the past decade. Beyond the simple, direct economic impact of greater purchasing power of those with a greater marginal propensity to consume, there have been important political externalities as well, and democratic consolidation has proceeded apace. With more liberal political as well as economic regimes taking at least a tentative hold in the region, national and foreign direct investment has been spurred. This has generated a positive, somewhat self-reinforcing cycle, of liberalization–trade–prosperity, conducive to human development. More importantly, as a greater portion of the populace enjoys the benefits of trade that is freer than before (even if still not free), significant constituencies have arisen to advocate for the deepening of liberalizing trade reforms. All this bodes well for any investor seeking to do business in Latin America.

In the following pages, we will briefly touch on each of these points (globalization, middle class, democracy, and markets) individually, before moving on to the main challenges confronting the investor interested in doing business in Latin America.

Globalization

Globalization has had a major impact on the political, social, and economic transformation of Latin America. By and large, globalization can be both good and bad for a country or region; the results depend on a country's ability to make the most of the trade opportunities globalization presents. Technological access plays a big role in determining how well an individual country economy can succeed in the international economy. Particularly with the intensification and pervasiveness of the digital world, borders are shrinking and personal communications have become instantaneous. The rapidity of information exchange through the internet with email, Twitter, blogs, Facebook, and other social media tools, has created an environment that is more data rich and accessible than ever before in world history. The information age has tremendous relevance for business, especially international business.

Due to technological advances, people can make consumption and business decisions more rapidly, with more timely and accurate information. Business advancements, new strategies, and more efficient business models focused on different ways of promoting, selling, and distributing products have provided countless new ways for people to increase not only their incomes but their ways and quality of life.

The opening of previously closed markets and the globalization of trade have led to a higher quality of life for most, but not all, people. Marked inequalities persist, particularly so in Latin America. Darker issues related to globalization concern the rise of inequality due to the remuneration of more productive factors of production, labor mobility and displacement, cultural conflicts, and socioeconomic challenges arising from the presence of foreign competition on national soil, the different patterns of social welfare states among trading nations, and—in Latin America in particularly—the illegal trafficking of drugs and people. Nonetheless, globalization has presented not only many complex challenges but tremendous opportunities as well. Again, this is particularly so in the case of Latin America. Mexico alone accounts for more US trade than the BRIC countries combined.

In the face of the concrete costs of the temporary and transitional adjustments globalization obliges upon its participants, the benefits outweigh the costs. Almost every country wants to be a major player on the world economic stage today, or at least not be left out. This is why liberal trade zones have gathered strength in the years following the defeat of communism by capitalism during the Cold War. Even regions known for mercantilist, strategic trade policies (such as Latin America, for instance) have since pushed forth with trade agreements such as NAFTA, CAFTA, MERCOSUR, and the Andean Pact, in addition to a whole host of bilateral arrangements to liberalize trade between nations.

Despite troubles associated with economic and political integration in the Euro Zone from 2009 to 2013, freer (if not free) trade negotiations have become a key factor in the promotion of business activity and business development within and among the nations of Latin America. These changes have not been easy to do, especially given the poor quality of the political class in Latin America. The fact that these changes have occurred is significant in its own right. All the signs point to a credible commitment by the region as a whole, with certain notable exceptions, that Latin America has turned its back on its trade-restricting mercantilist past, and has embraced the opportunities and challenges of the globalized economy.

The rise of a would-be populist brand of pseudo-socialist governments led by Venezuela and principally grouped in the ALBA coalition will be, throughout this book, the exception that proves the rule.[3] Particular attention will be paid to this phenomenon in separate sections in the appropriate chapters of this book.

Rising Middle Class

The middle class in Latin America is defined by those who fall into the income bracket of $10–$50 per capita daily. Some 30% of the Latin American population falls into the middle class category by this definition, an increase of some 50% and 50 million people in the past decade. The surge of the Latin American middle class has been due to the jobs created by economic growth (World Bank News, 2012).

Critics will cry that globalization has been disruptive, and that the benefits of trade and growth are not widely spread, which is true. Despite the inequality associated with the initial stages of globalization and growth, a proper perspective must be kept. Living standards are better than ever in the world today, and Latin America is not the exception (Ridley, 2013). The middle class in Latin America is larger than ever, and lives better than ever. More important still, consumer preferences in Latin America are becoming more strongly oriented toward higher quality, value-added goods and services that developed economies such as the US can produce.

In fact, it can be said that the main strength of Latin America's economic growth has been based on the expansion of her middle sectors. The growth of the middle class has augmented domestic demand and spurred economic growth, leading to the gradual reduction of poverty in the region as a whole. Even more importantly, the surge of the middle class has led to the advancement of democracy and greater pragmatism in economic policies (OECD, 2010). As relatively more political certainty takes hold, the region starts to look like a more attractive investment option, particularly given the political uncertainty that has gripped the United States and, most especially, Europe.

Due to lessons learned from the Latin American debt crisis of the 1970s and 1980s, and the ensuing neoliberal reforms associated with the Washington Consensus, Latin America resisted and recovered fairly well from the Great Recession of 2009. It is poignant to note that the same cannot be said of the bloated pseudo-socialist welfare regimes of many European countries, such as, among others, Greece, Italy, Portugal, and Spain.

The expansion of the middle sectors and the economy as a whole has indeed attracted new investors to the region, increasing FDI flows. This is important, as Latin America still has high rates of poverty and, thus, low rates and levels of accumulated savings to finance full investment opportunities. According to the World Investment Report, Latin American nominal FDI inflows grew by 104% from 2005 to 2010, while FDI outflows grew 124% in the same time frame. These patterns of growth in outlays demonstrate the importance of the Latin American economy in the eyes of world investors (World Investment Report, 2012). These trends show no sign of abating significantly, laying down the framework of interest behind this book: Latin America is open for doing business.

Democratic Consolidation and Spread of Markets

The rise of the middle class has fueled not only economic progress but political modernization as well. Middle class growth and political pragmatism generally proceed apace. The political upheavals and civil wars are increasingly seen as things of the past. The civil wars ended in the late 1980s through the mid-1990s. Since then, relatively smooth, stable, and predictable elections have been the norm. Even as governments have alternated in power, for the most part the commitment to monetary and fiscal discipline and liberalizing trade reforms has remained relatively constant. With the advance of markets has come the advance of democracy, and vice versa. This has been, and will continue to be, tremendously important for the political and economic development of Latin America, as foreign investors are keen to see concrete commitments to property and other civil rights before they put their money into a country.

Of the countries in the Latin American region, Argentina and Chile are perhaps the only ones that have exhibited an economic and political environment similar to that of the US and Western Europe, at least for some periods of their history. For the most part, the other Latin American nations are fledgling countries eager to achieve levels of economic growth and human development similar to those of the advanced nations of the world. Then the menace of the 21st-century variant of populist socialism afflicts countries such as Venezuela, Ecuador, Bolivia, and Nicaragua (the ALBA nations), and threatens others. Even the countries not on the ALBA path are threatened by corruption from within.

These issues will be treated more in depth in subsequent chapters.

SOME OF THE MAJOR CHALLENGES TO DOING BUSINESS IN LATIN AMERICA

The major challenges to doing business in Latin America can also be rendered in a simple narrative. Even though doing business in Latin America is, more and more, a winning proposition, the reader should be forewarned that substantial hurdles still need to be cleared. The Latin American region is a long way off from becoming part of the developed world. One of its main challenges on the path to full development of its political, social, economic, and business opportunities is lack of infrastructure. Infrastructure takes on many meanings, beyond the simple physical one of common parlance. The optimal exploitation of business opportunities and attainment thereby of full developmental potential depends on not just physical infrastructure, but also technological, regulatory, political economic, and cultural and social infrastructure. These issues will be discussed in more depth elsewhere in the book.

Limitations in physical infrastructure alone can be daunting, if only because the geography in Latin America can be quite difficult to negotiate. For example, Bolivia is a landlocked, mountainous country. Outside the capital city of La Paz, the road network is frankly primitive. Peru is also a very mountainous country with a very treacherous road system. The difficulty of accessing Brazil's Amazon region is, of course, legendary. The lack of access to the areas outside the capital cities or developed coastal regions limits the growth potential and business opportunities in these countries. With proper political prioritization of economic initiatives, these problems of poor infrastructure and limited national integration could be resolved in relatively short order. However, this political will is starkly lacking.

To the infrastructural difficulties one can add the cultural differences an American business person, for example, would encounter when seeking to do business in a largely Spanish-speaking region. Issues of punctuality, meeting management, bodily expressions, and etiquette will surely surface. Tolerance of rule breaking and corruption can be shocking to outside observers. If these issues weren't enough, the unresolved social issues have a habit of creating social conflict that directly impacts the conduct of business, such as farm and mine invasions, for instance, or road blockages.

This type of political uncertainty is a hindrance to investment, and the creation of business and job opportunities. Compounding this problem is the poor quality of Latin American political institutions, which, unfortunately, are still plagued by rampant corruption, rendering the governments of the region markedly incompetent and ineffective as it pertains to the attainment of basic development goals. The single exception seems to be those political arrangements that tie Latin American countries to the developed world, be it the UN, the US, or Europe, by way of political pacts, trade agreements, etc. The fact remains that state weakness and incompetence lead to lingering doubts as to the commitments of the region and particular countries to democracy and markets. Importantly, in many countries of Latin America, state weakness has enabled narco-trafficking organized crime to penetrate the highest echelons of political power.

Latin America is often misunderstood due to the difference in the dynamics of business evolution that the region has in comparison with North America or Europe. To understand Latin America one must understand both the trends and the businesses that are leading the growth of the region and the culture.

MAJOR BUSINESS TRENDS IN LATIN AMERICA

The strength of Latin America is based on the expansion of middle sectors, which augmented the domestic demands, the reduction of poverty in many countries, and the advancement of democracy and the pragmatism in economic policies (OECD, 2010).

The expansion of the middle sectors has attracted new investors to the region, increasing the FDI flows. According to the World Investment Report, Latin American FDI inflows grew 103% from 2005–2010, and FDI outflows grew 124% in the same time frame. The growth demonstrates the importance of the Latin American economy. The economic crisis that began in 2007 affected the rhythm of growth in the region, but in 2010 the recovery was forthcoming. Agwaral and Aramswami (1992) mentioned that a firm interested in offering services or products to foreign markets has to choose between which FDI entry mode is the right one for the economy. The most common entry modes for Latin America are greenfield projects, and mergers and acquisitions.

A greenfield investment or project is considered as an investment in a production plant or services in an area where there is no development or infrastructure. A greenfield project is focused on developing a new business in a country without the exclusion of the business that will be engaged. It is usually developed by a parent company that is in need of infrastructure to develop a service or product in a certain region or country.

A merger and acquisition (M&A) is a category for two different business transactions. The reason for grouping them in the same category is that a merger could lead to an acquisition in the long run. An acquisition is the process by which a company takes interest in another company by the purchase of more than 50% of the company's shares, to establish ownership. A merger could be defined as the combination of two or more companies. One of the companies will be retaining the identity, usually the larger of the companies involved.

The FDI inward stock has increased from $111,337 billion in the 1990s to $1,772,278 billion in 2010. The same tendency could be observed in the FDI inward stock: in 1990 the stocks were $56,645 billion and in 2010 they represented $732,781 billion. The reason for this shift could be analyzed by the growth from M&As and greenfield projects based on sales and purchases comparison. Table 1.1 presents recent M&A activity over a five-year period.

M&A had an impact during the economic crisis that can be demonstrated in the reduction of net sales and the net purchases when compared between the years 2007 and 2008. The M&A's sales and purchases recovered immediately for the year 2010, demonstrating the interest of the investor in the region. The same circumstance reflects on the deals where the sales and purchases grew more for the year 2010 than in the years before the economic crisis, demonstrating that the region has a dynamic economy and is attractive for new business ventures.

The other form of FDI investments, greenfield projects, reacted with the economic crisis of 2009, but recovered as rapidly as the M&A for the year 2010. Although M&As are more significant financially, there are more projects being offered from and to Latin America that are greenfield. Table 1.2 shows the greenfield FDI activity over the recent five-year period of time.

The trends indicate that Latin America is an attractive region for developing greenfield projects and for sustaining a negotiation concerning an M&A. Although there is still a trend based on commodities based on exportation, there has been investment

Table 1.1 M&A Sales and Purchases

Year	2005	2006	2007	2008	2009	2010	2011 (Jan–May)
Latin America and Caribbean (net sales millions of dollars)	14,563.00	12,768.00	20,648.00	15,452.00	(4,358.00)	29,481.00	9,024.00
Latin America and Caribbean (net purchases millions of dollars)	10,013.00	28,064.00	40,195.00	2,466.00	3,740.00	15,710.00	5,979.00
Latin America and Caribbean (net sales deals)	147.00	250.00	425.00	378.00	221.00	400.00	161.00
Latin America and Caribbean (net purchases deals)	80.00	132.00	174.00	146.00	116.00	192.00	68.00

Source: Elaborated by the authors based on information from the World Investment Report (UNCTAD, 2011)

Table 1.2 Greenfield FDI projects

Year	2005	2006	2007	2008	2009	2010	2011 (Jan–Apr)
Latin America and the Caribbean (world as destination, millions of dollars)	5,358.00	7,961.00	12,074.00	20,023.00	16,164.00	19,946.00	9,838.00
Latin America and the Caribbean (world as source, millions of dollars)	65,433.00	64,461.00	63,847.00	125,406.00	109,094.00	118,195.00	58,257.00
Latin America and the Caribbean (world as destination by source, number of projects)	86.00	128.00	226.00	219.00	230.00	273.00	92.00
Latin America and the Caribbean (world as source by destination, number of projects)	568.00	588.00	820.00	1,169.00	1,229.00	1,180.00	524.00

Source: Elaborated by the authors based on information from the World Investment Report (UNCTAD, 2011)

in other sectors, including technology, manufacturing, and services (Latin American Monitor, 2011). Businesses from all over the world, such as Flextronics from Singapore, Compal and Wistron from Taiwan, Jabil and Sanmina SCI from the US, TPV Technology from China, and Celestica from Canada, established overseas production bases in the Latin American region. The businesses mentioned handled revenues of approximately $198 billion,[4] and their portfolio includes clients of companies such as Apple, Inc., Alcatel-Lucent, Cisco, Dell, Sony, IBM, General Electric, Hitachi, and other leaders.

Concerning the trend of M&A in Latin America, Bloomberg (2011) mentioned, "while the region did experience moderate growth compared to other regions, it was Latin America M&A activity that jumped the most, followed by North America." Based on the study by Bloomberg (2011), Latin America is one of the most attractive regions where acquisition will be based (ranked third) and had a significant expectation of private equity/venture capital firms activity during the year 2011. Table 1.3 summarizes and compares M&A activity worldwide.

The trend in Latin America focuses on the attractiveness of its economy, the possibility of expansion, and the capacity of creating new business ventures. Although there are more greenfield projects than M&As, there is more profit on joining and/ or buying a business than creating one in a financial perspective. Latin America is the new region for investment, attracting firms around the world, depending on the

Table 1.3 Worldwide M&A activity

Region	Expectation of most active buyers	Most attractive acquisition targets	Expectation of major activity in private equity/venture capital firms
Central Asia	13%	6%	12%
Asia Pacific	45%	23%	36%
Africa/Middle East	3%	7%	1%
Western Europe	7%	18%	9%
Eastern Europe	n/a	6%	3%
South & Central America	7%	15%	8%
North America	22%	25%	31%

Source: Elaborated by the authors based on information from Bloomberg (2011)

necessities. The different industries in which M&As and greenfield projects revolve will be described in the following chapter.

DESCRIPTION OF POPULAR BUSINESS VENTURES

Business ventures in Latin America involve different sectors and different strategies for entering the market. Greenfield projects are booming after the economic crisis, based on the fact that new markets developed as a consequence. Concerning profits, the most profitable industry in Latin America is petrol/gas, which is characterized by public–private unions. Table 1.4 illustrates the major industries and their sales activity. Petro/gas seems to present large opportunities for potential investors.

Other business ventures that are attractive have been telecommunications; mostly dominated by seven different companies, including Carlos Slim's[5] conglomerate America Movil. The broadband growth projected concerning the years 2008–2013 for Latin America is 17%, and for wireless it is 7%, according to TeleGeography (2011). Latin America's growth is the second highest in the world, surpassed only by Africa concerning broadband and wireless. In 2009, mobile subscribers totaled 88.2% of the population, which can be compared only to 90.4% in North America (Euromonitor, 2010). The largest telephone markets in Latin America include Brazil, Mexico, and Argentina, with an average of 100 million mobile subscribers.

This tendency suggests that the mobile industry is booming while the fixed line is growing slowly. The reason for this behavior is the costs, which in the long run are lower for the mobile industry than the fixed line. An example of this behavior is the growth in Guatemala, with an average of 1,196 mobile subscriptions per 1,000 persons (Figure 1.2).

The retail industry has grown significantly in the past five years with the expansion of Wal-Mart in Central America and Brazil, Cencosud in Chile, and Carrefour

Table 1.4 Petrol/gas industry sales activities

Industry	Sales in millions of dollars	Share of total
Telecommunications	$98,502.00	11%
Metal industry	$33,028.40	4%
Petrol chemistry	$24,665.00	3%
Petrol/gas	$371,146.30	40%
Multisector	$64,912.10	7%
Electric energy	$44,794.20	5%
Construction	$10,520.40	1%
Retail	$68,909.30	7%
Cement	$15,138.70	2%
Beverage/liquor	$38,170.70	4%
Automobile	$54,530.40	6%
Food	$26,948.10	3%
Agroindustry	$40,629.40	4%
Total	$931,895.20	100%

Source: Elaborated by the authors based on information from America Economía (2010)

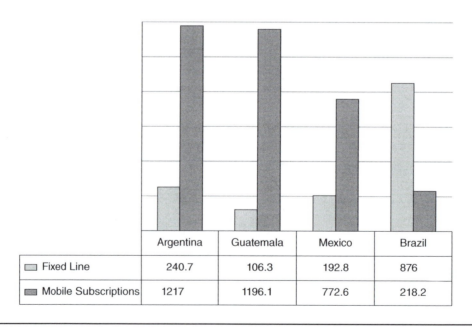

	Argentina	Guatemala	Mexico	Brazil
Fixed Line	240.7	106.3	192.8	876
Mobile Subscriptions	1217	1196.1	772.6	218.2

Figure 1.2 Fixed-line and mobile telephone subscriptions (2009) per 1,000 people

Source: Elaborated by the authors based on information from Euromonitor (2010)

Table 1.5 Global online population

Region	2009	2010	2012
North America	259	266	292
Europe	415	475	500
Asia Pacific	645	846	1033
Latin America and Caribbean	178	204	255
Middle East and Africa	135	173	241
Total	1632	1964	2321

Source: Elaborated by the authors based on information from IMAP (2010)
Note: The data for 2012 are projected

in Brazil. The retail industry represents $68,909.30 million in Latin America, with three major companies leading in sales. The retail industry, in terms of transactions, in Latin America is valued at $1.4 billion (IMAP, 2010). The online population that could be reached in the retail industry in Latin America was due to grow 43% by 2012, which is one of the major potential markets in the world given the fact that the internet is still a growing industry, in comparison to Europe or Asia Pacific.

One sector that is growing in Latin America is the mining industry. The potential markets concentrate in Brazil, Chile, Argentina, Peru, Mexico, and Colombia. In Brazil the company Vale Do Rio Doce (VALE) is the second-largest mining company in the world. VALE was privatized in 1997 and is responsible for more than 50% of Brazil's mineral output. The opportunity for the market is in equipment supplies for the mining industry because of the company's size. Other mining companies include Anglo American, ArcelorMittal, and MMX. The gold industry in Brazil projects an output of 100 tons per year by 2013, and it will be one of the major producers in the world for the mentioned year (US Commercial Service, 2010).

In the case of Colombia, the carbon industry represents 15% of the total exports for the year 2010 and the ferronickel industry represents 2%. The growth from 2009 to 2010 in carbon is equivalent to 11%, or $598 million, the same tendency for the ferronickel industry, with a growth of 33%, or $241.40 million.

The mining industry represents a significant 4% of the total revenues obtained by companies in Latin America. Markets such as Colombia and Brazil are significant for investing and developing strategies of investment. The popular ventures in Latin America are focused on retail, telecommunications, multisector business, and mining industries. The sectors in which investment is directed are practically raw material or special services.

CONCLUSION

This chapter has provided an introductory overview of the general important issues facing Latin America, and those interested in doing business there. The

Table 1.6 Colombia: exports (FOB)

Year	US$ millions		Net weight in tons	
	2010	2009	2010	2009
Total exports	$39,819.50	$32,853.00	112,486,495.00	103,446,928.50
Carbon	$6,015.20	$5,416.40	72,226,880.00	68,684,309.10
Ferronickel	$967.30	$725.90	140,824.60	169,571.60

Source: Elaborated by the authors based on Dirección de impuestos y aduanas nacionales de Colombia (2010)

topics covered briefly here will be shown to be integral to economic progress and the continued business development of the region. The risks notwithstanding, it is fair to say that now is still a good time to get in on the ground floor. Globalization has set forth tremendous opportunities, paving the way to a fuller appreciation of the need to facilitate the doing of business. In this sense, globalization has provided access to foreign markets and capital, as well as ideas, and, perhaps most importantly, the incentives to innovate and modernize. It is this greater degree of openness, which makes the region a prime attraction for would-be investors, entrepreneurs, and established ventures seeking to expand internationally.

Overall, business development in Latin American countries has shown incredible potential and, we believe, will continue to do so. Interested individuals who read the rest of this book will be well informed and ready to make current and well-informed business decisions about doing business in Latin America.

NOTES

1. This number excludes Puerto Rico, which is not an independent country, and the smaller Caribbean countries as well.
2. ECLAC (Economies of Latin America and the Caribbean) is the commission that forecasts economic climate in the region (see http://www.cepal.org/default.asp?idioma=IN). LAC = Latin American Caribbean.
3. ALBA, or the Bolivarian Alliance of the Americas (ALBA).
4. For more information concerning this data consult Table IV.1 in the World Investment Report.
5. Carlos Slim Helu is, according to *Forbes* (Kroll, 2010), the number-one billionaire in the world and one of 67 of the most powerful people in the world.

REFERENCES

America Economía (2010) Las 500 empresas de América Latina en el 2010. Obtained from http://rankings. americaeconomia.com/.

Bloomberg (2011) *2011 M&A outlook*. Obtained from: http://about.bloomberg.com/pdf/manda.pdf.

Direccion de impuestos y aduanas nacionales de Colombia (2010) Export statistics, obtained from http:// www.colombiatrade.com.co/links/direcci%B3n-de-impuestos-y-aduanas-nacionales.

Euromonitor (2010) Latin America enjoys mobile telephone boom. Euromonitor Global Market Research, obtained from http://www.euromonitor.com/.

IMAP (2010) Retail industry global report 2010. IMAP reports for 2010, obtained from http://www.imap. com/imap/media/resources/IMAPRetailReport8_23CB9AA9C6EBB.pdf.

Kroll, L. (2010) The world's billionaires. *Forbes*, obtained from http://www.forbes.com/2010/03/10/worlds-richest-people-slim-gates-buffett-billionaires-2010_land.html.

Latino.Foxnews.com (2012) Obtained from http://latino.foxnews.com/latino/news/2012/10/12/study-ranks-mexico-as-world-4th-best-investment-destination/.

Laura (2010) Top ten largest countries in the world, obtained from http://voices.yahoo.com/top-10-largest-countries-world-5807056/html/ (accessed 11/3/12).

OECD (2010) Latin American and the Caribbean economic outlook 2010, obtained from http://www.oecd.org/dev/americas/latinamericaneconomicoutloo2010.htm.

Ridley, M. (2013) Obtained from http://www.rationaloptimist.com/blog/global-outlook-rosy-europe's-outlook-grim.aspx.

Rosenberg, M. (2011) Most populous countries today, obtained from http://geography.about.com/cs/worldpopulation/a/mostpopulous.htm (accessed 11/3/12).

TeleGeography (2011) GlobalComms insight, obtained from http://www.telegeography.com/research-services/globalcomms-insight/index.html.

UNCTAD (United Nations Conference on Trade and Development) (2011) *World investment report 2011*, obtained from http://unctad.org/en/docs/wir2011_embargoed_en.pdf.

US Commercial Service (2010) Mining industry overview and exporting opportunities in Latin America. Trade Winds Forum for the Americas, obtained from http://www.globalvirginia.com/Information/Documents/Latin_America_Mining_Guide.pdf.

World Bank (2013) Obtained from http://data.worldbank.org/indicator/SP.POP.TOTL.

World Bank News (2012) Obtained from http://www.worldbank.org/en/news/2012/11/13/crecimiento-clase-media-america-latina.

World Investment Report (2012) Towards a new generation of investment policies, UNCTAD, obtained from http://unctad.org/en/PublicationsLibrary/wir2012overview_en.pdf (accessed 11/3/2012).

Business Case

Miami Herald (2012) Open English expands across Latin America, obtained from http://www.miamiherald.com/2013/02/17/3239707/open-english-expands-across-latin.html.

Moreno, A. (2013) Andres Moreno's blog, obtained from http://andresmorenoblog.com/.

TechCrunch (2012) Open English lands US $43 million from insight, Redpoint to bring online language ed to Latin America, obtained from http://techcrunch.com/2012/07/26/open-english-43m/.

In case you are interested in the advertisement, visit the following web page: http://www.openenglish.com/anuncio-de-TV-aprender-ingles.do.

2

THE ECONOMIC HISTORY OF
LATIN AMERICA

From independence to the debt crisis of the 1980s

GENERAL INTRODUCTION

In most economic histories of Latin America the development of export economies, commodity cycles, and the advent of industrialization efforts typically acquire significant importance, especially in the period between independence from the European imperial powers in the early 19th century and the Great Depression.

International trade has always been an important part of the economic equation for both Latin America and her trading partners. For much of her post-independence history, trade has been a complement to Latin American industrialization. As a case in point, railroads constructed for the rapid exports of locally produced goods or extracted natural resources produced important externalities for purposes of the domestic market development. The cases of Mexico and Argentina stand out in this regard.

This chapter provides a comprehensive discussion, analysis, and summation of how Latin American economic history played a role in its development, its stagnation, and now again in its redevelopment. A great deal of evidence is presented that clearly and convincingly supports the notion that Latin America has been very economically active, has lots of human and natural resources, and is extremely rich in opportunities for a variety of business ventures. With proper political and economic management Latin America will be an attraction to various business entrepreneurs.

The twin issues of trade and development have always been intertwined in Latin America, spawning a historical debate, still unsettled, between those who would look inward for development prospects, and those who would look outward. Basically, it has always boiled down to a debate between export-led growth advocates and proponents of import substitution industrialization (ISI) and other state-led industrialization efforts. The debate continues to this day.

Despite the benefits Latin America has derived from trade with the world, nationalist sentiments and insecurities have always held significant political and intellectual sway in the region. They still do. A significant portion of Latin Americans believe that trade benefits the rich countries more than their own. However, this doesn't stop Latin Americans from hungering for any and all things from the developed world, especially Europe and the United States. In light of the fact that many Latin American countries are fast becoming rich themselves, new approaches to economic history and international trade are now coming into vogue.

Far too often, for far too long, past economic inquiries found what they sought to see: an unhealthy and increasing dependence of the "south" (developing economies) on the "north" (developed economies). However, recent orientations in economic history have allowed for new questions to be asked, and new answers to be found. As a consequence, new interpretations of Latin American economic history are being innovated, to the benefit of understanding, particularly as regards the present business climate in Latin America. This is a positive development, pointing the way toward a more fruitful understanding of the key to future prosperity in Latin America, increasing openness to trade.

The question of openness to trade is important, not least because Latin American intellectuals and supposed experts on the region have reflected a tendency to externalize blame for all locally engendered problems. Sadly, this was the case in the 19th century, and the tendency is still pervasive today. The fact is that poor economic performance in Latin America has been due to the interrelated mechanics of poor domestic politics and policies. Thanks precisely to the contacts established through international commerce, Latin America has learned a lot from the developed world, but not enough.

One of the key things Latin America has not sufficiently learned from the developed world is the importance of institutional quality for the course of a country's economic development. Public institutions in Latin America are still today of tremendously poor quality. Curiously enough, this fact is effectively ignored by international organizations with a focus on the region, such as ECLAC and BID, which tend to stress the need for governments in the Latin American region to collect more tax revenues, more so than they stress the need to ensure quality control in that public spending.

Nonetheless, there is an emerging consensus that scholars must focus on the quality of political institutions in the region if the economic policies of the region are to attract foreign and domestic capital and investment, and thus spawn economic growth. This runs the gamut from property rights to public investment in quality education. One cannot survey the economic history of Latin America, and its economic performance under evolving trade regimes, without focusing on Latin American institutions and their dismal failures to take advantage of the opportunities offered by world markets over time.

It is safe to say that Latin American economies pose conundrums for economic historians in several respects. Bright economic futures have rapidly become eclipsed for seemingly nonsensical reasons. In 1820, Latin America as a whole produced 20% more output than the United States, reaching a 2.1% share of world GDP, as compared to 1.8% for the United States.

Table 2.1 Shares of world GDP, 1820–2030

	1820	1950	1973	2003	2030
Western Europe	23.0%	26.2%	25.6%	19.2%	13.0%
USA	1.8%	27.3%	22.1%	20.7%	17.3%
Japan	3.0%	3.0%	7.8%	6.6%	3.6%
Rich	27.9%	59.9%	58.7%	49.6%	36.4%
China	32.9%	4.6%	4.6%	15.1%	23.8%
India	16.0%	4.2%	3.1%	5.5%	10.4%
Latin America	2.1%	7.8%	8.7%	7.7%	6.3%
Africa	4.5%	3.8%	3.4%	3.2%	3.0%
Rest	72.1%	40.1%	41.3%	50.4%	63.6%
Latin America as % of USA	1.2:1	0.29:1	0.39:1	0.37:1	0.36:1

Source: Adapted from Maddison (2008)

Even in per capita terms, Latin America was not always an underdeveloped region relative to the United States. In 1700, the British colonies in North America had a per capita GDP below that of the Caribbean and Mexico, and just on par with the average for the entire Latin American region (Coatsworth, 2005). The reason why Latin America did not keep on par with the North American pace of modernization, and economic and political development is tied to the institutional legacy left behind in Central and South America, and the Caribbean, by the Latin countries of Europe, Spain, Portugal, and France.

Economies like Argentina, Mexico, and Cuba once looked promising as cases of successful development. Unfortunately, they would on account of internal defects quickly become emblematic symbols of self-induced failure. Latin American development failures were typically the result of bad economic and commercial policies, crafted in response to the changing circumstances of the world economy. These failures were all too often rationalized away by blaming foreigners. The fact is that the reason for Latin America's failure to fully develop according to her true potential has more to do with internal domestic policies and the political economy of trade, than trade with foreigners itself.

To a great extent, the poverty of political institutions in Latin America is an inherited trait, passed on from the patterns of conquest followed by Iberian imperial powers. The basic institutions that determined the patterns of economic organization were imported from Portugal and Spain. The conquest and enslavement of entire populations of indigenous peoples created perverse incentives for the creation of inefficient, yet persistent, institutions. The persistent colonial legacy was one of insufficiently broad property rights, slavery, and discriminatory caste systems that worked in conjunction to create great disincentives to capitalist development and progress (Coatsworth, 2005).

Latin America did not commence her independence period with the most helpful of institutional legacies. Whereas the United States, Australia, and New Zealand provide the best examples of the exportation of pro-growth institutions, this was not the case in Latin America, which inherited Iberian institutions, culture, and norms. Whereas Anglo-Saxon cultures prioritized the establishment of the rule of law, always a boon to foreign investment, Latin American cultures developed around the political concept of the *caudillo*, or strongman. Rich in natural resources, Latin America followed in many cases the model of the extractive state, a dissuader of national and foreign investment. Here, Latin American geography worked against her economic development, as Anglo-Saxons did not tend to settle where mortality rates from disease proved to be high, affecting negatively institutional development in Latin America. This was important because the very patterns of growth and development are determined in large part by the quality of local institutions (Acemoglu, Johnson, and Robinson, 2001). Although not as bad as the African case, the Latin American countries did not, by and large, inherit the Anglo-Saxon model of flexible and efficient institutions, but rather went seeking ones that stifled growth.

Many of the Latin American regions were rife with tropical diseases, which served as disincentives for European migration. European immigration was key to the development of Latin America. Areas that received large numbers of European immigrants tended to do better in terms of economic and, more importantly, political development than regions that did not receive European migrants (Acemoglu *et al.*, 2001). Simply put, Europeans were not as docile as Latin Americans. Where a small portion of elites ruled and property rights for all were not adequately protected, bad institutions tended to arise. Where Europeans and their descendants played a more major role, better institutions tended to flourish (Coatsworth, 2005). This point is best exemplified by the discovery of an inverse relationship between the degree of civilized advancement found at the time of Conquest and the level of economic progress detected after the time of Conquest. Regions better off before the arrival of the Europeans tended to be worse off relative to other regions after the arrival of Europeans (Acemoglu, Johnson, and Robinson, 2002). This was particularly true for cases such as Mexico and Peru, where the political economy of enslavement of indigenous peoples prevailed (Coatsworth, 2005).

After independence, the Latin American elites oversaw the region's difficult transition to economic growth, which would accelerate in the latter parts of the 19th century and into the 20th. Albeit imperfectly, Latin American elites consolidated political and economic power, undertook important changes in domestic laws and commercial codes, and managed to attract foreign capital so as to finance the infrastructure and export promotion projects that eventually led to Latin America's takeoff to industrialization (Coatsworth, 2005). A testimony to the eventual success of Latin American elites is borne out by the available economic data. Though in the 1820–1870 period per capita GDP growth in Latin America was negative, after that it was the highest in the world, in the period from 1870 up to World War I, slightly above even that registered for the US, Canada, New Zealand, and Australia.

Table 2.2 Per capita GDP growth, 1500–2001 (annual average compound growth rates)

	1500–1820	1820–1870	1870–1913	1913–1950	1950–1973	1973–2001
Western Europe	0.14	0.98	1.33	0.76	4.05	1.88
Canada, US, Australia, New Zealand	0.34	1.41	1.81	1.56	2.45	1.84
Japan	0.09	0.19	1.48	0.88	8.06	2.14
Western Europe	0.14	1.06	1.57	1.17	3.72	1.95
Asia excluding Japan	0	−0.1	0.42	−0.1	2.91	3.55
Latin America	0.16	−0.03	1.82	1.43	2.58	0.91
Easter Europe and USSR	0.1	0.63	1.18	1.4	3.49	−0.05
Africa	0	0.35	0.57	0.92	2	0.19
Rest	0.02	0.06	0.82	0.65	2.83	1.75
World	0.05	0.54	1.3	0.88	2.92	1.41

Source: Maddison (2005)

THE ILLIBERAL IBERIAN LEGACY IN LATIN AMERICA

Latin America underwent a series of liberal reformist governments in the late 19th century. This brought about many changes, but not the enduring establishment of liberal governments and liberal societies more generally. The independence movements were an elite affair in Latin America, and allowed the political, economic, and social elites to preserve their status. The independence movement that swept Latin America in the early 19th century was nominally a copy of the American Revolution, but it was something that Latin Americans at the time were essentially ill prepared to adopt.

In a most fundamental sense, the separations from Spain created countries out of colonies, but they were countries largely in name only. The new countries lacked the components of national integration, such as national identity. Very few people could actually read, even fewer could vote. This was true in large countries such as Brazil, Argentina, and Colombia, as well as smaller countries in Central America. Literacy tests and property requirements further restricted the eligible population, which was of course confined exclusively to men.

The failure of true liberalism to take root in Latin America was due to many factors; chief among them was the continued prevalence of old ways. Corruption and illiteracy doomed early liberal political reforms, as the main task of the elites was to remain elite. Social mobility was kept low, even as political, social, and economic inequality were kept high. Latin American leaders were products of their times, and their culture predisposed to modes of political and economic thinking somewhat distinct from the more truly liberal Anglo-Saxon schools of thought. In addition, the liberal elites shared a privileged socioeconomic background with the more conservative elements of Latin American society, which they were not willing to give up in exchange for the power of new ideas.

Groups that possess political power are the ones that create economic institutions. Political power can be traditional, such as those de jure manifestations of political power, which are regulated by formal political institutions. There is also de facto political power, which gives groups the ability to capture the political decision-making apparatus for their own private gain. As paradigmatic changes occur in formal political institutions, i.e. the change to democratic regimes from authoritarian ones, a distribution occurs in the de jure political power. This provides an incentive for displaced, yet still powerful, elites to invest in de facto forms of political power. This is what happened throughout Latin American history (Acemoglu and Robinson, 2008).

It wasn't liberal-minded democrats that declared independence from Spain, rather it was the conservatives. The conservatives basically figured they would be economically better off without monopolistic economic ties to the Spanish crown. However, for the most part, Latin American conservatives remained fervent supporters of the primacy of the Catholic Church in Latin America, and mercantilist trade policies that sought to channel and control trade. A notable exception was Mexico, where the Juarez government in the middle of the 19th century seriously restricted the previously uncontrolled and corrupt power of the Catholic Church. Still, even in Mexico, these moves engendered stiff political opposition, and the internal divisions were reflected in a bloody civil war at the dawn of the 20th century.

The main liberal ideas to take hold were those related to economics. In a clear break with old world mercantilism, free trade was seen as inextricably linked to human progress, peace, and prosperity. This was true not only in Mexico, but in countries as far down south as Brazil, Argentina, and Chile, as well as countries in Central America. In truth, the founding fathers of the new Latin American republics hoped little would change with the newfound political status of independence. The main objective was for the political, social, and economic elites to concentrate the benefits of economic exploitation of the region's vast resources. Unlike in the United States, there were no visions of a democracy of small farmers, and dispersed political and economic power.

The practice of corrupt elections contributed to the failure of true republican liberalism to take root in Latin America. Elections were to be in form only, for the true desire of Latin American elites was basically to preserve the status quo of the *ancien régime*, which had prevailed during the colonial era. Fraud, official intimidation, and voter manipulation were, and sadly still are, typical characteristics of Latin American elections and politics in general. Political strongmen, known as *cuadillos*, were largely the main factors determining not only political recruitment but also political participation, which thus affected political outcomes.

1820–1870

In the 19th century, Latin America complemented the market demands of the developed world nicely. It exported raw materials and commodities needed for consumption and industrialization in the developed world. Manufactured goods and textiles came, first, from Britain and then increasingly the United States to Latin America.

The dominant international player in Latin America in the early 19th century was Great Britain, not the United States.[1] Nevertheless, the overall trade pattern outlined above continued throughout the 19th century. By the early 20th century, however, the US had overtaken Great Britain as the main trading partner for Latin America as a whole. There were notable exceptions such as Argentina, which continued strong trade ties with the British. Argentina exported cattle hides and wool to Great Britain, and Great Britain exported textiles to Argentina.

Trade links between Argentina and Britain became so strong that it used to be said that when London caught a cold, Buenos Aires caught pneumonia (Salvucci, 2008, pp. 249–292). This quote, obviously, captures not only the strength of trade ties between London and Buenos Aires, but also the asymmetric effects of economic dependency, an issue that would acquire particular political-economic importance as the years went on.

Other countries in Latin America developed unique comparative advantages that they exploited to trade with Europe and the United States, and to a lesser extent, one another. Whereas Argentina exported meat, wool and grain, Chilean exports were for the most part centered on wheat, silver, and copper. Peru exported guano and nitrates. Ecuador exported cacao. Brazil exported coffee, rubber, and cacao. Mexico exported precious metals, mainly silver, while the Caribbean and Central America relied on the exports of sugar, bananas, and, in the cases of countries like Guatemala, coffee.

Latin American trade, then as now, brought benefits to everybody involved. The people that embarked upon trade with Latin America in the 19th century were risk takers. Betting on Latin America in the 19th century, or overseas trade in general, was far from a sure thing. Large gains made from successful voyages had to compensate the risk of major losses on another. Many investors from developed countries that took the risk of investing in trade with Latin America reaped big rewards commensurate with the significant levels of risk they undertook at the time. However, it would be a stretch to claim that the developed countries became developed because the poor countries became progressively underdeveloped. Trade between Latin America and Europe or North America was generally a very small percentage of total economic activity for the developed areas.

The typical trade pattern in the 19th century was that Latin American countries provided the raw materials in exchange for manufactured, industrial goods. Economic agents from the developed world would also provide the value added on Latin American export products such as sugar, tobacco, and coffee. Europeans and North Americans bought gold, coffee, sugar, fruit, lumber, dyes, and spices from Latin Americans. Latin America provided Europe, especially, with the opportunity to diversify its bland diet with new foods like corn, potatoes, beans, tobacco, cacao, tomatoes, pineapples, and peppers. Europeans and Americans found their diets augmented in ways that their domestic agricultural industries could not provide. Exotic tropical produce became a form of luxury good in developed economies.[2]

The consumer benefits of the increased range, variety, and quality of foodstuffs notwithstanding, the fact is that Europe could have made do without these consumer goods. However, the converse was not true. Latin America needed Europe, even if

Europe only wanted Latin America. Latin America needed the imports of manufactured goods that European economies provided, given the relative lack of innovative, entrepreneurial, and technical talent in Latin America at the time.

One key export from Latin America to Europe was precious metals, namely gold and silver. This is a clear example of trade benefits to the more developed world of trade relations with the less developed world. Precious metals exported from Latin America to Europe benefitted the developed economies by augmenting the money supply, which at the time was made up of precious metals. This facilitated greater trade and specialization. Greater trade and economic specialization was directed not only toward Latin America, but other regions of the world as well. Furthermore, the inflationary effects in Europe due to the inflow of precious metals from Latin America further encouraged trade to exploit differences in inflation rates between economies. Incentives to trade grew as aggregate income was effectively redistributed from the working class to the investment class. As trade expanded, so did the demand for money. Herein lie the trade facilitation benefits of Latin American exports of precious metals to the developed world.

Without a doubt, Latin American exports of precious metals fed the European demand for money as trade relations grew in number and complexity. There were other important consequences as well to the imports by Europeans of precious metals from Latin America. Government finances, for one, were improved. Insofar as liberal ideas grew in importance, this enabled public institutions to begin playing a more complementary role to market forces in developed countries. There is no denying that the role of public institutions in society was stimulated by the revenues from the Latin American region. Latin American exports of precious metals to the developed economies facilitated the workings of the new, increasingly complex economic machine founded on freer markets.

As always, the economic effects of trade were uneven for the most part. Given their lower technological status, Latin American countries probably benefitted more by the time savings measure of the benefits of trade than the developed countries, which had a technological advantage. Latin American trade was more important for maritime powers like England and Spain than for countries like France, Belgium, or Germany. But the importance of foreign trade to Latin America to England, and to a lesser extent Spain and Portugal, provided important cost-cutting opportunities and benefits of specialization to leading trading firms in England, which naturally facilitated trade with regions other than Latin America itself.

The unquestionable benefits of trade to Latin America notwithstanding, the following of an export-led path to economic growth and development had domestic political implications in the Latin American countries. Export elites naturally favored the depreciation of the currency, because that grew the receipts for the goods they exported; growing export revenues could then be used to purchase more domestic goods. One non-tradable, domestic good that was typically purchased was, of course, land. Dating back to colonial times under the Spanish crown, land acquisition was culturally prized in most Latin American countries. This tended over time to concentrate the distributions of wealth in ways that would later be exploited as points of political contention.

In the 19th century, Latin American export economies were not sufficiently diversified, so they tended to depend on the export of commodity goods produced on plantations, or mineral products extracted from mines. Commodity products were subject to volatile swings in prices and thus profits. Lacking sophisticated financial centers such as New York or London, Latin American export economies could not attract foreign capital to make up the difference when commodity prices fell. Although the Latin American economies prospered as never before under the export-led models, they were subject to recurrent boom and bust cycles.

Latin America sold agricultural products; she bought manufactured goods. Although international trade certainly benefitted Latin America during the 19th century, the fact remains that the prices of what Latin America sold, agricultural products, fluctuated more widely than the prices of what it bought, manufactured goods. Consistent, positive performance was not a mainstay of the Latin American economies in the 19th century.

Political and economic instability were serious impediments to progress. What Latin America lacked in the 19th century were efficient, capable, and relatively trustworthy and credible institutions, mainly public, but also private. Prudent fiscal and commercial policies were, as a whole, not practiced, so there was only so much that could be expected of the monetary institutions, such as they were at the time. All that said, the independence of Latin American countries, the breaking of Spanish crown monopolies, the opening up to trade and insertion of the Latin American economies into the burgeoning international economy were sum positives for the region. Importantly, it was by way of imports that Latin Americans gained access to new physical and ideational technologies on better ways to manufacture better products and, indeed, societies. The qualitative nature of imports was important, as the importation process provided access to modern technologies and ideas.

SUMMING UP THE LIBERAL ERA

Latin American politics in the post-independence period present a puzzle. If change was the order of the day, why did very little seemingly change? After all the declarations of independence, liberty, and equality for the Latin American masses, little changed when independence from the European countries was declared. However, it is important for the reader to take note that what happened in this period was the introduction of liberal political and economic ideas that were to take root only gradually and much later, but take root they did.

Latin American elites managed to form an imperfect coalition predicated upon weak, non-autonomous political institutions based upon informal contractual arrangements between political and economic elites. This worked to the benefit of export elites and elites in the nascent banking and industrial sectors and, importantly, to foreign capital interests. Key to this system working was credible guarantees against foreign expropriations (Coatsworth, 2005).

Latin American elites continued to idolize things European as more advanced than they were, which, after all, was the sad truth. Paris tended to be regarded as the center for fashion and style; London remained the apex of economic efficiency for Latin Americans. In a nutshell, European modes were superior and local traditions were expressions of an inferior culture. Latin American elites, the only political actors that mattered in the 19th century, wholeheartedly accepted the point of view that European modes of dress, etiquette, living, etc., were the only ones worthy of emulating. This point of view persisted long after formal independence from Spain. It should be recognized that Brazil only became independent from Portugal and declared slavery illegal. Even then, these moves were largely only cosmetic. For the most part, Latin America in the 19th century was a conservative bastion of non-liberal practices, fronted by a plethora of liberal ideas plastered in the new constitutions of the nascent "republics."

Latin American elites either did not believe in liberal principles or they did not believe in them enough. Substantial political, economic, and social progress did not happen. Politically, the elites did not want to share power, especially with people of lower classes and different races. Economically, the entrenched powers simply did not wish to compete with foreign companies, much less with national ones. Economic progress, as in prosperity, was fine, as long as it accrued to entrenched elites. Political progress, as in power sharing, was not. Political equality between people of different races and ethnicities was not something Latin American elites could even contemplate in the late 19th century.

Intellectual currents in vogue during the 19th century were manipulated by elites to concord with the practice that effectively excluded the lower social economic and political classes from political participation. The ideal state in Latin American terms, broadly understood, could be taken to be as *Order and Progress*. This was actually the motto displayed on the Brazilian flag. The phrases are important not just for their expression, but the *order* of their expression, which implies clearly that there is no progress without there first being order.

The premium placed on scientific progress, and social evolution in the mode of Darwin, led many to champion the idea that European races were superior. However, the argument was not sufficiently extended to European institutions, which would have had the effect of extending political and social participation and suffrage. As always, political-economic, as well as social-cultural, arguments got in the way. It was, and still is in many respects, common for Latin Americans to believe that what was European, and white, was right. There has always been since the colonial age a Latin American predisposition to associate things European with progress and civilization. This, curiously enough, typically extended only to the trappings of European, and by extension, Western society, but not its fundamentals. The luxurious trappings of civilizations of European descent proved seductive, but not the workings of the institutions that made them possible, such as access to the political system, power sharing, etc. As a result, Latin American elites copied the trappings of the largely decadent European social elite, but not the workings of modern institutions of European influence, such as democracy, republicanism, market economies, etc.

In a restricted social sense, Latin American customs were really not much different than North American ones. Latin Americans discriminated against indigenous peoples and cultures, afro-descendants, and people of mixed blood, much as North Americans did. In a political and economic sense, tremendous differences grew over time. Whereas the Emancipation Proclamation issued under President Abraham Lincoln freed American slaves in 1865, slavery was still legal in Brazil as of 1887. Although not directed at African descendants, forced labor of indigenous populations was common in countries such as Guatemala during the coffee booms of the late 19th century. Elsewhere, the disenfranchisement of indigenous populations was the rule, not the exception to the norm.

Even in the post-independence period, Latin American political institutions took on the twin beliefs that liberty and equality were the way to go, but that the region had a way to go before it got there. The blame for Latin American lack of advance in this respect was typically placed on the lower classes, which were typically of non-European descent.

Latin American culture also played an influential role in impeding the taking root of more liberal political and economic institutions and traditions. Latin American culture is and has been largely fatalistic. In their crafting of their constitutions, Latin Americans were, and have been, influenced by focusing on what is ideally possible more than what is true. Quite unfortunately, this practice has run into the reality that what is true supersedes the ideal. It is, for instance, quite common to see Latin American constitutions "guarantee" all sorts of "human rights" that extend far beyond the minimalist conception that might occur to an American mindful of the Bill of Rights.

These notions of sociological progress can be founded on dominant sociopolitical thinking at the time. The imperative toward progress had the consequence of pushing towards more, not less, racial, cultural, social, political, and economic progress, even though that was not the intent of Latin American elites at the time. Latin American elites of the 19th century found it difficult to divorce superior ideas from the race, culture, and ethnicity of the people originally holding them. If the Europeans first propagated the ideas of political and economic liberalism, it must have been meant only for Europeans or peoples of European descent. This was a convenient belief, inasmuch as peoples of European descent typically controlled industrial and agricultural production in virtually all Latin American countries in the 19th century, as well as the 20th century. This tendency held even as non-Europeans penetrated the ranks of the Latin American elites. It was not uncommon for Latin American elites "tainted" by non-European blood to seek to hide their indigenous origins.

Despite all the limitations, the impact on Latin American history of new liberal political and economic ideals, of markets and democracy, cannot be underestimated. It is commonly supposed that the discovery of the New World opened up new modes of cheaper international trade. However, price gaps between continents remained stable until the advent of the free trade model in the early 1800s and the innovation of new, cheaper transport technologies. It was due to such technological and, most importantly, *ideational* innovations that a boom global trade in animal products, grain, etc., became possible (O'Rourke and Williamson, 1994, 1999; O'Rourke, Taylor, and Williamson, 1996).[3]

In the final sense, it can hardly be doubted that, for Latin America, the seeds of change were sown in the colonial era. European settlers had a primal goal in mind: to enrich themselves via the market and free trade (Denoon, 1983). It was not only the Industrial Revolution that led to this important effect on wage–rent ratios. The surge in liberal economic and trade policies had an effect as well, lowering transaction costs of trade, even as technological innovation lowered the transportation costs. As the share of trade in national accounts became more important, the positive effects of more liberal trade had external effects throughout the economies. Liberal institutions flourished around the principles of market economies and freer trade between nations (O'Rourke and Williamson, 2005).

Attempts have been made to argue that international trade benefitted rich countries like the United States and the Europeans more so than Latin American countries. This is an incorrect reading of the facts. Although significant, the importance of trade with Latin America to rich countries' development has been exaggerated. Technological innovations in industry and agriculture were the true determinants of growth in what would become the developed countries. Europe, and to a lesser extent North America, had been developing the institutional prerequisites for industrial takeoff for centuries, prior to the explosion of trade with Latin American in the 19th century.

Despite the benefits of trade all around, the true causes of economic prosperity (or failure) were to be found domestically, not internationally. The models for reference purposes would be the developed countries in the 19th century. Domestic institutional innovations in key European countries were the true causes of growth of domestic and international markets, rather than the existence of international markets for exports and imports. As of 1500, Europe had an estimated 70 universities. Education and the dissemination of knowledge spawned new inventions and discoveries, in shipping technologies, in meteorology, and astronomy. Major advancements in mathematics and physics led to improved telescopes, microscopes, thermometers, barometers, clocks, watches, and the steam engine. These factors had been developing in European and North American societies for centuries and had no counterparts elsewhere in the world (Maddison, 2008). Institutional innovations like limitations on the powers of governments also incentivized wealth accumulation. These factors were the true reasons behind the economic success of these economies vis-à-vis the underdeveloped economies of Latin America, a fact only recently coming to be discovered in Latin America.

Modern scholars have perhaps been overly seduced by the greater amount of international trade data available relative to other economic activities for centuries past. That, coupled with romantic stories of exploration, the *Conquista* in Latin America, and imperial rivalries, has always made for fascinating reading. However, the fact is that Europe and North America developed more from within than from some supposed reliance on unjust international trade. Moreover, the technology-deprived backward economies of Latin America benefitted disproportionately from access to developed economies goods, services, institutions, and ideas. Even if trade with Latin America was not all that important for Europe and North America, it certainly was for Latin America. Moreover, trade would not have been all that important in the aggregate, but on the micro level, great opportunities surfaced and great fortunes were made.

For all its political mythology and rank hypocrisy, the independence movement had accomplished some significant advancements. Chief among these was a change in outlook, a testimony to the power of new ideas. The new Latin American republics looked more towards the modern British political and economic models of political and economic organization, instead of the Latin Iberian ones. This involved what would accumulatively become a sea change in attitudes related to politics, economics, and even society.

THE ECONOMIC STRUCTURE OF LATIN AMERICA IN THE 19TH CENTURY

Latin America during the 19th century was abundant in many resources, particularly natural resources. The region, however, suffered scarcity in labor. Labor mobility was restricted in the internal economies of most Latin American countries, due to the pervasive influence of retrograde institutions overly influenced by Iberian traditions that were non-conducive to economic growth and development.

Latin America would not have been able to respond to the opportunities offered by the world economy had it not been for the easy access it had to the European immigrant market. This was particularly true for the southernmost part of Latin America. Strong immigration flows from Europe to southernmost Latin America brought an influx of highly valuable entrepreneurial and technical talent. The influx of ideas challenged homegrown Latin American political and social institutions. The Europeans were not as docile as Latin Americans when it came to exclusion from political affairs.

Liberal ideas were exported from North America and Europe to Latin America, to profound political, social, and economic effects. Where indigenous populations remained important, coercive measures were politically implemented to spawn labor mobility. However, indentured service and slavery would gradually be forced out. The conservative influence of the Catholic Church waned, to the benefit of political, social, and economic progress.

Foreign financing was important to the development of large-scale economic activities, such as the exploitation of natural resources, such as oil and minerals. It was also important to the spawning of the great plantation structures of the banana and sugar industries. Foreign participation in forms other than financial was important to the development of the coffee industry in countries such as Guatemala, where the local German population was instrumental in developing the industry. This industry, as were many others in Latin America, was to focus on exporting to external markets abroad.

1870–World War I: The Export Boom

Between 1870 and 1930, the Latin American economies failed to achieve macro-economic stability on what could be regarded as a regular basis, due to the inability of governments to handle their exchange rates under a proper stable system. However, the introduction of railroad and modern transport systems provided substantial learning opportunities and positive externalities that enabled Latin American economies to modernize by imitation, at least in comparison to where they were before, without world trade. In countries like Brazil and Mexico, the railroads were an important impetus for economic modernization, although true modernization would not begin until after World War II. The immersion of Latin America into export markets brought about important productivity improvements in export sectors, although the transmission effects to other sectors were always slow.

The advent of the export age brought about not only national investment, but international investment as well. However, as profits from trade grew, so did the thinking that economic dependency was a peril to be dealt with. Trade boomed among Latin American countries in the years between 1870 and 1914, the beginning of World War I. In Mexico, Argentina, Brazil, Colombia, Cuba *et al.*, trade increased significantly. Even though it may not have been a very significant part of the total economy of the developed countries, the dramatic increase in the importance of trade was certainly a factor to notice in Latin America. Then, as now, trade benefitted not as much the developed countries as the Latin American, which tried to control it.

The initial gains from trade naturally benefitted the economic agents that invested in land, since it was agricultural products that were typically being exported from Latin America. This aspect was further deepened where railroads were built to favor export enclaves, i.e. railroads that went directly from the farms or mines to the ports for exports. However, the general story is that trade benefitted Latin America tremendously. The boom in exports created a small, but important, middle class of merchants and clerical workers that deviated strongly from the previous categorization of Latin American society, which was basically rich and educated or ignorant and poor. As the export sector went, so did Latin American modernization, inasmuch as the creation of a new middle class of educated, not rich, yet aspirational people set the basis for the creation of the foundations of modern Latin American democracies.

Though trade benefitted Latin America in the aggregate, there were important microeconomic effects, which, as always, ended up having macro results. Since farm or mine products conformed the primary export, international trade favored the landed classes relatively more than the poorer classes, although these latter also benefitted. Along with the growth in trade came a relative boom in middle-class occupations like merchants and civil professionals dedicated to the transactions of trade. Suffice to say, these beneficiaries of trade constituted the minority of the population in the bulk of Latin American countries, not because of trade, but because of archaic, anti-liberal policies regarding trade.

Though the turn towards exports surely created an economic boom, the reality was that this boom also created an economic dependency on the continued willingness of foreign investors to choose Latin America instead of other regions of the world. In the context of the prevailing sociopolitical culture, the safe havens required by foreign investors tended to be roughly translated to order and peace maxims, typically prejudicial to the legitimate political interests of the non-elites.

Inasmuch as Latin American economies became more acceptant of the realities of the benefits of free trade, they became more dependent on the economic prospects of their trading partners. This postcolonial economic dependence would eventually become a focal point of Latin American political contention, as if there were ever a choice between competing in the world economy or not.[4]

Nationalist rhetoric aside, there has always been a significant degree in Latin America of what Mexicans would call *malinchismo*, roughly translated as a preference for what is foreign. This surely drove the imports of European and, to a lesser extent, American, manufactured and luxury goods in the 19th and 20th centuries. It is very common, still today, for Latin Americans to criticize everything American, while yearning to display American brand goods, such as Coca-Cola and Hilfiger, and listen to—and copy—American music. In this context, Latin American economic nationalism must be taken with a grain of salt, especially when expressed at a popular level. It is when it becomes official government policy that it becomes a problem.

Latin American economic expansion up to the Great Depression was primarily fueled by the growth of exports. However, export-led growth produced uneven effects in Latin American countries. Export sectors were important as pioneering new forms of economic activity, and learning, but they did not employ the bulk of local labor forces. Typically, export-led growth focused on the exploitation of Latin America's abundant natural resources. This tended to foment the expansion of land tenure structures focused on extraction of existing resources, instead of the production of non-existing ones. Importantly, the "curse of the riches" worked against the development of entrepreneurial cultures, such as those that developed in countries less richly endowed in resources such as England, Holland, and, more recently, South Korea, Taiwan, and Japan.

Exports not only increased as a share of GDP for many Latin American countries, Latin America's structural participation in world trade also increased from 7.1% to 8.6% in the time period from 1899–1913. As trade ties with the developed world progressed, precious metals declined in overall importance as produce, meat, and natural resources like oil and minerals grew in importance. Coffee, sugars, and spices also were important sources of export revenues.

Argentina in the late 19th and early 20th centuries provides the best example of export-led growth. However, virtually all Latin American economies improved with their insertion into the international economy. At first, Latin American economic dependence was focused on Europe, but as the North American economy began to catch up with and surpass Europe, the Latin American economies made the transition. As the European economies fell into slowdown in the interwar years, Latin American economies turned towards the US economy as an increasingly important export market.

Table 2.3 Latin American export performance, 1860–1929

	1859/1861	1899/1901	1911/1913	1927/1929
Value of Exports (Millions of USD)				
Latin America	$292	$664	$1,493	$2,954
Argentina	$13	$163	$437	$964
Latin America excluding Argentina	$279	$501	$1,055	$1,989
Share of World Trade		7.1%	8.6%	9.2%
Share of Exports from the Third World	41.8%	37.4%	38.4%	36.4%
Commodity composition (% of export totals) Traditional products				
Agricultural and forest includes sugar, tobacco, leather, rubber	41.2%	28.5%	24.5%	16.9%
Mineral includes precious metals, guano, nitrates	18.8%	14.2%	13.0%	6.6%
Coffee	18.2%	18.5%	18.6%	18.0%
Dynamic Products				
Agricultural includes cereals, wool, meat	3.9%	22.2%	24.4%	27.7%
Mineral includes copper and tin	0.2%	1.2%	4.7%	14.2%

Source: Adapted from Ocampo (2006)

Many factors conflated to create a favorable export climate for Latin America in the decades following 1870. Technological innovations reduced transport costs in the 19th century. This improved the terms of trade for Latin American economies focused on exporting commodity products. However, after World War I, prices for commodity goods grew increasingly volatile.

Export-led growth in Latin America engendered capital and labor movements. London was the main source of external financing for Latin America for the 19th century and the early part of the 20th. However, over time, other European powers increased their capital financing to the Latin American region, as did the United States. Foreign capital was instrumental in the financing of infrastructure projects such as the construction of roads and railways, which helped integrate the national economies of Latin America, as well as increase their participation in world trade.

Immigration flows between the developed world and Latin America were basically the inverse of what they are today. People from the first world immigrated to Latin America, not vice versa. Countries like Argentina absorbed a huge quantity of southern European immigrants, particularly Italians. Brazil and Chile absorbed massive relative numbers of immigrants from Europe, who brought with them entrepreneurial attitudes and competencies, and technical skills largely unknown to the Latin American region. Chinese immigrated to countries like Peru. Of course, large contingents of slave labor were brought also, forming important parts of the population in the Caribbean, and to a lesser extent Central America.

Table 2.4 Latin America in the world economy

	1820	1870	1913	1929	1950	1980	1990	2000
Per capita GDP								
Western Europe	$1,232	$1,974	$3,473	$4,111	$4,579	$13,197	$15,966	$19,002
USA, Australia, New Zealand, Canada	$1,202	$2,419	$5,233	$6,673	$9,268	$18,060	$22,345	$27,065
Japan	$669	$737	$1,387	$2,026	$1,921	$13,428	$18,789	$21,069
Asia excluding Japan	$577	$550	$658		$634	$1,494	$2,117	$3,189
Latin America	$692	$681	$1,481	$2,034	$2,506	$5,412	$5,053	$5,838
Africa	$420	$500	$637			$894	$1,444	$1,464
World	$667	$875	$1,525		$2,111	$4,520	$5,157	$6,012
Inter regional disparities (%)								
Latin America vrs. USA	55.1%	27.9%	27.9%	29.5%	26.2%	29.1%	21.8%	20.8%
Latin America vrs. World	−103.7%	77.8%	97.1%		118.7%	119.7%	98.0%	97.1%
Latin America vrs. Africa	164.8%	136.2%	232.5%		280.3%	352.3%	349.9%	398.8%
Latin America vrs. Asia excluding Japan	119.9%	123.9%	225.2%		395.5%	362.2%	238.7%	183.1%
Latin America's share of world output	2.2%	2.5%	4.4%		7.8%	9.8%	8.3%	8.4%

Source: Adapted from Ocampo (2006)

Demonstration effects came into play as well. Latin American development was undoubtedly inspired and determined by its political and economic relations with the developed countries. The influence overall of the developed world on the developing world of Latin America was positive, and it was not confined to the realm of consumer goods, capital inputs, and the importation of ideas of markets, democracy, and progress. There were concrete results that redounded to the benefit of mankind. A case in point is the Panama Canal. Had it not been for the United States, Panama—and the Panama Canal—would likely not have come into existence.

By the middle of the 19th century, Latin America was in the midrange of the income hierarchy of world regions. In this time period, it was claiming an increasing share of total world gross product.

Latin American countries did not succeed in developing their internal economies. As a result, Latin American governments were particularly dependent on tariff duties as sources of revenues. Investment patterns suffered with the booms and busts of international trade, further disrupting the supply of investment for important domestic economy developmental projects. The largest countries of Latin America—Argentina, Brazil, Chile, and Colombia—suffered these types of volatile revenue swing.

The export era of Latin America has been incorrectly labeled the *laissez-faire* age. This is not true. Latin American countries typically have turned to inflationary measures and currency depreciations to recover their competitiveness in world markets. Governments forced labor in countries like Guatemala, and intervened to ensure that the revenues from exports of agricultural and mining products did not accrue to the working classes, in many cases.

THE IMPACT OF EXPORT-LED GROWTH ON THE DIVERSIFICATION OF THE SOCIOECONOMIC STRUCTURE

Latin America's early model of export-oriented growth was largely confined to the export of primary products or commodities for industrial use in the developed countries, "the North." Export-led growth in Latin America typically spawned debates centered around the issues of the distribution of the benefits generated by exports, particularly of natural resources, as well as the backward and forward linkages associated with export-oriented sectors. On the distributive debate, the issue typically centered on the division of the profits between national and foreign players, but also on the distribution among national economic agents. These issues have never been resolved in Latin America. Landowners typically resist governmental attempts to tax exports and land.

Latin American tariff policies were oriented to stimulate import-substitution industrialization, a prerequisite to the imperative of modernization, which Latin American elites had assumed. Countries such as Chile, Mexico, Colombia, and Brazil were actively protectionist. Despite Latin America's reliance on trade, governments in the region never hesitated to practice economic protectionism in order to shield local economic actors from the rigors of international markets. Latin America had the highest tariffs in the world in the 19th century (Coatsworth and Williamson, 2003). Taxes were one thing; government spending was another. Where governments chose to invest in physical and human capital in the 19th century and the early part of the 20th, the economies of the region improved. Unfortunately, Latin American governments, then as now, did not always prove to be wise spenders of public revenues.

Export activities had important backward linkages that introduced new innovations into the rest of the economy. Mineral exportation activities spawned processing plants. Sugar processing plants also arose in response to the needs of the sugars export sector. Technological innovations like refrigeration made the transportation of meat possible. This, too, spawned the birth of meat-processing plants. The surge in new employment opportunities spread benefits throughout society. As incomes grew in Latin America, a consumer class arose and, with it, domestic demand grew. Local consumers demanded not only foreign products, but also domestically grown produce, further fueling Latin American development.

Latin America did not only benefit from her exports, but imports as well. While it is true that national demand for foreign manufactures benefitted foreign exports to Latin America, the importation of these manufactures facilitated local industrialization as well. The exportation of goods involved forward linkages such as processing requirements. The cement and beer industries tended to be characterized by backward linkages, through which materials, money, and information flowed between firms and suppliers, creating a network of economic interdependence. The high costs of transportation worked to the favor of national industries as well.

An important benefit of the export-led growth era was the transmission of technological know-how and entrepreneurial attitudes lacking in traditional Latin American cultures. Trade promoted greater specialization, innovation, and the diffusion of ideas and institutions. International trade spawned greater specialization and innovations in banking, insurance, and shipping. To participate in world trade, Latin America had to adopt the rules of the game of the international economy. As Latin American trade with the other regions of the world became more congruent with world rules than local shenanigans, the prospects for the general enrichment of the general population through free trade reforms increased. Latin America had to innovate new financial institutions to facilitate trade, which over time would have positive external effects on economic growth and development in the region (Cárdenas, Ocampo, and Thorp, 2000a, Ch. 1; Bulmer-Thomas, 2003, Ch. 5).

Industrialization began during the export-led boom (Gomez-Galvarriato and Williamson, 2009). The countries that experienced the most success during the export age were Argentina, Chile, Cuba, and Uruguay. Colombia, Peru, and Venezuela also benefitted tremendously. Brazil stagnated in the 19th century, but rebounded in the 20th.

DISCUSSION OF MONETARY REGIMES

The exportation of primary goods by the Latin American economies was subjected to various booms and busts over the course of the 19th century. In the 19th century, Latin American economies as a general rule either adhered to the gold standard or the silver standard. In the 1870s, silver depreciated strongly versus gold. Certain economies, like those of Mexico and Central America, found themselves facing a continuing devaluation of their exchange rate. As exports were strengthened, so was the political and social position of the economic elites involved heavily in these sectors.

The economies of the Latin American region have always found difficulties in keeping the balance between domestic and external performance under fixed exchange rate regimes. Due to lack of a domestic manufacturing base, demand for imported manufactured goods was inelastic. Trade deficits for Latin American countries, therefore, tended to be more persistent, even under normal economic conditions of growth. Changing terms of trade in a fixed exchange rate system had economic consequences, primarily on output levels.

Gold Standard

Strong arguments have been made in favor of a monetary standard like gold. The case of Argentina in the decades leading up to World War I is a clear example, experiencing nearly 6% growth, combined with a low inflation rate of 2.6% per annum (Della Paolera and Taylor, 2003). Similar arguments are made for other standards, namely silver. When the price of silver dropped in the last three decades of the 19th century, countries on the silver standard effectively saw their currencies depreciated and their export sectors concomitantly fortified. This helped countries like Peru (Thorp and Bertram, 1978) and Colombia, as well as Central America (Perez-Brignoli, 1989).

It bears remembering that Latin America was originally a prized region for its production of mineral wealth, such as gold and silver. A country on a silver standard, like Mexico, would perceive benefits if the currency depreciated, because that would help its exports. On the other hand, its export receipts for silver would decrease, complicating matters to say the least. Currency depreciations also created obstacles to access to foreign capital markets, raising the effective price of debt servicing from abroad, a much-needed venue for the capital to fund nascent Latin American industrialization and modernization efforts.

Adherence to the gold standard by the Latin American economies based on the exportation of primary commodities meant that these same would undergo large inflows of gold. Export growth, and hence national economic growth, would inherently be accompanied by what amounted to a lax monetary policy. By the same token, trade deficits would imply an outflow of gold.

The persistence of weak and corrupt political institutions prevalent in the entire region made adherence to the gold standard difficult for many Latin American countries in the 19th century. Some argue that the gold standard for Latin America proved to be a disaster, as it fueled a preference for imports and degraded the competitiveness of Latin American exports. Typically, appreciating exchange rates brought about rising imports, and a profound growth in the introduction of new technologies and ideas, albeit at the cost of deteriorating current account balances in the short run. The stability of prices was one benefit of the gold standard applied in those times, even if macroeconomic stability did not always follow. In the end, the costs of adhering to a disciplined monetary regime, such as was the gold standard, need to be balanced against the benefits of what would have surely been inflationary political and economic schemes, as judged by modern Latin American history in the 20th century.

1900–1920

The coming of the 20th century marks the advent of the US as a regional power in the American hemisphere. This implied, in principle and practice, a certain dominance of political, economic, and even social affairs in Latin America. Whereas the Monroe Doctrine declared the Americas as a region destined for democracy, the US had little power to make this so in the early 1800s. By the early 1900s things had changed. The Roosevelt Corollary to the Monroe Doctrine made this explicit. The 1898 Spanish-American War marked the decline of Spain as a world power in Latin American affairs, and the ascent of the United States in its place. US foreign policy formally established its right to intervene militarily in Caribbean and Central American affairs when the US saw fit, usually to protect the commercial interests of powerful US citizens or industries.

The political implications of nascent American power on Latin America were direct. In point of fact, one result of US intervention in Latin America was not only the Canal of Panama, but also Panama itself. The US sought in Colombia a territorial concession in the territory in the area of Panama in order to build a canal across the isthmus. To this notion, the Colombian government was opposed. As a result, the US gave at least tacit backing to those who would create the new nation of Panama, which subsequently granted the concession of the construction of the Panama Canal by the United States (Greene, 2009).

American interventions in the Central American regions were, of course, not confined to the creation of such public goods[5] as the Panama Canal. The US was to later become involved in numerous "Banana Wars," which were justified in the name of protecting US lives and property, albeit pointedly not democracy (Lake, 1989). The prolific US intervention in Central American affairs in the interests of American "lives and property" would prove to be both cause and consequence of the stifling of the progress of liberal political and economic institutions in the region. One modern consequence of this is that Latin Americans have an overwhelming tendency to blame every endogenous drawback of theirs on the influence of the United States.

The admixture of demands for greater political democracy and liberal economic markets did not always proceed apace. Mexico, right next to the US, was where the great political upheaval took place in the second decade of the 20th century. After a prolonged struggle, in which millions of people died, a liberal government based on democratic principles was formally implemented, but it was one in which the main aspirations of the working classes and rural classes went largely ignored. The same occurred throughout Latin America.

With the advent of World War I, the flows of manufactured exports from the developed world to Latin America were interrupted. This created incentives for local production, which engendered increasing demands for local protectionist measures, typically through increasingly prohibitive tariffs imposed on manufactured goods from abroad. The development of local manufactures was limited by the small size of the domestic markets and poor economic integration on national scales. Latin American countries typically lacked the quality public institutions necessary to implement national strategies of economic integration over the long run. It was not unusual for the export sectors of Latin American countries to be better integrated with foreign economies than with their own national economies.

Latin America returned, by and large, to the gold standard after World War I. However, this was not to last. To avoid the most difficult structural adjustments and deflationary conditions, several countries—such as Mexico, Argentina, and Brazil—rapidly abandoned the gold standard. This was perceived as an economic necessity. As demand conditions for primary commodities in the developed world fell off, the Latin American export sectors were particularly hard hit. Inflows of gold declined precipitously, and balance of payments problems surged.

The Great Depression hit Latin America particularly hard. As demand conditions in the developed economies plummeted, so did the markets for exports from the regions. Inasmuch as the Latin American economies depended on a relatively constrained basket of exports to pay for an increasing array of manufactured and luxury imports, the balance of payments problems for countries in the region severely worsened and output levels dropped dramatically. Particularly hard hit in the Great Depression were Argentina, Chile, Brazil, Mexico, Colombia, and the nations of Central America.

The demand for Latin American primary commodity exports was derived demand, dependent on the ups and downs of the demand conditions prevalent in the developed world, Europe, and the US. Given their reliance on exports, Latin American economies were, in a large sense, extensions of the European economies, scarcely reliant on their own internal, domestic demand conditions for further economic growth. Countries such as Brazil, Colombia, and the nations of Central America, relied on coffee exports. Mexico, Peru, Bolivia, and Chile exported minerals. Argentina and Cuba exported foodstuffs. The clients in all cases tended to be countries from the developed world.

The acceptance of the imperatives of globalization and the adoption of export-led growth models proved decisive for the development of Latin America. The ability to integrate to foreign economies was crucial for the success of the political economic bargains attained by Latin American elites. Foreign financed and induced technological advancements, such as railroads and refrigerated transportation, made possible, and credible, the promise to return greater economic benefits by allying abroad (Coatsworth, 2005).

Despite the benefits of contacts with the developed world that increased commerce provided, Latin America had not optimized its exploitation of the opportunities provided by an increasingly connected world economy. It inherited the legacy of Spanish institutions and social structure, not Anglo-Saxon ones. There was precious little understanding of the social and political infrastructure needed for true political, economic, and social development and modernization. Nonetheless, with the onset of the Great Depression and the collapse of the world economy, Latin American governments took it upon themselves to become stewards of national economic development in the coming decades, albeit to differing degrees of "success."

THE IMPORT-SUBSTITUTION-INDUSTRIALIZATION ERA

The Great Depression dealt a deathblow to the Latin American export model. As demand conditions in the US as well as Europe fell off, the export markets for Latin American economies collapsed, as commodity prices plummeted. The global financial system fell into chaos and uncertainty as countries, even the UK, abandoned the gold standard, causing FDI flows to dry up, leaving Latin America dearly short of capital. As markets for Latin American exports fell off, the Latin American countries experienced negative pressures in their external finance sectors, as well as in their fiscal situations and balance of payments accounts.

Beginning with the Smoot-Hawley Tariff Act in the US in 1930, a run of protectionist beggar-thy-neighbor policies characterized the disintegration of free trade commercial regimes. As the developed economies fell into the illiberal practices of trade restrictions, Latin American countries also were prone to follow. Ill-advised multiple exchange rates were experimented with, particularly in countries that didn't use the dollar as a medium of exchange. Fiscal pressures meant that nearly all Latin American countries were pressured to abandon their foreign debt obligations.

As foreign sources of financing dried up, balance of payments accounts were stressed. Multiple policy responses failed to rebalance matters. As protectionism, exchange controls, devaluation, import controls, and the employment of multiple exchange rates failed, the measure of last recourse was all too often the decision to default on foreign debt.

The advent of the Great Depression brought great shocks to the Latin American region. With the collapse of the world economy came a drastic reduction in the demand of raw materials from the developed world to the underdeveloped world. Intellectual opinion in Latin America turned against the great dependency that was perceived in the economic relationships between the rich "North" and poor "South." Declining terms of trade between North and South were commonly signaled as causal factors of poverty between the two regions.

In 1938, the Cardenas Administration in Mexico, in a bold move, nationalized US oil companies. The US let it stand. Despite the negative implications for the commercial interests of the US, the Roosevelt administration gave way, understanding it could not wholly impede the nationalist aspirations of its Latin American neighbors. Thus, the Good Neighbor Policy was born, entailing as well the repealing of the Platt Amendment, which had given the US the "right" to interfere in Cuban politics. Upon the advent of World War II and the struggle against global fascism, the US was brought closer together with its Latin American neighbors, at least some, and in part.

Having adopted as a nationalist imperative the need to modernize politically, socially, and economically, but lacking capital to pay for industrial inputs, Latin American countries turned towards import-substitution-industrialization (ISI) as the means to achieve their developmentalist aims. ISI policies were promoted, based on the idea of commercial protectionism, transfer of riches, and the creation of burgeoning local, middle classes, whereby local, protected, industries would tend to local demand. ISI was, essentially, an infant-industries argument. Latin American countries were to adopt ISI policies in order to produce self-sufficient development, based on the expansion of the internal market. ISI was essentially a state-led regime, whereby the state not only implemented protectionist trade policies, but also nationalized key industries, and subsidized strategic industries such as power, which were determined to be of critical importance for the purposes of national economic development.

This time, the industrialization emphasis was not to be tied to the needs of the export sectors. Instead, the development of the internal, domestic markets was to be the focus. The ISI trend was led by the big countries of Latin America, such as Mexico, Brazil, and Argentina, but was also followed by the smaller countries of Central America.

In the 1930s a paradigmatic change in economic thinking was under way. The classical economics underpinnings of the free trade regimes were apparently discredited, and pro-interventionist policies, later known as Keynesian economics, became the new normal. Under the new economic philosophy, domestic demand could and should be stimulated by activist fiscal and monetary policies. These ideas took sway in Latin America, where the suspension of foreign debt obligations and the creation of national banks restored in the short run domestic credit and financial markets.

Latin America as a whole embraced the Keynesian notions of activist monetary and fiscal policies, controls on free trade, as well as the ISI notions aimed at substituting the importation of manufactures and agricultural goods. ISI policies needed to complement Keynesian demand management policies, so that Latin American countries did not unduly stimulate the demand for imports, and thus exacerbate their balance of payments problems. Domestic demand did, indeed, recuperate partly, and with varying degrees of success throughout the Latin American region, leading to increasingly greater levels of state intervention in subsequent decades, even when decreasing marginal returns on public investments set in.

Only time would reveal the long-term costs of unmitigated state interventionism. After adopting the Keynesian fiscal and monetary policies and ISI commercial policies, Latin American governments no longer were inclined to adopt the views that industrialization was for developed countries and exports of primary commodities for developing countries. The imperative was to pursue both industrialization and growth in the export sectors. Latin American countries all hoped to regain their former access to the developed world markets, which they had enjoyed prior to the Great Depression and World War II.

ISI policies were based on a certain economic nationalism, which eventually led to the nationalization of foreign investments in Latin America. The most famous case was the nationalization of the oil companies by the Cardenas administration (1934–1940) in Mexico. The onset of World War II actually provided a strong exogenous push for Latin American industrialization, as Western industrialized nations directed their industrial outputs to the existential war against fascism. Keynesian monetary policies were apparently validated as domestic inflation lowered the pressures of foreign debt holdings. As Latin American countries imported less, while continuing to export to the US, the financial and economic engine of the war effort against global fascism, trade balances improved, as did the holdings of international reserves. Domestic financing of new types of ISI investment drive was greatly facilitated under these unique historical conditions for Latin America. It is important to note that Latin America had the tremendous good fortune of avoiding the destructive consequences of World War II, but able to participate as a supplier of raw materials for the Allied cause.

Latin American governments became more activist and interventionist in their national economies than they had been in the past. However, there was a general outright rejection of the collectivist alternatives presented by the Nazis and the Soviets in the 1940s. Latin American countries continued to rely on their export sectors as sources of foreign exchange and fiscal revenues. ISI regimes validated protectionist policies, while the adoption of Keynesian economic schemes provided the rationale for an increasingly activist state that aimed to direct national economic development drives. National economic development drives strove to modernize not only the nascent industrial sectors, but also the traditional agricultural sectors.

For the most part, Latin American governments assumed the tasks of implementing trade restrictions, tariff controls, capital controls, and FDI controls. In addition, the state assumed such important tasks as infrastructure developments, in terms not just of highways and railroads, but also banking systems. Social infrastructure was also the goal of public investments in health, education, and a modicum of social safety net legislation.

As demand conditions stabilized in the developed countries in the postwar period, the international reserves that Latin America had accumulated diminished in short order. Volatile price swings made export models predicated on the selling abroad of primary commodities an unviable proposition. This was especially so given that the protectionist measures adopted in the interwar years still applied. The creation of a liberal world order after World War II was to rely tremendously on the Bretton Woods scheme and the General Agreement on Tariffs and Trade, which, importantly, made strong exceptions for agricultural and textile sectors, areas where Latin America would have otherwise held a strong comparative advantage.

THE COLD WAR

The main thinkers in the ISI tradition were Raúl Prebisch and Celso Furtado. The Dependency School of economic thought that they helped establish was neo-Marxist and neo-Keynesian in outlook, blaming the structure of world trade and national economies for the development of underdevelopment in Latin American, as well as the rest of the Third World. The marriage of Keynesianism with ISI philosophy was summed up into a cogent theory backed by the United Nations Economic Commission for Latin America (ECLAC, or CEPAL by its Spanish initials). Industrialization was essential if the Latin American "periphery" was to break the chains of dependency on the industrialized "center," which was the developed world. Essential to this process was the achievement of scale economies through regional economic integration. It was particularly hoped that economic integration would provide efficiency incentives for domestically protected industries. These ideas were widely shared by others that partook of the general Keynesian consensus, such as the US government at the time, American big capital, and multilateral bodies such as the International Monetary Fund, the IBRD, and the World Bank.

Upon the ending of World War II, however, new grounds for US intervention in Latin America arose; quite specifically, the specter of communism. Latin Americans were forced to choose between falling into the US sphere of influence, or that of the USSR. Given what was at stake for Latin American elites they gladly chose to be US allies. Latin America would remain stalwart commercial partners of the West, while the US would benignly overlook the fact that Latin American countries had a proclivity to adopt authoritarian political regimes that looked after the interests of the political and economic elites, who happened to be US allies. Latin America had since its independence always opted, in general, for authoritarian regimes of a conservative order, but after World War II the authoritarian regimes could claim the added legitimacy of US backing.

Given the structural inequities of Latin American societies dating back to the colonial era, it was not surprising that communist insurgencies took root throughout the region, promising falsely, as they did, equality and progress. An early success for the communists was the rise to power in Guatemala via free and fair elections in Guatemala of the governments of Juan Jose Arevalo and Jacobo Arbenz, which had known, overt communist sympathizers in areas of influence in their governments. This was followed by the overthrow of the dictator Fulgencio Batista in Cuba by the later declared communist forces led by Fidel Castro. The comforting simplicity of the authoritarian law-and-order model preferred by US investors and the American government had come to an abrupt end. The failed US-backed Bay of Pigs Invasion in Cuba became legendary throughout Latin America, representative as it was thought to be of American determination to oust each and every government not to its liking. Though US influence waned as one went further south of the border between the US and Mexico, it became engrained in Latin American culture that the US was behind every counterinsurgency movement and coup that occurred during the Cold War. The truth was that the US did not invent the figure of the Latin American military dictator, but it did choose to do business with such, as an alternative to communist regimes such as those found in Cuba and Vietnam. These notions explain a great deal of the "anti-American" sentiment still prevalent among Latin Americans today.

An unintended, yet positive, consequence of the victory of the democratic allies in World War II over the forces of fascism was the yearning for more democratic governments in Latin America. All over the world, liberal ideas took hold. It was modern and progressive to give power to the people; it was reactionary not to do so. Illiberal communist movements took advantage of the new worldview, especially in the Third World, where American and pro-Western allies backed imperialist and authoritarian stooges in the name of "law and order." Whereas the drawbacks of the authoritarian status quo were evident, those of the totalitarian communist future were not. The communists had the advantage, and exploited it, especially in Latin America, promising a more inclusive, democratic, less oppressive future to the excluded peoples of Latin America, which the Americans, the West, and their authoritarian satellites in the Third World had been only too content to ignore. The communists took able advantage of the fact that the Western powers were also imperialist powers, eventually forced by the power of new ideas to let their empires go.

The go-to response of the Latin American elites to nullify the threat of a communist takeover of their governments was their traditional tool of political influence, the military coup d'état. Though criticized as a tool of American imperialism, the coup was, in fact, a homegrown Latin American political method exploited upon occasion by an opportunistic American foreign policy eager to avoid the worst-case scenario of seeing totalitarian communist regimes sprout up all over Latin America. It was deemed easier to deal with pro-market authoritarian regimes (Kirkpatrick, 1982).

Though communist takeovers were rather limited, insurgencies sprouted up all over Latin America. Countries such as Brazil, Colombia, Chile, Argentina, Guatemala, and the rest of Central America were affected. Of greater impact was the aforementioned surge in protectionist, statist regimes throughout the region of Latin American in the 1950s, 1960s, and 1970s. Countries such as Argentina, Brazil, Mexico, and Venezuela saw state involvement in their economies grow tremendously, even though the quality of their institutions did not grow apace with their public revenues and spending. The guiding principle was the state rectorship of political, economic, and social progress of the nations, enabled by the protection of national industries along the lines of "infant industries" argument, whereby national industries would be entitled to protection so that they could grow large enough to be able to compete against the dominant multinational firms from the "North" (Franko, 2007).

The communist takeover of Cuba focused American attention on the problems of underdevelopment in Latin America. The US created the Alliance for Progress to foster the conditions of economic growth and political development in order to blunt the attractiveness of radical communist political programs in Latin America. Though modest in its aims, many of the proposals contained in the Alliance for Progress were considered radical in the conservative circles of Latin America, particularly proposed tax and agrarian reforms, and state-financed social assistance policies.

Latin American industrialization depended at first on the linkages generated by the export sectors and domestic trade protection. The industrialization process in the region received strong positive jolts due to exogenous shocks emanating from the Great Depression and World War II. With the theoretical and institutional backing of CEPAL, the Latin American industrialization strategy became explicitly tied to trade protectionism, controlled exchange rates, development banks, financial sector regulation, fiscal incentives, and public spending on infrastructure. In some cases, like PEMEX in Mexico, the state became actively involved in the running of state-run monopolies in key strategic sectors, such as oil, energy, and telephony.

Protectionism grew haphazardly and without an overall rationale as the Latin American governments proved incapable of overcoming the mercantilist pressures of different sectors, particularly those that had already attained a modicum of state protection. Mercantilist demands for trade protectionism were not only directed at American and European companies seeking to penetrate the Latin American market, but Latin American competitors as well. As a result, the efforts at great economic integration in Latin America were never fulfilled in the ISI era.

Perhaps emboldened by the successful Mexican takeover of American oil enterprises, many Latin American countries took a hard line against FDI in natural resource sectors in the region. FDI was negatively affected by the economic nationalism implicit in ISI regimes.

ISI coupled deepened import-substitution strategies with export promotion policies, all led by a redefined role for the state in national economic development.

EVALUATING THE ISI REGIME

The effects of the postwar modernization drives in Latin America were substantial. Perhaps most importantly, a burgeoning middle class was created. Latin America began the move toward an urban society, as opposed to an agricultural, *latifundista* society.

The positive interpretation of ISI points to the high growth rates achieved in the postwar period up until the 1980s. However, others question the results of ISI, pointing to the fact that increases in productivity, capital goods investments, and research and development were disappointing. Latin America's lack of productivity and efficiency was made evident when the economic crises hit at the end of the 1970s (Yáñez, Ducoing, and Jofré, 2010).

Stability in fiscal, monetary, and commercial policies has strong growth implications. Policy uncertainty can have strong negative impacts on investment, as business investors will hold off from investing until uncertainty subsides. The economic consensus seems to hold that inconstancy in policy can adversely affect growth conditions (Pereira, Singh, and Mueller, 2011). Where this leaves ISI is open to interpretation. On the one hand, on a very general level, the rules of the game for operating in Latin America dictated that one could expect a high and heavy hand of state intervention, justified on the domestic industrialization principles embodied under the relatively firm ISI regimes. On the other hand, each intervention and regulation stipulated by such regimes seemed to lead to ever more interventions.

Overall, exports experienced average growth rates of approximately 5% from the mid-1950s to 1980, while the average GDP growth rate for Latin America was about 4.5%.

Table 2.5 Shares in total population and total product

	Share in total population (percent)	Share regional GDP (percent)		GDP per capital (1975 dollars)		Growth Rate of GDP per capital (percent per year)	
	1980	1950	1980	1950	1980	1950–1980	1980–88
Brazil	35.6	22.2	34.2	$637	$2,152	4.2	0.2
Mexico	20.2	18.5	23.1	$1	$2,547	3	−1.3
Argentina	8	21.2	11.8	$2	$3,209	1.8	−1.9
Colombia	7.5	7.2	6.3	$949	$1,882	2.3	1.4
Venezuela	4.3	7.2	7.1	$1,811	$3,310	1.5	−1.8
Peru	5.1	4.9	3.9	$953	$1,746	2.1	−1.7
Chile	3.2	5.7	3.4	$1,416	$2,372	1.8	0.2
Uruguay	0.8	3.1	1.2	$2,187	$3	1.4	−1.2
Ecuador	2.3	1.4	1.6	$638	$1,556	3.1	−0.9
Guatemala	2	1.6	1.2	$842	$1,422	1.8	−2.4
Dom. Rep	1.7	1.1	1.1	$762	$1,114	13	0.2
Bolivia	1.6	1.4	0.8	$762	$1,114	13	−3.3
El Salvador	1.3	0.8	0.5	$612	$899	2.3	−0.4
Paraguay	0.9	0.8	0.7	$885	$1,753	3.30	−1.1
Costa Rica	0.6	0.5	0.6	$928	$2,157	2.9	−3
Panama	0.5	0.5	0.5	$928	$2,157	2.9	−3
Nicaragua	0.7	0.5	0.4	$683	$1,324	2.3	−3.4
Honduras	1	0.6	0.4	$680	$1,301	1.4	−1.8
Latin America						2.7	−1.4

Source: Adapted from Cardoso and Fishlow (1989)

Table 2.6 Growth rates in the 1960s and 1970s

Country Name	1961–69	1970–79
Argentina	4.111	2.928
Brazil	5.904	8.474
Chile	4.368	2.476
Colombia	5.079	5.811
Costa Rica	5.938	6.344
Guatemala	5.5	5.864
Mexico	6.782	6.434
Panama	8.083	4.71
Paraguay	4.275	7.917
Peru	5.252	3.936
Uruguay	1.304	2.699
Venezuela	4.812	3.966
United States	4.656	3.321

Source: Authors' calculations, based on World Bank data

As Table 2.6 shows, growth rates were healthy in the 1960s and 1970s for many Latin American countries, both big and small. While Argentina grew at an average annual rate of 4.11% in the 1960s, only to experience a slowdown to 2.928% in the 1970s, Brazil grew at close to 6% in the 1960s, and more than 8% in the 1970s. Costa Rica grew at an average annual rate of near 6% over the two decades, as did Mexico. Colombia and Guatemala also grew at average annual rates for these decades in excess of 5%.

While Latin America experienced a 116% increase in its per capita GDP from 1950–1980, the US increased its per capita GDP in the same time frame an estimated 95%. Asia, excluding Japan, surpassed the Latin American increase by some 20 percentage points. Notably, Japan reflected an almost 600% increase in its per capita GDP from 1950–1980.

During this time period, Latin America underwent the greatest increase in the GDP per capita. In other words, the standard of living rose tremendously.

The economic results for leading Latin American economies in the 1960s and 1970s were impressive. Brazil saw its GNI per capita (constant $2,000 US dollars) increase by some 136% in the 1960 to 1980 time period. Similarly, Mexico and Paraguay saw this indicator of economic standard of living increase by more than 100%. Colombia and even Guatemala saw increases of approximately 70% in their GNI per capita from 1960–1980. Peru, Uruguay, Honduras, and Chile saw more modest increases in the order of the 30% range.[6] More generally, Latin American GDP grew by more than 5% per annum in the 1950–1980 time period. The Latin American share of world GDP grew from 7.8% in 1950 to 8.7% in 1973.

By the 1970s, it appeared that Latin America was firmly on the developmentalist path. ISI policies had resulted in growth in the stocks of capital in the region, which translated into productivity gains, as measured against the Latin American economic past. The Asian Tigers that pursued even stronger export-led growth models experienced

Table 2.7 GNI per capita in constant terms (constant 2005 US dollars)

Country Name	1960s	1970s	1980 over 1960
Argentina	20.03%	14.49%	38.67%
Brazil	27.07%	64.65%	136.14%
Chile	18.84%	9.16%	38.97%
Colombia	18.84%	36.07%	69.80%
Guatemala	25.46%	35.43%	76.02%
Honduras	11.58%	26.60%	37.33%
Mexico	39.29%	33.25%	103.59%
Nicaragua	38.84%	−26.86%	6.26%
Paraguay	12.54%	64.69%	115.85%
Peru	22.95%	3.01%	34.95%
Uruguay	1.27%	9.56%	30.27%

Source: Authors' calculations, based on World Bank data

Table 2.8 Shares of world GDP, 1820–2030

	1950	1973
Western Europe	26.2%	25.6%
USA	27.3%	22.1%
Japan	3.0%	7.8%
Rich	59.9%	58.7%
China	4.6%	4.6%
India	4.2%	3.1%
Latin America	7.8%	8.7%
Africa	3.8%	3.4%
Rest	40.1%	41.3%
Latin America as % of USA	0.29:1	0.39:1

Source: Adapted from Maddison (2008)

even greater growth in GDP and productivity rates. Important in this regard was that the trade protectionist aspect of ISI closed off Latin America to important aspects of technological transfer. The inward focus of ISI in the larger countries of Latin America, such as Argentina, Brazil, and Mexico, led to a loss of relative participation in the increasingly globalized economy in the decades following World War II.

Economic growth spurred other important changes in the social and political spheres. The adoption of the interventionist state led to social welfare policies in education and health, and a modicum of social safety net legislation. A negative byproduct was the growth in the strength of labor unions, which tended to grow more radicalized over time. Latin American trades unions would push for greater concessions over time, to the detriment of the national competitiveness and efficiency of the labor markets of the regions.

Table 2.9 Latin America exports as a share of world total

Latin America/World	1953	1963	1973	1980
Total	10.10%	6.80%	4.70%	4.80%
Food	23.90%	15.10%	13.10%	12.50%
Raw materials excl. fuels	11.00%	9.20%	7.40%	8.50%
Fuels	19.50%	27.00%	11.40%	9.30%
Chemical	2.70%	1.40%	1.60%	1.80%
Machinery	0.00%	0.20%	0.70%	1.10%
Other manufactures	2.60%	2.50%	2.70%	2.70%

Source: Adapted from Ocampo (2006)

ISI, as its name would tell, contained an inherent bias against the agricultural sectors. However, the state tried to compensate with fiscal incentives existing for companies that imported heavy machinery for the agricultural sector, and heavy infrastructure investments that lowered transportation costs considerably. State actions, such as the introduction of banks, oriented toward the agricultural and rural sectors. In Guatemala, the National Coffee Association (ANACAFE, its Spanish acronym) took on such measures as training small farmers, and introducing new farming and fertilization technologies to spur quantity and quality gains.

The Latin American share of total world trade fell off from 10.1% in 1953 to 4.7% by 1980. Its share of world exports in food and fuels fell from roughly 23.9% and 19.5% to 12.5% and 9.3%, respectively, in the same time period. By 1980, Latin American exports of machinery accounted for 1.1% of the world total, in spite of the industrialization efforts of import substitution.

The composition of Latin American exports changed in the period from 1953–1980. Food exports went from comprising 52.7% of the total of exports in 1953 to 26.9% by 1980. The structural participation of raw materials in export totals also declined, from 19.4% to 11.9% in the same time frame. Fuel exports, however, showed a significant increase, from 19.6% to 37.5%. Other manufactures similarly showed a significant increase, from 6.8% in 1953 to 14.3% of the export total by 1980.

Institutions matter for economic development. As pointed out by Hayek, countries that inherited common law traditions have better property rights and financial markets. The clearest cases are those of Korea and Germany, where the same people were divided into two countries with very different institutional contexts. On the liberal side, based on markets and republican principles, the economy flourished, while the illiberal, dictatorial side, floundered (Acemoglu *et al.*, 2001). ISI regimes lent themselves inexorably to rent-seeking mercantilist practices on the part of Latin American businessmen afraid to compete on the world market. ISI had the explicit aim of reducing Latin American dependence on foreign imports of machinery and capital equipment. However, as the industrialization process took off, Latin American industries proved extremely dependent on the importation of capital inputs. Far from being temporary, protectionism became a way of life for government officials and Latin American businessmen in

Table 2.10 Composition of Latin American exports

	1953	1963	1973	1980
Total	100.00%	100.00%	100.00%	100.00%
Food	52.70%	37.80%	38.60%	26.90%
Raw materials excl. Fuels	19.40%	18.40%	15.40%	11.90%
Fuels	19.60%	31.40%	21.20%	37.50%
Chemical	1.20%	1.40%	2.60%	2.90%
Machinery	0.10%	0.60%	4.60%	6.00%
Other manufactures	6.80%	10.20%	17.00%	14.30%

Source: Adapted from Ocampo (2006)

general. The fear of foreign competition prevented the regional economic integration measures from ever taking off in optimal fashion. Public investments in infrastructure and services often led to massively wasteful and inefficient boondoggles.

Of course, without the efficiency incentives provided only by free trade regimes, the giant Latin American business concerns in banking, airlines, telephony, power, etc., never became efficient. The ISI model promoted by the Economic Commission for Latin America and the Caribbean, or ECLAC, became a massive transfer of wealth from the consuming to the capitalist classes, shielding as they did the latter from having to compete, innovate, and answer to consumer demands. Augmenting the problem was the fact that these enterprises were often state run, a complete disaster from any rational economic point of view. Alongside these direct state interventionist policies were grandiose state social programs that were universally characterized by clientelism, cronyism, and corruption.

The massive expansion of state-run enterprises and social programs, in the name of national development, had the effect of draining the coffers of the state, which had to look over the running of economies that were, in Latin America, unduly burdened by the coexistence of enormous informal economies that pointedly did *not* pay their "fair share" of tax burdens to the state. Large deficits and inordinate levels of public debt became the norm in Latin America. This norm was financed in the 1970s by ever-growing levels of foreign indebtedness, facilitated by low interest rates made possible by the influx of "petrodollars" into the world financial system. When the global economic slowdown occurred at the end of the decade of the 1970s, and interest rates rose again, the foreign debt incurred willingly by Latin American governments became unsustainable, leading to the debt crisis of the 1980s.

As could be expected, ISI would prove to have the most success in the large countries, which had sufficient market size to achieve some modicum of scale economies. Brazil and Mexico had the most success, but Chile, Uruguay, and Venezuela also reflected differing levels of success with the ISI regime. Given the obvious drawbacks to achieving scale economies in small Latin American countries, such as those of Central America, an important impetus was given to the processes of regional economic integration.

CONCLUSIONS

For all its numerous drawbacks, the ISI experience left Latin America industrialized, with all the sociopolitical implications that implies. In its industrialization efforts, the nations of Latin America had managed to create a politically active middle class. The introduction of not just a modernizing, but a modern state apparatus introduced influential innovations to the region in the way of public spending in health, education, and social safety nets. Importantly, the modern Latin American middle class would prove to be an important demander of the aforementioned services in education, health, and social safety net services that would in the end help make Latin American labor more productive.

Latin America has left behind the days when its comparative trade advantages rested solely in the agricultural sector. In fact, the region as a whole has moved past the industrial state, to a regional economy based more on services than even industry. Nevertheless, the legacy of the method, import substitution, that the Latin American countries chose to industrialize, still leaves a negative imprint on the doing business climate for foreign investors. Latin American businessmen are almost universally mercantilistic, looking always to the state for protection from foreign competition at every turn. That said, the region has moved towards greater economic openness amid an increasingly globalized economy, and via free trade pacts, which slowly but surely have introduced liberalizing economic and trade reforms into the economies of the region. This is good news for foreign investors seeking to do business in Latin America, as freer trade policies are increasingly institutionalized into free trade pacts from which the local governments are ever more reticent to back out, and which the peoples of Latin America are ever more inclined to demand, on account of a greater quantity and quality of goods and services they find available when foreigners come to do business in their countries.

The economic results of ISI regimes unfortunately proved to be questionable. The growth in incomes in Latin America barely outpaced that which transpired in the US, and fell behind Asia, particularly Japan, in the same time period. The shutting off of Latin American economies from the competitive pressures of the global economy meant that Latin American enterprises became less and less competitive over time, and ever more reliant on growing protectionist measures. The scaring away of foreign capital diverted important resources to the Asia region, which reflected more dynamic growth over the period. Technological progress in the Latin American region was also stunted. Importantly, the region was shut off from the exchange of ideas necessary for the full development of nations in integral terms, political, economic, and social. When the economic crisis of the 1980s hit Latin America, the region found itself overspent, over-indebted, inflationary, and with little internal resources to spark the regional economy back into a healthy growth spiral. After decades of seeking economic independence, Latin America was forced to go, cap in hand, to the developed world for economic resources and technical know-how to get her economies back on track. This would prove to be a painful process, involving the much maligned neoliberal structural adjustment processes succinctly summed up in the Washington Consensus.

On the plus side, the ISI experience benefitted Latin America with greater levels of employment and, importantly, insulated in large part the regional economy from the negative impact of exogenous shocks emanating from the global economy. On the downside, ISI regimes only helped to create large, inefficient, non-competitive industries, which over time acquired great political power.

On the downside, ISI policies in the end created major economic distortions and imbalances that reflected a massively inefficient use of scarce economic resources. ISI regimes suffered from constant balance of trade and payments crises. This defeated the purpose of striving for insulating Latin America from the ups and downs of the world economy. There were also unintended consequences in the realm of income distribution, as industrial workers obtained relatively high salaries, while rural workers did not. In addition, ISI regimes tended to be associated with high levels of deficits and inflation rates. In the end, that was the legacy of the ISI regimes—unsustainable levels of state intervention, debt, and inflation.

Thanks to the implementation of the structural adjustment reforms of the neoliberal recovery strategy, Latin America found herself much more able to weather negative exogenous economic shocks, both as compared to her own past, as well as other regions. In Figure 3.3, in the next chapter, it can be seen that, whereas in the 1980–1983 time period, wherein the US suffered two recessions, the US still managed to reflect an average annual growth rate for the period of 1.21%, versus 1.07% for Latin America. The advanced economies reflected a 1.57% average annual growth rate and the world as a whole a 1.9% growth rate for the 1980 to 1983 period. This is made all the more striking when one considers that LAC is a region exclusively comprising developing countries, which should grow their GDPs at average annual rates several points above the already developed countries. Nevertheless, when the onset of the 2008–2009 world economic crisis hit, the Latin American nations were well prepared, having already applied for almost two decades the lessons of relative fiscal and monetary discipline. When the economic crisis hit in 2008–2009, Latin America found herself with moderate rates of inflation, deficits and debt, unlike the developed world. Latin America's average annual GDP growth rate for the 2008–2011 period was 3.34%, higher than the world average, and much higher than that of the US and the advanced economies, which had 0.2% and 0.29%, respectively, while the European Union reflected a negative average annual growth rate for the period. The most current data, then, shows that Latin America is better positioned for growth in the coming years than are Europe and the United States.

NOTES

1. It is worth noting that the first major proclamation of US foreign policy, the Monroe Doctrine, had Latin America in mind, and its main goal was to dissuade the British against excessive meddling in the political and economic affairs of Latin America.

2. These luxury goods would prove quite sensitive to changes in income and price movements, making Latin America susceptible to booms and busts in developed economies over time.

3. Trade between peripheral regions, such as Latin America, and center regions, such as Europe, would inevitably affect the ratios between wages and rent. In the center economies, trade would cause wage–rent

ratios to rise, as the ratio of prices of imported agricultural products to the prices of exported manufactured goods would invariably fall. The opposite would happen in the peripheral economies.

4. The absurdities of the economic argument notwithstanding, it made (and still makes to this day) for good political red meat. Short-run focused, populist, left-wing Latin American politicians can always make headway with protectionist, nationalist rhetoric, so long as the general populace remains uneducated and ignorant in Latin America.

5. The Panama Canal was a public good to the world in the sense that it promoted world economic integration and spurred commerce as a whole, even though to the specific detriment of the Colombian nation, in the particular.

6. Authors' analysis based on World Bank data, April 2013.

REFERENCES

Acemoglu, D. and Robinson, J. A. (2008) The persistence and change of institutions in the Americas. *Southern Economic Journal, 75* (2), 282–299.

Acemoglu, D., Johnson, S., and Robinson, J. A. (2001) The colonial origins of comparative development: an empirical investigation. *American Economic Review, 91* (5), December, 1369–1405.

Acemoglu, D., Johnson, S., and Robinson, J. A. (2002) Reversal of fortune: geography and institutions in the making of the modern world income distribution. *Quarterly Journal of Economics, 117* (November), 1231–1294.

Bulmer-Thomas, V. (2003) *The economic history of Latin America since Independence* (2nd ed.). Cambridge, UK: Cambridge University Press.

Cárdenas, E., Ocampo, J. A., and Thorp, R. (Eds.) (2000) *Industrialisation and the state in Latin America: The post war years, an economic history of twentieth-century Latin America,* Vol. 3. Palgrave Press and St. Martins.

Cardoso, E. and Fishlow, A. (1989) Latin American economic development: 1950–1980. Working Paper No. 3161. National Bureau of Economic Research, November.

Coatsworth, J. (2005) Structures, endowments, and institutions in the economic history of Latin America. *Latin American Research Review, 40* (3), October.

Coatsworth, J. H. and Williamson, J. G. (2003) Always protectionist? Latin American tariffs from Independence to Great Depression. *Journal of Latin American Studies, 36* (2), May, 205–232.

della Paolera, G. and Taylor, A. M. (Eds.) (2003) *A new economic history of Argentina,* Vol. 1. Cambridge: Cambridge University Press.

Denoon, D. (1983) *Settler capitalism: The dynamics of dependent development in the southern hemisphere.* Oxford: Clarendon Press.

Franko, P. (2007) *The puzzle of Latin American development* (3rd ed.). New York: Rowman and Littlefield Publishing Group, Inc.

Gomez-Galvarriato, A. and Williamson, J. G. (2009) Was it prices, productivity or policy? Latin American industrialisation after 1870. *Journal of Latin American Studies, 41,* 663–694.

Greene, J. (2009) *The canal builders: Making America's empire at the Panama Canal.* New York: Penguin Press.

Kirkpatrick, J. J. (1982) *Dictatorships and double standards: Rationalism and reason in politics.* New York: Simon & Schuster.

Lake, A. (1989) *Somoza falling: A case of Washington at work.* Boston: Houghton-Mifflin Co.

Maddison, A. (2005) Measuring and interpreting world economic performance, 1500–2001. *Review of Income and Wealth, 51* (1), 1–35.

Maddison, A. (2008) The West and the rest in the world economy: 1000–2030: Maddisonian and Malthusian interpretations. *World Economics, 9* (4), October–December.

O'Rourke, K. H. and Williamson, J. G. (1994) Late 19th-century Anglo-American factor price convergence: Were Heckscher and Ohlin right? *Journal of Economic History,* 54, 892–916.

O'Rourke, K. H. and Williamson, J. G. (1999) *Globalization and history: The evolution of a nineteenth-century Atlantic economy*. Cambridge, MA: MIT Press.

O'Rourke, K. H. and Williamson, J. G. (2005) From Malthus to Ohlin: Trade, industrialisation and distribution since 1500. *Journal of Economic Growth, 10*, 5–34.

O'Rourke, K. H., Taylor, A. M., and Williamson, J. G. (1996) Factor price convergence in the late nineteenth century. *International Economic Review, 37*, 499–530.

Ocampo, J. A. (2006) Latin America and the world economy in the long 20th century. In K.S. Jomo (Ed.), *The great divergence: Hegemony, uneven development and global inequality*. New Delhi: Oxford University Press.

Pereira, C., Singh, S. P., and Mueller, B. (2011) Political institutions, policymaking, and policy stability in Latin America. *Latin American Politics and Society, 53* (1), 59–89.

Perez-Brignoli, H. (1989) *A brief history of Central America*. Berkeley: University of California Press.

Salvucci, R. (2008) Export-led growth, 1870–1930. In Bulmer-Thomas, V. *et al.* (Eds.), *The Cambridge economic history of Latin America* (2 vols.). Cambridge: Cambridge University Press, Vol. 2, 249–292.

Thorpe, R. and Bertram, G. (1978) *Peru, 1890–1977: Growth and policy in an open economy*. New York: Columbia University Press.

Yáñez, C., Ducoing, C., and Jofré, J. (2010) La industrialización por sustitución de importaciones y la frustración de la modernización económica, Chile 1890–2000. CLADHE II. México DF: México.

3

THE BUSINESS CLIMATE IN LATIN AMERICA

INTRODUCTION

The important issues of the Latin American economy pertinent to the foreign investor wishing to do business in the region pertain to the matters of trade. In this chapter, we treat the matters of the increasing involvement of the Latin American countries in the globalized economy, and her continued efforts to pursue economic integration via trade treaties, from the perspective of the investor wishing to do business in Latin America. For this we rely on conventional indicators typically used, such as the Global Competitiveness Index (World Economic Forum), Index of Economic Liberty (Heritage Foundation), the Ease of Doing Business Index (World Bank), and the Human Development Index (United Nations), to name but a few.

This chapter gives an overview of the evolution of the Latin American economy and its business climate, to explain how it got to where it is today, and to give a better picture of where it might be going. We begin with the historical perspective of the doing business climate in Latin America, which covers in quick order the legacy of the Import-Substitution-Industrialization (ISI) regimes and the debt crises. This is important to do, because the significance of current trends can be gauged only from this perspective, which takes into account the progress already made. Based on important lessons learned, Latin America has greater macroeconomic stability than either the United States or the Euro Zone countries today.

After reading this chapter, the reader should have a strong, general grasp of the broadly considered business climate in Latin America, and the strong commitment and harsh measures that the region has had to demonstrate in order to achieve today what should be considered one of its strongest comparative advantages: a climate conducive to doing business.

Latin America has undergone profound changes in its business climate. Once the purview of state privileged mercantilists and landed oligarchs, the private sector in the Latin American region has learned to embrace world trade, adopt foreign business practices, and excel at them. Although the region has a long way to go, particularly as regards the failure of public institutions to catch up to the efficiency and results-orientation of the private sector, its climate for doing business is remarkably different than it was in the past.

Part of this success is due to the much-maligned Washington Consensus (Williamson, 1989), which among other things recommended the privatization of state enterprises, trade liberalization, and the freeing up of restrictions on FDI. This new market orientation engendered a new culture of openness and competency where, before, closed-mindedness and protectionist inefficiencies reigned. The true winner in all this, of course, was the Latin American consumer, who has benefitted from a wider range of higher-quality products at accessible prices. Once shown the benefits of freer markets, Latin Americans turned out to like them.

The institutional and preference shift toward markets and commerce provides great opportunities for American businesses seeking new growth outlets in world markets. With the US still recovering mildly in 2012 from a severe recession in 2008–2009, and Europe mired in its unsolved problems of political and economic integration, brought to the fore by the sovereign debt crisis in Greece, as well as Italy, Spain, Portugal, Ireland, England, France, and even Germany, the emerging markets have been declared the engines of growth for the foreseeable future. Latin America is chief among these emerging regional markets. In fact, the President of the International Monetary Fund (IMF), Christine LaGarde, points out: "The new Latin America can provide some lessons to the advanced countries—such as saving for a rainy day, and making sure that risks in the banking system are under control" (LaGarde, 2011).

LATIN AMERICAN DEBT CRISIS

As far as Latin America is concerned, the debt crisis refers to the phenomenon whereby countries of the region reached the point of being unable to service and/ or repay their foreign debt. In the two decades prior to the 1980s, Latin American countries had, in order to finance their so-called infrastructure and industrialization projects, accumulated massive debts from international creditors. This was easy enough to do during periods of high economic growth. The international creditors included organizations like the World Bank, but also private banks looking for safe investment outlets for their petrodollars. Latin America, as a whole, increased its foreign debt four-fold in the 1975–1983 period, an alarming increase surpassed only by the rate of increase in its schedule of debt service, which increased more than five-fold in the same time period.[1]

The global economy entered into a worldwide recession at the end of the 1970s and the onset of the 1980s. After the successful organization of the OPEC oil cartel, oil prices grew sky high, causing problems for Latin American oil-importing countries. The rise in oil prices induced Latin American countries to incur greater, unsustainable levels of foreign debt. Oil-producing nations in Latin America, such as Mexico, believed oil prices would continue to rise, so they too incurred greater amounts of debt, which would later prove to be unsustainable.

Interest rate increases in the developed world at the end of the decade of the 1970s caused an increase in debt payments. This made it much more difficult for the debtor countries in Latin America to even service their foreign debts, much less pay them back. Declining terms of trade in dollar terms translated into declining purchasing power coupled with more onerous debt servicing schedules for the countries of Latin America, which were suffering through a general decline of the prices of the goods they sold. Eventually, the debt levels of Latin American countries became unsustainable.

Mexico was the first country to effectively declare itself in default, i.e. unable even to service its foreign debt. In direct consequence of Mexico's announcement, private banks halted lending to Latin America, which, naturally, aggravated the process. Adding insult to injury was the fact that good portions of the loans to Latin America were short-term. Upon refusal of the international creditors to refinance these loans, the crisis was compounded significantly, as the debts became immediately due.

The pressing concern became how to avoid a global financial panic. New loans were issued, but this time under strict conditions, which often included the intervention of the IMF. The IMF pushed the structural adjustment conditions, which it felt were necessary to guarantee any future loans. Debt restructuring was to include the reduction of public-sector consumption in Latin American countries, the liberalization of their economies, making them more open to trade with efficient, rational exchange rate schemes in place, and, upon prior accomplishment of pre-established conditions, explicit debt relief for the Latin American countries that simply could not pay back the inordinate sums of debt they had borrowed and irresponsibly spent.

The Latin American debt crisis that occurred with the onset of the 1980s was grave in its immediate consequences. Economic growth in real terms stalled and real incomes plummeted. Inflation soared, as Latin American governments sought to monetize their debts by printing worthless money. Progress on mitigating poverty and other social issues stalled, as public spending became increasingly oriented to pay public debt.

For the most part, Latin American countries had no option but to abandon the failed ISI models of import substitution industrialization. Real interest rates soared as capital, both national and foreign, flowed out of the Latin American region, having the effect of depreciating national exchange rates. This compounded the problem of foreign indebtedness, bringing to the breaking point even the largest Latin American countries, such as Mexico, Brazil, and Argentina, among many others.

The Onset of the Latin American Debt Crisis

Latin American countries showed themselves unable to sustain their excessive debt loads, and it was clear that the pace of indebtedness was unsustainable. The major Latin American economies were effectively bankrupt. The largest of the Latin American nations had borrowed heavily, supposedly to fund public investment projects that

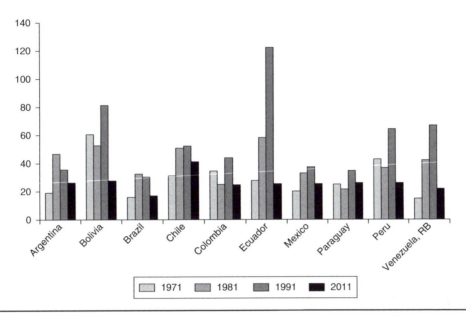

Figure 3.1 External debt stocks, as a % of GNI, selected Latin America countries, 1971, 1981, 1991, and 2011[2]

Source: Authors' calculations based on World Bank data, May 2013

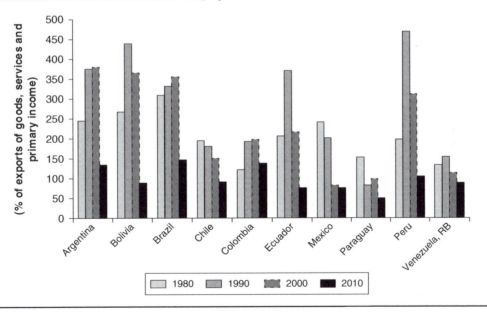

Figure 3.2 External debt stock, selected Latin America Countries, 1980, 1990, 2000, and 2013[3]

Source: Authors' calculations based on World Bank data, May 2013

would ultimately propel them into economic prosperity, and leave behind the days of generalized poverty and inequality; however, truth be told, the money was ill spent on boondoggle public investments, publicly run public monopolies and the like, generating little in the way of sustainable projects that created true wealth over the long term.

The decade of the 1970s put an end to two myths that held sway in Latin America. In the first place, an end was put to the Keynesian myth that, by governmental fine-tuning, the macroeconomy could be made to supersede the boom and bust nature of the business cycle, that economic growth could be indefinitely projected into the future. The second myth that came to an end in the 1970s was that the Latin American nations could propel themselves into the category of productive, competitive nations on a world scale by pursuing the ISI strategy. Both stratagems entailed heavy state involvement in the economy, which is a problem for business in and of itself, but one that compounds exponentially only when dealing with countries where institutions are corrupt. At any rate, the world suffered through severe global recessions in the decade of the 1970s, recessions that were accompanied by high inflation rates, leading to the coining of the term "stagflation." As global interest rates rose to curtail inflation, this put an end to the days of easy money for the debt-hungry Latin American nations. In the short run, of course, the debt-servicing schedule of the heavily indebted nations of Latin America increased tremendously, eventually becoming unsustainable, and forcing the Latin American nations to effectively declare themselves in default and unable, or unwilling, to pay.

The major state spending initiatives implied in the ISI regimes would prove to have their limits. A major economic slowdown hit the developed world at the beginning of the 1980s. The major advanced economies of the world suffered an economic slowdown, if not serious recession, at the onset of the 1980s. Canada experienced a GDP contraction of −2.859%, Germany −0.788%, and the US −1.942%. World economic growth decelerated strongly from 2.243% in 1981 to 0.713% in 1982. Latin America contracted 0.5% in 1982, and another −2.769% in 1983. The Latin American region went from a GDP growth rate of 6.485 in 1980 to −2.769 by 1983, a drop-off of more than 9 percentage points. GDP in current US dollars fell off by more than 18%, from $836 to $682 billion. Investment as a percentage of GDP fell off from 24.7% to 18.24% from 1980 to 1983. Inflation soared from the already high levels of 53.45% in 1980 to more than 102% in 1983, nearing 475% by 1990. The current account balance for the region declined from −3.3% of GDP in 1980 to −5.6% in 1982. External debt as a percentage of GDP went from 27% in 1980 to more than 51% in 1983. Just the total debt service of the external debt went from 5.119% in 1980 to 8.682% in 1982. Interest payments in service of the debt went from 2.37% of GDP to 4.86% by 1983. The total debt service as a percentage of exports of goods and services went from 17.47% in 1980 to more than 30% by 1983.[4]

Argentina experienced back-to-back contractions of −5% in 1981–1982. Bolivia contracted at near −4% for both 1982 and 1983. Chile contracted an astounding −10% in 1982, and again −3.78% in 1983. Paraguay also contracted more than −3% for both 1983 and 1983, while Uruguay contracted an amazing −9% in both 1982 and 1983. Even oil-rich Venezuela contracted −2% in 1982, and −3.76% in 1983. The world as a whole barely escaped a technical recession with just 0.42% growth in 1982.[5] After decades of trying under ISI regimes, Latin America had not achieved the goal of economic "independence" from the rest of the world.

Table 3.1 Average annual inflation rates in Latin America in the 1980s[6]

Country	1980–1984	1985–1989
Argentina	310.06	1190.68
Bolivia	570.32	1656.78
Brazil	144.92	727.69
Chile	22.02	19.76
Colombia	22.25	24.34
Costa Rica	38.56	15.61
Dominican Republic	10.66	29.66
Ecuador	26.57	44.82
El Salvador	13.63	24.73
Guatemala	6.02	18.24
Guyana	19.21	37.89
Honduras	8.19	5.69
Jamaica	17.66	13.59
Mexico	66.57	80.00
Panama	5.31	0.57
Paraguay	28.44	28.44
Peru	103.16	966.61
St. Lucia	6.86	3.19
St. Vincent and the Grenadines	7.88	2.17
Uruguay	42.07	73.82
Venezuela	n.d.	35.72

Source: Authors' calculations based on IMF data

Many of the problems Latin America faced at the onset of the 1980s were of its own making. Lax monetary policies fueled hyperinflation. Argentina experienced an average annual inflation rate of more than 300% in the first half of the 1980s, and of more than 1000% in the latter half of the same decade! Brazil, too, suffered from hyperinflation rates, passing from an average annual inflation rate of nearly 145% in the 1980–1984 time period, to more than 700% in the 1985–1989 period. Peru similarly went from an average annual inflation rate of more than 103% in the first half of the decade, to more than 966% in the latter half. By these figures, Mexico's inflation rate averages of 66.57% and 80% for the 1980–1984 and 1985–1989 time periods seem responsible by comparison.

Many Latin American countries experienced negative trade balances at the onset of the 1980s. Argentina had an average annual trade deficit of −2.51% of GDP in the 1980–1984 time period, compared to −5.8% for Brazil, −8.8% for Chile, −6.26% for Paraguay, and −6.3% for Peru. Countries of Central America also suffered trade deficits, with Guatemala posting an average annual trade deficit for the 1980–1984 time period of −4–45%, Honduras −7.7%, Panama −5%, and Costa Rica −10.44%. Oil-rich Venezuela was notable in posting a 4.6% average annual trade surplus in the time period.

Table 3.2 Average annual trade balance as percentage of GDP for Latin American countries[1]

Country	1980–1984	1985–1989
Argentina	−2.51	−1.51
Bolivia	−3.30	−5.27
Brazil	−5.80	−0.24
Chile	−8.83	−4.17
Colombia	−3.59	−0.60
Costa Rica	−10.44	−4.14
Dominica	−18.98	−12.64
Dominican Republic	−6.04	−2.56
Ecuador	−3.64	−4.22
Grenada	−7.68	−7.24
Guatemala	−4.45	−4.30
Guyana	−35.34	−25.02
Haiti	−4.54	−1.61
Honduras	−7.73	−3.44
Jamaica	−11.72	−6.44
Mexico	−1.50	−0.31
Nicaragua	−12.25	−15.83
Panama	−5.00	5.28
Paraguay	−6.26	−4.38
Peru	−6.30	−3.01
Trinidad and Tobago	−2.78	−3.36
Uruguay	−4.10	−0.15
Venezuela	4.60	−0.75

Source: Authors' calculations based on IMF data

Confronted with the realities of market economics, Latin American countries were "forced" to abandon their ill-advised ISI policies wholesale. Most nations adopted an export-led growth and industrialization strategy. This came to be known as the neoliberal structural adjustments advocated by the IMF. It was John Williamson who coined the term "Washington Consensus." The Washington Consensus centered on the policy recommendations of respect for property rights, fiscal and monetary discipline, liberalization of exchange rates and interest rates, modernization of the bloated and inefficient public sector through privatization and deregulation schemes, and the reorientation of public spending towards education, health care, and infrastructure investment (Williamson, 1989).

THE WASHINGTON CONSENSUS: THE PAINFUL RESTORATION OF COMPETITIVENESS

Instead of the discredited ISI policies, Latin American countries found themselves with few realistic options but to adopt the unpopular neoliberal strategies

Table 3.3 Latin America, selected economic indicators[8]

Variable	1980–1989	1990–1999	2000–2009	2010–2018
Gross domestic product, constant prices, % change	2.12	2.98	3.16	4.05
GDP based on purchasing-power-parity (PPP), % share of world total	10.60	9.27	8.54	8.64
Investment, % of GDP	20.83	20.95	20.98	21.55
Gross national savings, % of GDP	19.46	18.48	20.68	19.53
Inflation, end of period consumer prices	178.01	108.96	6.97	5.71
Volume of imports of goods and services	4.09	10.97	4.88	7.76
Volume of imports of goods	5.54	11.43	4.44	8.12
Volume of exports of goods and services	6.25	8.56	3.81	5.76
Volume of exports of goods	6.73	9.16	2.97	5.60
Terms of trade of goods and services	−2.81	−0.17	1.62	1.01
Terms of trade of goods	−3.27	−0.75	2.33	1.49
General government revenue, % of GDP	n.d.	26.48	26.80	30.73
General government total expenditure, % of GDP	n.d.	30.97	29.15	33.21
General government net lending/borrowing, % of GDP	n.d.	−4.49	−2.35	−2.48
General government gross debt, % of GDP	n.d.	n.d.	52.15	48.94
Current account balance, % of GDP	−2.02	−2.43	−0.29	−1.88
External debt, total, % of GDP	44.46	35.85	31.52	23.02
External debt, total, % of exports of goods/services	297.10	245.84	142.20	106.64
External debt, total debt service, % of GDP	7.45	8.43	10.42	6.43
External debt, total debt service, % of exports of goods/services	50.88	53.99	43.84	27.88
External debt, total debt service, interest, % of GDP	3.76	2.27	1.95	0.95
External debt, total debt service, interest, % of exports of goods/services	25.30	15.20	8.75	4.42

Source: Authors' calculations based on IMF data

associated with the IMF's structural adjustment policies. The Latin American region struggled to regain its competitiveness, implementing policies that sacrificed short-term growth in order to regain economic competitiveness in the long term.

Latin America found herself with little option but to take the IMF's advice, in return for the money and official backing she would need to repay her debts. Although politically unpopular, the IMF reforms went a long way towards advancing free market principles in the Latin American regions. The IMF structural adjustment reforms were painful to implement. The 1980s has been called the "lost decade" for Latin America, as growth was close to zero, actually negative in per capita GDP terms, and living standards suffered in the short term as well. An important source of rejection was the perceived loss of national sovereignty by the peoples of Latin America.

The success or failure of the much-maligned Washington Consensus depends on how you look at it. As a development program, the results leave much to be desired. However, that was not its intended purpose. The intended purpose was to restore the fiscal and monetary sectors of the Latin American economies, as well as introduce economic stability. Whereas the region as a whole grew by only some 2.12% by the 1990s, the average annual growth rate for the decade had restored to 2.98%. Importantly, despite two US recessions in the 2000–2009 periods, the average annual growth rate for the region proved to be 3.16%, and projects to be higher in the 2010–2018 periods, with an estimated 4.05%, despite an uncertain outlook in the US and depression in many countries in the Euro Zone.

Whereas Latin America's share of world GDP declines two percentage points from the high of 10.6% reflected in the 1980s, this is to be expected as a consequence of the restoring of internal imbalances that afflicted the Latin American economies in the 1980s. These were unsustainable to begin with, and the 8.64% average annual share of world GDP expected for Latin America in the 2010–2018 period is in line with her performance in the twentieth century. The important thing is that Latin America is now better suited to confront the future challenges that the increasingly dynamic world economy holds in store. Proof of this is that the average annual inflation rate for the region dropped from 178% for the 1980–1989 decade to 5.71% in the 2010–2018 time period.

The removal of barriers to trade translates into an average annual growth rate in imports of goods and services, from 4.09% for the 1980s to 7.76% in the 2010–2018 time period. The exports of goods and services falls from a growth rate of 6.25% in the 1980s to 5.76% in the 2010–2018 period, a fall of half of a percentage point. A notable fact is the change in terms of trade for the region, which reflected an average annual percentage change of −2.81% in the 1980s versus a 1.01% growth in the 2010–2018 period. The change is even stronger for the terms of trade of goods, which goes from −3.27% to 1.49% in the same comparative time periods. The negative current account balance shrinks also, from −2.02% average annual percent of GDP in the 1980s to −1.88% of GDP in the 2010–2018 time period.

The neoliberal reforms of the Washington Consensus were designed to rid Latin America of her unsustainable debt dependency. In this, the neoliberal reforms are to be considered an unqualified success. The external debt as a percentage of GDP falls from an average of 44.46% in the 1980s to 23.02% of GDP in the 2010–2018 time period. The external debt as a percentage of exports of goods and services falls from an average of 297.10% in the 1980–1989 time period to 106.64% in the 2010–2018 time period. Debt service as a percentage of GDP falls a full percentage point also in the same time periods, from 7.45% of GDP in the 1980s to 6.43% in the 2010–2018 time interval. Interest payments fall off significantly also, from 3.76% of GDP in the 1980s to 0.95% in the 2010–2018 time interval. Total debt service, as interest as a percentage of exports of goods and services fall off from 25.3% in the 1980s to 4.42% in the 2010–2018 time period.

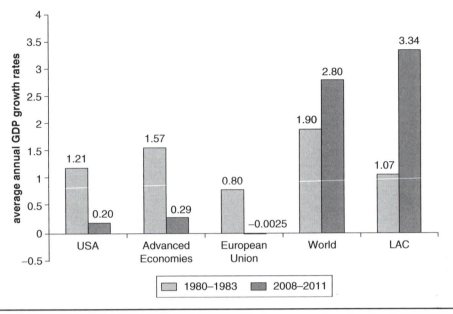

Figure 3.3 Economic recovery by region, 1980–1983 vs. 2008–2011[9]
Source: Authors' calculations based on IMF data, April 2013

Thanks to the implementation of the structural adjustment reforms of the neoliberal recovery strategy, Latin America found herself much more able to weather negative exogenous economic shocks, both as compared to her own past, as well as other regions. In Figure 3.3 it can be seen that, in the 1980–1983 time period, wherein the US suffered two recessions, the US still managed to reflect an average annual growth rate for the period of 1.21%, versus 1.07% for Latin America. The advanced economies reflected a 1.57% average annual growth rate and the world as a whole a 1.9% growth rate for the 1980–1983 period. This is made all the more striking when one considers that LAC is a region composed exclusively of developing countries, which should grow their GDPs at average annual rates several points above the already developed countries. Nevertheless, when the onset of the 2008–2009 world economic crisis hit, the Latin American nations were well prepared, already having applied for almost two decades the lessons of relative fiscal and monetary discipline. When the economic crisis hit in 2008–2009, Latin America found herself with moderate rates of inflation, deficits, and debt, unlike the developed world. Latin America's average annual GDP growth rate for the 2008–2011 period was 3.34%, higher than the world average, and much higher than that of the US and the advanced economies, which had 0.2% and 0.29%, respectively, while the European Union reflected a negative average annual growth rate for the period. The most current data, then, show that Latin America is better positioned for growth in the coming years than are Europe and the United States.

MACROECONOMIC PROFILE OF LATIN AMERICA

The global macroeconomic environment went through a systematic recovery phase after the global financial crisis of 2008. This process has left lessons about structural changes, that highly developed countries should implement controls to enhance macroeconomic stability and strategic management of fiscal and monetary policy. In this context, the Latin America and the Caribbean region estimate stable economic growth driven by strong domestic and external demand, in addition to efforts to improve productivity and business climate.

Comparison Between Latin America and United States

Latin America is the region composed of 32 countries: Antigua and Barbuda, Argentina, the Bahamas, Barbados, Belize, Bolivia, Brazil, Chile, Colombia, Costa Rica, Dominica, Dominican Republic, Ecuador, El Salvador, Grenada, Guatemala, Guyana, Haiti, Honduras, Jamaica, Mexico, Nicaragua, Panama, Paraguay, Peru, St. Kitts and Nevis, St. Lucia, St. Vincent and the Grenadines, Suriname, Trinidad and Tobago, Uruguay, and Venezuela.

Global Competitiveness Index

The Global Competitiveness Index is a comprehensive tool that measures the microeconomic and macroeconomic foundations of national competitiveness. If Latin America were a country, it would be in 61.5th position of 144 countries. That is not an excellent position but it is over the average of the countries. If we compare Latin America with the US, the US is better positioned in the ranking. The US is one of the ten best countries.

The Global Competitiveness Index has three principal groups of competitiveness components. In the Basic Requirements Sub-Index, Latin America is in 74.6th position. That position is pretty bad because it is below average of most countries. If we compare Latin America with the US, the US is better positioned in the ranking. The US is in 33rd position.

In the Efficiency Enhancers Sub-Index, Latin America is in 55.7th position. That position is good because it is above the average of most countries. If we compare Latin America with the US, the US is better positioned in the ranking. The United States is in 2nd position.

Finally, in the Basic Requirements Sub-Index, Latin America is in 62.7th position. That position is pretty good because it is above average of most countries. If we compare Latin America with the US, the US is better positioned in the ranking. United States is in 7th position.

Doing Business Project Index

The Doing Business Project Index provides objective measures of business regulations and their enforcement across 185 economies and selected cities at subnational and regional level. If Latin America were a country, it would be in the 100.9th position of 185 countries. That is a pretty bad position; Latin America is below average of most countries. If we compare Latin America with the US, the US is one of the best countries for doing business. United States is in 4th position of the ranking.

Table 3.4 Latin America and the Caribbean region, selected economic indicators[10]

Item	2013	2007–2012	2013–2018
Gross domestic product, constant prices, % change	3.38	3.69	3.79
Gross domestic product, current prices, USD	$6,007.49	$5,765.56	$8,039.95
Gross domestic product based on purchasing-power-parity (PPP) valuation of country GDP, Current Int'l	$7,589.59	$7,224.15	$10,166.55
Gross domestic product based on purchasing-power-parity (PPP) per capita GDP, Current Int'l Dollar	$12,818.20	$12,331.61	$16,265.48
Gross domestic product based on purchasing-power-parity (PPP) share of world total; %	8.70	8.61	8.62
Investment, % GDP	21.75	22.04	21.42
Inflation, end of period consumer prices, % change	6.07	6.41	5.35
Volume of imports of goods and services, % change	4.89	6.66	5.82
Volume of imports of goods, % change	6.17	6.53	6.02
Volume of exports of goods and services, % change	4.36	2.18	5.59
Volume of exports of goods, % change	5.69	1.75	5.67
General government revenue, % GDP	31.21	30.07	30.72
General government total expenditure, % GDP	33.57	32.75	32.77
General government net lending/borrowing, % GDP	−2.36	−2.68	−2.05
General government gross debt, % GDP	50.40	49.01	48.41
Current account balance, USD	−$102.28	−$99.54	−$191.13
Current account balance, % of GDP	−1.70	−0.95	−2.10
Direct investment, net, USD	$135.09	$121.45	n/a
External debt, total, USD	$1,492.83	$1,382.07	n/a
External debt, total, % of GDP	24.85	22.34	24.85
External debt, total, % of Exports of Goods and Services	112.77	102.54	112.77
External debt, total debt service, USD	$362.37	$359.17	n/a
External debt, total debt service, % of GDP	6.40	7.10	6.40
External debt, total debt service, % of Exports of Goods and Services	27.37	30.29	27.37
External debt, total debt service, interest, USD	$56.14	$57.58	n/a
External debt, total debt service, interest, % of GDP	0.94	1.11	0.94
External debt, total debt service, interest, % of Exports of Goods and Services	4.25	5.06	4.25
External debt, total debt service, amortization, USD	$306.23	$301.59	n/a
External debt, total debt service, amortization, % GDP	5.10	5.50	5.10
External debt, total debt service ,amortization, % Exports of Goods and Services	23.30	25.40	23.30

Source: Authors' calculations based on IMF data for 32 countries

It has ten principal aspects for measuring the facility for doing business. The first aspect is Starting a Business. In this aspect, Latin America is in 98th position. That position is pretty bad because it is below average of the countries. If we compare Latin America with the US, the US is better positioned in the ranking. United States is in 13th position.

Table 3.5 Latin America and Caribbean region vs. United States, 2013[11]

IMF table: LA and Caribbean Region vs United States	LA	US
Gross domestic product, constant prices, % change	3.38	2.12
Gross domestic product, current prices, billions, USD	$6,007.49	$16,198
Gross domestic product per capita, current prices, USD	$10,165.23	$51,056
Gross domestic product based on purchasing-power-parity (PPP) per capita GDP, Int'l dollar	$12,818.20	$51,056
Gross domestic product based on purchasing-power-parity (PPP) share of world total,%	8.70	18.65
Inflation, end of period consumer prices, % change	6.07	1.83
Volume of imports of goods and services, % change	4.89	3.58
Volume of Imports of goods, % change	6.17	4.10
Volume of exports of goods and services, % change	4.36	4.32
Volume of exports of goods, % change	5.69	4.31
Population, millions	590.98	317.26
General government revenue, % of GDP	31.21	33.19
General government total expenditure, % of GDP	33.57	40.47
General government net lending/borrowing, % of GDP	−2.36	−7.28
General government gross debt, % of GDP	50.40	111.72
Current account balance, billions, USD	−$102.28	−$499.25
Current account balance, % of GDP	−1.70	−3.08

Source: Authors' calculations based on IMF data

The second aspect is Dealing with Construction Permits. In this aspect, Latin America is in 101.26th position. That position is pretty bad because it is below average of the countries. If we compare Latin America with the US, the US is better positioned in the ranking. The United States is in 17th position.

The third aspect is Getting Electricity. In this aspect, Latin America is in 87.4th position. That position is pretty good because it is above the average of the countries. If we compare Latin America with the US, the US is better positioned in the ranking. The US is in 19th position.

The fourth aspect is Registering Property. In this aspect, Latin America is in 105.8th position. That position is bad because it is below the average of the countries. If we compare Latin America with the US, the US is better positioned in the ranking. The US is in 25th position of the ranking.

The fifth aspect is Getting Credit. In this aspect, Latin America is in 81st position. That position is pretty good because it is above the average of the countries. If we compare Latin America with the US, the US is better positioned in the ranking. The US is in 4th position.

The sixth aspect is Protecting Investors. In this aspect, Latin America is in 77.6th position. That position is good because it is above the average of the countries. If we compare Latin America with the US, the US is better positioned in the ranking. The US is in 6th position.

Table 3.6 Regional comparison between Latin America and the United States[12]

Indicators : LA Region vs United states	LA	US
Global Competitiveness Index, World Economic Forum	61.49	7
GCI Subindex A Basic requirements	74.60	33
GCI Subindex B Efficiency enhancers	55.70	2
GCI Subindex C Innovation and sophistication factors	62.73	7
Doing Business	100.93	4
DB starting a Business	98.04	13
DB Dealing with Construction Permits	101.26	17
DB Getting Electricity	87.38	19
DB Registering Property	105.77	25
DB Getting Credit	81.06	4
DB Protecting Investors	77.62	6
DB Paying Taxes	132.66	69
DB Trading Across Borders	103.67	22
DB Enforcing Contracts	99.38	6
DB Resolving Insolvency	102.42	16
Human Development Index, United Nations	73.16	4
Global Gender Gap, World Economic Forum	60.99	22
Travel and Tourism Competitiveness, World Economic Forum	59.57	6
Democracy Index, Economist Intelligence Unit	51.50	19
Freedom Status, Freedom House	N/A	N/A
Index of Globalization, KOF (0 to 100)	59.78	74.87855
Index of Economic Liberty, Heritage Foundation(0 to 100)	59.60	76
Transparency International	83.64	19

Source: Authors' calculations based on various indicators

The seventh aspect is Paying Taxes. In this aspect, Latin America is in 132nd position. That position is very bad because it is below the average of the countries. If we compare Latin America with the US, the US is better positioned in the ranking. The US is in 69th position.

The eighth aspect is Trading Across Borders. In this aspect, Latin America is in 104th position. That position is very bad as it is below the average of the countries. If we compare Latin America with the US, the US is better positioned in the ranking. The US is in 22nd position.

The ninth one is Enforcing Contracts. In this aspect, Latin America is in 99th position. That position is pretty bad because it is below the average of the countries. If we compare Latin America with the US, the US is better positioned in the ranking. United States is in 6th position.

Finally, the tenth aspect is Resolving Insolvency. In this aspect, Latin America is in 102nd position. That position is very bad because it is below the average of the countries. If we compare Latin America with the US, the US is better positioned in the ranking. The US is in 1st position.

Human Development Index

The Human Development Index introduced a new way of measuring development by combining indicators of life expectancy, educational attainment, and income.

If Latin America were a country, it would be in 73rd position of 186 countries. That is a pretty good position; Latin America is above the average of the countries. If we compare Latin America with the US, the US is one of the countries with the highest human development. The US is in 4th position.

Global Gender Gap Index

The Global Gender Gap Index is a framework for capturing the magnitude and scope of gender-based disparities, and tracking their progress.

If Latin America were a country, it would be in 61st position of 135 countries. That is a pretty good position; Latin America is above the average of the countries. If we compare Latin America with the US, the US is a country with a high Global Gender Gap Index. The US is in 22nd position.

Travel and Tourism Competitiveness Index

The Travel and Tourism Competitiveness Index analyzes the factors and policies that make it attractive to develop the travel and tourism industry in different countries.

If Latin America were a country, it would be in 59th position of 140 countries. That is a very good position; Latin America is above the average of the countries. If we compare Latin America with the US, the US has one of the most attractive travel and tourism industries. The US is in 6th position of the ranking.

Democracy Index

The Democracy Index is based on five categories: electoral process and pluralism; civil liberties; the functioning of government; political participation; and political culture. It classifies the countries in full democracies, flawed democracies, hybrid regimes, or authoritarian regimes.

If Latin America were a country, it would be in 52nd position of 167 countries. That is a pretty good position; Latin America is above the average of the countries, but it would be classified as a flawed democracy. If we compare Latin America with the US, the US is classified as a full democracy. The US is in 19th position of the ranking.

Index of Globalization

The Index of Globalization measures the three main dimensions of globalization: economic, social, and political.

If Latin America were a country, it would obtain 59.78 points of 100. That is a pretty good grade; Latin America is above the average of the countries. If we compare Latin America with the US, the US is a country with a high level of globalization. The US has 74.88 points of globalization.

Transparency International Index

The Transparency International Index scores countries on how corrupt their public sectors are seen to be.

Table 3.7 Index of Economic Liberty, scores for Latin America[13]

Country	Heritage overall score	Property rights	Freedom from corruption	Fiscal freedom	Government spending	Business freedom	Labor freedom	Monetary freedom	Trade freedom	Investment freedom	Financial freedom
Argentina	46.7	15	30	64.3	52.1	60.1	47.4	60.4	67.6	40	30
Belize	57.3	30	0	82.2	72.6	72.6	71.4	77.3	77.2	40	50
Bolivia	47.9	10	28	88.8	64.1	55.8	30.8	67.4	74.3	10	50
Brazil	57.7	50	38	70.3	54.8	53	57.2	74.4	69.7	50	60
Canada	79.4	90	87	79.8	44.8	91.7	82.3	75.2	88.2	75	80
Chile	79	90	72	77.6	83.7	70.5	74.2	84.6	82	85	70
Colombia	69.6	50	34	76.1	75.2	90.2	79.3	78.7	72.2	70	70
Costa Rica	67	50	48	82.9	90.1	58.3	60.4	75.4	85.1	70	50
Dominica	63.9	60	52	72	50.1	77	68.8	85.3	74.3	70	30
Dominican Republic	59.7	30	26	83.7	92.6	53.7	55.6	72.9	77.8	65	40
Ecuador	46.9	20	27	80.1	47.3	51.5	48	66.9	68.1	20	40
El Salvador	66.7	40	34	85.7	85.4	61.8	62	79.6	79	70	70
Guatemala	60	30	27	79.6	93.6	50.8	48.7	75.5	85.2	60	50
Guyana	53.8	30	25	67.9	61.1	66.3	75.4	75.9	71.2	35	30
Haiti	48.1	10	18	80.7	66.3	33.4	63.6	74.2	74.8	30	30
Honduras	58.4	30	26	85.3	79.2	61	26.8	73.9	77.1	65	60
Jamaica	66.8	40	33	77.5	67.7	84.3	69.3	76.1	75	85	60
Mexico	67	50	30	81.1	79.4	81.4	59.7	77.7	80.6	70	60
Nicaragua	56.6	15	25	78.7	65.1	51.2	62.2	73.2	85.4	60	50
Panama	62.5	30	33	86.2	77.8	72.5	40.1	75.9	74.8	65	70
Paraguay	61.1	30	22	95.9	85.4	59.1	25.6	79.8	82.7	70	60
Peru	68.2	40	34	79.9	89.1	72.3	67.1	84.3	85	70	60
St. Lucia	70.4	70	70	76.9	63.6	85.3	76.4	84.7	71.9	65	40
St. Vincent & Gren.	66.7	70	58	74.2	67.1	77.6	76.6	80.3	73.3	50	40
Suriname	52	40	30	71.6	72.5	40.2	77.5	66.7	66.3	25	30
United States	76	85	71	69.3	47.8	90.5	95.5	75	86.4	70	70
Uruguay	69.7	70	70	84.2	68.3	73.4	70.7	72.5	82.9	75	30
Venezuela	36.1	5	19	75.6	50.6	45.6	34.5	47.3	58.8	5	20
Latin America	59.6	45.0	35.5	74.3	64.5	63.0	57.6	73.3	73.0	54.5	55.5

Source: Authors' calculations based on Heritage Foundation data

If Latin America were a country, it would be in 84th position of 174 countries. That is a pretty good position; Latin America is above the average of the countries. If we compare Latin America with the US, the US is a country with a high level of transparency. The United States is in 19th position.

Index of Economic Liberty

The Index of Economic Liberty measures economic freedom using a scale from 0 to 100, where 100 represents the maximum freedom. It has four categories: rule of law; limited government; regulatory efficiency; and open markets.

If Latin America were a country, it would obtain 59.6 points of 100. That is a pretty good grade; Latin America is above the average of the countries. If we compare Latin America with the US, the US is a country with a high level of freedom. The US has 76 points. The country with the best score is Canada, with 79.4 points, and the country with the worst score is Venezuela, with 36.1 points.

The first pillar of the index is Property Rights. In this aspect, if Latin America were a country, it would obtain 45 points of 100. That is a pretty bad grade. If we compare Latin America with the US, the US is a country with a very high level of property rights. The United States has 85 points. The countries with the best scores are Canada and Chile, with 90 points, and the country with the worst score is Venezuela, with 5 points.

The second pillar of the index is Freedom from Corruption. In this aspect, if Latin America were a country, it would obtain 35.5 points of 100. That is a very bad grade. If we compare Latin America with the US, the US is a country with a high level of freedom from corruption. The US has 71 points. The countries with the best scores are Canada and Chile, with 90 points, and the country with the worst score is Venezuela, with 5 points.

The third pillar of the index is Fiscal Freedom. In this aspect, if Latin America were a country, it would obtain 74.3 points of 100. That is a very good grade. If we compare Latin America with the US, the US is a country with a lower level of fiscal freedom than Latin America. The United States has 69.3 points. The country with the best score is Paraguay, with 95.9 points, and the country with the worst score is Argentina, with 64.3 points.

The fourth pillar of the index is Government Spending. In this aspect, if Latin America were a country, it would obtain 64.5 points of 100. That is a pretty good grade. If we compare Latin America with the US, the US is a country with a low level of government spending freedom. The US has 47.8 points, very close to the country with the lowest grade. The country with the best score is Guatemala, with 93.6 points, and the country with the lowest score is Canada, with 44.8 points.

The fifth pillar of the index is Business Freedom. In this aspect, if Latin America were a country, it would obtain 63 points of 100. That is a pretty good grade. If we compare Latin America with the US, the US is one of the countries with the highest levels of business freedom. The US has 90.5 points, very close to the country with the highest grade. The country with the best score is Canada, with 91.7 points, and the country with the lowest score is Haiti, with 33.4 points.

The sixth pillar of the index is Labor Freedom. In this aspect, if Latin America were a country, it would obtain 57.6 points of 100. If we compare Latin America with the US, the US is the country with the highest level of labor freedom. The United States has 95.5 points. The country with the lowest score is Honduras, with 26.8 points.

The seventh pillar of the index is Monetary Freedom. In this aspect, if Latin America were a country, it would obtain 73.3 points of 100. That is a very good grade. If we compare Latin America with the US, the US is a country with a similar level of monetary freedom. The US has 75 points. The country with the best score is Dominica, with 85.3 points, and the country with the lowest score is Venezuela, with 47.3 points.

The eighth pillar of the index is Trade Freedom. In this aspect, if Latin America were a country, it would obtain 73 points of 100. That is a very good grade. If we compare Latin America with the US, the US is a country with a very high level of trade freedom. The US has 86.4 points, very close to the country with the highest grade. The country with the best score is Canada, with 88.2 points, and the country with the lowest score is Venezuela, with 58.8 points.

The ninth pillar of the index is Investment Freedom. In this aspect, if Latin America were a country, it would obtain 54.5 points of 100. That is a very bad grade. If we compare Latin America with the US, the US is a country with a high level of investment freedom. The US has 70 points. The countries with the best score are Chile and Jamaica, with 85 points, and the country with the lowest score is Venezuela, with 5 points.

The tenth pillar of the index is Financial Freedom. In this aspect, if Latin America were a country, it would obtain 55.5 points of 100. That is a pretty good grade. If we compare Latin America with the US, the US is a country with a high level of financial freedom. The US has 70 points. The country with the best score is Canada, with 80 points, and the country with the lowest score is Venezuela, with 20 points.

CONCLUSIONS

Latin America is a competitive region in the world economy. If it were a country, the region would rank in the top half of the nations of the world, in terms of general competitiveness. That might not sound like a great ranking, but, particularly if one takes her protectionist past and the last twenty-year trend into account, the changes are generally positive and projected to continue in the right direction. This provides strong incentives for investors thinking of doing business in Latin America. First movers are likely to benefit greatly from making early forays into the Latin American business sectors.

The general regional rankings don't tell the whole story. The global competitiveness context includes the very poor-performing state institutions, which are, excepting the countries linked to the 21st-century socialism initiative embarked upon by the late president of Venezuela, Hugo Chavez, in the process of improving. Due to widespread public frustration with state corruption, political instability in the form of massive demonstrations has racked Brazil, just ahead of the World Cup tournament to be held there in 2014. Like the much-vaunted Arab Spring, this has the potential to spread all over the region, because corruption is as Latin American as salsa music. This has obvious implications for the business climate. However, on the upside, opportunities to invest outweigh these downside risks. On top of rampant inequality, and highly corrupt and inefficient public institutions, the protests in Brazil were triggered by the heavy investments directed at the World Cup tournament, when so much of the population suffered from the effects of bad government. Nevertheless, even Brazil will weather this political storm, as the left-leaning Rousse government had, prior even to the protests, already taken strong first steps to fight corruption.

Latin America scores better on the quality of her private institutions, on such issues as corporate ethics, efficiency of boards of directors, the strength of auditing and accounting standards, and protection of investor interests. Moreover, Latin America scores well on efficiency enhancers, which include such items as the quality of universities and, in particular, business schools. Staff training is another area where many Latin American countries score well. An American investor seeking to do business in Latin America would find himself quickly in contact with well-trained business persons, a strong critical mass of which speak English.

The Human Development Index scores tell us of the persistence of structural problems, such as poverty and inequality, and strong lags in terms of public goods such as security, education, and health. This, again, is tied to the corruption in the public sector, which taxes businesses and formally employed citizens, but provides few benefits in return. This is true not only in countries like Guatemala, but also in large countries like Brazil. Nevertheless, strong progress has already been achieved, and everything points to the trend being towards more progress. Poverty rates may be over 50% in Guatemala, but were more than 80% a few decades ago. Countries like Chile, Peru, Uruguay, and Costa Rica have turned the corner on their development paths, and have demonstrated strong commitments to forge the stable business climate necessary to attract foreign investors. As rule of law conditions improve in Latin America, public-sector efficacy and efficiency will improve, enlarging the state's ability to finally work positively on behalf of the region's poor population.

The good news is that, due to globalization and freer trade, the correct institutional reforms are under way, albeit haltingly. As indicated by the data from the Heritage Foundation, Latin America has an overall score on economic liberty of 59.6 out of a maximum possible score of 100. Make no mistake, this is a strong improvement over the region's protectionist past, and, in particular, the ISI strategies pursued under the misguided notions of Keynesianism and neo-Marxist and structuralist economics. Latin America has improvements to make on the protection of property rights and, in particular, public-sector corruption (35.5). Although improvements need to continue, the region has progressed on matters relating to labor and investment freedom, as well as financial freedom. Overall, the strong points for the region are its good scores on fiscal freedom. The tax and spending climate in Latin America certainly isn't what the business investor would find in Europe and even the US these days. In terms of monetary, trade, and business freedom, the Latin American region has made strong progress, scoring over 70, well above her general score of 59.6 on general economic liberty. This is all good news for the American investor interested in doing business in Latin America. However, a caveat applies. Foreign investors seeking to do business in Latin America would be wise to avoid the political risks associated with potential investments in the countries linked to or flirting with the ALBA initiative. From the previous chapter, on economic history, we know that Latin America has gone through pro-business and anti-business phases in her past, and even twenty year trends can be quickly reversed by leftist, populist demagogues seeking to capitalize on the frustrations of Latin America's numerous poor population. The countries to avoid outright would be Venezuela and Cuba, of course, and the ones to watch closely and consider only under strict scrutiny would be Ecuador, Bolivia, and Nicaragua. Even Argentina has to be put on a watch list, given the power grabs of the Kirchner government, which tellingly include moves against central bank independence, a surefire route to the inflationary days of macroeconomic instability of her past.

Overall, the business climate in the region of Latin America and the Caribbean is good, and improving. The economies of the region are cognizant of the principles of competitiveness, and improving the business and investment climate. Latin America ranks slightly better than middling on competitiveness, and is sorely held back by the poor quality of her public institutions. Public institutions are not transparent, and that leads to corruption, clientelism, and cronyism in politics, which obviously holds back improvements needed to make Latin America more friendly towards market-friendly principles. Still, economic liberty is on the rise, which is a good sign, and, if history is any guide, political liberty will eventually follow. The indicators presented in this chapter make clear that democracy is the order of the day in Latin America, always a good sign for potential investors, provided that the democratic institutions are respected by the politicians in power. This isn't always the case in Latin America. The realm of the political institutions is a matter we leave to another chapter.

NOTES

1. Authors' analysis based on World Bank data. World Bank. World Development Indicators, online database: http://databank.worldbank.org/data/views/variableSelection/selectvariables.aspx?source=world-development-indicators (accessed May 2013).

2. World Bank. World Development Indicators, online database: http://databank.worldbank.org/data/views/variableSelection/selectvariables.aspx?source=world-development-indicators (accessed May 2013).

3. Ibid.

4. Authors' own calculations based on IMF data from WEO, April 2013.

5. Analysis based on World Bank data, April 2013.

6. International Monetary Fund. World Economic Outlook, online database: http://www.imf.org/external/pubs/ft/weo/2013/01/weodata/weoselgr.aspx (accessed May 2013).

7. Ibid.

8. Ibid.

9. Ibid.

10. Ibid.

11. Ibid.

12. Authors' calculations based on various indicators, as follows (all accessed May 2013). Ease of Doing Business Index, 2013, World Bank: http://www.doingbusiness.org/rankings. Human Development Index, 2013, United Nations: http://hdr.undp.org/en/statistics/hdi/. Global Competitiveness Index,

2012–2013, World Economic Forum: www.weforum.org. Travel and Tourism Competitiveness Index, World Economic Forum: www.weforum.org. Global Gender Gap, World Economic Forum: www.weforum.org. Index of Democracy, 2012, Economist Intelligence Unit: http://www.eiu.com/Handlers/WhitepaperHandler.ashx?fi=Democracy-Index-2012.pdf&mode=wp&campaignid=DemocracyIndex12. KOF Index of Globalization: http://globalization.kof.ethz.ch/. Freedom in the World, Freedom House: http://www.freedomhouse.org/. Index of Economic Liberty, Heritage Foundation: www.heritage.org. Corruptions Perceptions Index, Transparency International: http://www.transparency.org/research/cpi/overview. International Monetary Fund, World Economic Outlook, online database: www.imf.org.

13. Heritage Foundation, Index of Economic Liberty: www.heritage.org (accessed May 2013).

REFERENCES

LaGarde, C. (2011) IMF chief praises Latinamerica which can provide "some lessons to the advanced world". Mercopress, South Atlantic News Agency, 27 November, obtained from http://en.mercopress.com/2011/11/27/imf-chief-praises-latinamerica-which-can-provide-some-lessons-to-the-advanced-world.

Williamson, J. (1989) What Washington means by policy reform. In Williamson, J. (Ed.), *Latin American Readjustment: How Much has Happened*. Washington: Institute for International Economics.

4

CULTURE AND BUSINESS

LATIN AMERICAN BUSINESS CULTURE MISTAKES

Parker Pen in Mexico

Parker Pen is a well-recognized company, founded in 1888, specializing in pen design. The company decided to launch a marketing campaign in Mexico. The aim for the campaign was to respond to the problems that the consumers had with a brand of pens that used to spill ink in shirts or pants. The marketing campaign in English was as follows: "It won't leak in your pocket and embarrass you."

The company decided to translate this slogan but the translation team did a terrible mistake with the word "embarrass" and translated it as "embarazar" in Spanish. The problem is that "embarazar" in Spanish means getting pregnant. In the end the slogan was understood in Spanish as follows: "It won't leak in your pocket and get you pregnant."

American Airlines in Mexico

American Airlines was born in 1934 when American Airways changed its name after some subsidiaries were incorporated in the company. The company started flying on September 6, 1942, and started its Super Saver campaign (discounts) in 1977. In October 2007 the company celebrated its 65th anniversary of flying to Mexico, with more than 360 flights a week.

Although American Airlines knew the market, it failed in the campaign when announcing the leather seats incorporated in its new airplanes. The slogan was supposed to read "Fly in leather;" in Spanish that was written as "vuele en cuero." The problem is that, in Mexican culture, "en cuero" means naked. Basically the advertisement was read as "Fly naked."

INTRODUCTION

Globalization has substantially increased the number of business ventures in international markets. Since we live in a "borderless" business environment, not only are the opportunities to entry in a world market greater, but also the barriers. One of the major barriers to successful business operation is culture. No matter what the business activity may be, culture is always present. Culture affects business operations in different ways. While English may be considered the "lingua franca" or the language of international business, it is not always useful when transacting business. The host country's native language is important. Mistranslations and misinterpretations of information can cause significant problems and become a major deal breaker. Miscues regarding pricing and promotion are common in business transactions. However, when these errors are translated into a country's native language, more complex problems emerge. Probably the major element that needs to be recognized is the fact that foreign business cultures are different and they must be respected. No business person who wants to establish a business relationship should ever impose his/her beliefs on the host country. The bottom line is that the global business person needs to learn the culture, language, and needs of the host country clients. This is the only path to gaining respect, trust, and a competitive edge (Gullestrup, 2007).

The opening case presents an example of two mistakes that companies made because they did not pay attention to the details of culture. Both of these cases could have been avoided. The companies had to admit their mistakes, and repair their image and reputation. Moreover, these blunders have a negative impact on the sales levels of companies. Some people will refuse to buy a product from a company that is insensitive to a country's culture and language. Lesson learned: pay attention to all dimensions of culture when doing business in Latin America.

Because of the constant change that has been occurring in Latin American countries, it is imperative that global business people learn to be cross-culturally competent. The failure to acquire cultural knowledge can have a significant cost impact on a company's brand. The lack of understanding of culture can have both short- and long-term effects on business dealings because it will strain relationships, negate trust, and decrease confidence in business interactions. Knowing these cultural attributes can determine whether business negotiations are composed of implicit or explicit features (Deari, Kimmel, and Lopez, 2008).

This chapter focuses on the cultural factors that affect the ability to conduct business in Latin American countries. The chapter presents issues regarding customs, social structures, religion, and communication. Each one of these factors can have an influence on the transaction of business in any one of the Latin American countries. Being aware of these cultural dimensions can be a major strength for those business people who do business in Latin America.

HISTORICAL INFLUENCE

The historical influences of Spain and Portugal have their left mark on Latin America. The traditions that were brought from afar have become embedded in the patterns of living of Latin American people and continue to exist in present-day cultures of all Latin American countries (Becker, 2011, p. 148). The personality traits, attitudes, and beliefs that came with the immigrants have become the central determinants of how the present Latin American cultures see, think, and act in their environments. Decisions they make are based on their cultural orientations. As such, business and consumer decisions are all connected (linked) with the culture of the country and its people. The issue of cultural literacy is critically important for any person wanting to do business in Latin America. Knowing the relationship of family, religion, and language, for example, can be a determining factor in many business decisions, so becoming a student of culture is an absolute necessity.

WHAT ARE CULTURE AND MANAGEMENT VALUES IN LATIN AMERICA?

Discussions of values and attitudes are important for all as part of business transactions. It has been found that honesty and responsibility were extremely high when surveying business people in Latin America. Other values, like civility, cheerfulness, helpfulness, obedience, and optimism, came after the two major values. It is interesting that self-direction, imagination, independence, intellect, and open-mindedness were considered the least important values among business executives. As we have stated previously, relationships are critical in business dealings. These relationships are related to values that each person possesses. Traits such as loyalty, trust, and organizational flexibility require good relationships (Davila, 2004). An example will illustrate. Workers in Argentina approach conflict through arbitration, discussion, and intervention. In the Dominican Republic the method of dealing with relationships or conflict is generally autocratic. Mexicans are generally concerned with others and hence want to resolve a conflict as amenably as possible. Latin Americans generally associate themselves with their respective "in-group" without regard to the entire organization. They like social structures that are established on friendship. By and large the cultural framework in the country will determine the human resource practices, particularly when it comes to recruitment. Physical appearance age, and social contacts and birthplace may be critical in the selection process. This is expressly evident in Chile (Dávila, 2005).

People's perception of the world and how they react to ideas is a function of their culture. No other variable is as important as culture when doing business in a foreign land. Culture is at the core of understanding people's perspectives on products, services, and ideas. It has a huge effect on almost every marketing activity.

There are a variety of definitions of culture one could present as a foundation for understanding a people in any geographic area of the world. One general definition that we believe applies to the Latin American environment can be presented as follows: "Culture is a complex cognitive system that comprises people's beliefs, knowledge, know-how, rules and value. Within this context, people can form different types of identities such as individual and collective. An example of these would be: an individual identity would be composed of an individual's personal identity while a collective identity relates to a religious community, a national group, political party or economic entity" (Stockinger, 2010, p. 6).

A manager doing business in Latin America might be surprised to see many employees doing their work in front of a religious painting or image. The association of local religious denominations with work is common in many Latin American countries. In Mexico, many workers like to do their work in front of a picture of the Virgin of Guadalupe. This is one of the many examples of how culture can have an impact on business (Dávila, 2005).

It is critical that the manager of a business in Latin America understand that culture is the most important lens that people use to understand the world they live in and the surroundings with which they interact (Becker, 2011, p. 148). Without the understanding of the culture of a business client, the dealer is going to lose the sale on almost every account.

National Culture and Subcultures

Culture is passed on from one generation to another. The elements of the culture are molded and embedded into traditions that dictate a person's thinking, family composition, and the community's patterns of living. While traditions and customs are always difficult to change, when enough pressure is presented, old ways give way to new ideas about how to live, work, and engage in social discourse. Globalization has introduced new technology and new ways of doing things. The advent of 24/7 information cycles has substantially changed cultures in various Latin American countries. Yes, there are those secluded areas in the altiplano of Peru, the depths of the Amazon in Brazil, and the mountains of Bolivia, but even in these remote areas, the internet has made its mark and connected people who never knew what existed outside of their city, village, or barrio. As such, attitudes and values that have been around for decades and centuries can change because of new information. As they change or are modified they also shape the management styles of managers in organizations.

In Latin America a manager is viewed as an expert, in contrast to the view held in the US that a manager is basically a problem solver or resource allocator. Traditions and customs affect the internal and external ideas of how the hierarchy of the organization is structured. Latinos look at organizations from a "pecking order" point of view, or from the position where they are located in the organization (Becker, 2011, p. 149).

Figure 4.1 is a comprehensive diagram of how the cultural variables interact with the culture as a whole. Each variable has a unique impact on the cultural composition and each person's experience in family, religion, and education—for example, which will mold and shape their profile as a person, and how they see social and business situations.

While globalization has been occurring over the past 25 years, it has slowly forced Latin Americans to think differently. The business practices and processes that have historically been part of the daily lives are now changing to accommodate global

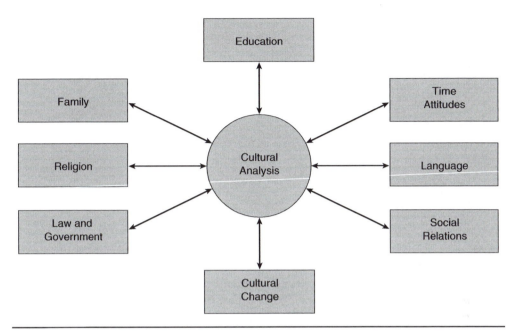

Figure 4.1 Cultural analysis

Source: Adapted from Hill (2011, p. 54)

business practices. This is happening because success in business requires a management process, which operates congruently with contemporary global business practices. An example of this is using English as a means of negotiating business transactions. Even though English is being required for many business transactions, the international business manager needs to know and understand the local cultural differences that exist in various parts of the country or region where business is conducted. The cultural differences in rural areas are many times unlike those in large cities and, as such, it is important that the international managers recognize the differences and respect their impact on the business activities that are being conducted (Becker, 2011). So, culture is a huge concern for business managers.

Latin American countries have similar but different cultures. While there are a variety of definitions of culture, most experts define culture as "the sum total of the beliefs, rules, techniques, institutions and artifacts that characterize human populations … It is interesting to note that culture cannot be observed but can be learned by understanding the social world in which it exists" (Ball *et al.*, 2012, p. 64). When we examine the totality of a society, we can observe the two dimensions of social and cultural. Social is meant as the interactions of people with culture or beliefs, rules, techniques, and patterns of behavior. The elements mentioned above make up the cultural framework that allows a society to identify itself and operate within the larger regional and national settings. Some societies believe their "way of life" is superior or the best, and hence are ethnocentric about their country, and its products or processes. This can sometimes be an obstacle to the successful conduct of business (Ball *et al.*, 2012).

Social Structures

When one thinks of Latin America, one thinks of poverty, constant change in governments, and instability. Crises and revolts have been part of the life and culture of Latin America. For decades, inequality in income and in status has been a major issue. Because of the inequality and dislocations that have affected Latin American people, there have been social and political uprisings throughout the continent. The Venezuela situation with President Hugo Chavez is an example. Mr. Chavez's changes in the public structures in his country have given rise to uncertainty. The demands of the indigenous people of Bolivia, led by the election of Evo Morales, as a person who recognizes the issues of inequality, and his efforts to increase the quality of life for the underprivileged groups, is another example. In Colombia there has been significant reduction in drug movement.

From another perspective, social structures relate to how a society is organized. It refers to the relationships of the society and its people and how they organize themselves. Most societies have two major parts—one is that of the individual (Western culture), the other is the group (collective) or Eastern cultures (Hill, 2011). The social structure also focuses on how societies are created in terms of classes or casts. How mobile a person is in a society will determine its social structure. For example, American society allows for just about unlimited mobility. Being part of a social structure can have a serious impact on one's ability to achieve economic independence and innovative capabilities. Those individuals who seem involved in a social class that does not permit mobility are clearly constrained. As such their ability to develop businesses, achieve economic rewards, and be an active consumer of goods is constrained or limited (Hill, 2011).

The social structure in Latin American culture begins with the family. The family is the major social entity around which everything else revolves. Family comes first before anything else in the life of most Latin Americans.

Figure 4.2 provides a picture of how social relationships operate in Latin American culture. The concentric circle demonstrates that the family is the center of all business and cultural activities. As we move out from the center of the circle, loyalty and obligations are significantly affected.

Historically and currently, the family is the place where all relationships begin and end. From a very young age Latin Americans recognize that the core of their being starts with the family. Loyalty to the family is everything to Latin Americans. As they move away from the family structure, there is less loyalty and less inclination for close relationships. Personal relationships with close family and close friends supersede any other relationship or activity. A detached approach seems to be the prevalent way of engaging other people in Latin America. This social structure has implications for business in terms of product and service sales strategies, and also for the human resource recruitment process (Becker, 2010).

Groups are important in Latin America business and social situations, but they work well only when the members of the group are known to one another. Strangers, while greeted politely and engaged, are not the primary concern of Latin Americans. Clearly this has major implications for business relationships and transactions

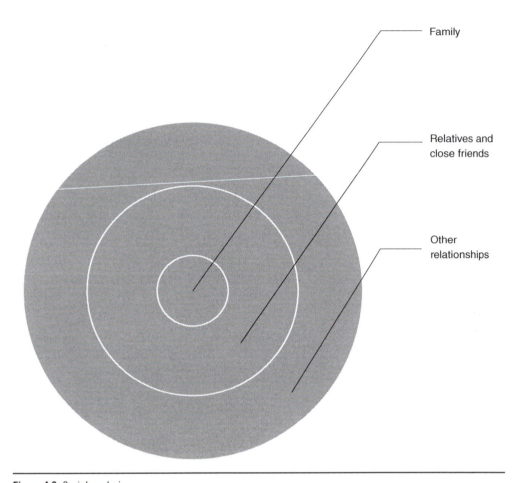

Family

Relatives and
close friends

Other
relationships

Figure 4.2 Social analysis

Source: Adapted from Hill (2011, p. 54)

(Becker, 2010). This leads us to the issue of social stratification, or hierarchal levels or classes.

Social Stratification

We can look at people from a variety of different dimensions. The more we know about the relationship of culture to negotiation and the transaction of business the better a business person is going to be in achieving his/her economic goals. For decades, Hofsteder's perspective on culture, the characteristics of people in different cultures, and how these characteristics affect business transactions has been a foundation for business people. It remains an important vehicle for explaining and understanding why people in different cultures behave the way they do. In Table 4.1 we outline the cultural dimensions and where they are indicated in Latin America. It provides definitions of the cultural dimensions that exist in various Latin American countries.

Table 4.1 Cultural dimensions

Cultural dimension	Definition or description of cultural dimension	Country and geographic area
Power distance	Members of an organization in a country accept the fact that power is distributed unequally. As such, national cultures can have low power distance in which there is an attempt to reduce the inequalities. Latin American countries have registered a higher power distance score, meaning that those people with less power expect that power is to be allocated unequally. Additionally, it means that a higher power distance score is related with income inequality. This dimension would suggest that organizations and governments centralize their power and put others with less power in lower levels of the organization.	Latin American countries
Individualism/ collectivism	According to the individualistic dimension, people are independent, or able to take care of themselves and their own affairs without depending on others. In contrast, the collectivistic dimension states that societies care for the other members of society. This is exemplified in a country like Ecuador, where family and other groups are a nuclear part of society.	Ecuador
Masculinity/ femininity	This dimension focuses on the relationship of how gender roles are viewed and followed in a society. It relates to issues of feminine qualities such as modesty, and masculine qualities like success and performance.	Latin America has a distinct view on women's role in society

Source: Hofstede (2009)

By and large, consumer behavior is controlled by culture. As such marketers need to identify, interact with, and integrate culture into their company's marketing campaign. Throughout Latin American business environments, cultural similarities exist. Using Hofstede's framework as a platform or foundation for understanding culture in Latin America, we can make some estimations as to how people may react to certain products or services that marketers are offering in the respective countries. Throughout Latin America Hofstede's study found that people have high uncertainty avoidance and a low individualism rating. As such they have low tolerance for ambiguity. On another scale it was found, using Hofstede's dimensions, that Latinos have a high risk avoidance rating and thus prefer business communications that avoid ambiguity. With further study, the investigators found on a different dimension that Latinos are predominantly collectivists rather than individualists. This confirms our previous discussion, which indicated that Latinos have very close family ties and historical alliances that many times overshadow other cultural characteristics. While these are only a few of the cultural factors that have been identified to have a major impact on business relations and associations, it would behoove all business people to study and become familiar with these and other cultural dimensions (Quillen, 2013). Another element of culture that has an influence on thinking and behavior is religion.

Religions

Religion is a very important part of the life of Latin American citizens. Figure 4.1 summarizes the religions that exist in Latin America. Those colored pink show that the predominant religion is Catholic or Christian. Clearly Christianity is the predominant belief structure in all of these countries. Generally Roman Catholicism is the dominant religion of most people who live in just about any country of Latin America. It reflects the historical roots that each country has with its European ancestors. While business people may not always recognize it, religion does in fact have a major impact on a society (Gillespie & Hennessey, 2011), and thus may have an impact on the development and conduct of a business enterprise. The way people think and act is many times affected by their religious inclination. The rules and beliefs can determine what products and services a person purchases. It is difficult and risky to make generalizations regarding the relationships between religion and business practices and consumer behavior (Hill, 2011). There is some evidence to suggest that there may be some relationship between religion and business practices. In a global environment, it is evident that Catholics, Protestants, and other religions have demonstrated entrepreneurial and sustainable economic activity (Hill, 2011).

In many parts of Latin America, especially the areas populated by the indigenous people (Bolivia, Ecuador, Guatemala, Mexico, and Peru) there have been some major conflicts and divisions due to different aspects of religious beliefs. The friction is derived from different sects, and the relationship between religions and politics. Some of these conflicts have led to serious and bloody violence and death. Areas in the southern part of Mexico have witnessed outbursts that have created major alienation and anger among many of the communities. The political establishments that create turmoil as a strategy to disrupt and topple political leaders and regimes have manipulated some of the religious sects in Bolivia, Guatemala, Ecuador, and Peru. This interface has been seen in various parts of Latin America. Because religion plays a major role in the lives of Latin Americans and touches so many people, it is an easy path via which to reach large groups of people (Cevallos, 2005).

All of these social factors are really without merit unless there is a viable communication system. No society can function normally without an effective level of personal communication.

Personal Communication

Successful business development requires business people to address the intercultural challenges that each country in Latin America presents. To conduct any business activity, communication is required, and communication is almost always cultural. Since culture and communication are so intimately intertwined there is always an opportunity for miscommunication. When a business person understands the culture, he/she can also understand the dimensions of communication. Because culture has such major impact on how people see the world, it influences the content and character of the communication. Understanding the factors that affect cross-cultural communication can reduce differences in interpretation and establish trust in the dialogue (LeBaron, 2003).

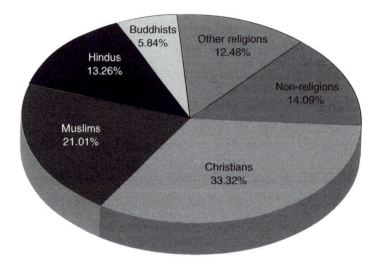

Figure 4.3 World religions by percentage
Source: CIA World Factbook 2010

Globalization has upped the ante with regard to proper and effective communication in global business. Successful competition in global markets requires business people to be knowledgeable about the customs and communication styles of foreign clients (Chaney and Martin, 2009). Many communication skills are highly visible at the outset of most intercultural meetings. How one is perceived on the first meeting can linger and have an impact through the business interaction. Things such as the initial greeting, proper introductions, dress appearance, and non-verbal communications are important dimensions that affect the way people come across to one another in a dialogue (Chaney and Martin, 2009). One of the most important skills to have in intercultural transactions is that of being a good listener who avoids sensitive topics that may create a distance between the parties. Certain non-verbal gestures can create uncertainty and awkwardness. Being aware of communication protocols regarding the presentation of non-verbal communication can go a long way in enhancing effective communication (Chaney and Martin, 2009). In some Latin American countries, prolonged eye contact is important and has value in creating a good contact with the client or business person (Chaney and Martin, 2009).

For people doing business in Latin America, communication is at the core of the business transaction. Knowing how, when, and to what extent to communicate with existing and potential business clients and partners is a skill all foreign Latin American business people must acquire. Business people must learn the differences between high- and low-context cultures. This means that, in a low-context culture, a person is direct and to the point in her/his interactive communication. Low-context communication means that people say what they mean in direct language without any round-about conversations. In a high-context culture just the opposite happens.

The interactive communication requires a diplomatic and polite transaction of words and ideas as the parties exchange ideas and views on particular products, processes, or ideas (Tompkins, 2011).

One of the major effects of proper communication is the ability to negotiate business transactions. The high-context nature of Latin American people requires the establishment of relationships or social networks. These relationships are cemented with the notion of "confianza," or trustworthiness, that is endemic among Latin American business relationships. For example, Central Americans look for trust and confidence in their business relationships. This is a critical component to not only commence business negotiations but also to maintain them over time (LeBaron, 2003).

Communication is the silent language in Latin America. Latin Americans embrace (*abrazos*) between men—standing close together, a pat on the back, a tug and squeeze of the arm, energetically expressive motions, and non-verbal cues—all of which are important to communication in Latin America (Becker, 2011).

Latin Americans possess the characteristics of what anthropologists call "high-context culture." Their communication styles are carried out through non-verbal cues. That is, Latinos depend on silent language or indirect gestures to deliver their message. This is one reason that deals, negotiations, and agreements take longer. There is a need to elevate the level of trust so that the Latin is comfortable with the relationship he/she has with the foreign business partner. In common terms, each party must get to know the other so that this trust connection is solid and safe (Becker, 2011).

A leading social factor that is without a doubt at the foundation of transmitting and understanding the cultural interface between the Latin American countries and prospective investors or business developers is education.

Education

Latin American countries as a whole invest substantially in education. Public spending as a percentage of GNP in 2008 was about 4.85%, while the entire world spending was about 4.75% (UNESCO, 2011). Brazil invests a greater amount in education than most other Latin American countries (UNESCO, 2011). While enrollments in primary grades are growing in most Latin American countries, enrollments in secondary grades and universities are declining when compared to North America and Western Europe (UNESCO, 2010). The other aspect of Latin American education relates to the quality of education. Most of the Latin American countries are classified as at the bottom in terms of achievement when compared to OECD countries. Again Brazil is among the high-performing countries (Puryear, 2011). One of the distinguishing factors in Latin American education is that the rich students complete their education while the poor students do not keep pace with their rich peers. This dichotomy is a major factor that affects the present and future competitiveness of the region (Puryear, 2011). Moreover, the fact that Latin America is lagging in science and technology creates an even more challenging environment for business development and competitiveness. These are fundamental impediments that affect the development of human capital, which is so vitally important to economic development and entrepreneurship (Puryear, 2011). As business developers pursue their interest in Latin American investment possibilities, they need to think about cultural constructs that affect how the Latin American parties think about deal making, negotiations, and marketing.

CLASSIFICATION BY CULTURE

Components of Culture: Values, Spoken Language, and Body Language

This chapter's introductory cases present examples of the problems companies can encounter when they do not pay attention to cultural details. Entering the Latin American business environment presents not only many logistical and technical issues, but a variety of cultural challenges too. Culture is more complex than just language, and "how people live"; values, customs, religion, social structures, and patterns of living all have an impact on how business is conducted and partnerships developed. Each country in Latin America is different in some way, shape, or form.

Doing business in Latin America requires business people to adapt to the buyer and observe the customs of each country where business is conducted. Essentially there are four major cross-cultural constructs that every business person needs to understand and observe when transacting business in cross-cultural situations. These constructs are summarized in Table 4.2.

So What?

Any business exploring the opportunities of doing business in Latin America must think about how culture will affect its business negotiations and operations in a country or region. People's traditions affect human behavior, and ultimately have an impact on how they think, feel, and act. Culture is one of the main complex variables that business executives need to navigate in order to achieve business entry into Latin America. Business people in Latin America are inclined to be extroverted, impatient, talkative, and curious. Because Latin America is people oriented, they generally try to do things by seeking favors (Kamensk, 2010). The Latinos are much more collective, and prefer good interpersonal and cordial relationships individually and with groups. This attribute seems to be more important than professional expertise or competence. Some other characteristics that are very important to Latinos and that have an impact on business transactions are as follows.

- Time: Latinos have a poor allegiance to time and schedules. *Mañana* is generally the rule. Punctuality is not an important part of their life.
- Negotiations are generally slower in Latin America because there is a need for small-talk and the development of relationships. Within this context, Latin business people want to be in control, therefore it is important to measure the conversation so that no conflict arises.

Table 4.2 Cross-cultural constructs

Construct	Description
(a) Deal focused vs relationship focused	Deal-focused individuals are basically task-oriented individuals, while those who are relationship focused have people as their center of attention.
(b) Informal vs formal	Many times these two patterns are like oil and water. They can repel each other and cause conflict in the interaction.
(c) Rigid time vs fluid time	Many people watch the clock frequently. They are concerned about appointments, schedules, and dates. These rigid time adherers are many times fanatics about punctuality and due dates. In contrast, those from fluid time cultures are much more relaxed and casual about schedules, appointments, and due dates. These divergent perspectives can create frustration between the people who observe different constructs of time.
(d) Expressive vs reserved	Expressive people have a much different communication approach to that of reserved people. Many times, expressive people are constantly talking. They are direct; sometimes they are loud and have very real and direct eye contact. Noted for long silences or pauses. These divergent perspectives can create frustration between people trying to conduct business with one another.

Source: Gesteland (1999)

- Close together: one attribute that is universal among Latinos is their desire to sit close together. This is important to know because it is a custom important to "people interaction."
- Pleasure before business: to create and develop a relationship with clients and/ or partners, socializing is part of the relationship-building process. Dinners, entertainment, and social gatherings are very common before business is transacted.
- Impressions: it is important for business relationships in Latin America to leave a solid permanent impression about your company value system and attitude about business.

All of the aforementioned items illustrate a major concern that all Latin executives have, and that is whether they can trust the Anglo or foreign business acquaintance in business transactions (Carrasco, 2011).

So how do these cultural/behavior patterns fit in to doing business in Latin America? Based on the characteristics outlined in Table 4.2, we can say that Latin Americans are relationship focused, respect formal culture, and accept a polychromic (placing less emphasis on scheduling, time punctuality, and due dates) business culture with a very expressive cohort of people. With this information a business person can easily begin to analyze the environment and map out the proper approaches for negotiations, marketing, and managing people across cultures and borders. Without this information, foreign business people will significantly reduce their opportunities for the successful conduct of business.

The foregoing discussion has presented many of the cultural factors that impact the transaction of business. Next, a small example will illustrate the influence of culture in a business situation.

In order to introduce mobile handsets into a market like Venezuela, the supplier must be very familiar not only with purchasing habits, tastes, and willingness to purchase the product that is being sold, but also the culture. Understanding these factors starts with building a knowledge base about the major aspects of the culture and the target consumer. In Venezuela the seller of handsets needs to understand consumer habits and tastes. Additionally, the marketer needs to know how eager Venezuelan consumers are to buy the product. To achieve any success, the foreign business person in Venezuela has to acquire knowledge of the country's culture and the culture of the consumer in her/his target market(s). A country like Venezuela is a major consumer possibility for any marketer. With a large and generally educated population of 27 million people, there is a huge opportunity to sell a variety of goods and services. While Venezuela in some ways resembles the market composition of the US, it still requires a foreign business person to carry out extensive study of the culture in that country. Language, customs, and buyer attitudes have complicated structures. A failure to understand various dimensions of the consumer's habits and behaviors could be economically unrewarding (Rodríguez, Ciancio y Asociados, 2012).

This is just one of hundreds of business and cultural examples that exist among Latin American countries. Business people must not only be aware of cultural factors, but must also know how they affect the transaction of business. Studying, listening, and effectively communicating with country natives and experienced business people will significantly reduce the opportunity for error in business activity.

SUMMARY AND CONCLUSIONS

In this chapter we have given you a detailed understanding the component parts of how culture and business interact. Proper and accurate information about a country's culture is essential for the proper analysis and understanding of how culture interfaces with the business ideas and operations of your business.

Constantly updating and being aware of the general culture and business culture of Latin American countries is essential to success in those markets. No other area of business analysis is more important than understanding the culture of a country in which a business is going to invest. Almost everything else, such as finance, marketing, and technology management, is identical to what needs to be done in other environments. Since culture and how culture interacts with business is so complicated, it is necessary to read and reread the environment. The business person needs to make sure that he/she is on target with his/her assessment of the cultural details that relate to the business plans and strategies that are being developed for entry into the country.

It is literally impossible to successfully enter a country to do business without addressing cultural phenomena. Be open minded, focused, and deliberate in making culture a major part of your country analysis.

REFERENCES

Ball, D., Geringer, M., Minor, M., and McNett, J. (2012) *International business: The challenge of global competition* (12th ed.). McGraw-Hill: New York.

Becker, T. H. (2010) *Doing business in the new Latin America: Keys to profit in America's next-door markets.* Santa Ana, CA: Praeger.

Becker, T. H. (2011) *Doing business in the new Latin America: A guide to cultures, practices, and opportunities.* Santa Ana, CA: Praeger.

Carrasco, D. (2011) Borderlands and cultural encounters: Stories and rhythms of Latin(o) American lives, 2011–12 Series, University Center for the Humanities, Western Michigan University ScholarWorks at WMU, 27 October, obtained from http://scholarworks.wmich.edu/cgi/viewcontent.cgi?article=1014&context=humanities_events.

Cevallos, D. (2005) 'Religion – Latin America: Indigenous peoples divided by faith. Interpress News Service (IPS), obtained from http://www.ipsnews.net/2005/05/religion-latin-america-indigenous-peoples-divided-by-faith/.

Chaney, L. H. and Martin, J. S. (2009) Communication skills needed for successful interactions with America's largest trading partners. *Proceedings of the 74th Annual Convention of the Association for Business Communication*, 4–7 November, Portsmouth, Virginia.

CIA World Factbook (2010) Obtained from https://www.cia.gov/library/publications/download/download-2010.

Davila, A. (2004) Culture and business practices in Latin America: Opportunities for research and challenges for management. In Schweickart, N. and Kaufmann, L. (Eds.) *Lateinamerika – Management. Konzepte–Prozesse–Erfahrungen* [Management in Latin America – Concepts, processes and experiences]. Wiesbaden: Gabler.

Dávila, A. (2005) How culture affects work practices in Latin America, obtained from http://www.wharton.universia.net/index.cfm?fa=viewArticle&id=901&language=english.

Deari, H., Kimmel, V., and Lopez, P. (2008) Effects of cultural differences in international business and price negotiations: A case of a Swedish company with operations in e.g. South America. Unpublished master thesis. Sweden: Växjö University.

Gesteland, R. (1999) Patterns of cross-cultural business behavior marketing, negotiating and managing across cultures. Copenhagen Business School, 1–5.

Gillespie, K. and Hennessey, H. D. (2011) *Global marketing* (3rd ed.). United States/United Kingdom: Southwestern Cengage Learning.

Gullestrup, H. (2007) *Cultural analysis: Towards cross-cultural understanding.* Copenhagen: Copenhagen Business School.

Hill, C. (2011) *International business.* New York: McGraw-Hill.

Hofstede, G. (2009) *Hofstede's five cultural dimensions: Structure model: Identity and image*, obtained from http://www.eurib.org/fileadmin/user_upload/Documenten/PDF/Identiteit_en_Imago_ENGELS/z_-_De_vijf_cultuurdimensies_van_Hofstede__EN_. pdf.

Kamensk, K. (2010) Culture: Cross-cultural perspectives, obtained from http://www.scribd.com/doc/.http://www.scribd.com/doc/75338841/Culture.

LeBaron, M. (2003) Culture-based negotiation styles, obtained from http://www.beyondintractability.org/essay/culture-negotiation.

Puryear, J. (2011) *How do Latin American schools compare?* Banco Itau Holding.

Quillen, C. (2013) VP of Operations at Davinci Meeting Rooms, LLC.

Rodríguez, Ciancio y Asociados (RC&A) (2012) Venezuela, doing business guide, obtained from http://www.integra-international.net/files/guides/venezuela.pdf.

Stockinger, P. (2010) Intercultural communication: A general introduction. NATO Regional Cooperation Course (NRCC), North Atlantic Treaty Organization, NATO Defense College, Via Giorgio Pelosi, 1, Cecchigonola.

Tompkins, P. S. (2011) Practicing communication ethics: Development, discernment, and decision making. Boston: Pearson.

UNESCO (2010) Latin America and the Caribbean, obtained from http://www.unesco.org/new/en/communi cation-and-information/portals-and-platforms/goap/access-by-region/latin-america-and-the-caribbean/.

UNESCO (2011) Latin America and the Caribbean, obtained from http://www.unesco.org/new/en/education/themes/leading-the-international-agenda/education-for-all/advocacy/global-action-week/gaw-2011/2011gaw-latin-america/.

5

ECONOMIC CLIMATE OF DOING
BUSINESS IN LATIN AMERICA

INTRODUCTION

Monetary Policy Under Inflation Targeting

The macroeconomic climate of the two decades prior to the 21st century reflected significant turbulence, particularly in the area of price stability. From 1980 onward, Latin America underwent radical inflationary spirals, associated with the twin crises of public debt and balance of payments. This led to the 1980s being called the "lost decade of Latin America." The significant economic costs of recession and recovery notwithstanding, there were significant lessons learned that, in fact, were and are applied, and these have a lot to do with the relative macroeconomic stability that today characterizes most of the countries of the region. Nowhere was the progress made more striking than in the area of inflation.

In this chapter we present a detailed overview of the economic climate that exists in Latin America. From a macroeconomic and a microeconomic point of view, we discuss the dynamic economic environment that has existed over time, where the economy is presently, and what we believe the economic future of the region offers for business and economic development.

A few graphics will help to illustrate the true progress that has been made in the area of price stability. The following figures present the annual inflation rates for the 1980–2011 time period for different regions, which are defined by the World Bank in its World Development Indicators.

After decades of application of Keynesian economics, the 1980s began with double-digit inflation in many countries, particularly those of the Third World. After 1982, the general price level began to rise throughout the region, with the increase reaching full force at the end of the decade. Along with Sub-Saharan Africa, the Latin America and the Caribbean region suffered the episodes of highest inflation in the world. The high points were reached, respectively, in 1991, with 22.1% in the case of

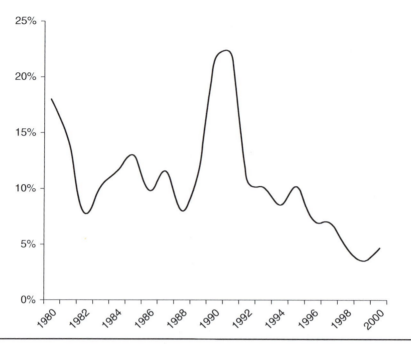

Figure 5.1 Latin America and the Caribbean, inflation rates, 1980–2000[1]

Source: Based on the World Development Indicators; authors' calculations based on World Bank data

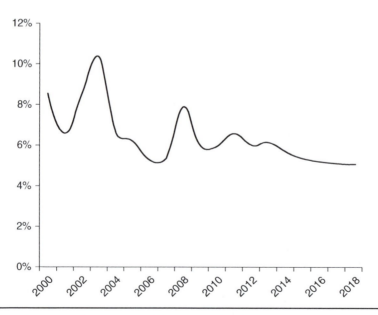

Figure 5.2 Latin America and the Caribbean, inflation rates, 2000–2018[2]

Source: Based on statistics from the IMF; authors' calculations based on World Bank data

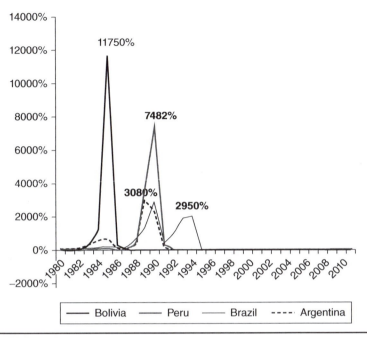

Figure 5.3 Latin America and the Caribbean, annual inflation rate of selected countries[3]
Source: Authors' calculations based on World Bank data

the LAC region. This is where the Washington Consensus kicks in, registering perhaps its greatest benefits, whipping inflation in the region. Thanks to the neoliberal structural adjustment reforms in matters of deficit and debt spending, and sounder monetary and fiscal policies in general, general price level increases fell below 5% by the end of the 1990s. The IMF projects a modest inflation rate of 5.1% into the medium term in the future, 2018.

Figure 5.3 presents the inflation rates for selected countries of the Latin American region, from 2000. It shows the countries that went through the most severe periods of hyperinflation, with inflation rates into the thousands of percent. Figure 5.4 shows those countries that had more "moderate" rates of inflation, in comparison to the countries in Figure 5.3. For the most part, these countries had inflation rates under 150%, with the exception of Suriname, which reached an inflation rate of 368.5% in 1994.

Given the severe distortions in the price mechanism, thanks to decades of state intervention under the Import-Substitution-Industrialization (ISI) regimes and excessive Keynesianism in the macroeconomic sphere, the monetary policy of the countries of Latin America had to undergo drastic changes in order to restore monetary credibility and stability into the markets. According to Luis Jácome (2006), the structural changes that countries in the LAC region generally underwent were characterized by the following factors: (a) strengthening of the institutional order; (b)

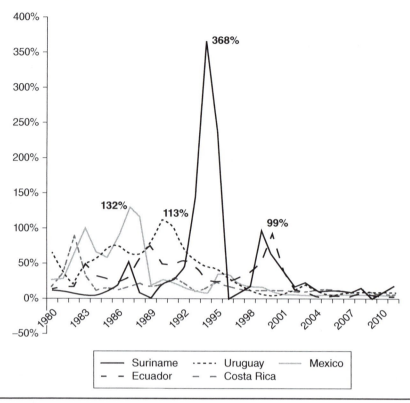

Figure 5.4 Latin America and the Caribbean, annual inflation rate of selected countries[4]

Source: Authors' calculations based on World Bank data

exchange rate flexibility; (c) change over to inflation targeting as a general monetary policy; and (d) the conduct if monetary policy adopts as its core principle the short-run management of bank liquidity, especially in emerging markets (Jácome, 2006).

Inflation targeting was a pillar of the structural adjustments that the LAC region needed to implement in order to recuperate some semblance of monetary and fiscal discipline. Inflation targeting basically means the following. The central bank is first made to be autonomous, and independent of political interference. The central banking authorities then typically announce publicly their inflation targets for the year, in order to raise their audience costs in a transparent fashion, and thereby acquire credibility over time, as the authorities then do whatever is perceived as necessary in order to comply with the inflation target. Typically, the inflation target cannot be changed during the year (Jácome, 2006). Implicit in all this is that, for the central bank, job one for the monetary authorities is inflation. Not only was inflation to be the main job; in large part, it was to be the only job. Thanks to the neoliberal reforms of the Washington Consensus, Latin American central banks do not assume the task of stimulating the economy. Since then, the overriding objective is price stability, and central bank credibility is deemed of utmost importance in this task, so that inflationary expectations can be kept under rein. Inflation targeting was officially adopted by sixteen emerging countries in the wake of the hyperinflationary spirals of the 1980s and the 1990s; among these were Brazil (1999), Chile (1999), Colombia (1999), Mexico (2001), and Peru (2002). The results speak for themselves, since these countries succeeded in reducing their inflation rates to single digits, below 5% in most cases. Guatemala formally adopted inflation targeting in 2005.

The adoption of inflation-targeting monetary policy schemes is good news for national and foreign investors alike. This is borne out by the facts, as net inflows of FDI to Latin America grew from $8.4 billion in 1990 to roughly $170 billion by 2011, according to World Bank figures.[5] This is borne out in Figure 5.5.

The positive impact on FDI flows, outside of recession and recovery years, should be no surprise. Inflation targeting results in lower inflation rates, lower expected rates of inflation, lower volatility in the general price level, all this with null negative effects on a country's macroeconomic performance in general. As a last prize, inflation-targeting monetary policy regimes bring about favorable exchange rates and international reserves in light of interest rate volatility. Whether or not the specific announced inflation targets are met, the key point is that the authorities demonstrate a credible commitment to price stability. Moreover, the comparative referent point is the Latin American past. Thanks to the Washington Consensus's structural reforms, hyperinflation is dead.

FINANCIAL LIBERALIZATION

Financial liberalization is a 20th-century phenomenon, which Latin America could not escape, no matter how much some political and business leaders may have tried to resist progress. This is one area where the benefits of globalization

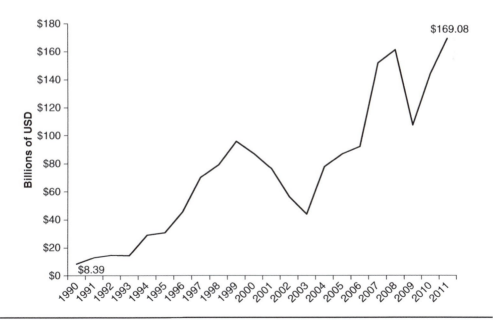

Figure 5.5 Evolution of foreign direct investment, net inflows, current US dollars

Source: Authors' calculations based on World Bank data

were truly reaped. From the 1980s onward, chaotic events and painful disruptions were characteristic of the adjustments the peoples of Latin America had to suffer. It was perhaps to be expected that Latin America had to close painfully the 20th century, a century marked by two world wars, the Cold War, and the constant painful adjustments of countries that found themselves in the full-fledged processes of political, social, and economic modernization.

In the second half of the 20th century, the political and economic consensus at an international level focused on the search for measures, policies, and reforms to spur the world economy. Attention was thereafter focused on economic liberalization as a mechanism that would permit developing countries to recover their wealth-producing capacity. Key to this engine of growth whereby economic growth could fuel human development was the role that FDI would play. Capital account movements would prove to be key among and between countries and regions, thereby permitting gradual increases in savings and investment.

The process of economic and financial liberalization started in the 1970s, as the abandonment of the Bretton Woods system became progressively more official. The Bretton Woods system had been implemented after World War II with the goal of both freeing and controlling capital movements, so as to facilitate financial and macroeconomic stability and independent monetary policies. A big problem arose as governments confronted the Triffin dilemma, whereby the desires of countries to maintain dollar reserves were strongly set back due to the loss of confidence in the US, on account of America's current account deficit (Chowla, 2011).

Other factors supported economic liberalization. Among these were: (a) the need of the US to import capital to finance its central government deficits, made necessary by greater expenses associated with the temporary Vietnam War and the permanent Social Welfare spending programs; (b) financial innovation, and the desire to evade new and bothersome financial regulations; (c) greater ease to make deposits, loans, and emit loans in dollars—in Europe; (d) competition to acquire a greater proportion of world financial services, under strategic private-sector pressure; and (e) the arrival of a dominant ideological paradigm in the neoliberal Washington Consensus.

The emerging economies of Latin America, motivated by the imperatives of attracting foreign direct investment, began promoting their economic liberalization by the end of the 1980s. Latin America began offering a supply of investment-friendly incentives just when the world was demanding more liberal capital flows. The IMF, the World Bank, and the bilateral trade agreements supported the institutional processes of trade and financial liberalization contemplated in the Washington Consensus. One positive outcome was the return of foreign capital to Latin America, which had been scared away in large part during the ISI regimes, infamous for their capital controls. Since the Washington Consensus, Latin America has been much more investment friendly, a factor that has paid off, judging from the greater inflows of FDI to the LAC region.

In large measure, the Washington Consensus was the best set of policies that Latin America could have applied in order to re-establish a friendly business climate for the foreign investor (Ferreiro *et al.*, 2007). Countries of the LAC region, guided by the market fundamentals of the Washington Consensus, acquired gradual advances through the progressive adoption of common-sense, albeit painful, economic and financial reforms. The reforms came in the form of first-, second-, and even third-generation reforms. First, the LAC countries adopted flexible exchange rates to promote their own competitiveness in the increasingly globalized international economy. Interest rate controls were done away with, and capital accounts were liberalized. In the phase of second-generation reforms, barriers to entry to foreign capital were eliminated, central bank independence was established, and public banks were, for the most part, closed. Third-generation reforms began in the 21st century, focused more on the lessons learned from the inflationary crises, those applicable to central banking.

Thanks to that controversial set of reforms, the LAC region as a whole has undergone substantial deregulation and privatization of state enterprises, has adopted the creed of property rights, and enjoys competitive interest rates and exchange rates determined by markets. Importantly, the region has opened itself up to trade. In other words, Latin America is open for business.

The benefits of economic and financial liberalization should be borne out in the statistical data. Figure 5.6 and 5.7 present the tendencies in foreign commerce in the periods before and after the Washington Consensus.

In Figure 5.6, one can see different regions of the world twenty years before and after 1990, roughly the year that the Washington Consensus came into norm and a year after the fall of the Berlin Wall. One can see that, in the twenty-year period between 1991 and 2011, the portion of foreign trade as a percentage of GDP grew significantly over the prior twenty-year period. The greatest increase, of course, is reflected by China, followed by Canada, the European regions, Asia, and the LAC region; these registered the greatest increases in trade as a percentage of GDP with respect to the 1970 to 1990 period.

However, if one looks at Figure 5.7, one sees that the LAC region has much yet to do in the way of effective trade liberalization. Foreign commerce as a percentage of GDP, although greater than before in Latin America, still increased by only 6 percentage points in the 1991–2011 period over the 1970–1990 period. This compares poorly to the structural change reflected by the world as a whole (54% vs. 41.2%), South Asia (154% vs. 71%), East Asia and Pacific (62.8% vs. 37.8%).

Even though the LAC region has maintained a fair rhythm of progress as far as trade liberalization is concerned, it can still do better. But the change of direction is clear, so the future expectations are exceedingly positive in this regard, in general. The LAC region has strong potential to grow its foreign trade component, due, in large part, to the fact that many of its constituent member countries are emerging market economies. The emerging economies of Latin America, such as Guatemala, Costa Rica, Panama, Colombia, Peru, *et al.*, understand that they have the most to gain from adopting greater trade and financial liberalization measures.

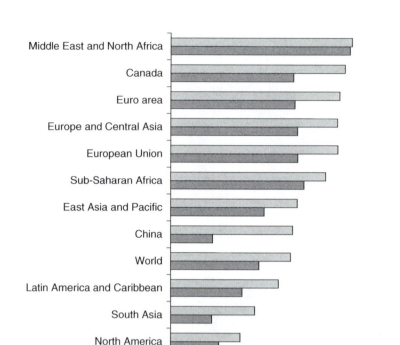

Figure 5.6 World's regions: maximum growth rates of trade as a percentage of GDP, by period, 1991–2011[6]

Source: Authors' calculations based on World Bank data

Figure 5.8 depicts those countries that have shown the greatest increases in the proportional share of trade in GDP. As one can see, there is substantial participation of the smaller countries of the Central American and Caribbean regions in the countries that have most reflected an increase in the share of GDP accounted for by foreign commerce. Once again, the two periods under comparison are the twenty years before and after the Washington Consensus.

In general, one can observe that the countries in question accelerated significantly their shares of foreign trade with respect to their GDPs in the two decades following the Washington Consensus. Guyana is a surprising case, which went from an already high rate of 131.5% share of foreign trade as a percentage of GDP in the 1970–1990 periods to a 215.8% share in the 1991–2011 period. Other impressive increases were reflected by Puerto Rico, Panama, Honduras, Paraguay, and Mexico.

A direct conclusion of what we have seen so far is that economic liberalization facilitated the ability of the foreign sector to maximize its potential. Nevertheless, prudence requires maintaining some semblance of balance of trade, in order to avoid vulnerability to severe macroeconomic shocks. On the other hand, economic

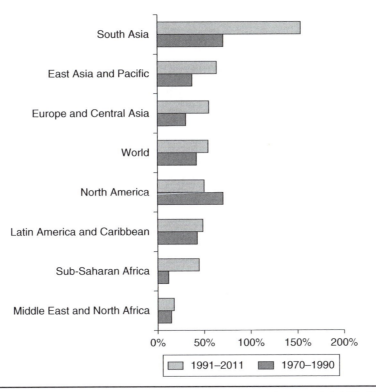

Figure 5.7 World's regions: maximum growth rates of trade as a percentage of GDP, by period, 1970–1990, 1991–2011[7]

Source: Authors' calculations based on World Bank data

liberalization implies a certain level of free-hand dynamism in the capital accounts of the different regions and countries, in the extent that they are pertinent to the economic performance of said countries and regions. Figures 5.9 and 5.10 depict the behavior of the FDI inflows to different regions in the first decade of the 21st century.

In general, the tendency in the FDI flows can be divided into three phases in the 2000–2001 time period. This holds true for the main regions of the world, as well as key Latin American countries (Figure 5.9). The first phase consists of a fall in FDI flows (in GDP percentage terms) in the years between 2000 and 2003, consistent with the first recessionary period of the new century. From 2004 to 2007, the second phase consists of a significant recuperation that reached maximum levels in 2007. After that, from 2008 to 2011, another significant decline occurs on account of the severe economic and financial recession that passed through the developed economies first and foremost in those years. It bears mentioning that Latin America survived better these external shocks than did the developed economies, thanks in the most part to the region's having followed the recipes for financial and monetary discipline of the

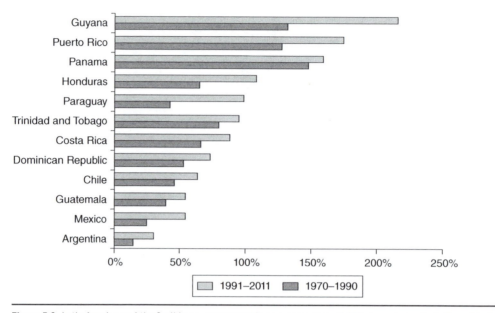

Figure 5.8 Latin America and the Caribbean: average trade as a percentage of GDP, by period, selected countries[8]
Source: Authors' calculations based on World Bank data

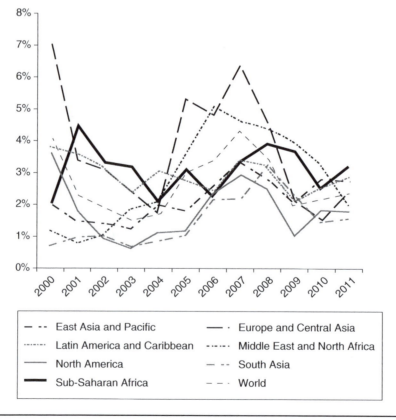

Figure 5.9 World's regions: foreign direct, net inflows (percentage of GDP), selected countries[9]
Source: Authors' calculations based on World Bank data

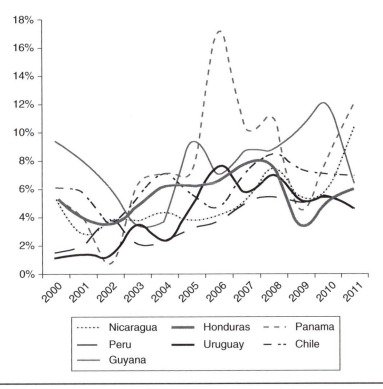

Figure 5.10 Latin America and the Caribbean: foreign direct investment, net inflows (percentage of GDP), selected
countries[10]

Source: Authors' calculations based on World Bank data

Washington Consensus in the wake of the 1980s debt crisis. Latin America began her
recovery in 2009, whereas the region of Asia began her respective recovery in 2010.
Countries operating under exceptional conditions, such as Panama, suffered the biggest declines in the GDP shares of FDI, whereas Peru, Uruguay, and Chile suffered
much more modest declines.

Figure 5.10 details how the FDI flows obeyed accelerated cycles of rise and decline
in most regions of the world—a clear indication of a bubble phenomenon. The
greatest manifestation, of course, occurs in the European region. The Latin American region, as a whole, suffers a significant decline as a result of the 2008–2009 economic contraction, but the greatest drop in FDI shares of GDP occurs in the region
of Europe. In fact, the drop in relative share of FDI in GDP occurs less in the LAC
region than for the world region as a whole. This is a clear signal that the LAC region
has gotten something right; Latin America has learned the market lessons of the past,
which is a useful data point for foreign investors to consider today when deciding
where to invest their money.

Up until now, the impetus towards economic liberalization of the LAC region
economies has borne fruit, and constitutes a particular boon for foreign investors.
On the external economy front, there has occurred a substantial amplification of the
horizons of the market's goods, services, and capital, as always under the pertinent

imperatives of the current account balance, which roughly measures import versus export performance. In addition, economic liberalization has improved long-run economic prospects in the region, particularly as concerns foreign investors. Savings and investment are particularly incentivized from the opening up of the capital accounts. Nevertheless, since the dawn of the 21st century, it has been critically shaped by the severe recession in the United States and frank depression in the Euro Zone, led by Germany, and prospects of new capital inflows are severely dampened. With eyes toward the future, Latin American countries need to redouble their efforts to attract FDI away from the dead markets of Europe, which are proving exceptionally reticent to abandon their mercantilist, protectionist practices that deprive their economies of national competitiveness, employment, and prosperity. It remains to be seen whether the US will be a leader or follower in terms of market lessons for betterment of the climate for doing business in the Americas in the years to come.

True to historic form, after the 2008 economic crisis, protectionist sentiments set in worldwide. After the crisis, even international organizations, governmental institutions, and think-tanks have engaged in a discussion as to whether the trend towards greater economic freedom bears maintaining. Given the significant general contractions in the economies of not only specific countries of Latin America, but also the region as a whole, and especially the developed world, many countries in the developing world have fallen to increasing the regulation and control of FDI inflows. This is surely in response to the fact that the FDI flows to developing countries in the LAC region have both increased and become more volatile. This is why some argue that financial liberalization hasn't helped the LAC countries as much could have been hoped, on account of foreign investors' ability to price risk. Still, judging from the results and, more importantly, the trends, the LAC region is one of the most attractive investment opportunities in the world.

Figures 5.11–5.14 prove useful to contrast the economic growth rates before and after the liberalization period. From them, the reader can see the minimum and maximum rates of economic growth, according to the period of evaluation and regions of the world as well as the top ten growing countries of the LAC region. The least growing economies are shown in the Figure 5.11.

An immediate interpretation could be that the economies of the LAC region grew less in the 1991 to 2011 period than in the two decades prior. However, that ignores the obvious reality that the growth observed in the 1970 to 1990 period was achieved by short-run measures that effectively bankrupted the Latin American countries. In contrast, the more moderate GDP growth rates registered in the 1991 to 2011 period reflect sounder macroeconomic and financial policies oriented towards the long-run interests of the Latin American countries and the region as a whole. Whereas the short-run benefits, in terms of sporadically high growth rates, won't be there, the risks for long-term investors of sharp rises and falls also will be absent. One strong indicator that the LAC region economy is more resilient than in years past is that it resisted better the 2008 to 2009 economic crisis that plunged the US and the European Union into a severe recession; Latin America not only suffered a less pronounced recession, she also recovered faster than did the developed economies, a sign of long-term economic health that should provide positive market signals to foreign and national investors alike.

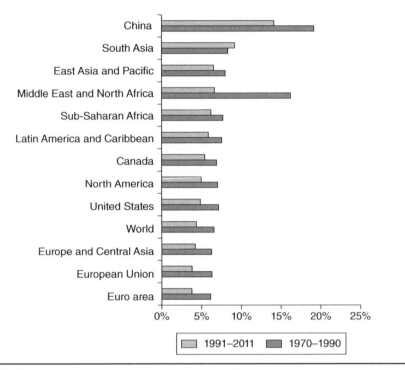

Figure 5.11 World's regions and selected countries: economic growth maximum and minimum rates, by period[11]

Source: Authors' calculations based on World Bank data

Figure 5.12 World's regions and selected countries: economic growth maximum and minimum rates, by period[12]

Source: Authors' calculations based on World Bank data

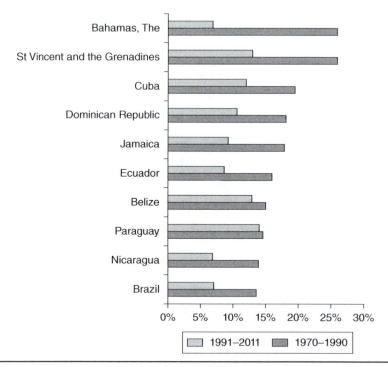

Figure 5.13 Latin America and the Caribbean: countries with the highest economic growth maximum rates[13]

Source: Authors' calculations based on World Bank data

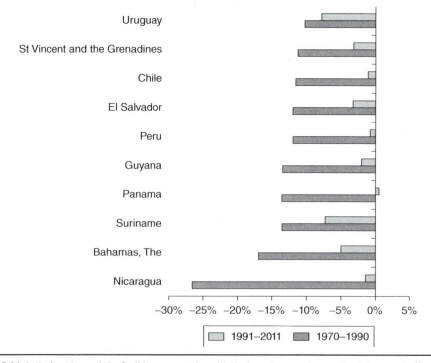

Figure 5.14 Latin America and the Caribbean: countries with the lowest economic growth minimum rates[14]

Source: Authors' calculations based on World Bank data

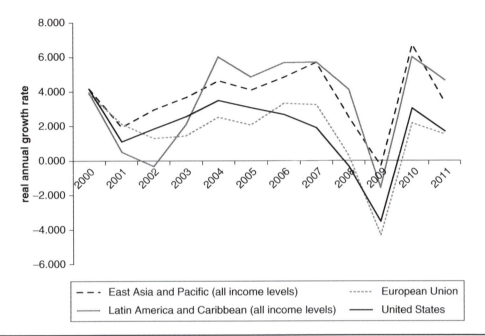

Figure 5.15 Evolution of real annual growth rates during the 2009 recession[15]

Source: Authors' calculations based on World Bank data

Table 5.1 Latin American financial flows[16]

	2009	**2010**	**2011**	**2012**	**2013**	**2014**
Financial Flows						
Current account balance	−22.2	−60.6	−77.5	−109.7	−144.6	−184.3
Capital Inflows	173.2	319.8	278.5	230.7	258.3	298.5
Private inflows, net	155.3	298.4	267.4	223.5	250.4	289.9
Equity inflows, net	119.9	153.9	161.5	124.4	145.7	178.7
FDI inflows	78.3	112.6	155.0	118.8	131.3	158.7
Portfolio equity inflows	41.6	41.3	6.5	5.6	14.4	20.0
Bonds	40.7	48.8	49.0	61.0	57.6	50.0
Banks	−0.3	27.4	14.0	11.0	12.0	15.9
Short-term dept flows	−4.5	67.2	42.7	27.0	35.0	45.0
FDI outflows	—	—	—	—	—	—

Source: Authors' calculations based on IMF data

COMPOSITION OF PRODUCTION

The economic cycle manifests dynamic rhythms characterized by distinct phases of growth, deceleration, contraction, and recovery. Its tendency is generally propelled by the evolution of the leading world economies, given the ups and downs of aggregate demand in the developed economies. Figure 5.19 presents the participation in

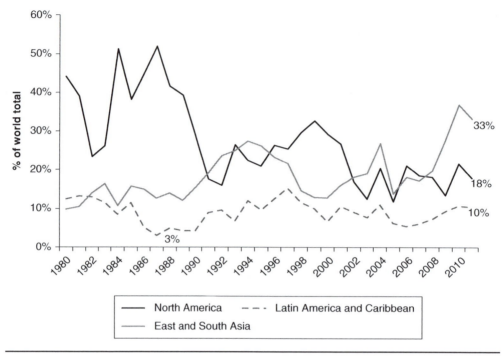

Figure 5.16 Evolution of net FDI flows 1980–2011[17]

Source: Authors' calculations based on World Bank data

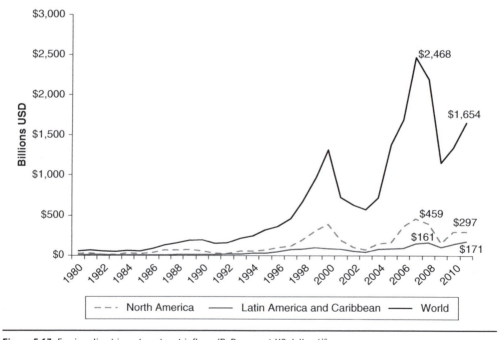

Figure 5.17 Foreign direct investment, net inflows (BoP, current US dollars)[18]

Source: Authors' calculations based on World Bank data

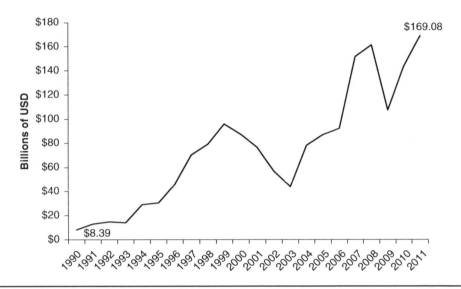

Figure 5.18 Evolution of foreign direct investment in Latin America and Caribbean, net inflows (BoP, current US dollars)[19]

Source: Authors' calculations based on World Bank data

the global product that different regions of the world have, based on data from the first decade of the 21st century.

According to World Bank estimates, the world produced in 2011 a global world GDP of $70,020 billion. Taken as a region, Europe and Central Asia constituted about 31.6% of the total, North America 23.9%, East Asia and the Pacific 26.8%, Latin America and the Caribbean 8.3%, and the rest divided among the remaining regions of the world. Even though the first two regions represent some 55.5% of the world GDP, they have lost relative product share over the years. As a case in point, the East Asia and Pacific region went from a 25% world GDP share in 2000 to a 21.2% share in 2007, recovering to obtain a 26.8% share in 2011. In a positive direction, the LAC region has also increased its world product share some 1.6 percentage points in the same time period. Although the LAC region has failed to achieve the competitiveness levels of the Asian regions, important lessons have been learned, and true progress is being made in the doing business climate.

Latin America is among the emerging market economies that are occupying a progressively important place in the world economy. Figures 5.20 and 5.21 depict the tendencies in the real economy, according to different regions.

Figure 5.20 shows that, while the US has lost relative global product share, down to 21.4% in 2011, China has increased its share to 18.7% in 2011, up from 11.3% in 2000. Although the LAC region has not enjoyed the same boom in world product share, it is the region that suffered the least during the last severe recession of 2009, with a contraction of 1.6% in 2008 and a 6% recovery in the following year.

Figure 5.21 presents the relative share in world GDP of the LAC region, divided into three different regions. For 2011, the World Bank estimated the GDP of the LAC

Table 5.2 Latin American economic indicators

	2009	2010	2011	2012	2013	2014
Real Expenditure Growth						
1. GDP at market prices	−1.9	6.1	4.3	3.5	4.1	4.0
2. Private consumption	−0.8	6.0	5.1	3.6	4.0	3.8
3. Government consumption	4.0	4.1	2.9	3.1	3.2	3.4
4. Fixed investment	−10.2	12.8	8.6	6.6	8.3	8.0
5. Exports, GNFS	−9.7	11.4	6.2	5.6	6.4	6.6
6. Imports, GNFS	−14.8	22.3	9.7	7.6	8.1	8.0
Contribution to GDP Growth						
1. Private consumption	−0.5	4.0	3.3	2.4	2.7	2.5
2. Government consumption	0.6	0.6	0.4	0.4	0.5	0.5
3. Fixed investment	−2.3	2.6	1.9	1.5	1.9	1.9
4. Net exports	−2.3	2.5	1.4	1.3	1.6	1.6
Share of GDP						
1. Private consumption	63.7	61.8	62.0	61.9	61.7	61.5
2. Government consumption	16.7	16.3	16.1	15.8	15.7	15.6
3. Fixed investment	19.4	19.9	20.3	20.9	21.8	22.7
4. Change in stocks	0.3	5.1	4.7	4.9	4.7	4.5
5. Total investment	..	..	..	..	..	..
6. Exports, GNFS	20.0	20.0	21.3	20.6	19.5	18.5
7. Imports, GNFS	20.4	21.0	22.6	22.6	21.9	21.3
Miscellaneous						
1. Nominal GDP (USD billions)	3,949.8	4,884.9	5,489.4	5,802.3	6,492.0	7,237.0
2. Population (millions)	564.6	571.1	578.4	585.7	593.2	600.7
3. Real per capita GDP growth	−3.2	4.8	3.1	2.3	2.8	2.8

Source: Adaptation of World Bank table

region to be $5.8 billion. Of this, South America captured 74.4% of the total, Central America 23.6%, and the Caribbean 2.1%. As one can see, the Central American and Caribbean regions have lost relative regional product share, with 7.1 and 4.9 percentage points fewer in 2011 than in 2000. South America has risen as the economic powerhouse of the LAC region, gaining 12 percentage points of relative regional product share in the same time frame.

The dynamic tendencies of globalization, adapted as a result of the technological innovation, scientific progress, and modernization of the ways of life of Latin American consumers in particular, among other factors, have resulted in changes in the distribution of product; whereby not only do certain regions gain relative to others, but also where certain economic sectors gain relative to others. Figures 5.22 and 5.23 present a comparison of the structure of production for the years 1987 and 2007, for different regions of the world.

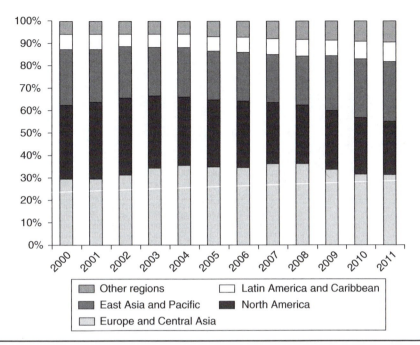

Figure 5.19 World's regions, composition of world GDP by region[20]

Source: Authors' calculations based on World Bank data

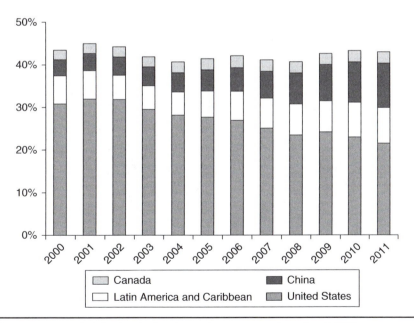

Figure 5.20 Latin America, Caribbean and selected countries percentage share of world GDP[21]

Source: Authors' calculations based on World Bank data

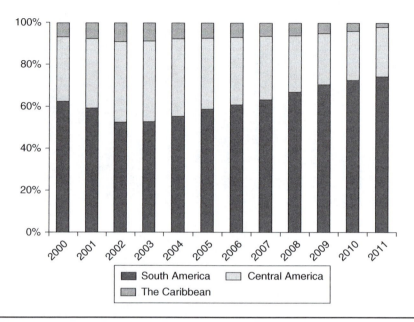

Figure 5.21 Latin America and the Caribbean: composition of Latin American GDP, by sub-region[22]

Source: Authors' calculations based on World Bank data

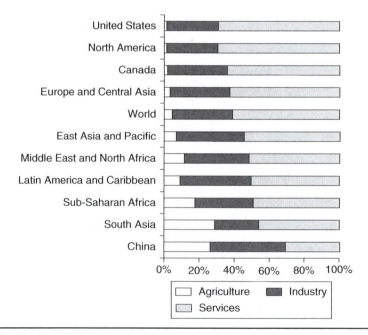

Figure 5.22 World's regions and selected countries: structure of GDP, by general productive sector, 1987[23]

Source: Authors' calculations based on World Bank data

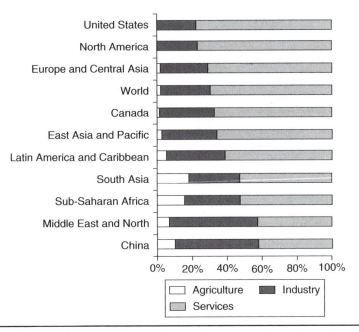

Figure 5.23 World's regions and selected countries: structure of GDP by general productive sector, 2007[24]

Source: Authors' calculations based on World Bank data

According to the World Bank, the economic structure of the world economy was distributed in 1987 into the different conventional economic sectors of agriculture (5.6% of GDP), industry (33.8%), and services (60.6%). By 2007, the relative share of agriculture for the world had dropped to 2.9%, that of industry dropped to 27.6%, whereas services increased its relative share to 69.5%. This means that, in these twenty years, the supply of product in the world market shifted significantly toward more services, by an increase of 8.9 percentage points more. The economy of the LAC region went from being 9.9% agriculture to 5.8%, from 40.4% industry to 33.4%, and from 49.8% services to 60.8%.

Figures 5.24 and 5.25 reflect the distribution of employment across the different regions, and within the LAC region specifically. Figure 5.24 demonstrates that the agricultural sector of the LAC region takes approximately 15.4% of the employment force, compared to 22.6% for the industrial sector and 61.9% for the services sector. By comparison, the US devotes almost nothing of its labor force to agriculture, but 20.6% to industry and 78% to the services sector. In Figure 5.25 we can see that the Caribbean and Central American economies in particular devote a substantial part of their labor forces to the services sector. More than half of the countries of the LAC region devote more than 60% of their labor force to the service sector.

AN OVERVIEW OF HUMAN DEVELOPMENT

The Human Development equation is important for the doing business climate in the LAC region for many reasons. The greater the standard of living, the greater

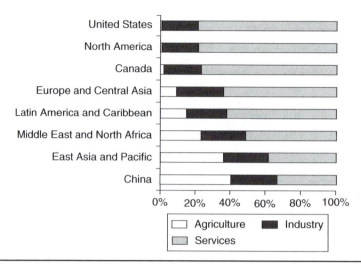

Figure 5.24 World's regions and selected countries: distribution of employment, by general productive sector, 2007[25]

Source: Authors' calculations based on World Bank data

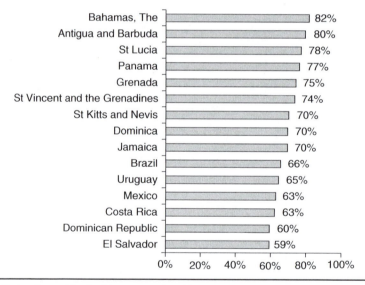

Figure 5.25 Latin America and the Caribbean: countries with the highest average GDP share of service sector, 2000–2011[26]

Source: Authors' calculations based on World Bank data

the levels of consumption there will be, and the greater number of sustainable business opportunities as well. Human development is, of course, made possible only by economic growth and the creation of wealth and employment, for which reasons a sound business and investment climate is imperative. The LAC countries now understand this. The UN publishes an annual Human Development Report, which shows that the world is growing progressively more egalitarian than ever

Table 5.3 Human Development Index scores, by region, several years[27]

Region of the world	1980	1990	2000	2005	2007	2010	2011	2012	Increase over 1980
Arab States	0.443	0.517	0.583	0.622	0.633	0.648	0.65	0.652	47.18%
East Asia and the Pacific	0.432	0.502	0.584	0.626	0.649	0.673	0.678	0.683	58.10%
Europe and Central Asia	0.651	0.701	0.709	0.743	0.757	0.766	0.769	0.771	18.43%
Latin America and the Caribbean	0.574	0.623	0.683	0.708	0.722	0.736	0.739	0.741	29.09%
South Asia	0.357	0.418	0.47	0.514	0.531	0.552	0.555	0.558	56.30%
Sub-Saharan Africa	0.366	0.387	0.405	0.432	0.449	0.468	0.472	0.475	29.78%
World	0.561	0.6	0.639	0.666	0.678	0.69	0.692	0.694	23.71%

Source: Authors' calculations based on data from the UN Development Program (2013)

before, with the stand-out countries of the southern regions achieving significant advances in human development. Nevertheless, significant inequalities persist, which wouldn't be a problem but for the conditions of stark poverty lived in by the lowest 20% (UNDP, 2013). The LAC region has many countries with high structural poverty rates, which it will take significant efforts to reduce. Nevertheless, progress is possible, as the cases of Chile, Peru, and Brazil.

The Human Development Index (HDI) comprises indicators along three dimensions: (1) longevity; (2) educational achievement; and (3) control over the resources necessary for a dignified level of quality of life. The HDI takes on a value between 0 and 1, with values closer to 1 implying higher levels of human development.

As can be seen, the LAC region increased its HDI significantly in the thirty years since 1980. The LAC region saw a 29.09% increase in its quality of life, as measured by the UN HDI. While this is substantial, and ahead of the world increase of 23.71%, it pales in comparison with the achievement of East Asia and the Pacific, which saw an increase of 58.10% in its HDI, and the South Asia region, with 56.3%. These increases in the quality of life in the LAC region have far-reaching consequences for the market opportunities present in the region. A direct consequence is the growth of the Latin American middle classes, with burgeoning consumption patterns, led most strikingly of all by female consumers. The business opportunities to be had by the reduction of poverty across the LAC region and the growth of a brand-conscious consumer class are simply too numerous to mention.

According to the UN, in the LAC region, the southern area has the important cases of Brazil and Chile, which have obtained a particularly positive level of progress. Figure 5.26 shows the human development rankings; these demonstrate how approximately half of the countries of the LAC region have been classified as having High Human Development, whereas another twelve countries have been classified as having Medium Human Development.

The best rankings in the LAC region are obtained by Barbados, Chile, and Argentina, with respective rankings of 38, 40, and 45, achieving the same category

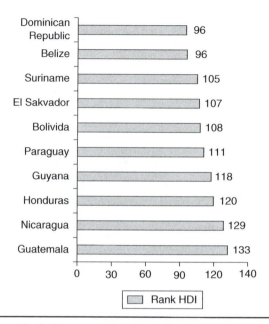

Figure 5.26 Latin America and the Caribbean: countries with medium human development, 2012, 186 countries[28]

Source: Authors' calculations based on data from the UN Development Program (2013)

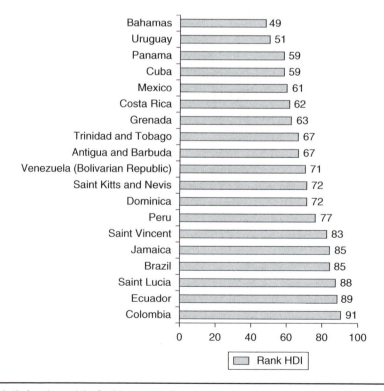

Figure 5.27 Latin America and the Caribbean: countries with high human development, 2012 186 countries[29]

Source: Authors' calculations based on data from the UN Development Program (2013)

of High Human Development as the United States, Canada, and Hong Kong, which have respective rankings of 3, 11, and 13. Nevertheless, also in the region are countries like Haiti, with a ranking of 161, being the only country in the LAC region to be characterized as having Low Human Development. It bears remembering that the HDI is, like any such metric, a flawed indicator, as revealed by the fact that Cuba is classified as having High Human Development, when it is a dictatorship that gives its people very few freedoms. Venezuela would be another example of a basket-case economy, sustained only by oil revenues, but that still suffers from significant breaches of human rights and scarcity of basic goods. These exceptional cases notwithstanding, the point is that significant progress has been made in the quality of life of the countries in the LAC region, and this is good for future business opportunities.

The UN explains that there has been satisfactory progress made on the human development front by the nations of the south. The UN considers these countries to be examples of structural changes that the developing nations in the rest of the region, and other regions, should follow, to achieve the full growth potential that globalization offers (Programa de las Naciones Unidas para el Desarrollo, 2013). Figure 5.28 shows the relationship between GDP per capita in selected countries of the LAC region, and their coefficient scores on the GINI index, an index designed to measure inequality of income (values closer to 1 reflect greater inequality). As one can see in the figure, as GINI scores fall, level of GDP per capita grows.

Countries of the LAC region such as Argentina, Chile, and Uruguay attribute their economic and social progress to having lessened the worst effects of poverty associated with inequality.

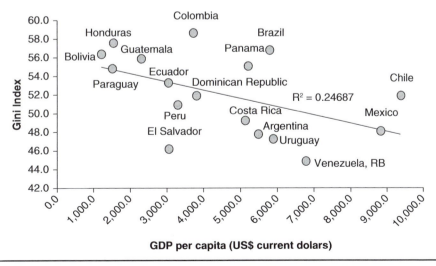

Figure 5.28 Latin America and the Caribbean: relation between the GINI index and the GDP per capita, 2006[30]

Source: Authors' calculations based on World Bank data

LATIN AMERICAN COMPETITIVENESS

As has been discussed already, the LAC region as a whole can be said to be enjoying an upward trend in its competitiveness. On both the fronts of economic growth and human development, the region has come a long way; importantly, the business sectors see the need to tend to the remaining social ills if the region is to become truly competitive.

As things stand now, the region has competitive offerings in geography, commerce, and logistical operations, plus strong efforts to augment the productivity of human as well as physical capital, particularly as the human quality of life improves, with access to education and health services. According to the Economic Commission for Latin America and the Caribbean, the LAC region is projected to grow 3.2% in 2012 and 4% in 2013. Thanks to the fiscal and monetary policy discipline implemented during the structural adjustment reforms of the Washington Consensus, the region still has significant policy space if it needed to act counter-cyclically in case of any forthcoming adverse external shocks. Latin America has effectively turned the tables on the past, as the region is now in a position to dictate the lessons of market fundamentals to the developed world, including the United States and Europe (OECD, CEPAL, 2012).

The countries of the LAC region have strong competitive advantages to attract investment, which has been borne out in the data we have covered. To this effect, Tables 5.4–5.6 compare results in the areas of opening businesses, registering of property, and paying of taxes that the LAC region obtained with respect to other parts of the world, according to the World Bank's Doing Business indicators (World Bank, 2013a).

As can be seen, Latin America has an advantage in that it requires the least capital to open a business: 3.7% of GDP per capita. On the other hand, it demands the highest number of procedures, which implies higher transaction and uncertainty costs. Opening up a business in the LAC region will on average cost approximately 33.7%

Table 5.4 World's regions: indicators about business openings, 2013

Indicator	Latin American & The Caribbean	OECD	East Asia & The Pacific	Middle East & North Africa	Europe & Central Asia	South Asia	Sub–Saharan Africa
Procedures (number)	9	5	7	8	6	7	8
Time (days)	53	12	36	23	14	19	34
Cost (% of income per capita)	33.7	4.5	22.4	29.8	6.8	21.6	67.3
Minimum capital requirement (% of income per capita)	3.7	13.3	13.4	72.3	5	17.8	116

Source: World Bank (2013a)

Table 5.5 World's regions: indicators about property registry, 2013

Indicator	Latin American & The Caribbean	OECD	East Asia & The Pacific	Middle East & North Africa	Europe & Central Asia	South Asia	Sub–Saharan Africa
Procedures (number)	7	5	5	6	6	6	6
Time (days)	67	26	80	33	30	100	65
Cost (% of property value)	6	4.5	4.1	5.9	2.7	7.2	9.4

Source: Authors' calculations based on World Bank data

of GDP per capita, which is high for Latin American citizens but low for foreign investors, especially Americans, who seek to do business in the region.

In the LAC region, the cost of registering a property over the value of the same is lower with respect to the Asian and Sub-Saharan African regions, and almost as low as in the Middle East and North Africa. Even though the registering of property implies the greatest number of procedures on a global scale, the time taken in these processes is less than one would see in Asia.

Latin America has good news to report on the doing business front, a fact that especially comes into light if one compares among countries. Figures 5.29 and 5.30 compare the ten countries of the LAC region that reported the lowest costs in opening of businesses, in terms of GDP per capita, and the lowest costs of registering a property, in terms of percentage share of the value of the property.

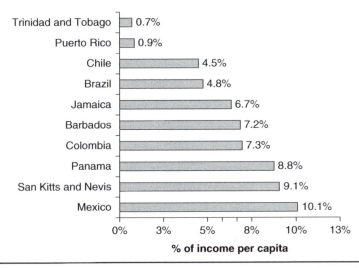

Figure 5.29 Latin America and the Caribbean: business opening costs of selected companies, 2013[31]

Source: Authors' calculations based on World Bank (2013a)

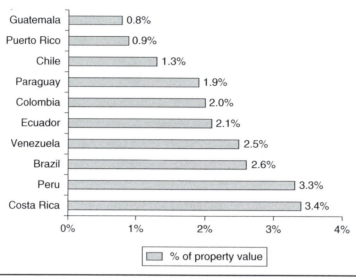

Figure 5.30 Latin America and the Caribbean: property registry costs of selected countries, 2013[32]
Source: Authors' calculations based on World Bank data

By way of a general overview, it bears mentioning that twenty-one countries of the LAC region registered lower costs of opening a business, in terms of percentage of GDP per capita, than did the Asian regions. It is indeed surprising that, in relative terms, it is cheaper to start a business in Trinidad and Tobago and Puerto Rico than it is in China, or even the United States, which have 2.1% and 1.4% percentage shares of GDP per capita as start-up costs, respectively. The ten countries in Figure 5.30 all have lower costs to register a property than Canada (3.4%), the United States (3.5%), and China (3.6%).

In general terms, the tax burden is high on businesses in the LAC region, a problem that is accentuated by the pervasiveness of a large tax-evading informal sector. The foreign investor operating in Latin America will find that the problem is not the tax rate in itself, but the discretionary forms of paying taxes, and the unfair competition posed by informal tax evaders. Nevertheless, it is common for governments in the region to give tax incentives to foreign firms that come to invest in free-trade zones. Other regions have higher tax rates, as does Sub-Saharan Africa, for instance.

On fiscal aspects in the LAC region, Bolivia, Argentina, Venezuela, Paraguay, and Panama have the lowest taxation rates, in terms of percentage rates of profit, with 0, 2.7, 6.1, 9.6, and 12.5, respectively. These are lower rates than those found in China, Canada, and the United States, which have respective rates of 6.2%, 8.4%, and 27.6%. Chile and Mexico, for their part, make fewer tax payments in comparison to China and Canada. These countries and Ecuador, Argentina, Brazil, Colombia, Peru, and the Dominican Republic all make a lesser amount of tax payments than is required in the United States. Comparing 2013 with 2012, the governments of Jamaica, Uruguay, Costa Rica, and Panama have all reduced the number of tax

Table 5.6 World's regions: indicators about taxes payments, 2013

Indicator	Latin American & The Caribbean	OECD	East Asia & The Pacific	Middle East & North Africa	Europe & Central Asia	South Asia	Sub – Saharan Africa
Payments (number per year)	30	12	25	19	28	30	39
Time (hours per year)	367	176	209	184	260	311	319
Profit taxes (%)	21.5	15.2	16.7	11.9	9.1	17.1	19
Labor taxes and contributions (%)	14.4	23.8	10.9	16.5	22.1	8.7	13.3
Other taxes (%)	11.3	3.7	6.9	3.9	9.3	14.4	25.5
Total tax rate (% of profit)	47.2	42.7	34.5	32.3	40.5	40.2	57.8

Source: Authors' calculations based on World Bank (2013a)

payments it is necessary to make in their countries: 50%, 42.1%, 25.8%, and 15.4%, respectively.

Countries of the LAC region run the gamut on the doing business rankings from the very pro-market Chile to economic basket cases like Venezuela and countries in line with its so-called revolution of 21st-century socialism, such as Ecuador, Bolivia, and Nicaragua. In this line, Figure 5.31 presents the ranking obtained by the top five countries from South America, Central America, and the Caribbean.

As Figure 5.31 shows, Chile, Puerto Rico, Peru, Colombia, and Mexico all placed in the top fifty countries for doing business. The majority of the countries of the Central American region obtained inferior rankings as compared to the rest of the countries in the LAC region. However, even though Guatemala and Costa Rica obtained inferior rankings, it bears mentioning that they climbed twelve and five places, respectively, in the 2013 Doing Business report, as compared to the 2012 report.

CONCLUSIONS

The economic climate is conducive to doing business in Latin America. Inflation is whipped in key countries, and even erstwhile anti-US countries like Ecuador are dollarized. Gone are the days of bloated government and unsustainable public debt. Financial flows have been greatly liberalized, and trade in the region is freer than it has been in more than half a century. Gone also are the days when Latin America was merely a source of raw materials. Today, the modern Latin American economy is oriented more toward services than agriculture, and even industry has displaced agriculture in most countries.

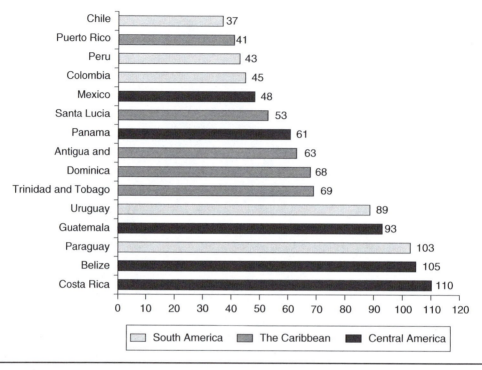

Figure 5.31 Latin America and the Caribbean: the four countries per sub-region where it is easier to do business, 2013[33]

Source: Authors' calculations based on World Bank data

The benefits of sound macroeconomic fundamentals, however, have not been optimized. This is due to the lack of second- and third-generation reforms, which are needed in the political sphere. Due to this, Latin American still has progress to make on the human development front. Poverty still afflicts more than a quarter of the population in Latin America, also one of the most unequal regions of the world. This would not be a problem in and of itself, except that it lends credence to populist politicians who would threaten to undermine the great progress Latin America has made in its macroeconomic environment, and its business and investment climate. The realm of the political institutions is a matter we leave to another chapter.

NOTES

1. World Bank. World Development Indicators, online database: http://databank.worldbank.org/data/views/variableSelection/selectvariables.aspx?source=world-development-indicators (accessed May 2013).
2. Ibid.
3. Ibid.
4. Ibid.
5. LAC figures exclude, for lack of data the following countries or territories: Curacao, Puerto Rico, Sin Maarten (Dutch part), St. Martin (French part), and the US Virgin Islands.

6. World Bank. World Development Indicators, online database: http://databank.worldbank.org/data/views/variableSelection/selectvariables.aspx?source=world-development-indicators (accessed May 2013).
7. Ibid.
8. Ibid.
9. Ibid.
10. Ibid.
11. Ibid.
12. Ibid.
13. Ibid.
14. Ibid.
15. Ibid.
16. International Monetary Fund, World Economic Outlook, online database: http://www.imf.org/external/pubs/ft/weo/2013/01/weodata/weoselgr.aspx (accessed May 2013).
17. World Bank, World Development Indicators, online database: http://databank.worldbank.org/data/views/variableSelection/selectvariables.aspx?source=world-development-indicators (accessed May 2013).
18. Ibid.
19. Ibid.
20. Ibid.
21. Ibid.
22. Ibid.
23. Ibid.
24. Ibid.
25. Ibid.
26. Ibid.
27. United Nations. Human Development Index, 2013, online database: http://hdr.undp.org/en/statistics/hdi/ (accessed May 2013).
28. Ibid.
29. Ibid.
30. World Bank. World Development Indicators, online database: http://databank.worldbank.org/data/views/variableSelection/selectvariables.aspx?source=world-development-indicators (accessed May 2013).
31. Ibid.
32. Ibid.
33. Ibid.

REFERENCES

Banco Mundial (2013) *Doing business 2013*. Banco Mundial.

Chowla, P. (2011) Ha llegado la hora de un nuevo consenso. Bretton Woods Project.

Ferreiro, J., Gómez, C., Rodríguez, C., and Correa, E. (2007) Liberalización financiera en América Latina: efectos sobre los mercados financieros locales. Universidad del País Vasco. Universidad Autónoma Nacional de México.

International Monetary Fund (IMF) (2013) World economic outlook, online database, obtained from http://www.imf.org/external/pubs/ft/weo/2013/01/weodata/weoselgr.aspx (accessed May 2013).

Jácome, L. (2006) Metas de inflación en América Latina: Lecciones para Guatemala. Jornadas Económicas, Banco de Guatemala.

OECD, CEPAL (2012) Perspectivas Económicas de América Latina 2013: Políticas de PYMES para el cambio estructural.

Programa de las Naciones Unidas para el Desarrollo (2013) Obtained from http://www.undp.org/content/undp/es/home.html.

United Nations Development Program (UNDP) (2013) *Human development report 2013. The rise of the South: Human progress in a diverse world.* UNDP.

United Nations Human Development Index (n.d.) Online database, obtained from http://hdr.undp.org/en/statistics/hdi/ (accessed May 2013).

World Bank (2013a) Doing business 2013, smarter regulations for small and medium-size enterprises. Comparing business regulations for domestic firms in 185 economies (10th ed.). International Bank for Reconstruction and Development/World Bank, obtained from http://www.doingbusiness.org/~/media/GIAWB/Doing%20Business/Documents/Annual-Reports/English/DB13-full-report.pdf.

World Bank (2013b) Ease of doing business index (2013) Obtained from http://www.doingbusiness.org/rankings (accessed May 2013).

World Bank (n.d.) Online database. www.worldbank.org (accessed May 2013).

6

POLITICAL CLIMATE

INTRODUCTION

For various items on the Doing Business Index and the Global Competitiveness Index, as pertains to public institutions, regional constructs are created. To create regional indicators, we use structural participation in regional GDP as factor weights. The idea behind using a weighted regional indicator is to give the reader an easy way to assess the Latin American region as if it were a single country. The items on the Global Competitiveness Index that are of particular interest are those that pertain to the realm of public institutions.

In this chapter the overall political climate of Latin America is treated, with three main issues in mind: the twin threats of corruption and populist socialism, to which Latin American societies are vulnerable if not prone; and the need to recuperate a strong (not large) state in order to impose law and order, for the benefit of the investment and business climate and general welfare of the population in Latin America.

OVERVIEW OF THE POLITICAL CLIMATE IN LATIN AMERICA

Latin America is on the path toward democratic consolidation, having progressed from the process of democratic transition. However, several dangers loom large on the business climate in Latin America; these are corruption, populist socialism, and crime. The chief priority for the Latin American nations interested in achieving competitiveness, prosperity, and peace is to restore law and order, and respect for the principles of republican democracy.

Politically, progress has been made. However, Latin American history is a chronicle of missed opportunities, so in that light any perceived political risks loom large in the Doing Business calculus. At least they should. Latin America is still undergoing its democratic wave, which began after the military regimes felt sure enough that they had defeated the existential communist threat, which they perceived threatened the way of life their societies had been based on. In the past, it was believed that authoritarian regimes were the lesser evil, compared to the communist alternative. Once communist insurgencies were defeated, democratic transition began in countries such as Argentina, Brazil, Chile, Guatemala, and El Salvador, among many other cases. Latin America has certainly made strong progress towards democratic consolidation, but much progress is still needed, particularly as regards the quality of Latin American democratic institutions.

A distinct new threat is democratic populism, which uses democracy to get into power. Previously, communist insurgents vowed to destroy the state in an outright struggle. Now, their socialist heirs purport to undermine the regimes of capitalist democracy from within. There is no need to suffer the costs of civil war when elections can be won using the public coffers as promise and payback. A new generation of Latin American populist leaders quite expertly use redistributionist rhetoric to get into power by relatively free and fair elections, and then use all the levers of power to degrade democratic institutions from within, in order to stay in power. This has occurred in Nicaragua, Venezuela, Ecuador, Argentina, Bolivia, and Honduras, to name but a few examples.

The case of Honduras is emblematic. Allowing then President Zelaya's shenanigans to continue, illegally, in power eventually led to a "democratic coup" in that country in 2009. The military ousted President Zelaya, who was attempting to run again, contrary to that country's constitution. It bears remembering that, after the military regimes, the democratic consensus was that a key pillar of democracy was to be the alternation of those in power, so re-elections were widely proscribed. Nevertheless, repeat offenders have surfaced throughout Latin America.

The chief example is Venezuela, with the late Hugo Chavez being perhaps the most notorious illiberal, yet "democratically elected," political leader. Rafael Correa in Ecuador follows in his stead, as does Daniel Ortega in Nicaragua. In Guatemala, there was a major scandal when the then wife of the President Alvaro Colom tried to succeed him in office, until the Supreme Court declared she was constitutionally prohibited from doing so. Thereupon, the first lady divorced the president, but to no avail as far as the top courts were concerned. Although the eventual result in Guatemala was the correct one, great general uncertainty loomed throughout 2011 as to what course the elections, and the country, would take. It is impossible to quantify the costs of such political uncertainty to the general business climate and the market economy, but the effect is certainly negative. Worse still, these types of cheap trick are not confined to countries such as Honduras and Guatemala, the erstwhile "banana republics" of years gone by. Most definitely, the new trend, and political risk, is for Latin American heads of government to not want to leave.

These political dirty tricks have profound business implications. In the first place, it is typical of would-be repeaters to engage in the usual practice of Latin American populists of raising the scepter of the bogeyman of the Yankee Imperialists. Attacking the United States for each and every homegrown defect is a tried and true political tactic in Latin America. This, in itself, raises political risks and costs for Americans seeking to do business in Latin America. However, the costs of populism do not stop there. In order to cling to power, Latin American populists use the promises of a growing welfare state to buy votes through rank clientelistic practices. The sad truth is that Latin America is vulnerable to such banana republic shenanigans because large portions of the populations still live in poverty.

Poverty and Inequality

Poverty still afflicts some 30% of the population in Latin America. Poverty has been falling in the past two decades, but the rate of reduction has slowed. Poverty has only been able to be reduced on account of positive economic growth and contained inflation, according to the report "Social Panorama of Latin America 2012," published by the Economic Commission for Latin America and the Caribbean (ECLAC). According to this report, in 2011, 168 million Latin Americans (29.4% of the regional population) lived below the poverty line. Thanks to economic growth, wages have been rising for the poor, and this, not social programs, was the main reason for the reduction in poverty rates (United Nations, ECLAC, 2013).

The executive secretary of ECLAC, Alicia Barcenas, states: "Current poverty and indigence rates are the lowest for three decades, and this is good news, but we are still facing unacceptable levels in many countries. The challenge is to generate quality jobs as part of a development model based on equality and environmental sustainability" (CEPAL, United Nations, 2012).

Table 6.1 Poverty rates and rural-over-urban differentials[1]

Country	2000–2011: Urban	2000–2011: Rural	2000–2011: National	Urban–Rural Divide
Argentina	6.5	n.d.	n.d.	n/a
Nicaragua	30.9	70.3	48.3	39.4
Peru	18	56.5	27.8	38.5
Guatemala	35	71.4	53.7	36.4
Ecuador	17.4	50.9	28.6	33.5
Bolivia	51.1	77.6	60.6	26.5
Haiti	34.3	55.5	48	21.2
Paraguay	23.9	44.8	32.4	20.9
Colombia	30.3	46.1	34.1	15.8
Mexico	45.5	60.8	51.3	15.3
Jamaica	12.6	25.1	17.6	12.5
Dominican	36.5	48.4	40.4	11.9
Honduras	59.8	71.6	66.2	11.8
El Salvador	31	42.4	42.5	11.4
Costa Rica	22	29.3	24.8	7.3
Chile	19.7	23.7	20.2	4
Uruguay	14.3	6	13.7	−8.3

Source: Authors' calculations based on World Bank data

In most countries of Latin America, poverty rates are still relatively high, especially in the rural areas. This divide obeys the region's initial endowments and governmental focus on agricultural competitiveness. Certainly, Latin America is a region primed to supply the world with key inputs in the areas of foodstuffs and minerals. This competitive advantage needed no governmental protection, which only introduced rigidities into the political economic systems, weak to begin with. Nevertheless, the fact is that the poverty rates can be as much as 20 or 30 percentage points higher in the rural areas than in the urban areas. In this aspect, the national poverty rates, already dismal, don't tell the whole story. Higher poverty rates in the rural areas translate into exceedingly high rates of political vulnerability and risk, as ill-fed, under-educated rural voters are more susceptible to populist false promises that, over time, work to introduce uncertainty into the local investment and business climates of the countries of Latin America.

So, although progress has been made, poverty rates are still high. This makes the political system vulnerable to populist socialists bent on deforming the market economies to their political needs. When this happens the business climate suffers, not the least from policy uncertainty and loss of property rights. Adding fuel to the potential fire posed by still high poverty rates, Latin America is one of the most unequal regions in the world. Inequality itself is not a problem but, coupled with poverty, it is, because the poorest segments of the population cannot consume or participate adequately in the market economy.

Table 6.2 illustrates how much more the richest quintile possesses of the nations' income than the poorest quintile. For purposes of comparison, we can take the US as a comparative referent. It should be noted that it is said in some circles that the US is a highly unequal society, where the richest 20% of the population possess 8.42 times the income share of the poorest 20%. However, virtually all the Latin American countries are in double digits, and even in such countries as Chile the richest 20% possess 13.54 times the income share of the poorest 20%. In Guatemala the figure is 19.56, Brazil 20.55, and Honduras nearly 30%, at 29.67.

Crime

Crime is a major area of concern in Latin America, particularly in Central America, the Caribbean, and Venezuela. Central America is the world's most violent region, and Honduras, Guatemala, and El Salvador are perennials on the list of most violent countries. Violence, of course, is not pervasive, because Argentina, Chile, Peru, and Costa Rica have escaped the grip of violence such as has engulfed the region. As a whole, the region posts some 25 murders per 100,000 inhabitants, but that ranges from the lows of 3 and 4 posted by Argentina and Chile, to the 45, 69, and 92 posted by Venezuela, El Salvador, and Honduras. The Caribbean Small States, as a region, posts a figure of 35 murders per 100,000 people. (All figures are for the 2009–2011 time period.) Obviously violent crime scares away foreign investment, but also national investment and entrepreneurship.

For Latin America as a whole, it has been estimated by the Inter-American Development Bank (BID, by its Spanish initials) that the economic cost of crime and

Table 6.2 Income share of richest quintile divided by poorest quintile[2]

Country Name	1995–2010
Belize	30.71
Honduras	29.67
Bolivia	27.85
Brazil	20.55
Colombia	20.05
Guatemala	19.56
Paraguay	17.31
Panama	17.08
Costa Rica	14.51
El Salvador	14.31
Chile	13.54
Peru	13.45
Ecuador	12.54
Venezuela	11.55
Mexico	11.35
Dom. Rep.	11.30
Argentina	11.27
Uruguay	10.35
St. Lucia	9.24
USA	8.42
Jamaica	8.22

Source: Authors' calculations based on World Bank data

violence is more than 14% of regional GDP. The figures varied heavily from nearly 25% of GDP in El Salvador and Colombia (24.9% and 24.7%, respectively) to 11.8% in Venezuela, 10.5% in Brazil, and 12.3% in Mexico, to 5.1% in Peru (Londoño and Guerrero, 1999). In a more recent study focused on Central America, the World Bank estimated the economic costs of crime and violence to be 7.7% for Guatemala, 10.8% for El Salvador, 9.6% for Honduras, 10% for Nicaragua, and 3.6% for Costa Rica (World Bank, 2011).

Crime and violence do not just reduce to delinquency in Latin America. They take political overtones, which directly impact the climate for doing business in the region. The direct intent of the efforts during the peace processes that engulfed the Latin American region upon the end of the Cold War and the transition toward democratic governments, was to weaken the state apparatus, on the premise that state power for law and order purposes was evil in and of itself. In the first place, this was not true. Civil war violence started with communist terrorism, throughout the region. More importantly, the weakening of the state proceeded too far, enabling not only criminal groups to displace state power, but also anti-establishment associations to engage in ever more violent protests to make their political point, be this against mining activities, education reform, or whatever. Figure 6.2 shows how Latin

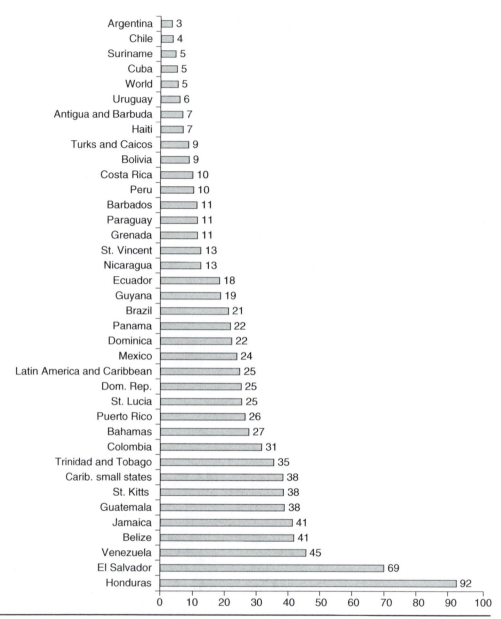

Figure 6.1 Homicides per 100,000 inhabitants, 2009–2011[3]

Source: Authors' calculations based on World Bank data

American nations fare in the realm of political violence and instability, both areas that greatly denigrate the climate for doing business in the region.

Latin America certainly suffers from criminal and political violence. Criminals and political dissenters alike feel empowered to take violent measures into their own hands to protest against the inequities of the system, and do so with impunity. Latin American governments, particularly in countries where the military

Table 6.3 Economic Costs of Crime and Violence as % of GDP

	Guatemala	El Salvador	Honduras	Nicaragua	Costa Rica
Health Costs	4.3	6.1	3.9	4.5	1.5
Institucional Costs	1	1.5	2.6	1.6	1
Public Security	0.7	0.9	1.6	1	0.4
Justice Administrations	0.3	0.7	1	0.7	0.6
Private Security Costs	1.5	1.8	1.9	2.3	0.7
Homes	0.5	0.4	0.5	0.6	0.2
Businesses	1.1	1.4	1.4	1.8	0.5
Material Costs	0.8	1.4	1.2	1.5	0.4
Total	7.7	10.8	9.6	10	3.6

Source: World Bank, (2011)

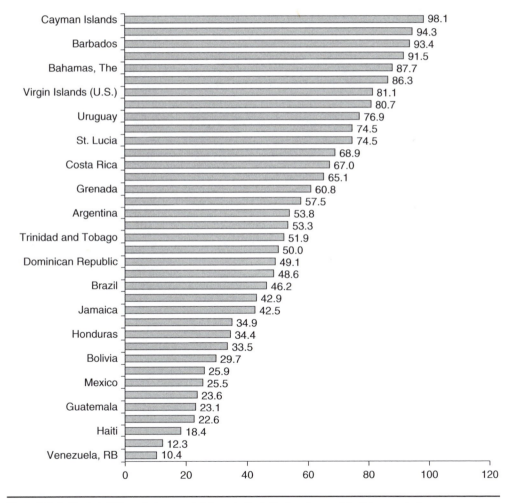

Figure 6.2 Political stability and absence of violence in the Latin American and Caribbean region[4]

Source: World Bank, Worldwide Governance Indicators

handily beat the communist revolutionaries, such as Guatemala, feel hamstrung to apply the self-same law and order techniques that would be applied in the United States at the first instance of violent public protests against business interest, private property, or the public order in general. Adding insult to injury, corruption in the public institutions is another factor that weakens the state's ability to act for the common good in Latin America. The next section deals with this topic.

Corruption and Transparency

Corruption is notoriously hard to prove, let alone measure. Therefore, it is prudent to gauge as many measures as are available. The World Bank takes another such measure, "Control of Corruption," as part of its Worldwide Governance Indicators. Here, higher scores are better than lower ones. It is interesting to note that the best scores in the region of Latin America and the Caribbean go to the Caribbean island states. Chile, Uruguay, and Costa Rica all score well on control of corruption, but if clear and evenly applied rules of the game are what you're interested in, the it is worth taking a look at the Caribbean. As usual, the countries of Venezuela, Bolivia, Ecuador, and Nicaragua populate the bottom of the pile. A curious fact is that the communist state of Cuba scores relatively well on all measures of corruption. This might pick up the fact that, while the rules of the game in that communist country are all wrong, at least you know what they are. There is certainly less uncertainty in Cuba as compared to Venezuela, for example—the latter country abusing discretionary state power at every turn, whereas in Cuba state power trumps from the outset. It can scarcely be said an investor would not know that.

The Corruption Perceptions Index is elaborated by the organization Transparency International. Figure 6.4 shows the ranking each country obtained in the 2012 report. Transparency International attempts to measure the public's perceptions of the situation of corruption in each country. Venezuela is, not surprisingly, at the bottom of the pile as far as Latin American countries go, with a ranking of 165 out of 183 countries. Ecuador and Bolivia also rank quite poorly. Pro-market Chile ranks well, indicating the application of lessons learned and an understanding of the importance of public institutions for the national achievement of global competitiveness. Uruguay and Costa Rica rank well. Certain Caribbean countries like St. Vincent and the Grenadines, the Bahamas and Barbados rank quite well. Investors seeking to do business in Latin America would do well to look at the most transparent countries, not omitting to take into account the small island states eager to do business on correct terms.

Yet another measure of corruption is taken by the Heritage Foundation, which prepares the Index of Economic Liberty. One of the components of the general score (from 0 to the best score of 100) is *freedom from corruption*. Once again, Chile, Uruguay, and Costa Rica obtain the best scores, representing Central America and the "deep south" of Latin America. What the Heritage scores reflect is that corruption in public institutions continues to be the single most important factor impeding the Latin American countries from having first-class, competitive business and investment climates.

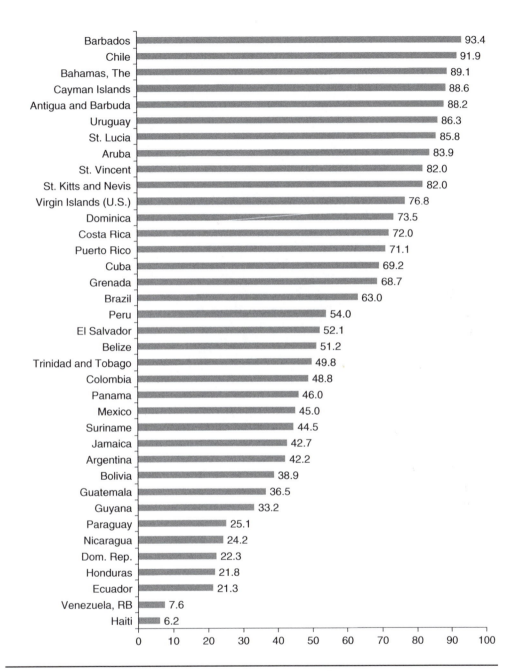

Figure 6.3 Control of corruption in the Latin American and Caribbean region[5]

Source: World Bank, Worldwide Governance Indicators

The Global Competitiveness Index takes measures of the quality of institutions as its first pillar of competitiveness. The weighted rank for the Latin American region in the matter of public institutions is 96.2. This weighted average rank runs the gamut from the high rank of Chile, with 28, Costa Rica (55), and Uruguay (36), to Argentina

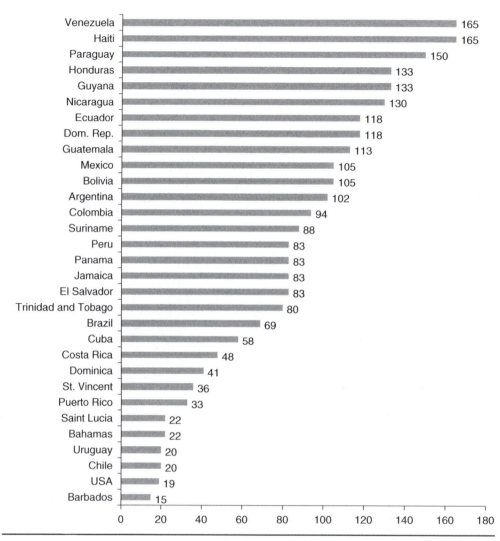

Figure 6.4 Latin America and the Caribbean, Corruptions Perception Index, 2012[6]

Source: Transparency International, 2012

(138), Haiti (143), and Venezuela, which, with a rank of 144, comes in dead last in the world in the matter of quality of public institutions. Generally, the ranks of Latin American countries on the quality of public institutions lag far behind their overall rank on competitiveness. One can only imagine how much better the business and investment climate would be in Latin America if public institutions were less corrupt. One can see that, on the measure of Government Services for Improved Business Performance, the regional weighted rank of 79.1 is far behind the regional rank on Global Competitiveness as a whole: 61.5. Argentina, El Salvador, Honduras, Mexico, and Venezuela stand out as cases where the government needs to improve its services to the business sector.

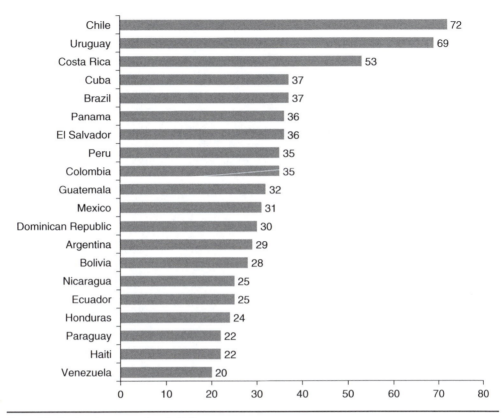

Figure 6.5 Freedom from corruption, 0–100[7]

Source: Based on Heritage Foundation data

On the matter of property rights, Latin America has at long last begun to get the message of their importance for global competitiveness. The regional weighted average rank of 74.7 is a middling rank, but in places such as Uruguay, Panama, Costa Rica, Chile, and even protectionist, interventionist Brazil, substantial gains in the protection of property have been made. Generally, due to the lack of competence and ethics in the public institutions, the protection of intellectual property rights lags behind normal property rights. The weighted average regional rank would be 88.1. Poor-performing countries in this area are Argentina, Dominican Republic, Ecuador, El Salvador, Guatemala, Haiti, Paraguay, Peru, and Venezuela.

On the several items that the World Economic Forum measures in order to gauge corruption and the quality of public institutions, the Latin American region generally needs to improve. On the Diversion of Public Funds and Public Trust in Politicians, the weighted average regional ranks are 110.2 and 111, respectively. On Wastefulness of Government Spending, the weighted regional rank is 107.8, and 119.9 for the Burden of Government Regulation. As would be expected, the worst rankings in the realm of Irregular Payments and Bribes go to the countries in the region that most flirt with socialism. These are Argentina (126), Bolivia (143), Venezuela (134),

Table 6.4 Public institutions, property rights and competitiveness[8]

Country	GCI Global Competitiveness Index	1st pillar: Institutions	Public institutions	Property rights	Intellectual property protection	Gov't services for improved business performance
LA Region Wtd	61.5	92.7	96.2	74.7	88.1	79.1
LA Region Simple	83.7	105.1	107.8	95.7	100.3	91.6
Argentina	94	138	138	135	134	135
Bolivia	104	119	113	128	88	89
Brazil	48	79	80	51	75	79
Chile	33	28	28	37	61	20
Colombia	69	109	122	96	89	69
Costa Rica	57	53	55	59	68	73
Dom. Rep.	105	126	132	89	119	99
Ecuador	86	131	128	120	115	n.d.
El Salvador	101	134	134	99	133	117
Guatemala	83	124	130	102	121	95
Haiti	142	143	143	143	144	138
Honduras	90	118	123	107	90	128
Mexico	53	92	100	71	77	57
Nicaragua	108	114	117	123	98	78
Panama	40	69	73	43	38	11
Paraguay	116	135	135	132	136	133
Peru	61	105	118	98	127	81
Uruguay	74	36	36	41	49	107
Venezuela	126	144	144	144	143	139

Source: Based on World Economic Forum data

and Ecuador (109). Paraguay (121) and Haiti (131) are quite poor performers on this front, too, as are Dominican Republic (106) and El Salvador (102). Corruption is simply widespread in Latin America, affecting the competitiveness of the whole region. The foreign investor interested in doing business in Latin America needs to know this in order to make informed risk calculations.

The poor quality of public institutions affects the business clime in important ways, namely the business costs of crime and terrorism. On the Business Costs of Terrorism, the region ranks relatively well, with 61.7. However, in countries with political violence, like Colombia, it pulls down its national rank to last place, with 144. Bolivia, Ecuador, El Salvador, Guatemala, Nicaragua, and Peru all have quite poor rankings. When it comes to the Business Costs of Crime and Violence, the weighted regional ranking is telling: 123.3. Here the reader can see that the best-ranking country, Chile, obtains only a halfway decent rank of 65, followed by Uruguay with 88. Argentina, Bolivia, Brazil, Colombia, Dominican Republic, El Salvador, Guatemala, Mexico, Panama, Paraguay, Peru, and Venezuela are particularly hard hit by crime. This is

Table 6.5 Corruption in public institutions[9]

Country	Diversion of public funds	Public trust in politicians	Irregular payments and bribes	Judicial independence	Favoritism in decisions of government	Wastefulness of government spending	Burden of regulation	Transparency of government policymaking
LA Region Wtd	110.2	111.0	79.4	87.4	87.2	107.8	119.9	86.4
LA Region Simple	101.9	103.1	90.6	101.7	95.9	99.3	90.1	85.3
Argentina	140	143	126	133	143	136	134	137
Bolivia	67	62	143	97	58	68	59	130
Brazil	121	121	65	71	80	135	144	91
Chile	22	29	23	24	21	10	32	15
Colombia	130	100	96	96	105	104	110	83
Costa Rica	49	64	56	40	52	105	88	52
Dom. Rep.	142	138	106	120	144	144	83	69
Ecuador	109	77	109	128	81	79	101	96
El Salvador	110	135	102	116	125	130	78	125
Guatemala	132	122	73	103	96	121	53	41
Haiti	137	144	131	142	137	140	115	143
Honduras	101	109	87	69	115	125	93	79
Mexico	88	97	81	88	73	67	97	64
Nicaragua	104	91	98	134	102	75	81	120
Panama	77	101	71	132	103	37	44	33
Paraguay	136	140	121	141	131	124	39	86
Peru	103	127	72	125	82	49	128	88
Uruguay	26	21	28	29	32	95	89	26
Venezuela	143	137	134	144	142	143	143	142

Source: Based on World Economic Forum data

Table 6.6 Poor public performance in justice and criminal system[10]

Country	Efficiency of legal framework in setting disputes	Efficiency of legal framework in challenging regs.	Business costs of terrorism	Business costs of crime and violence	Organized crime	Reliability of police services
LA Region Wtd	94.7	81.9	61.7	123.3	123.5	90.6
LA Region Simple	101.3	97.9	95.1	121.7	117.4	104.3
Argentina	129	142	42	115	120	131
Bolivia	104	99	136	109	128	122
Brazil	84	61	11	122	122	60
Chile	23	21	50	65	54	14
Colombia	97	89	144	136	140	74
Costa Rica	73	47	77	108	92	46
Dom. Rep.	95	119	73	127	110	143
Ecuador	130	138	127	131	130	116
El Salvador	123	117	129	143	144	118
Guatemala	110	98	123	144	143	137
Haiti	143	143	99	138	135	136
Honduras	102	77	131	142	141	125
Mexico	100	85	117	135	139	134
Nicaragua	112	125	116	105	113	94
Panama	47	80	87	118	95	52
Paraguay	127	124	106	121	124	138
Peru	118	105	119	125	126	128
Uruguay	63	46	19	88	33	71
Venezuela	144	144	100	140	142	142

Source: Based on World Economic Forum data

due to the poor quality of political institutions in Latin America. Another factor that needs to be mentioned is the misdirected and undue influence of the human rights discourse that has taken shape in Latin America. After the wave of military dictatorships in Latin America, international organizations and left-wing groups are wont to see a return to the militarism of the past in any expression of state power. As such, the Latin American governments face strong disincentives to implement law and order measures that a foreign investor from the United States or Europe would naturally just take for granted. The results are high business costs of crime and violence.

So far we have seen that Latin America is progressing. First-generation reforms, embodied in the structural adjustment recommendations of the Washington Consensus, were applied, with success. Order was restored to the public finances. Monetary and fiscal discipline have been applied, and inflation has been whipped, as has been the problem of public indebtedness. However, second-generation reforms, those pertaining to the quality of public institutions carrying out economic and social policies, have largely not been applied, outside a small group of countries, captained by Chile, Uruguay, Costa Rica, and perhaps Peru. Some would include Panama in this category. The lessons of this are that the most pro-market and pro-trade states are the freest of corruption and the most progressive as well.

Lack of state reach impacts the business and investment climate in important ways. One is the inability to invest optimally in the betterment of the competitiveness climate of the country. Infrastructural investments in Latin America are run by mercantilist principles, not those of free trade and markets. Where poverty is an issue, like the Central American countries of Honduras and Guatemala, the government has scant resources to invest in programs to reduce poverty, and what is spent in this realm is spent badly, obeying more the principles of clientelism and cronyism than actual poverty reduction. The continuation of poverty, due to the lack of conviction in pro-market policies, is then used to attack market economics for the benefit of populist politicians. In this context, a reasonable, efficient investment of tax revenues in social programs for the poor should be looked at as the price of doing business in these Latin American countries. The problem is the lack of confidence that rampant corruption inspires. There is no guarantee that tax income will be spent on the promised programs, and every likelihood that it will not. This creates a negative spiral in Latin American countries, particularly those strategically located in Central America, wherein corruption breeds informal economic activities that are unregulated and untaxed. This "robs" state coffers, and further impedes state investment in security, infrastructure, and poverty reduction.

Underfinanced State

As a general rule, it is a myth that the state is underfunded in Latin America. The real phenomenon is that state income via taxes is insufficient to invest in poverty reduction, social safety net programs, and corruption. A sound level of tax revenues as a percentage of GDP would be 20%. In countries such as Argentina, state income is more than 40% of GDP, in Brazil, 37%, and 28.1% in Colombia. Even in pro-market Chile, state revenues are almost 24% of GDP. State revenues are reported lowest in terms of percentage of GDP for Guatemala. The general recommendations are to boost state coffers in order to enable the state to invest in education, health and infrastructure, and, increasingly, security. Ostensibly, these types of public investment would all redound favorably to the benefit of the business and investment climate of the country in question. However, this promise is rarely kept in the strict sense. Social programs are famously fonts of corruption, clientelism, and cronyism in Latin America, particularly in the leftist regimes linked to Venezuela's cheap brand of populist socialism. In countries such as Ecuador, Nicaragua, and Venezuela, social programs ostensibly justified on grounds of poverty reduction are instead predicated on principles of vote maximization by the governments in power. Central America is another sub-region where the social programs are used more to bolster the electoral chances of politicians than actually reduce poverty and hunger.

Taken as a whole, it must be said that Latin Americans have not learned the lessons of progress. Curiously enough, those from the intellectual left who constantly

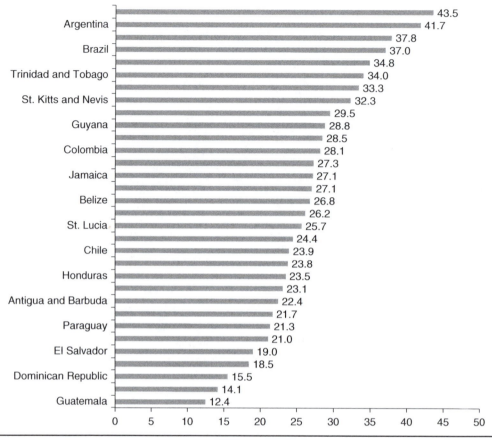

Figure 6.6 Tax revenues as share of GDP in Latin America and the Caribbean[11]
Source: IMF data

clamor for more state presence are the first to criticize the most basic expressions of state power, which is in the area of rule of law. Rule of law should, technically, be a matter of consensus. However, it is only pro-market countries that tend to respect this in Latin America. Chile, today, leads the pack. On matters of rule of law, the Caribbean countries outscore the region. This is because they depend heavily on financial investments, and financial markets are exceedingly well informed and efficient. With today's technology, options abound and are a keyboard strike away. Once again, among the poorest performers on rule of law are the pseudo-socialist regimes of Nicaragua, Bolivia, Ecuador, and Venezuela. A surprising, and exceedingly disappointing, case is represented by Argentina. With all her tangible economic resources and valuable human talent, Argentina should be a world-class, developed country. For lack of rule of law, Argentina is classified among the basket cases of Venezuela and Haiti. On the strict matter of rule of law, risk-averse investors would be well advised to stick to the large countries of Chile, Brazil, Costa Rica, and Panama. Profitable investment opportunities abound in other countries, to be sure, but the risk and uncertainty are much higher.

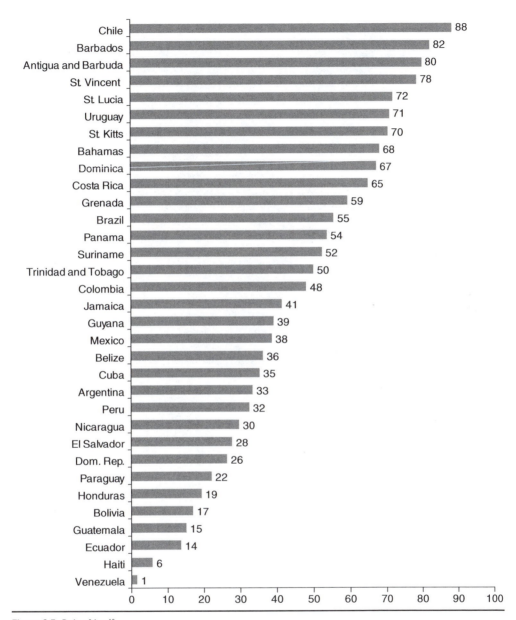

Figure 6.7 Rule of law[12]
Source: Based on World Bank data

Corruption matters, and should matter to the business investor first. On the matter of government effectiveness, once again, the pseudo-socialist countries of Nicaragua, Venezuela, Bolivia, and Ecuador score among the bottom of the barrel, as compared to the rest of their regional neighbors. Once again, the pro-market countries of Chile, Uruguay, Costa Rica, and the Caribbean small states lead the pack on matters related to effectiveness of government, with all the obvious implications this

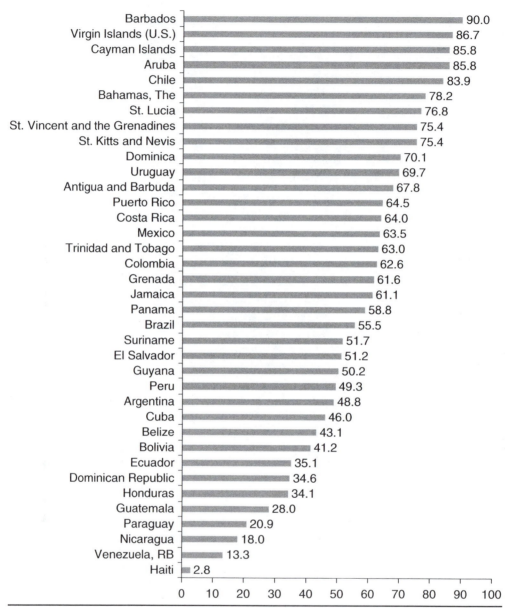

Figure 6.8 Government effectiveness in the Latin America and Caribbean region[13]

Source: Based on World Bank data

has for the business and investment climate in the region. However, the potential investor interested in doing business in the region of Latin America and the Caribbean should take note not just of the score, or rank, of a certain country in a certain point in time, but also the trend. As a case in point, in light of the bulk of data presented heretofore, it is clear that, although Peru does not achieve a particularly good score on Government Effectiveness, the country is making progress on matters related to

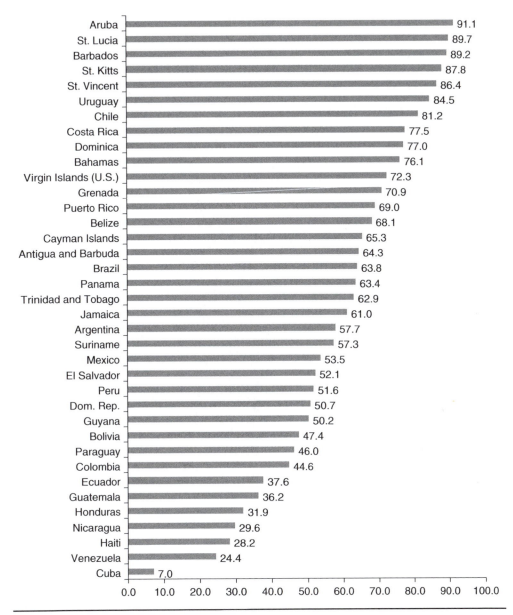

Figure 6.9 Voice and accountability[14]

Source: Based on World Bank data

pro-market economic policies and human development. What is surely noteworthy is that, once again, the socialist countries of Latin America are the poorest performers on government effectiveness, in spite of their being the most ardent advocates of government action.

The World Bank's measure of Voice and Accountability attempts to pick up how responsive governments are to the political preferences of the citizenry, under the premise that more responsiveness is better. Once again, the Caribbean small states surprise, leading as a group the entire region. Also, Chile, Uruguay, and Costa Rica lead the pack. Once again, the socialist countries of Venezuela, Cuba, Nicaragua, Ecuador, and Bolivia are near the bottom of the grouping. This, in conjunction with the other indicators analyzed, indicates governments that not only act against business interest, but also refuse to listen to societal clamor for needed reforms. The fact that different measures, taken by different organizations, continually pick up the socialist countries of Latin America as the perennial poor performers of the region should send a strong signal to would-be investors to be exceedingly wary of investing in these countries. Of course, investments made here could pay off, but the risk of loss is much greater.

TYPOLOGY OF POLITICAL SYSTEMS

The Index of Failed States relates a telling story. The reader should bear in mind that on this indicator a lower ranking is a *worse* score. Among the countries classified as stable are Chile, Uruguay, and Costa Rica. These are the countries most typically classified as the most pro-democratic and pro-market of the Latin American region. However, it is notable that Argentina also classifies, although it is an atypical case of a country rich in resources that nevertheless sub-optimizes them through exceedingly poor governmental orientation and public policies. With the scant exception of these few countries, the rest of the region is either in some degree of danger of being a failed state or in alert status, as in the case of Haiti. Haiti is already a failed state. Countries classified as being in varying degrees of danger of becoming failed states are the populist socialist nations of Bolivia, Ecuador, Nicaragua, and Venezuela. Also in varying degrees of danger are Colombia, Guatemala, and El Salvador. In Guatemala and El Salvador this is due to the growing influence of organized crime and the drug cartels. In Colombia, there are present not only drug lords but also violent terrorists; however, there seems to be in this case a determination by the government to vanquish at least the terrorists.

In the context of a globalized economy and complex interdependence of states, not investing in Latin America is not an option. However, the data show that there are countries more worthy of consideration of foreign investor attention, and these are Costa Rica, Chile, Uruguay, and the Caribbean small states. Although Argentina is definitely not a failed state, it is a state that is, today, with the current government, one that is frankly antagonistic towards business interests. This is borne out by the rest of the indicators presented in this, and other, chapters of this book.

The good news is that democracy and freedom have taken a foothold in Latin America and the Caribbean. Overall, for the 44 countries taken into account by Freedom House, 23 are fully Free, 10 are Partially Free and 1 is Not Free: Cuba. Colombia obtains a Partially Free classification on account of the political violence it continues to suffer due to the presence of violent terrorist groups. Similarly, Mexico suffers a tremendous load of violence due to its government's determination to win the war

Table 6.7 Index of Failed States[15]

Ranking (177)	País	Score/120 worst
7	Haiti	104.9
52	Colombia	84..4
62	Bolivia	82.1
67	Ecuador	80.1
69	Nicaragua	79.6
70	Guatemala	79.4
75	Honduras	78.5
82	Venezuela	77.3
93	El Salvador	74.4
95	Rep. Dom.	74.1
98	Mexico	73.6
99	Peru	73.5
101	Cuba	73.1
104	Guyana	71.4
105	Suriname	71.2
107	Paraguay	70.9
113	Belize	67.2
119	Jamaica	65.8
121	Grenada	65.0
122	Trinidad	64.4
123	Brasil	64.1
127	Ant & Barb.	58.9
132	Panama	56.1
134	Bahamas	55.1
135	Barbados	52.0
139	Costa Rica	49.7
145	Argentina	46.5
151	Chile	43.5
154	Uruguay	40.5

Alert

Danger

Stable

LAC Average Score		68.2
Latin America Average Score		66.4
Caribbean Average Score		72.3

Source: Fund for Peace

on drugs against the narco-cartels. Bolivia, Ecuador, Nicaragua, and Venezuela fall into the Partially Free category on account of election rigging, the oppression of dissenting opinions, and the general abuse of political power by those in power seeking to stay there. Cuba, of course, is a communist dictatorship, by definition Not Free.

Table 6.8 Freedom in the world, 2012[16]

Number	Free	Partly Free	Not Free
1	Antigua and Barbuda	Bolivia	Cuba
2	Argentina	Colombia	
3	Bahamas	Ecuador	
4	Barbados	Guatemala	
5	Belize	Haiti	
6	Brazil	Honduras	
7	Chile	Mexico	
8	Costa Rica	Nicaragua	
9	Dominica	Paraguay	
10	Dominican Republic	Venezuela	
11	El Salvador		
12	Grenada		
13	Guyana		
14	Jamaica		
15	Panama		
16	Peru		
17	Saint Kitts and Nevis		
18	Saint Lucia		
19	Saint Vincent and Grenadines		
20	Suriname		
21	Trinidad and Tobago		
22	Uruguay		
23	Puerto Rico		
Total	**23**	**10**	**1**

Source: Based on Freedom House data

Latinobarómetro takes measures of public opinion in Latin America on political matters. Latin Americans seem to want democracy. Democratic sentiment, as measured by the proportion of respondents who say that they would not accept a military government under any circumstances, is highest in the best economic performers, albeit not exclusively. The other countries are Costa Rica, Uruguay, Chile, and Panama, but also in corrupt countries such as Dominican Republic, Argentina, Ecuador, and Bolivia. The country least democratically attached is Guatemala.

The proportion of respondents willing to contemplate certain circumstances under which an authoritarian government might be preferable is highest in Paraguay, Dominican Republic, Brazil, El Salvador, Guatemala, Honduras, and Panama. The countries hardest hit by crime are in this group, not surprisingly.

Based on Latinobarómetro data, the Legitimacy of the Congress and Political Parties varies considerably across the region. Of course, hating politicians is also as American as apple pie, so these survey responses need to be taken into context.

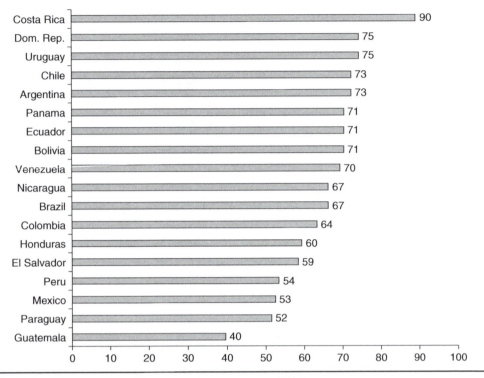

Figure 6.10 Latin American attitudes toward military government, 2011[17]

Source: Latinobarómetro (2011)

Nevertheless, in Bolivia, Colombia, Panama, Brazil, and Ecuador, the Congress is held in particular disregard.

Asked to rank what democracy needs most, a strong plurality identify Corruption as the key fault that needs fixing, with 48% of respondents indicating as much. In a related matter, another 31% respond with Transparency.

THE WAY OUT: PRIVATE AND PUBLIC PARTNERSHIP

The good news for Latin America is that its private sector is in much better shape than its public, political sector. This is relevant for both the political climate and the investment climate in Latin America. As free trade with advanced nations like the United States progresses, and US businesses invest in the Latin American region, there occurs a transfer of ideas and superior ways of organizing business and political life. This should eventually impact more positively on the Latin American political climate. A key example of this is NAFTA, the North American Free Trade Agreement, or CAFTA, the Central American Free Trade Agreement. Upon partnering with the US on trade, the Latin American countries have to commit to adopt modern, more agile, less burdensome rules and regulations, and apply them equally. Were it not for the American influence, corruption in Latin America

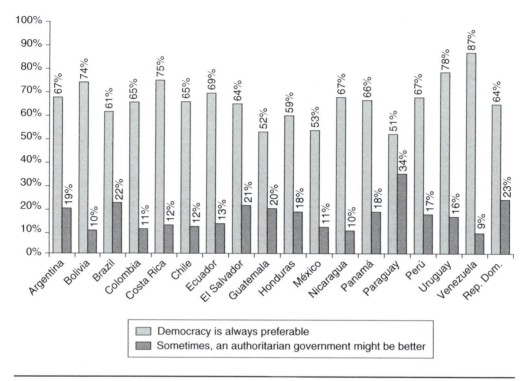

Figure 6.11 Support for democracy, 2010[18]

Source: Latinobarómetro (2011)

would persist yet longer, and be more profound. The first people to adopt modern methods are in the private sector.

In Table 6.9, the reader can see that, while public institutions receive a regional weighted rank of 96.2, private institutions receive 75.3, behind the overall competitiveness rank for the region seen in Table 6.4 (61.5), but still outperforming the public sector. Strength of Auditing and Reporting Standards receives a solid rank of 60.7, as does Efficacy of Corporate Boards, 61.1, and Strength of Investor Protection, 61.6. The investor seeking to do business in Latin America can take heart that there are reasons to believe that the political and business investment climate will continue to improve, based on key indicators from the private sector. Latin America ranks well in Quality of Management Schools (53), On-the-job Training (50.9), Availability of Research and Training Services (50.9), and Extent of Staff Training (57.4). These investments made by the Latin American private sector in the formation of competent, innovative human capital should, with time, have positive external effects on the quality of the political climate in the Latin American region.

THE LEFTIST THREAT IN LATIN AMERICA

The data from various organizations show that Latin America has not completely learned the lessons of the past. Due to poor institutions, and the political culture of

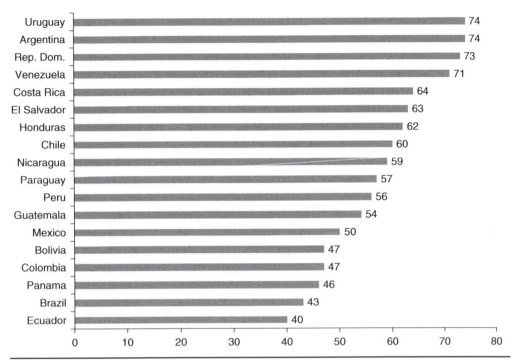

Figure 6.12 Legitimacy of political institutions[19]

Source: Latinobarómetro (2011)

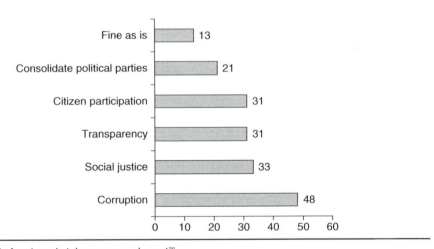

Figure 6.13 Latin America: what democracy needs most[20]

Source: Latinobarómetro (2011)

the *caudillo* strongman, which still reins in much of the region, countries in Latin America seem perennially susceptible to falling in the grip of socialist, populist governments. This is due to the continued presence of poverty in the region, and very low scores on matters of human development (seen in other chapters). This makes

Table 6.9 Private institutions[21]

Country	Public institutions	Private institutions	Ethical behavior of firms	Strength of auditing and reporting standards	Efficacy of corporate boards	Protection of minority stakeholders' interests	Strength of investor protection	Quality of management schools	On-the-job training	Availability of research and training services	Extent of staff training
LA Region Weighted	96.2	75.3	89.6	60.7	61.1	63.1	61.6	53.0	50.9	50.9	57.4
LA Region Simple	107.8	90.2	94.4	80.1	82.2	87.1	84.1	74.5	75.6	77.7	76.9
Argentina	138	135	138	120	107	128	94	34	65	60	78
Bolivia	113	124	114	128	138	115	110	120	104	107	103
Brazil	80	62	84	42	38	37	65	52	32	34	33
Chile	28	32	24	45	37	48	29	14	36	36	38
Colombia	122	76	112	84	66	82	5	74	80	75	99
Costa Rica	55	46	39	62	55	50	130	19	28	26	29
Dom. Rep.	132	89	111	73	98	63	52	88	78	84	76
Ecuador	128	129	131	107	115	111	110	94	99	105	90
El Salvador	134	119	118	90	83	117	130	99	79	81	81
Guatemala	130	82	74	65	39	106	110	43	42	53	40
Haiti	143	144	142	141	97	144	130	140	143	142	144
Honduras	123	90	79	57	63	72	130	109	82	94	63
Mexico	100	67	76	55	67	60	39	51	48	44	67
Nicaragua	117	107	101	96	119	125	80	98	116	124	97
Panama	73	55	64	36	76	39	94	82	40	43	43
Paraguay	135	112	123	102	108	107	52	124	117	121	107
Peru	118	66	93	49	54	71	17	49	81	85	84
Uruguay	36	40	34	71	72	49	80	54	55	46	86
Venezuela	144	139	137	99	129	130	140	72	111	116	104

Source: Based on World Economic Forum data

the political system vulnerable. Latin American populist political movements are all too eager to exploit the poverty and inequality that still characterize great parts of the region, in order to push for an anti-democratic and anti-capitalist agenda that is frankly hostile to business interests in the region, be they internal or external.

The leftist turn hasn't afflicted only small countries in Latin America, like Nicaragua, but rather large economies like Argentina, Venezuela, Ecuador, and Bolivia, too. Before the demise of the Venezuelan strongman Hugo Chavez, Venezuela led the ALBA countries, which included Ecuador, Bolivia, and Nicaragua as well, in a political movement he liked to call "21st-century Socialism." It is characterized mainly by attacks on private interests and the degradation from within of democratic institutions, so that regularly held elections are skewed to those in power. The end result is what was evident to all in the aftermath of Hugo Chavez's death in Venezuela in 2013, wherein his self-appointed successor won a rigged election that has thrown the country into political and economic uncertainty.

It is worth noting that Venezuela has strong allies in Latin America, namely the ALBA countries, as well as Argentina. Central American countries such as Guatemala have made irresponsible overtures to Venezuela as well. In Table 6.10, one can compare the traditional indicators for various countries associated with the Venezuelan ALBA initiative, Latin America (excluding the Caribbean countries),[22] and the US. A rapid review of the table demonstrates that, while the Latin American region as a whole would have a ranking of 61, Venezuela's ranking is more than twice as bad. As can be seen, Ecuador, Bolivia, and Nicaragua are also far below the regional ranking for competitiveness, with 85, 104, and 108, respectively. Argentina, a leftist country affiliated with the Venezuelan regime also reflects relatively poor competitiveness, with a ranking of 94 on the Global Competitiveness Index.

Another fact that stands out when comparing countries in the orbit of Venezuelan socialism is that none is a fully free democratic regime. Out of 185 countries sampled by the World Bank, Venezuela achieves a dismal ranking for Doing Business of 180, compared to a constructed ranking of 100.93 for Latin America. Argentina, Ecuador, Bolivia, and Nicaragua achieve individual rankings far worse than the Latin American region achieves as a whole, with rankings of 154, 124, 139, 155, and 119, respectively. The left-wing countries of Latin America also fare worse than the regional ranking in matters of starting a business and protecting investors. On the general item of Travel and Tourism Competitiveness, the ALBA countries fare worse than the regional average, although Argentina (not in ALBA) achieves a fair ranking of 61, out of 140 countries sampled by the World Economic Forum. In the realm of the Index of Economic Liberty, Venezuela, Argentina, Ecuador, Bolivia, and Nicaragua achieve scores (from 0 to the maximum score of 100) of 20, 30, 40, 50, and 50, respectively, compared to the 59.78 constructed score for the region of Latin America. On matters of corruption, the left-wing countries also fare poorly. Transparency International samples 176 countries for its Corruptions Perceptions Index. On the CPI, the Latin American region would obtain a ranking of 83.64, far better than the cases of Venezuela, Argentina, Ecuador, Bolivia, and Nicaragua, which obtain rankings of 165, 103, 118, 105, and 130, respectively.

Table 6.10 Indicators for Latin America, the US and ALBA countries[23]

Indicators for select countries	VNZLA	ARG	Ecuador	BOL	NIC	LA	US
Global Competitiveness Index, World Economic Forum	126	94	86	104	108	61.49	7
GCI Subindex A: Basic Requirements	126	96	75	94	104	74.60	33
GCI Subindex B: Efficiency Enhancers	117	86	100	122	119	55.70	2
GCI Subindex C: Sophistication and Innovation	135	88	93	100	116	62.73	7
Doing Business	180	124	139	155	119	100.93	4
DB Starting a Business	152	154	169	174	131	98.04	13
DB Dealing with Construction Permits	109	171	104	114	154	101.26	17
DB Getting Electricity	160	74	146	126	129	87.38	19
DB Registering Property	90	135	101	139	123	105.77	25
DB Getting Credit	159	70	83	129	104	81.06	4
DB Protecting Investors	181	117	139	139	100	77.62	6
DB Paying Taxes	185	149	84	180	158	132.66	69
DB Trading Across Borders	166	139	128	125	81	103.67	22
DB Enforcing Contracts	80	48	99	136	55	99.38	6
DB Resolving Insolvency	163	94	137	68	80	102.42	16
Human Development Index, United Nations	73	45	83	108	129	73.16	4
Global Gender Gap, World Economic Forum	48	32	33	30	9	60.99	22
Travel and Tourism Competitiveness, World Economic Forum	113	61	81	110	95	59.57	6
Democracy Index, Economist Intelligence unit	97	51	89	84	91	51.50	19
Freedom Status, Freedom House	Partly Free	Free	Partly Free	Partly Free	Partly Free	n.d.	Free
Index of Globalization, KOF (0 to 100)	50.9	58.94	54.16	53.79	55.11	59.78	74.88
Index of Economic Liberty, Heritage Foundation (0 to 100)	20	30	40	50	50	59.60	76
Transparency International	165	102	118	105	130	83.64	19

Source: Authors' calculations based on various indicators

COMMUNITY OF LATIN AMERICAN AND
CARIBBEAN STATES, OR CELAC

Although care should be taken by the foreign investor seeking to do business in Latin America to not read too much into it, there persists in the region a distinct anti-Americanism, more often expressed than practiced. This leads more to political actions that should embarrass Latin American political leaders than any negative implications on the trade and investment front. The recently founded Community of Latin American and Caribbean States (CELAC, by its Spanish initials) is perhaps the best example of how Latin American politicians can transform the political climate into a circus. CELAC is an organization that aspires to be some sort of "Organization of American States," without the US or Canada. It comprises 33 countries, with a population of some 600 million inhabitants, based on calculations from IMF data. Based on calculations from World Bank data, the region represents some $7 trillion international dollars and a per capita income of $12,000, also in international dollars, expressed in purchasing power parity terms. Taken as a region, CELAC would have a Human Development Index score of 0.721, classified by the United Nations as High Human Development. Sounds impressive, right?

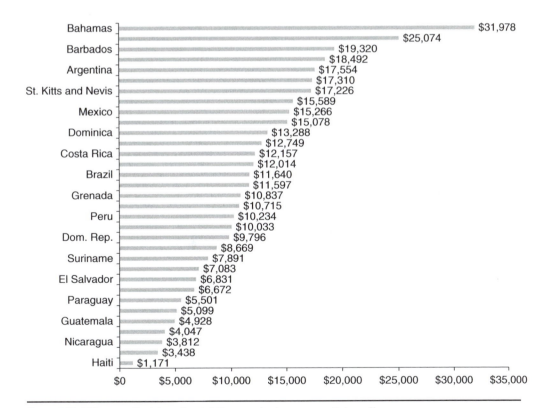

Figure 6.14 GDP per capita, international dollars, purchasing power parity terms[24]

Source: Authors' calculations based on IMF data

Table 6.11 Indicators for the Pacific Alliance[25]

Member Countries: Chile, Colombia, Costa Rica, Mexico and Peru

Subject Descriptor	2013	2007–2012	2013–2018
Gross domestic product, constant prices, % change	4.02	3.06	4.03
Gross domestic product, constant prices, billions, USD	$2,218.8	$2,055.5	$3,028.7
Gross domestic product per capita, current prices, USD	$10,254	$9,610	$13,259
Gross domestic product based on purchasing-power-parity (PPP) per capita GDP, Int'l dollar	$14,499	$13,871	$18,520
Gross domestic product based on purchasing-power-parity (PPP) share of world total, %	3.60	3.53	3.58
Inflation, end of period consumer prices, % change	3.21	4.22	3.00
Volume of imports of goods and services, % change	4.28	6.13	6.14
Volume of imports of goods % change	6.63	6.30	6.60
Volume of exports of goods and services, % change	3.90	4.17	6.36
Volume of exports of goods, % change	6.50	3.58	6.64
Population, millions	216.39	214.01	228.63
General government revenue, % GDP	23.74	23.47	22.92
General government total expenditure, % GDP	25.61	25.37	24.60
General government net lending/borrowing, % GDP	0.37	nd	nd
General government gross debt, % GDP	34.56	35.28	34.04
Current account balance, billions, USD	–$48.0	–$40.6	–$58.6
Current account balance, % GDP	–2.16	–1.29	–1.98

Source: Authors' calculations based on IMF data

In nominal terms, CELAC is, for practical intents and purposes, representative of the nations of the LAC region. In GDP per capita terms, as such, country achievements run from the $1,171 reported for Haiti, to the nearly $32,000 reported by the Bahamas. The nearly $7 trillion international dollars represented by the conglomeration of nations represents roughly 8% of world GDP. These figures are indicative for the LAC region as a whole, however, and are independent of the efforts of the socialist regimes aligned by and with Venezuela to form some sort of a counterweight to US influence in the region.

Taken as an economic whole, the GDP of the CELAC region is, indeed, impressive. And it is on these economic potentialities that the American business should focus when deciding to export to or invest in Latin America. Its economic potential on paper notwithstanding, CELAC lacks the institutional qualities of a serious organization, not to mention sound principles upon which to base a forward, future-oriented international organization. Proof of the silliness of this movement is borne out by the fact that the organization's president for 2013 is none other than Raul Castro, dictator of Cuba, a fact that was roundly condemned by Freedom House, an organization dedicated to the preservation and promotion of democracy in the world.

The election of Castro, head of a totalitarian regime, to head a Latin American organization supposedly founded to advance democracy and human rights, shows how politically immature and irresponsible the Latin American countries can still be. This can be frustrating for business people from the developed world to experience when they come to Latin America to do business. Under Venezuelan inspiration and Cuban leadership, CELAC represents little of value to the world of democracy, markets, and commerce, and the incentives and interests behind the initiative should be looked upon with suspicion by any objective observer. Fortunately for the foreign investor looking to do business in Latin America, the CELAC effort can be effectively ignored. Business risks can be substantially minimized by simply avoiding investing in countries of the ALBA initiative, or Argentina, for that matter. However, there are other more serious, and less laughable, Latin American initiatives that the more responsible, democratic and pro-market countries are engaging in. One such example is the Pacific Alliance.

The Pacific Alliance

For all its nationalist, anti-imperialist rhetoric, Latin America is still a good place to do business. The future is, on the whole, promising. Although a far cry from a unilateral declaration of freer trade and markets, the Latin American region as a whole has bet on increasing the levels of economic integration between its member countries.

The Pacific Alliance is a notable Latin American trading bloc founded in June 2012. It is was composed of Chile, Colombia, Mexico, and Peru originally, plus Costa Rica, which joined the Pacific Alliance in 2013. Its score on the Human Development Index, as a region, would be 0.764, which is considered High Human Development by the United Nations.[26]

The PA constitutes an ambitious trading bloc, representing more than 40% of the GDP of the LAC region and more than half of the exports from the LAC region. Were it an independent country, it would rank among the top ten economies of the world, equivalent to Russia and Brazil, and ahead of the United Kingdom. The GDP for the PA region is estimated to surpass $2,218.8 in current dollar terms. Based on calculations made from IMF data, the Pacific Alliance would have a GDP of some $3 trillion international dollars in purchasing power parity terms, and a GDP per capita estimated around $14,500, also in international dollars, in purchasing power parity terms.[27]

The PA nations together exported more than $567 billion in 2012, more than half again what the Mercosur nations exported in that same year. In terms of volume, both exports and imports are expected to grow at an annual rate of 6% for the 2013–2018 time frame. The macroeconomic environment for these countries taken as a region is also stable, and projected to remain stable through 2018. Fiscal balance is roughly achieved, and trade deficits in percentage terms of GDP are projected to not surpass in negative territory the baseline figure of -2% for the 2013–2018 time period. On a regional basis, per capita GDP stands at $10,254, when measured in current dollar terms, and $14,449 when adjusted for purchasing power parity, in terms of international dollars. This level of purchasing power is expected to keep the regional economy growing at a pace of 4% per annum, while maintaining in the respectable, stable region of 3% per year.

Sebastian Piñera of Chile assumed the first presidency of the PA bloc, and as of May 2013, the Colombian president, Juan Manuel Santos, is president of the PA bloc. Based on the principles of the free movement of goods, services, capital and persons, the PA aims to promote serious regional economic integration, and spur economic growth, human development, and competitiveness among its member countries.

The PA comprises the only two Latin American nations to have membership in the OECD, which are Mexico and Chile. Colombia is applying for OECD membership. The PA takes seriously the lessons learned from the Washington Consensus, and years of experience with functioning free trade agreements. Essential conditions for membership require the observance of the rule of law and democracy based on constitutional order.

It is important to note that the Alliance of the Pacific counts among its eager would-be partners both the United States and Canada, each of which enjoys free trade treaties with each of the nations in the Pacific Alliance. Japan has requested observer status as well.

POLITICAL RISK IN LATIN AMERICA

Political risk in Latin America should be a major concern for investors in the region. Defining political risk as the effect that a government could have on the Doing Business framework in the country could be the precise guide for developing

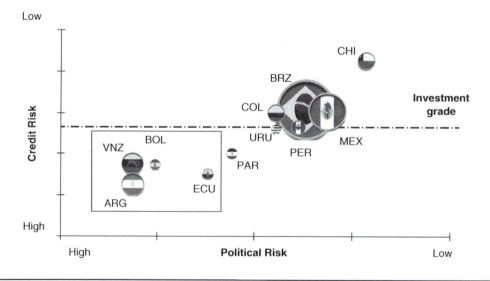

Figure 6.15 Credit risk/political risk

Source: Anthony (2012)

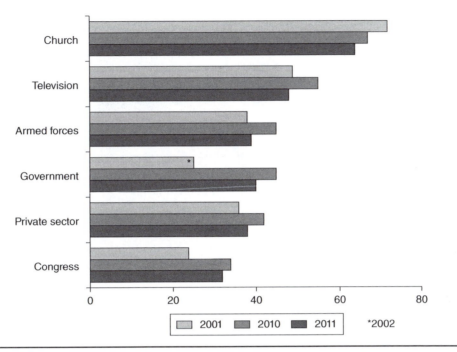

Figure 6.16 Trust in institutions

Source: *The Economist* (2012)

business in Latin American economy. As seen in different chapters, the economic risk leads to the indicators such as monetary policy and the economy of development in the region. Political risk represents the capability that government has on affecting business. The question is: "How much can government affect business?"

The first indicator for understanding political risk in Latin America is the credit rate. The credit rate is the interest rate that the government receives when issuing debt by bond or other monetary mechanism. If a country has a high risk, the interest rate will be higher; the same applies if the country has a low risk. Discerning this fact could be one of the best pieces of advice an investor can take.

Another important aspect to analyze political risk understands the confidence that the citizens have in the institution. For example, the institution that the citizens trust the most is the Church, followed by television, the armed forces, government private sector, and congress. The information gathered by the Latinobarómetro demonstrates that the most trustworthy institution is religion and the least trustworthy is the congress. The importance of this is that, in Latin America, the congress makes important decisions on the future of the country, and since they decide the future of the country, the lack of confidence is a major conflict when doing business. Another interesting aspect is that, despite the times, this has not changed in the past ten years, and the only institutions that have improved are the private sector and the government. Churches, television and the congress have lost confidence in recent years.

In conclusion, trust in Latin America is an important asset, and the trust that Latin Americans have in their institutions is an even better asset for decision making.

The lack of trust in the congress is a political risk in the country, because if the most important institution in a constitutional democracy is not trustworthy, the rules of the country could not be as easy to understand. For this reason, when Latinobarómetro (2012) asked about democracy as the best type of government, there were negative results when comparing 2010 to 2011, 60% questioned the veracity of the government. The consequences of the changes in government can be understood by the attitude of the government in Venezuela, where a *Caudillismo* based on the political system called *Populismo* established Hugo Chavez as head of state for more than ten years. The consequences of the lack of trust in the government led President Hugo Chavez to take over the power of the nation and, as a consequence, years later, expropriation was a discussion in Venezuela's political arena. The same discussion can be analyzed in Argentina, where companies have been expropriated (Repsol) without paying the proper price.

The lack of trust has driven the citizens of Latin America to think of dictatorship as a plausible solution. Venezuela demonstrated in the last election that, although the

Table 6.12 Trust in government

	Democracy is preferable to any other type of government				In certain circumstances authoritarian government can be preferable to a democratic one			
	2001	2010	2011	Change since 2010	2001	2010	2011	Change since 2010
Paraguay	35	49	54	5	43	33	25	–8
Argentina	58	66	70	4	21	13	15	2
Dominican Rep.	na	63	65	2	na	23	22	–1
Uruguay	79	75	75	nil	10	15	11	–4
Panama	34	61	60	–1	23	17	19	2
Chile	45	63	61	–2	19	11	14	3
Peru	62	61	59	–2	12	15	16	1
Ecuador	40	64	61	–3	24	12	23	11
Bolivia	54	68	64	–4	17	9	11	2
Colombia	36	60	55	–5	16	10	11	1
El Salvador	25	59	54	–5	10	19	16	–3
Venezuela	57	84	77	–7	20	9	14	5
Costa Rica	71	72	65	–7	8	12	14	2
Nicaragua	43	58	50	–8	22	9	15	6
Brazil	30	54	45	–9	18	19	19	nil
Mexico	46	49	40	–9	35	10	14	4
Honduras	57	53	43	–10	8	16	27	11
Guatemala	33	46	36	–10	21	17	22	5

Source: *The Economist* (2012)

government is not as transparent as it could be, it has a connection with most of the population given that, since the death of Hugo Chavez and the presidential election, his right hand, Nicolás Maduro, won the elections. This type of government perpetuating a certain type of politics is becoming more and more constant in Latin America. A few examples are presented below.

- Colombia: President Uribe and President Santos
- Venezuela: President Hugo Chavez and President Nicolás Maduro
- Argentina: President Kirchner and President de Kirchner
- Costa Rica: President Arias and President Chinchilla
- Brazil: President Da Silva and President Rousseff

The examples above have represented the perpetuation of the political movement that gave results according to the citizens of the countries. In some cases, such as Brazil and Colombia, the following of politics by a successor of the same party has given important results. In the case of Brazil, the country has become an example of the eradication of poverty and, in the case of Colombia, an example of the handling of drug lords and narco activities. Business has grown because the rules have become easier to understand and the results are goal oriented.

In the cases of Venezuela and Argentina, the results have worried the business sector since there has been a constant strategy in expropriation, irresponsible monetary policy, and a regular macroeconomic handling of the situation. The cases represent the main aspect of Latin America, its dichotomy.

One of the most important factors to consider is crime in Latin America. An example is Guatemala, in which 7% of the nation's GDP goes into the fighting of crime. This number is significant if you consider that the government of Guatemala constitutes 9% of the GDP, meaning that crime is almost as expensive as the government. The fight against drug lords from Mexico to Colombia has taken its toll on the citizens of each country and a variation in the political decisions in the fight. The problem is that the drug cartels have a better income and preparation than most of the governments. In the case of Colombia they can say that they have been victorious in the war against drugs after the falling empire of Pablo Escobar, but concerning Mexico the history is very different, since the cost of war has been extremely high in the population.

The political risk is that when devising strategies to fight drug lords, the government is diverted from its major concerns, and therefore the capability of the government is reduced for as long as the war lasts. The result is the redirection of budgets into security and, as a consequence, less budget in education, which can only lead to a deterioration of competitiveness in the region.

On a general note, it is exceedingly positive that Latin American nations have taken the lead in order to form a freer trade bloc that explicitly rejects the left-wing populism expressed by countries in the orbit of the ALBA nations. It seems that, for the foreseeable future, Latin America will run on two tracks, with those nations

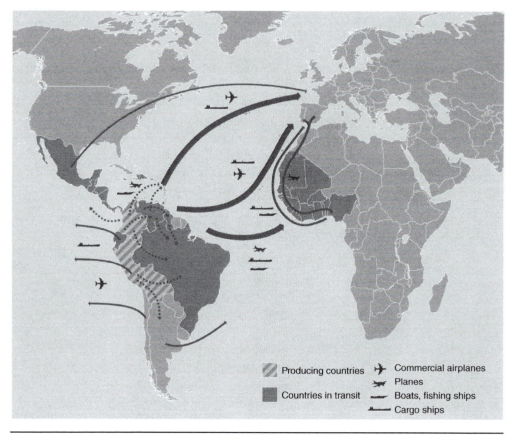

Figure 6.17 Map of drug-trafficking majors and routes

Source: Brombacher and Maihold (2009)

espousing the time-tested principles of free markets on the one hand, and those adhering to the failed policies of mercantilist socialism on the other. It would behoove the foreign investor to be aware of this, and to mind the difference. Investments are best made in countries that respect the principles of private property and the rule of law.

CONCLUSIONS

In this chapter we have covered the political climate in Latin America as it affects the business climate in the region. The main aspect that foreign investors seeking to do business in Latin America should take into account is the pervasiveness of corruption, and the dangers of crime and populist socialism in the region. The poor performance of political institutions degrades overall national competitiveness in general, and the quality of government services to improve business performance in particular. The business costs of crime and violence in the region are exceedingly high, posing a substantial disincentive and risk for those entertaining investing and doing business in Latin America. This needs to be stated with frankness.

Latin America is a competitive region in the world economy. If it were a country, the region would rank in the top half of the nations of the world in terms of general competitiveness. That might not sound like a great ranking, but, particularly if one takes the past twenty-year trend into account, the changes are generally positive and projected to continue in the right direction. This provides strong incentives for investors thinking of doing business in Latin America.

Latin America scores better on the quality of her private institutions, on such issues as corporate ethics, efficiency of boards of directors, the strength of auditing and accounting standards, and protection of investor interests. Moreover, Latin America scores well on efficiency enhancers, which include such items as the quality of universities and, in particular, business schools. Staff training is another area where many Latin American countries score well. An American investor seeking to do business in Latin America would find himself quickly in contact with well-trained business persons, a strong critical mass of which speak English.

The general regional rankings don't tell the whole story. The global competitiveness context includes the very poor-performing state institutions, which are, excepting the countries linked to the 21st-century Socialism initiative embarked upon by the late president of Venezuela, Hugo Chavez, in the process of improving. Due to widespread public frustration with state corruption, political instability in the way of massive demonstrations has racked Brazil, just ahead of the World Cup tournament to be held there in 2014. Like the much-vaunted Arab Spring, this has the potential to spread all over the region, because corruption is as Latin American as salsa music. This has obvious implications for the Doing Business climate. However, the upside opportunities to invest outweigh these downside risks. On top of rampant inequality, and highly corrupt and inefficient public institutions, the protests in Brazil were triggered by the heavy investments directed at the World Cup games, when so much of the population suffered from the effects of bad government. Nevertheless, even Brazil will weather this political storm, as the left-leaning Rousseff government had, prior to the protests even, already taken strong first steps to fight corruption.

The good news is that, due to globalization and freer trade, the correct institutional reforms are under way, albeit haltingly. As indicated by data from the Heritage Foundation, Latin America has an overall score on Economic Liberty of 59.6, out of a maximum possible score of 100. Make no mistake, this is a strong improvement over the region's protectionist past, and, in particular, the import-substitution-industrialization (ISI) strategies pursued under the misguided notions of Keynesianism and neo-Marxist and structuralist economics. Latin America has improvements to make on the protection of property rights and, in particular, public-sector corruption (35.5).

Although improvements need to continue, the region has progressed on matters relating to labor and investment freedom, as well as financial freedom. Overall, the strong points for the region are its strong scores on Fiscal Freedom. The tax and spend climate in Latin America certainly isn't what the business investor would find in Europe, and even the United States, these days. In terms of Monetary, Trade and Business Freedom, the Latin American region has made strong progress, scoring over 70, well above her general score of 59.6 on General Economic Liberty. This is all good news for the American investor interested in doing business in Latin America.

A caveat applies. Foreign investors seeking to do business in Latin America would be wise to avoid the political risks associated with potential investments in the countries linked to or flirting with the ALBA initiative. From Chapter 2, on economic history, we know that Latin America has gone through pro-business and anti-business phases in her past, and even twenty-year trends can be quickly reversed by leftist, populist demagogues seeking to capitalize on the frustrations of Latin America's numerous poor population. All in all, as mentioned earlier, presenting the greatest risk for investors would be Venezuela and Cuba; and the countries to watch closely and consider only under strict scrutiny would be Ecuador, Bolivia, and Nicaragua. As noted in an earlier chapter, even Argentina has to be put on a watch list, given the power grabs of the Kirchner government, which tellingly include moves against central bank independence—a surefire route to the inflationary days of macroeconomic instability of her past.

However, bright spots appear on the Latin American political horizon and should also be taken into account by the investor seeking to do business there. The private sector in Latin America is competitive, in spite of an underperforming political sector. As the quality of human capital grows in the private sector, positive externalities should transfer to the political sector, as national and foreign businesses demand less corruption and better public services, beginning with public security. All in all, the greatest risks for investors seeking to do business in Latin America would have to be Argentina, Venezuela, Ecuador, Bolivia, and Nicaragua. These countries suffer from the traditional defects that have afflicted Latin American political regimes since their inception, plus send every indication that the future trend will be towards some type of a pseudo-socialist, interventionist, over-regulated regime. Investors would be prudent to orient their investment capital towards more business-friendly countries such as Uruguay, Chile, Costa Rica, Colombia, Panama, and Mexico, to name but a few.

NOTES

1. World Bank. World Development Indicators, online database: http://data.worldbank.org/data-catalog/world-development-indicators (accessed May 2013).
2. World Bank. World Development Indicators, online database: http://datacatalog.worldbank.org/ (accessed May 2013).
3. Ibid.
4. World Bank. Worldwide Governance Indicators, online database. http://data.worldbank.org/data-catalog/worldwide-governance-indicators. Accessed May, 2013.
5. Ibid.
6. Transparency International. 2012. Corruption Perceptions Index, online database: http://www.transparency.org/research/cpi/overview (accessed May 2013).
7. Heritage Foundation. Index of Economic Liberty, online database: http://www.heritage.org/index/ (accessed May 2013).

8. World Economic Forum. Global Competitiveness Index, online database: http://www.weforum.org/ (accessed May 2013).
9. Ibid.
10. Ibid.
11. International Monetary Fund. World Economic Outlook, online database: http://datacatalog.worldbank.org/ (accessed May 2013).
12. World Bank. Worldwide Governance Indicators, online database: http://data.worldbank.org/data-catalog/worldwide-governance-indicators (accessed May 2013).
13. Ibid.
14. Ibid.
15. The Fund for Peace. Failed States Index, online database: http://ffp.statesindex.org/ (accessed May 2013).
16. Freedom House, Freedom in the World 2012, online database: http://www.freedomhouse.org/ (accessed May 2013).
17. Latinobarómetro Corporation. Latinobarómetro, online database: http://www.latinobarometro.org/latino/LATAnalizeSample.jsp (accessed May 2013).
18. Ibid.
19. Ibid.
20. Ibid.
21. World Economic Forum. Global Competitiveness Index, online database: http://www.weforum.org/ (accessed May 2013).
22. The Latin American rankings and/or scores are obviously calculated constructs; however, they are not simple averages. They are calculated in the following manner. First, the regional total GDP is constructed, taking the GDP figure in current US dollars reported for 2013 by the IMF. Then, each country's relative participation in that total is calculated in percentage terms. That percentage term for each county, its participation in the regional total GDP, is used as a weighting factor for its individual ranking. In other words, each country's rank or score is weighted by its relative participation in regional total GDP. The sum of all weighted scores gives us the regional rank or score.
23. Authors' calculations based on various indicators (all accessed May 2013): Ease of Doing Business Index 2013, World Bank, http://www.doingbusiness.org/rankings; Human Development Index 2013, United Nations, http://hdr.undp.org/en/statistics/hdi/; Global Competitiveness Index 2012–2013, World Economic Forum, www.weforum.org; Travel and Tourism Competitiveness Index, World Economic Forum, www.weforum.org; Global Gender Gap, World Economic Forum, www.weforum.org; Index of Democracy 2012, Economist Intelligence Unit, http://www.eiu.com/Handlers/WhitepaperHandler.ashx?fi=Democracy-Index-2012.pdf&mode=wp&campaignid=DemocracyIndex12; KOF Index of Globalization, http://globalization.kof.ethz.ch/; Freedom in the World, Freedom House, http://www.freedomhouse.org/; Index of Economic Liberty, Heritage Foundation, www.heritage.org; Corruptions Perceptions Index, Transparency International. http://www.transparency.org/research/cpi/overview; International Monetary Fund, World Economic Outlook, online database, www.imf.org.
24. Authors' calculations based on International Monetary Fund data. World Economic Outlook, online database: www.imf.org (accessed May 2013).
25. Ibid.
26. These are the authors' own calculations based on International Monetary Fund data from the World Economic Outlook online database, www.imf.org (accessed May 2013), and the United Nations Human Development Index, http://hdr.undp.org/en/statistics/hdi/ (also accessed May 2013).
27. Ibid.

REFERENCES

Anthony, S. (2012) *Political risk*. Obtained from http://estrategiaparatodos.wordpress.com/political-risk-in-latin-america-and-the-caribbean-smart-move-from-nimble-players-a-few-populists-and-a-giant-that-misses-one-more-opportunity/.

CEPAL, United Nations (2012) Press release: Social panorama of Latin America 2012, obtained from http://www.eclac.org/cgibin/getProd.asp?xml=/prensa/noticias/comunicados/9/48459/P48459.xml&xsl=/prensa/tpl-i/p6f.xsl&base=/prensa/tpl/top-bottom.xslt.

Corruptions Perceptions Index (n.d.) Transparency International, obtained from http://www.transparency.org/research/cpi/overview.

Ease of Doing Business Index (2013) World Bank, obtained from http://www.doingbusiness.org/rankings.

Economist, The (2012) The discontents of progress, obtained from http://www.economist.com/node/21534798.

Freedom House (2012) Freedom in the world 2012, online database, obtained from http://www.freedom-house.org/.

Freedom in the World (n.d.) Freedom House, obtained from http://www.freedomhouse.org/.

Fund for Peace (n.d.) Failed States Index, online database, obtained from http://ffp.statesindex.org/.

Global Competitiveness Index (2012–2013). World Economic Forum.

Heritage Foundation (n.d.) Index of economic liberty, online database, obtained from http://www.heritage.org/index/.

Human Development Index (2013) United Nations, obtained from http://hdr.undp.org/en/statistics/hdi/.

Index of Democracy (2012) Economist Intelligence Unit, obtained from http://www.eiu.com/Handlers/WhitepaperHandler.ashx?fi=Democracy-Index-2012.pdf&mode=wp&campaignid=DemocracyIndex12.

International Monetary Fund (n.d.) World economic outlook, online database, obtained from http://datacatalog.worldbank.org/.

KOF Index of Globalization (n.d.) Obtained from http://globalization.kof.ethz.ch/.

Latinobarómetro Corporation (n.d.) Latinobarómetro, online database, obtained from http://www.latino-barometro.org/latino/LATAnalizeSample.jsp.

Londoño, J. L. and Guerrero, R. (1999) *Violencia en América latina, epidemiología y costos*. Washington: BID.

Brombacher, D. and Maihold, G. (2009) The transatlantic cocaine business: Europe's options as it confronts new drug trafficking routes (WP). Real Instituto Elcano working paper, 14 December.

Transparency International (2012) Corruption perceptions index, online database, obtained from http://www.transparency.org/research/cpi/overview.

United Nations, ECLAC (2013) Social panorama of Latin America and the Caribbean. Santiago, Chile: United Nations.

United Nations (n.d.) Human development index, obtained from http://hdr.undp.org/en/statistics/hdi/.

World Bank (2011) *Crime and violence in Central America: A development challenge*. Washington, DC: World Bank.

World Bank (n.d.) World development indicators, online database, obtained from http://data.worldbank.org/data-catalog/world-development-indicators.

World Economic Forum (n.d.) Global competitiveness index, online database, obtained from http://www.weforum.org/.

7

ESTABLISHING BUSINESSES
IN LATIN AMERICA

INTRODUCTION

The Latin American economy is valued at 4.8 trillion dollars. This enormous market size, along with approximately 600 million citizens and an ever-increasing middle class has positioned Latin America as fertile environment for business development. While worldwide foreign direct investment (FDI) fell 18% in 2012, FDI in Latin America expanded by 7%. Countries like El Salvador, Peru, and Chile registered FDI investment of 34%, 48.7%, and 32.2% respectively (Winters, 2013). Clearly these statistics illustrate the great potential that exists for capable and interested investors.

This chapter focuses on the establishment of new business in Latin America. Its purpose is to define the strategies, the limitations, the opportunities, and the advantages of establishing a business in Latin America. Since Latin America has represented an important growth and an impressive recuperation since the economic crisis of 2009, it is common to hear about multinationals establishing in the region for expansion of new markets.

In this chapter the reader will be able to answer the following questions.

- What is a corporate strategy and how it is applied in Latin America?
- What are the new investment ventures in Latin America?
- How should a company handle a financial issue in Latin America?
- What are microcredits and how have they grown in the past years in the region?
- What is the situation in the physical infrastructure and how it affects supply chain?
- How should a manager manage the supply chain issues?
- What is the proper way to negotiate in Latin America?
- What is the best choice for establishing a new business venture?

CORPORATE STRATEGY IN LATIN AMERICA

Corporate strategy in Latin America has evolved depending on what the business is focused on. The business growth could be analyzed from 1983 onwards mainly because of the reduction in restrictions and the accumulation of debt in the governments (UNCTAD, 2007).

To understand corporate strategy one must understand the Latin American market. As McKinsey & Company (2011) reported, 315 million people would live in 198 large cities of Latin America by 2025, with a labor force of 50 million people, and a GDP growth of 3.8 trillion dollars.

America Economía (2011) divided the growing industries into petroleum production, technology, commerce, automobiles, steel, mining, and the gas industry. The reason for this division is that the Latin American market is very diverse, and its growth has been potentiated by market demands and FDI income.

Petroleum Production

Mexico, Venezuela, and Brazil direct this market with more than $325 million in sales. The corporate strategy has been to expand inside Latin America given the lack of offer worldwide. The creation of Petrocaribe—an agreement to give a preferential price to the countries that sign the agreement—stated a policy for Venezuela and PDVSA,[1] who developed a subsidiary based on the agreement, called PDV Caribe. The Petrocaribe agreement (2012) now provides petroleum for 18 different countries focused on Central America and the Caribbean islands.

Petrobras, the Brazilian petroleum company and leader in sales for Latin America, stated in the strategic plan 2020 that its focus is on the scale of prominence in biofuels, strength of peers, international presence, and commitment to sustainable development (Petrobras, 2009). The company's focus is on exploration and production, directing 79% of the international investments in the company to this sector seeking to lower production costs and incrementing the supply.

Pemex, the Mexican petroleum company, has taken a different route, focusing on the development of suppliers and contractors based on a policy of sustainability. Clean fuel has become a major strategy for the company based on the investment concerned in technology, which has created an important source of reducing costs and creating better efficiency.

Technology and Telecommunications

Technology has guided Latin America into the 21st century with important multinationals leading the list of top ten investors. Companies such as Telefónica and Google sum up to America Movil, Vivo, and Telesp to create a different industry characterized with different strategies.

America Movil, which during 2010 reported $44,220 million in sales with utilities adding up to $7,378 million, has become a reference in the communication industry. It controlled, by 2006, 70% of the Latin American market and has a strong influence in the AMXA index of Mexico. The strategy of America Movil has centered on a strong expansion and the acquisition of different companies concerning communication.

The recent permission to Costa Rica and the capacity of selling bonds through the Mexican Stock Market demonstrate why it has 211.3 million wireless subscribers, 24.7 million fixed lines, 12 million fixed broadband, and 8.6 million television subscribers (America Movil, 2011).

In the case of Telesp, the strategy is based on its nature as Telefónica's subsidiary in Brazil. Telesp has a regional strategy based on the plans of Telefónica, and expansion based on products focused on data, video, audio, and images. The Brazilian subsidiary reported 9,343 million in US dollars in 2010 and, in 2011, created a joint venture with AOL Latin America for media expansion.

Automobile Industry

In Latin America there are two countries that lead the automobile industry through the subsidiaries of General Motors, Ford Motor Company, Volkswagen, and Fiat: Mexico and Brazil.

The Mexican automobile industry is centered on General Motors and Ford Motor Company, which reported 21 million in US dollars in sales for 2010. Ford Motor Company bases its strategy on the principles of quality, clients, and continuing improvement in products, but also expansion on the Latin American market based on the diversity of the cars it offers. A similar strategy is that followed by General Motors, which is based on the multinational strategy, based on product quality and offering better options for the Latin American market.

The automobile industry in Brazil reports a more intensive market, with sales over 35 million US dollars during 2010. Fiat and General Motors focus the Brazilian automobile industry on providing neighbor countries.

Commerce Industry

The commerce industry in Latin America has to be divided in two: the e-commerce and the retail industries. Concerning e-commerce, growth has been linked with the telecommunications industry, which augmented the possibility of new consumers and the strategy of expansion based on these services. One company guiding this process is MercadoLibre. It has established itself in 14 different countries including the United States and Portugal. MercadoLibre is the largest platform for buying and selling through the internet in Latin America, which reported 85 million US dollars in 2007 and continued its growth after that (Forbes, 2008).

On the retail front, the retail industry is guided by different companies, including Wal-Mart (27 million US dollars in sales 2010), CBD (19 million US dollars in sales 2010), and Carrefour (14 million US dollars in sales 2010).

INVESTING IN NEW VENTURES

Latin American has not been stable during the past twenty years; the strategy has shifted since the civil war and Cold War conflicts started to diminish, and the political and economic strategies became important for the development of the countries.

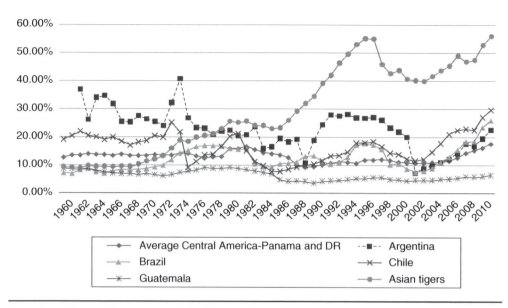

Figure 7.1 GDP per capita percentage of US GDP per capita

Source: World Bank 2011

The evolving strategies were guided by the economic growth of countries such as Chile, Brazil, and Argentina, which since 2002 have grown constantly and developed new markets. Colombia and Peru have experienced since the economic crisis a boost in their economy and they guide the markets through innovation in industries such as petrochemicals, energy, telecommunications, and retail. Figure 7.1 summarizes the per capita GDP.

When analyzing the fastest-growing companies in Latin America, Boston Consulting Group study took a sample from 2004–2009. This study found that the region was guided by Brazil (57%), followed by Chile, Mexico, and Colombia.

The industries vary but there is a tendency to establish businesses in communication, food processing, fuel and telecommunications, which has created a gap between these countries and the rest of Latin America. This shows the importance of the evolution of strategies, because small changes in the country strategy have shifted the economies to more productive states.

One important aspect is that technology has not been a main component of growth. The specialization in technology has been guided by the Asian Tigers. Meanwhile Latin American countries have been specializing in energy, retail, and food processing, which are main processes that in the 1980s were developed by those countries that changed their economic activity. The evolution of Latin America could be classified based on two main components: location and comparative costs.

Concerning location, Latin America is extremely close to the United States, making it a perfect destination for investments and the development of business ventures.

Table 7.1 Fastest-growing companies in Latin America

Company name	Country	Business
Molinos Rio de la Plata	Argentina	Food manufacturing and distribution
Alicorp	Peru	Food processing
Industrias CH	Mexico	Steel products
Randon SA	Brazil	Road and railroad load transport
Falabella	Chile	Retail centers
Grupo Nacional de Chocolates	Colombia	Food
America Movil	Mexico	Cellular telecommunications
Alpargatas	Brazil	Footwear, sporting goods, and textile
Petrobras	Brazil	Oil, gas, and energy
Vale	Brazil	Metals and mining
Compañía General de Electricidad	Chile	Energy
Companhia de Tecidos Norte	Brazil	Textiles
Weg	Brazil	Electric motors, power
CCR	Brazil	Highway concessions and inspections
TAM	Brazil	Passenger and cargo air transportation
Natura Cosméticos	Brazil	Fragrances and hygiene products
Cementos Argos	Colombia	Cement and concrete
Cencosud	Chile	Retailing, credit cards, and retail banking
Localiza Rent a Car	Brazil	Car rental
Minerva	Brazil	Food processing
Brasil Foods	Brazil	Food production
Mexichem	Mexico	Chemicals and petrochemicals
Marfrig Alimentos	Brazil	Meat and poultry processing
Ultrapar	Brazil	Fuel and chemicals
JBS	Brazil	Beef processing and export

Source: Boston Consulting Group (2009)

For example, it is quicker to fly from Buenos Aires to Miami than from Tokyo to Los Angeles, meaning that the longest flight from Latin America to the US is only 818.40 miles more than London, 704.76 more than from Madrid, and 643.32 more than from Paris. This comparison gives an interpretation of the proximity that Latin America has in comparison with other regions of the world.

For example Mexico is only 1,278.67 miles away from Miami and Medellin 1,348.40 miles. This added value in Latin America has led important companies such as Boeing (Brazil), Volkswagen (Mexico and Brazil), Ford (Mexico), Telefonica (Latin America), Microsoft (Argentina, Brazil, Chile, Mexico, and Colombia), McDonald's (Latin America), Kimberly Clark (Latin America), Accor (Brazil, Peru, Argentina, Chile, and Mexico), Oracle (Brazil, Costa Rica, Mexico, Puerto Rico, and Venezuela), and SC Johnson (Argentina, Brazil, Mexico, Uruguay, and Venezuela) to do business

Table 7.2 Strategic locations and distances

Flight distance

City	Destination	Miles
Buenos Aires	Miami	4321.29
Santiago de Chile	Miami	4056.75
Medellin	Miami	1348.40
Lima	Miami	2565.33
Mexico DF	Miami	1278.67
London	New York	3502.89
Madrid	New York	3616.53
Paris	New York	3677.97
Tokyo	Los Angeles	5506.76
Singapore	Los Angeles	8793.78

Source: World Atlas (2012)

in Latin America. A summary of strategic locations and their distances among Latin American countries is given in Table 7.2.

Comparative advantages have been centered in innovation and economic integration between South and Central America. Treaties such as NAFTA, CAFTA-DR, and Mercosur established a union in commerce between the countries and the United States. This integration also created important memberships, such as Caricom, which unites the Caribbean Community, SIECA, which united Central America, ALBA, which unites different South American countries and is led by Venezuelan Leader Hugo Chavez, and the SELA, which is the economic system for Latin America and the Caribbean.

The importance of these treaties is that they allow a more fluent economy and commerce between countries that gives as a result more flexibility and a wider expansion in the economies. For example, the Mercosur countries led in GDP growth from 2002 to 2011. Argentina had 6.70% growth, Uruguay 5.17%, Peru 4.82%, Colombia 3.48%, and Chile 3.35%. These statistics are based on data from the International Monetary Fund. Mercosur also helped to develop internal markets in Latin America, causing growth from 2002 to 2011 of 40 billion US dollars approximately, and with a considerable input to the world economy. Figure 7.2 outlines the details of the growth.

FINANCIAL ISSUES IN LATIN AMERICA

In financial issues, Latin America has been known for taking advantage of the global environment to become stronger in policy issues and, as a consequence of these actions, to lower long-term risk (Singh, 2008). Although Latin America started a deceleration in 2011, the financial markets continue to grow.

Mexico is one of the countries that is still growing financially because of the relation between its economy and the United States' industrial and monetary cycles.

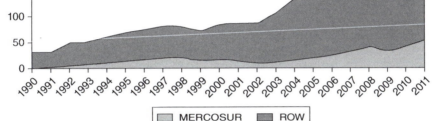

Figure 7.2 Exports to MERCOSUR and ROW

Source: UN Comtrade (2011)

In the case of Brazil, the financial markets have slowed down but they have had a sustained growth. Colombia, Chile, and Peru are expanding through commodities export. Venezuela and Argentina are the countries with lower growth based on the debt handling in the past year. Central America had sustainable growth because of the influence of the United States (Scotiabank, 2012).

When analyzing the financial markets, most countries with a stock exchange have been growing since 2009. In the case of the BOVESPA Index for Brazil, the lowest point was in 2008 when the movement in the stock was of only 30 million and, in 2013, the stock market was exchanging an average of 60 million, demonstrating an important improvement. The Chilean ISPSA Index also had a historical low in October 2008 when it traded a volume of 9 billion and actually, in 2013, the country was trading 32 billion. At the time of writing, the financial markets had reached stability, and were maintaining and attracting interesting investments for 2013.

Microfinance

Microfinance has been a model of growth for rural areas in Latin America. Microfinance projects started in the 1990s with the purpose of financing specific markets to expand growth. The main purpose of microfinance was to eradicate poverty, and to create a financial model that undermines risk and offers a better viability for a project. In Guatemala and Peru microfinance projects aimed their strategy at the sustainability of agricultural rural areas. In Guatemala, 81.7 million US dollars, an equivalent of 11.4% of Banrural's portfolio, is focused on agricultural operations and microfinances to develop. In Peru, the CMAC Sullana bank handles 11.6 million US dollars, which represents 15.2% of its portfolio for the development of rural areas (Wenner, 2007).

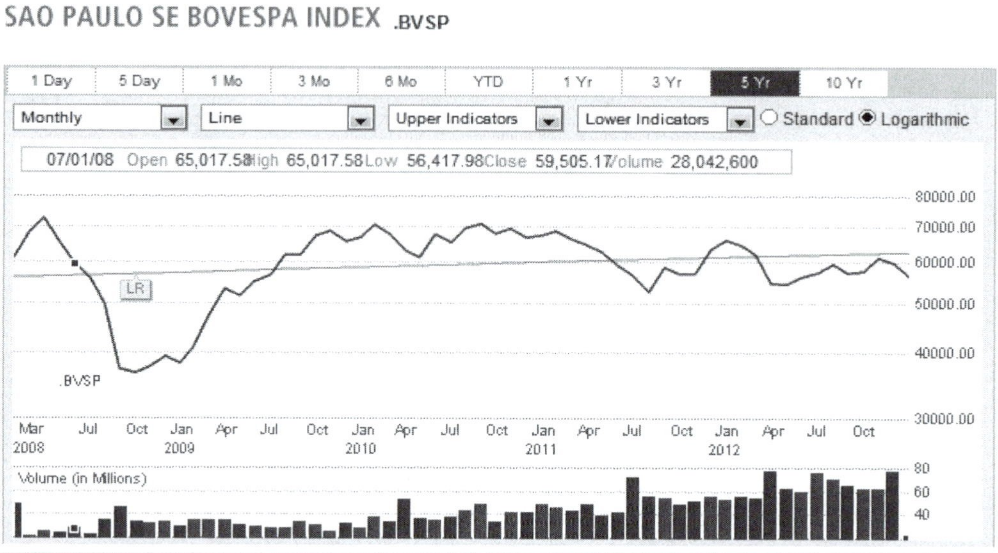

SAO PAULO SE BOVESPA INDEX .BVSP

Figure 7.3 BOVESPA index for Brazil

Source: Yahoo! Finance (2012)

The most important microfinance institutions in Latin America are listed below.

- CrediAmigo: a credit program offered by Banco do Nordeste do Brazil, which is the second largest microenterprise in Latin America
- Fundación para el Desarrollo Integral Espoir: one of the most efficient microfinance institutions and leaders in Ecuador; has a strong portfolio quality
- Pro Mujer: a program for women created in Bolivia, which combines efficacy with transparency
- Banco ADOPEM: bank created in Dominican Republic that has augmented the lending and deposit operations impressively in the past two years
- Banco Caja Social: concentrates on Colombian communities focusing on consumer credit; characterized by its impressive reach

DISTRIBUTION AND FOCUS: SUPPLY CHAIN MANAGEMENT ISSUES

The Supply Chain Council (SCC) establishes that the five biggest supply chain managements in the world are: (1) customer service; (2) cost control; (3) planning and risk management; (4) supplier/partner relationship management; and (5) talent (SCC, 2012).

In Latin America one of the major problems is the time it takes to reach a destination within the expected time. The best-ranked country according to the Logistics Performance Index of the World Bank (2012) is Chile, which is in position 39 of 155 countries. If Chile is analyzed based on timeliness, the country drops to rank 54, the category where Chile loses in comparison to other countries. Brazil is ranked 45 in the average but in timeliness it is ranked 49; Argentina is ranked 49 overall and its

Table 7.3 Top 20 microfinance institutions by deposits

Ranking						
2009	**2008**	**MFI**	**Country**	**Deposits Accounts**	**Deposits(US$)**	**General Trend**[†]
1	1	Banco Caja Social	Colombia	5,729,218	2,869,082,004	CNS
2	2	Caja Popular Mexicana	Mexico	3,514,028	1,449,700,914	CNS
3	3	Crediscotia	Peru	808,340	366,842,215	CNS
4	4	PRODEM FFP	Bolivia	569,829	338,991,459	MIC
5	n/a	COAC La Nacional	Ecuador	527,635	82,500,293	MIC
6	10	BancoEstado	Chile	503,682	425,261,602	MIC
7	4	Banco Los Andes ProCredit	Bolivia	381,416	415,389,164	MIC
8	6	CMAC Arequipa	Peru	340,367	346,762,116	MIC
9	9	BancoSol	Bolivia	333,488	342,864,051	MIC
10	7	Banco FIE	Bolivia	314,989	242,472,168	MIC
11	63	Banco ProCredit-El Salvador	El Salvador	301,135	202,470,700	MIC
12	11	MiBanco	Peru	223,862	849,069,550	MIC
13	7	Banco ProCredit-Nicaragua	Nicaragua	222,371	74,509,518	MIC
14	n/a	Comultrasan	Colombia	215,802	154,480,788	CNS
15	12	Banco ProCredit-Ecuador	Ecuador	202,245	179,393,791	MIC
16	n/a	CMAC Piura	Peru	197,999	383,530,084	MIC
17	n/a	CAME	Mexico	185,623	16,227,791	Only MIC
18	13	CMAC Cusco	Peru	184,863	205,664,273	MIC
19	19	Caja Nuestra Gente	Peru	166,075	149,005,966	MIC
20	n/a	Confiar	Colombia	162,596	108,904,363	CNS
Totals for 2008 (84 MFIs)				**14,376,679**	**9,537,606,293**	
Totals for 2008 (84 MFIs)				**18,167,731**	**12,400,989,369**	

n/a: Not available.

[†]By general trend is understood: MIC: Loans to microenterprise suepass 50% of toal loans. CNS: Consumer loans surpass 50% of toal loans.

*Only some MFIs supplied numbers for the volume of active loans and gross portfolio of loans.

timeliness rank places it in position 72. The comparison demonstrates that one of the supply chain management issues in Latin American countries is timeliness.

Central America has different challenges than just the time expected for a shipment. In Central America one of the major problems is road quality, which it grades in El Salvador as 4.8 over 10 and in Costa Rica as 2.5 over 10. Another problem is the road network, since only a few meters per square kilometer are paved roads. Nicaragua and Honduras represent an interesting case having an average of only 15 to 29 meters of paved road for each 131 to 159 meters. Figure 7.4 presents the roadwork density among Central American countries.

Table 7.4 Logistics performance index

Country	Year	LPI Rank	LPI Score	Customs	Infrastructure	International shipments	Logistics competence	Tracking & tracing	Timeliness
Chile	2012	39	3.17	3.11	3.18	3.06	3	3.22	3.47
Brazil	2012	45	3.13	2.51	3.07	3.12	3.12	3.42	3.55
Mexico	2012	47	3.06	2.63	3.03	3.07	3.02	3.15	3.47
Argentina	2012	49	3.05	2.45	2.94	3.33	2.95	3.3	3.27
Peru	2012	60	2.94	2.68	2.73	2.87	2.91	2.99	3.4
Panama	2012	61	2.93	2.56	2.94	2.76	2.84	3.01	3.47
Colombia	2012	64	2.87	2.65	2.72	2.76	2.95	2.66	3.45
Guatemala	2012	74	2.8	2.62	2.59	2.82	2.78	2.8	3.19
Ecuador	2012	79	2.76	2.36	2.62	2.86	2.65	2.58	3.42
Bahamas, The	2012	80	2.75	2.69	2.77	2.72	2.69	2.65	2.99
Costa Rica	2012	82	2.75	2.47	2.6	2.85	2.53	2.81	3.19
Dominican Republic	2012	85	2.7	2.53	2.61	2.83	2.74	2.49	2.97
Bolivia	2012	90	2.61	2.4	2.39	2.6	2.58	2.73	2.95
El Salvador	2012	93	2.6	2.28	2.46	2.57	2.6	2.6	3.08
Honduras	2012	105	2.53	2.39	2.35	2.7	2.44	2.35	2.9
Venezuela, RB	2012	111	2.49	2.1	2.17	2.54	2.33	2.57	3.18
Paraguay	2012	113	2.48	2.36	2.41	2.31	2.49	2.59	2.74
Jamaica	2012	124	2.42	2.22	2.27	2.43	2.21	2.43	2.91
Guyana	2012	133	2.33	2.29	2.15	2.35	2.33	2.14	2.67
Cuba	2012	144	2.2	2.18	2.08	2.12	2.21	2.26	2.31
Haiti	2012	153	2.03	1.78	1.78	1.94	1.74	2.15	2.74

Source: World Bank (2012)

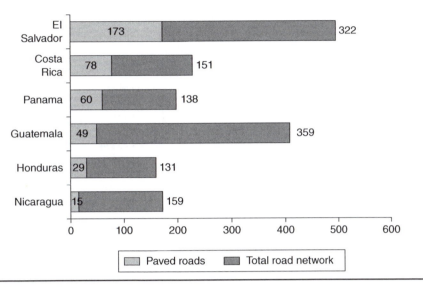

Figure 7.4 Road network density

Source: LCSSD Economics Unite, Optimal Path Analysis (2012)

The problem seems to be replicated in the port quality index and the linear shipping index in Central America. Panama and Guatemala are in the same category as Chile in terms of port quality infrastructure, but Honduras and Nicaragua are very behind these countries. Since commerce is developed as a region, this is an important challenge.

Two issues aggravate the supply chain management in Central America: (1) the cost of fuel and (2) the empty backhaul. Fuel is the major expenditure for trucking companies in Central America, followed only by labor. The cost of fuel is almost 50% of the total expenditure of a transport company, while security and insurance amount to an approximate 10%. The problem in Central America is aggravated when the cost of fuel rises, because this impacts directly on the trucking companies, creating a contraction of the supply.

The second problem is the empty backhauls in the region. Empty backhauls are all the transports that return to the country of origin without any merchandise, which means a lost cost. In this case Guatemala is the country that has most empty backhauls, followed by Panama, Nicaragua, and Costa Rica. For this reason logistical expenses in Central America are 36% of the total costs based on the final price of the merchandise (World Bank, 2012).

The most important aspect of the analysis is that Latin America is very diverse on the issues that are affecting the region. In the case of Central America there is an efficacy in some countries concerning ports, which is an efficacy in others concerning roads. In the case of South America the problem is that there are bottlenecks that lead to delays in the transfer of merchandise and a low rank in the Timeless index.

Supply Chain Issues

Mass merchandising has also created a large supply chain requirement that marketers must address (Becker, 2011). While countries in Latin America produce a wide variety of products, they have an underdeveloped supply chain management

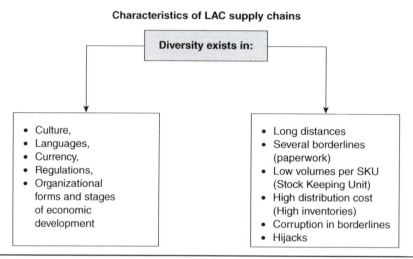

Figure 7.5 Characteristics of LAC supply chains
Source: University of Bayamon (2009)

(SCM) system. The significance of the supply chain is large since it stretches from small towns high in the Andean mountains to North America, Europe, and Asia. Different cultural traits among Latin American countries have an impact on a variety of SCM relationships. Supply chain challenges in Latin America are numerous and complex. Because the region has a number of internal vulnerabilities that hinder efforts to participate in global markets and influence supply chain decisions, it must strive to resolve these issues in order to make investment attractive.

Management of supply chains in Latin America is faced with a large assortment of logistically complex challenges. Bureaucratic and infrastructural hurdles impede the efficient and predictable flow of goods. Professionals need to invest time in logistics planning and better organizing inventories to deal with anticipated disruptions in supply chains. With experts expecting Latin American to experience a 6–8% growth in transportation, it would seem imperative to begin developing plans that would be able to address this growth in a timely fashion (Hestbaek and Cecolim, 2012).

Because of the existence of low-cost raw materials, and its ability to be a center for outsourcing, the region is fast becoming a significant player in the world economy. For this reason, Colombia presents significant opportunities for SMEs even though improvement in procedures and tools used in management of inventories is required.

In Argentina, there is a need for alignment among local businesses and suppliers' needs through the upgrading of technology.

Companies in Venezuela do not have leading-edge logistical tools and practices such as ERP systems. They could significantly benefit from outsourcing activities and opportunities.

In a high-context culture like Brazil there is a need for integration of material. For a long time it has been recognized that trust and long-term commitments are very important. Personal forms of contacts and maintenance of a relationship among suppliers are essential ingredients of the supply chain relationships in this country.

While logistical performance in Latin America is mixed, several items can increase improvement:

- Restructure customer procedures;
- Increase use of electronic filing;
- Security regulations and initiatives affect supply chain performance because of the history of corruption and drug trafficking, as such there needs to be major improvements in this area;
- Geographic obstacles need to be removed to the greatest extent possible. Countries in Latin America are investing heavily in infrastructure improvements and expanding export opportunities, which will resolve inadequate infrastructure and poor supply chain relationships that now exist in many Latin American countries. Additionally, with more utilization of privatized ports in Latin America primarily in Panama, Argentina, Mexico and Colombia significant opportunities are presented;
- Increased economic integration along with the implementation of risk assessment policies to reduce political risks that are found in a variety of locations among Latin American countries (Ruiz-Torres, Mahmoodi, and Ayala-Cruz, 2012).

Marketers operating in Latin America will face particularly difficult obstacles because the information they might want simply isn't there. Information about the country, locale, and region is in many cases difficult to obtain. Market studies are generally poor because Latin American businesses are loath to share information.

When traveling in just about any Latin American country one can experience, on main roads, substantially degraded infrastructure. Countries like Bolivia, Peru, Ecuador, Guatemala, Nicaragua, and Mexico all have significant infrastructure issues that many times can be barriers to investment in the regional areas of those countries. Generally, the major cities are in pretty good shape, but outside the major cities there is a different world for doing business, especially when supply chain activities are involved.

Concerning the growth in trade, physical infrastructure and supply chain management have become very important aspects when investing in a country. Latin America and the Caribbean have demonstrated, from 2005 to 2010, 88% of net growth in container traffic between ports.

With regard to the Global Competitive Index (GCI) infrastructure in Latin America, we can see it has an average score of 3.75 on a 10-point index. Mexico, Argentina, and Costa Rica rank as the best countries in terms of infrastructure, but the rank of these countries is between 75 and 79 on a 138-point index. The worst countries in terms of infrastructure in Latin America are Nicaragua, Paraguay, and Venezuela. Venezuela has had a setback over the past ten years because of lack of investment in this matter.

With reference to transport, the Latin American average score is 3.48. The best country in this category of transport is Mexico, with a rank of 57 out of 138. The rest of the countries rank very low, with Paraguay being the worst ranked in the list. Electricity and telephony are aspects that have improved with globalization and rank Latin America with a score of 4.01 out of 10, being led by Mexico, Argentina, and Costa Rica.

McKinsey established in 2007 the main supply chain risks in Latin America, and the concern of the investors when analyzing a strategy based on these issues. Risk reduction in Latin America focuses on performance contracts with suppliers and service providers. Specifying this element into contracts is one way to minimize, if not eliminate, the risk. The second decision to minimize risk is to avoid the redundant suppliers and product designers that create bottlenecks, and in a financial aspect to use currency hedges to minimize economic impact.

A total of 24% of the Latin American organizations surveyed do not use formal methods to assess risk in supply chain management. This can be ascertained from the GCI index and the problems that Latin America is facing in this issue.

NEGOTIATION IN LATIN AMERICA

Understanding negotiation partners is as important as understanding cultural dimensions. Geert Hofstede (2011) established that there are four important aspects for understanding cultural dimensions: power distance, individualism, masculinity, and uncertainty avoidance.

The uncertainty avoidance index explains how tolerant a society is with regard to uncertainty. In the case of Latin America, the ranking is 80/100, which means that the Latin American society has a low level of tolerance for uncertainty. Concerning power distance, Latin America has a rank of 70/100, which explains that there is inequality in society, and that opportunity is not stressed as a feature that each country should have. Masculinity, which is related to discrimination between genders, ranks 48/100, which indicates that there is some discrimination in the countries, but that this is not pre-eminent. Latin American society is collectivist and not individualist, as its ranking of 15/100 shows, which means that its peoples prefer working in groups.

The description above gives an understanding of culture in Latin America, which could be described as intolerant to uncertainty, socially unequal, and with some discrimination between genders and collectivists.

Cross-cultural negotiations consider the cultural dimensions when trying to understand how to achieve a win-win negotiated settlement. Negotiations in Latin America are influenced by social factors such as trust and respect. As mentioned earlier, in Latin America family and society relationships are very important. As such, negotiation could take place in a business environment or in a social environment such as a restaurant or the house of one of the negotiators (Inbel, 2011).

Latin America is a culture that values presentation when negotiating. It is important to be prepared when participating in negotiations. Basically, that means making sure your wardrobe is appropriate and that the person you are negotiating with is at the same level as you. Being in the same position businesswise is very important because it shows respect and commitment to what you are negotiating. It is important to take this into account because, if you send the wrong person (i.e. a person at a lower level than the person with whom you are negotiating), the negotiation is likely to fail.

Table 7.5 Infrastructure 2010–2011: Latin America and the Caribbean, and selected comparators

Country/Economy	Infrastructure 2010–2011		A. Transport		B. Electricity and telephony	
	Rank	Score	Rank	Score	Rank	Score
Hong Kong SAR	1	6.77	1	6.69	1	6.85
Korea, Rep.	18	5.59	12	5.73	30	5.44
Barbados	23	5.37	29	4.82	15	5.93
Chile	40	4.69	37	4.56	48	4.83
Panama	44	4.53	46	4.15	44	4.92
Trinidad and Tobago	45	4.53	58	3.94	38	5.12
China	50	4.44	31	4.73	69	4.14
Uruguay	53	4.29	75	3.54	42	5.03
El Salvador	59	4.13	66	3.78	56	4.49
BRIC average	n/a	4.10	n/a	4.27	n/a	3.93
Brazil	62	4.02	67	3.76	65	4.28
Jamaica	65	3.91	51	4.05	86	3.76
Guatemala	66	3.9	76	3.48	64	4.31
Latin America and Caribbean average	n/a	3.75	n/a	3.48	n/a	4.01
Mexico	75	3.74	57	3.96	92	3.51
Argentina	77	3.63	89	3.17	73	4.08
Costa Rica	78	3.62	111	2.78	59	4.45
Colombia	79	3.59	101	2.94	68	4.24
Honduras	85	3.51	82	3.30	88	3.73
India	86	3.49	39	4.50	115	2.49
Peru	88	3.47	94	3.08	84	3.86
Ecuador	96	3.18	99	2.96	95	3.39
Bolivia	100	3.04	122	2.59	94	3.49
Guyana	103	2.92	100	2.95	102	2.90
Dominican Republic	107	2.83	79	3.38	121	2.28
Venezuela	108	2.82	123	2.58	98	3.06
Nicaragua	111	2.73	102	2.90	112	2.55
Paraguay	125	2.46	139	2.10	104	2.82

Source: World Economic Forum (2011)

Another aspect of Latin American negotiations is punctuality. This feature is not the most important for Latin American culture, since they value more being prepared and dressed for the occasion than being at a meeting at a specific time. Although European cultures value punctuality, in the case of Latin America it is not as important, so if the person you are negotiating with is late, do not take it as an act of disrespect.

Hand gestures in Latin America are very common, specifically when negotiating. It is very important to focus on the kinesics of the person with whom you are negotiating since their body language will tell you what the negotiator is trying to say even if the words do not match the body language. It is very important to start the negotiation with a strong handshake and by looking into the eyes of your counter-part—this is a gesture of respect.

Eye contact throughout the negotiation is very important because it shows you are paying attention to the conversation and that you are aware of what the person is talking about. It is convenient to use appropriate hand gestures such as open palms, because these will let the negotiation flow based on the expression of body language. Always use body language that leads to a further negotiation and not body language that closes a negotiation.

MAKING THE CHOICE

To make a choice in Latin America, the first step is to accept that, in the region, every country is as different in its capabilities as in its weaknesses. In Central America, a considerably small region, the decision to establish a new business venture in Guatemala could be settled by the proximity with Mexico and the United States, but there are weaknesses such as violence and uncertainty that affect the country. If you want to choose El Salvador it could be because the country is dollarized, which makes transactions easier, but if you want to choose Costa Rica you might base your choice on the size of the middle class.

South America is similar to Central America in these scenarios. Venezuela has been politically unstable in the past ten years, but investments concerning oil and gas have augmented considerably, although when making an oil investment in Venezuela, the government of Venezuela owns 60% of the business (Embassy of the Kingdom of the Netherlands in Venezuela, 2011). Argentina has had difficult economic circumstances, which have affected investments, and Chile has remained stable since the 2000s, which makes it evident that Latin America is a region of contrasts.

When making a choice, take into account the product that you are introducing to the region or the investment you are planning to make. The main problems when investing in Latin America could be summed up as follows: lack of knowledge of the market, and logistical problems. In terms of the first problem, company managers could enlighten themselves by asking questions such as those listed below.

- Why am I entering the market?
- If I am entering the market to expand to other countries, do I know about the Free Trade Agreements?
- What is the economic and social situation in the country I am planning to enter?
- What logistical problems am I going to face?

These questions are important because they help to establish the opportunities and the issues around entering Latin America. To make an efficient choice, one has to analyze, along with the information offered, the type of business that the company is going to develop or how the business in going to tackle the various challenges.

Based on these issues, we interviewed the CEO of one of the fastest-growing companies in the food industry in Latin America, Pollo Campero. Pollo Campero registered 300 million in US dollars in revenues in 2006, and was present in the US, Latin America, Europe, and Asia (Hispanic Business, 2007). Once a company has made the choice to enter the market then it needs to understand the legal systems as they are presented in Latin America.

Legal Systems in Latin America

Legal systems in Latin America are mostly based on the civil law code, which is influenced in most countries, with the exception of Brazil, by the Spanish legal tradition. Some countries in Latin America, such as Argentina, have been influenced by the Spanish, French, and Italian legal systems, which can make an important difference between Latin American countries. The legal systems often act under no "stare decisis," which is a legal principle for judges to respect prior established decisions. In the case of Latin America, prior decisions are important but they can be changed (Peoples, 2004).

Central America is ruled by the civil law in most countries except for Belize, which is guided by the common law. South America is also ruled by the civil law, with the exception of Guyana and Suriname, which are ruled by the common law. The countries ruled by civil law were inspired by Roman law and are focused on traditional law. One example of traditional law is, in Peru, when you offer a compensation package or a Christmas present for three consecutive years, it becomes law and has to be applied in every subsequent year.

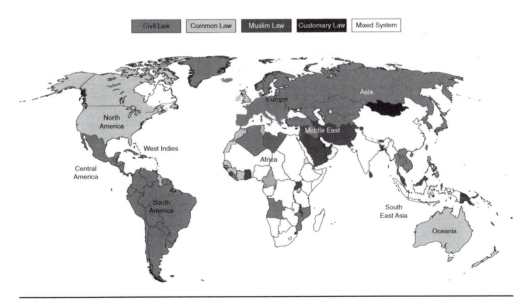

Figure 7.6 Types of world legal system

Source: University of Ottawa (2012)

Another important aspect to consider is the language that the law will be discussed in and how the contracts are going to be enforced. Concerning the language, almost all countries in Latin America have legal problems resolved in Spanish; the exceptions are the following countries: Belize resolves in English, Brazil resolves in Portuguese, French Guyana resolves in French, and Suriname resolves in Dutch.

Business Contracts

Concerning the formation of legal contracts in Latin America, Ferrari (1994) establishes the following common ground when enforcing contracts in Latin America.

- Contracts
  - All legal systems in Latin America require a consent or agreement from the parties as a manifestation of mutual assent. The consent must be effective and enforceable. The agreement must be free from illegality, fraud, and other defects that can affect the parties.
  - An agreement will exist when there is a complete coincidence between the parties and the will of enforcing the contracts.
  - There is not an established amount of time between the offer and the acceptance.
  - A contract can be acceptable if the person is not present but he is negotiating by telephone or any other means, but it is valid only if the person negotiating the deal is operating the machine personally.
  - South American systems allow the parties to reach an agreement expressly or implicitly, which means that an agreement manifested by words is as acceptable as an agreement manifested by a signature.
  - A tacit agreement or implied agreement is accepted when the conduct or acts of the person negotiating presume an agreement.
  - Most contracts are handled by offer and acceptance, which means that the acceptance of an agreement may vary from the offer; if a declaration of will exists to bind the contract, then the offer is taken as an expression of interest.

- Offer
  - An offer is considered definite as long as it includes all the terms that have been negotiated and there will be no modification further on.
  - The revocability of an offer should be stated in the document negotiated. If a document is negotiated irrevocably, then it cannot be revocable. The same circumstance applies if the document has been negotiated to be revoked, it can be revoked.
  - Brazil, Colombia, and Peru adopted a German rule, which states that an offer is irrevocable in a specific period of time, if it is specified, or in a reasonable limit of time, if it is not specified.

- Acceptance
  - Most South American legal systems state that acceptance of an offer cannot be inferred by silence.

- o The acceptance of the offer can be taken as valid if the person has accepted the same terms as the ones presented in the last offer or in the definite offer.
- o The time limit for an offer is presented by the offeror; the time limit expressed in the offer should be respected. If the offeror did not state a time limit, the courts will determine a reasonable timing for the offer.
- o Late acceptance constitutes a new offer in Argentina, Peru, Colombia, and Brazil, which are inspired by a German law. In Venezuela and Uruguay a late acceptance is acceptable when the offeror agrees to it.

- Conclusion of contracts

  - o The conclusion of a contract can be handled by four different theories of declaration, expedition, reception and information.
  - o Declaration sends a contract when there is a declaration of acceptance concerning the terms offered. Chile and Peru have this system.
  - o The theory of expedition focuses on when the contract is sent to the persons that have signed a copy.
  - o Reception theory focuses on when the contract has been formally received and accepted.
  - o The information theory is when the offeror takes notice of the acceptance concerning the offer.

A final issue to consider regarding legal systems in Latin America relates to the informal system. The informal system remains outside the government apparatus and is usually complex. Communities and the absence of state usually create informal systems (Barton, 2004) to conduct business. In these cases an agreement can be made outside the law when negotiating with communities in Latin America.

Employment Contracts and Agreements

An area of business that is critically important for business functioning is employment contracts and employment arrangements. Since human resources are critical to the success of any business, it is important for businesses to create an employment environment that is conducive to recruiting competent and high-quality management talent. While there has been a tradition of hiring people associated with a family or selected groups, changes have occurred in Latin America that are more relevant to business success. In order to survive in business it is necessary to recruit talent that will meet the needs of the business and allow it to achieve its goals. As such, Latin American companies have changed their approaches to recruiting and hiring human resources. Contracts and employment agreements have become part of the process. These new arrangements have given the businesses another avenue for aligning human resources with the needs of the business. Several reasons exist for the change in contract and agreement development among countries in Latin America. Several economic crises in Mexico and Argentina have led to a clearer understanding among companies of how to hire human resources. Latin America businesses have developed a more comprehensive perspective on contract and agreement strategy with regard to hiring talent.

Table 7.6 Leave of absence and vacations in Argentina

The Employment Contract Law prescribes the following general rules regarding

A. <u>Paid leave of absence</u>: (Argentina)

   (i)   Birth of employee's child: two (2) calendar days;
   (ii)   Marriage: ten (10) calendar days;
   (iii) Death of the spouse or concubine, children, father, or mother: three (3) calendar days;
   (iv)   Death of a brother or sister: one (1) calendar day; and
   (v)   Examination at a high school or university: two (2) calendar days per examination, with a maximum of ten (10) calendar years per hour.

B. <u>Vacations</u>

Employees are entitled to a minimum and continued period of paid annual

Vacations of:

   (i)   14 calendar days when seniority does not exceed five years;
   (ii)   21 calendar days when seniority is between five and 10 years;
   (iii) 28 calendar days when seniority is between 10 and 20 years; and
   (iv)   35 days when seniority exceeds 20 years.

Source: Baker and McKenzie (2008)

Essentially, there are two types of hiring method that are common in Latin America. The first is known as a regular employment, which establishes an indefinite term for the employment contract. One aspect of this employment arrangement is that, in some Latin American countries, the regular employment contract could have benefits or not, depending on the type of business. Some countries in Central America have a similar employment system, which could include benefits such as social security and recreation, while the other regular employment may be seen as an "indefinite consultancy" that does not include benefits.

An important element of these employment contracts is that they include a trial period, which is usually three months. This trial period is to help the company find out if the person hired is able to perform the job. If and when the person is not able to perform the job, the company gives fifteen days' notice that the person will not be hired after the three months.

The second type of contract is a fixed term. The fixed term establishes a length for the person hired that may vary from one year to three. The fixed-term contract could include benefits but this is not mandatory, since the figure of fixed term is used for consultancies.

Another aspect important in contracts is working hours. Working hours are recognized to be eight hours per day, and normally work schedules are from 8:00 a.m. to 5:00 p.m., not counting the hour for lunch. The time of entrance may vary from company to company, depending on which sector they work in. Also, other companies include the lunch hour in the working hours. It is very common that, after eight hours of work, the rate per hour goes up, as this is considered as "working after hours." This is in long-term contracts. The limit of extra hours per month is 30 hours at the most, or 200 hours per year.

Table 7.7 Enforcing contracts

Economy	Enforcing contracts
Argentina	1
Nicaragua	2
Chile	3
El Salvador	4
Antigua and Barbuda	5
Guyana	6
Mexico	7
Venezuela, RB	8
Dominican Republic	9
Guatemala	10
Haiti	11
St. Vincent and the Grenadines	12
Ecuador	12
Puerto Rico (U.S.)	14
Uruguay	15
Barbados	16
Paraguay	17
Peru	18
Brazil	19
St. Kitts and Nevis	20
Bahamas, The	21
Panama	22
Costa Rica	23
Jamaica	24
Bolivia	25
Colombia	26
Grenada	27
St. Lucia	28
Belize	29
Dominica	30
Trinidad and Tobago	30
Honduras	32
Suriname	33

Source: World Bank (2012)

Another important factor relating to agreements and contracts in Latin America is the enforcement of contracts. According to the World Bank Doing Business report (2012), enforcing contracts measures the efficiency of the judicial systems focused on the resolution of commercial disputes. The enforcement of contracts is measured by the time, the cost, and the procedures that concern the resolution of the conflict.

Concerning this aspect, the Doing Business report establishes that, in Latin America, Argentina is the best country for enforcing contracts, and Suriname and Honduras the worst.

Argentina's process of enforcing a contract is 590 days, 150 for filing and service, 320 for trial and judgment, and 120 for enforcing the judgment. In comparison, Honduras has a process for enforcing contracts of 920 days, divided by 60 on filing and service, 680 on trial and judgment, and 180 on enforcing the judgment.

If we compare Argentina and Honduras to the US, which is ranked fourth in enforcing contracts, the duration of the enforcing of contracts is 370 days, divided into 30 days for filing and service, 240 for trial and judgment, and 100 for enforcement and judgment.

On a global perspective, the problem in Latin America is the duration of the process. East Asia and Pacific countries have an average for enforcing contracts of 522 days, Eastern Europe and Central Asia countries have an average of 414 days, the OECD high-income countries have an average of 510, and Latin America has an average of 727. If you compare Argentina to the average by country, it will be below average in all the aforementioned regions.

Latin America has only three more procedures than Eastern Europe, and the cost of the claim is cheaper only than East Asia, demonstrating that the problem of enforcing contracts in Latin America will be the duration of the enforcement.

An important issue to consider regarding contracts and agreement in Latin American countries is to remember that each country has its own legal system and procedures. One of the most recurrent problems in Latin America is the assumption that the legal system is the same in every country.

SUMMARY AND CONCLUSION

Latin America is a region of contrasts and, based on the contracts, there is an important opportunity for growth. Concerning new business ventures, there is a tendency to enter Latin American markets by M&A rather than greenfield projects; the reason for this is that it is advisable that a company has a partner in Latin America that understands the process because this will help that company acclimatize faster. M&A sales reached in 2010 the amount of 29,484 net million dollars and constituted 192 net purchases deals. The impact of this strategy justifies that it is a good business investment to consider a business partner with which to enter the market.

Considering that Latin America is one of the most attractive economies to target, expansion to the market is a must if a company is in need of new markets. Latin America is an adaptable but complicated region; adaptable because there are only two languages used in business there. These are Spanish and Portuguese in Brazil, but in every country the use of English for business transactions has become essential. As a result, adaptability to the market, the way of life, and doing business is certainly easier than in other regions.

The complicated characteristics of the region are the political and social circumstances that are present in the region. In this case the augmented violence in the region and drug trafficking have become major problems for Colombia, Central America, and Mexico. The political circumstances surrounding business could affect the process of doing business in Latin America; events like this happened with YPF in Argentina and Nestlé in Venezuela.

The problem in logistical issues is mostly based on the agencies that are improving by the year and that create an opportunity to do business more easily and with a more targeted agenda. In this case logistics is very important for developing business in Latin America because the biggest market is the middle class, which is interested in the price.

The existence of free trade agreements in the region have improved the Doing Business status in the region, and Latin America is getting more integrated, which means a great opportunity for creating businesses in the region. The capacity for multinationals to expand to the region has become apparent over the past years since the markets have become more accessible.

Concerning negotiations, the difference between the United States and Latin America is that business is often carried out over a meal, coffee, or a drink. It is usual to engage in a relationship with one's counterparts, and to continue a cordial relation into the near future.

Latin America is a region of contrasts and a region of opportunities. The importance thing is to find the balance between the country and the opportunities to create better investments.

NOTE

1.   PDVSA is one of the largest oil companies in Latin America. Its capital is owned by the government.

REFERENCES

America Economía (2011) Encuestas de negocios para América Latina. Obtained from http://mba.americae-conomia.com/biblioteca.

America Movil (2011) Relevant events, obtained from http://www.americamovil.com/amx/en/cm/about/events.html?p=28&s=38.

Baker & McKenzie (2008) Overview of Labor and employment law in Latin America, obtained from http://digitalcommons.ilr.cornell.edu/cgi/viewcontent.cgi?article=1047&context=lawfirms.

Barton, B. (2004) Informal legal systems in Latin America, obtained from the following address: http://lanic.utexas.edu/project/etext/llilas/ilassa/2004/barton.pdf.

Becker, T. H. (2011) *Doing business in Latin America* (2nd ed.). Westport, CT: Praeger.

Boston Consulting Group (2009) Latin America influential groups, obtained from http://www.thebostonconsultinggroup.es/documents/file15481.pdf.

Embassy of the Kingdom of the Netherlands in Venezuela (2011) Exports and imports concerning Latin America, obtained from http://paisesbajos.embajada.gob.ve/index.php?option=com_content&view=article&id=9&Itemid=13&lang=en.

Ferrari, F. (1994) Formation of contracts in South American legal systems. University of Loyola, obtained from http://digitalcommons.lmu.edu/cgi/viewcontent.cgi?article=1334&context=ilr.

Forbes (2008) Entrepreneurship in Argentina, obtained from http://www.forbes.com/2008/03/21/mitra-entrepreneur-argentina-tech-ebiz-cx_sm_0321mitra.html.

Hestbaek, P. (Senior Vice President) and Cecolim, A. (Managing Director) (2102) *Latin Trade*: Special supplement: logistics. *Latin Trade*, January/February, obtained from https://www.google.com/#q=Cecolim+and+Hestbaek,+2012&spell=1.

Hispanic Business (2007) Pollo Campero expanding footprint in the US, obtained from http://www.hispanicbusiness.com/2007/5/21/pollo_campero_expanding_footprint_in_us.htm.

Hofstede, G. (2011) Dimensionalizing cultures: The Hofstede model in context, Article 8, Universities of Maastricht and Tilburg, Netherlands, hofstede@bart.nl, obtained from http://scholarworks.gvsu.edu/cgi/viewcontent.cgi?article=1014&context=orpc.

Inbel (2011) Tips for negotiations with Latin American business partners. Interview with Gerardo Müller Albán, CEO of INBEL (Intercultural Business Euro Latin, www.inbel.eu) on the differences between Germans and Latin Americans in business, obtained from http://www.inbel.eu/download/Local%20Global%20Interview%20Inbel%20Müller%20Alban.pdf.

LCSSD Economics Unite, Optimal Path Analysis (2012) Competitiveness report for Central America, obtained from http://www-wds.worldbank.org/external/default/WDSContentServer/WDSP/IB/2013/02/05/000333037_20130205101024/Rendered/PDF/750980WP0Logis00Box374299B00PUBLIC0.pdf.

McKinsey (2011) Building globally competitive cities, obtained from http://www.mckinsey.com/mgi/publications/Building_globally_competitive_cities/PDFs/MGI_Latin_America.pdf.

Peoples, L. (2004) A legal and cultural primer. Oklahoma City University, obtained from http://www2.okcu.edu/law/lawlib/pdfs/guide_summerabroad_000.pdf.

Petrobras (2009) Petrobras strategic and business plan, obtained from http://trade.gov/td/energy/PETROBRAS%20Strategic%20&%20Business%20Plan%202009-2013%20OTC%2020091.pdf.

Petrocaribe (2012) Energia para la Unión, obtained from http://www.petrocaribe.org/.

Ruiz-Torres, A. J., Mahmoodi, F., and Ayala-Cruz, J. (2012) Supply chain management research in Latin America: A review. *Supply Chain Forum: An International Journal, 13* (1), 20–36.

Scotiabank (2012) Latin America regional outlook, obtained from http://www.gbm.scotiabank.com/English/bns_econ/latin.pdf.

Singh, A. (2008) The financial market crisis and risk for Latin America, obtained from http://www.imf.org/external/np/speeches/2008/031708a.htm.

UN Comtrade (2011) Mercosur data, obtained from http://comtrade.un.org/.

UNCTAD (2007) Foreign direct investment from Latin America and the Caribbean, obtained from http://www.unctad.org/en/docs/iteiit20071a2_en.pdf.

University of Bayamon (2009) Monitoring report, obtained from http://www.upr.edu/docs-ms/P-UPR-Bayamon-Monitoring-Report.pdf.

University of Ottawa (2012) World legal systems, obtained from http://www.juriglobe.ca/eng/index.php.

Wenner, M. (2007) Managing credit risk in rural financial institutions in Latin America, obtained from http://www.grade.org.pe/upload/publicaciones/archivo/download/pubs/ELLABRIEF_130131_ECO_Mic_BRIEF3.pdf.

Winters, R. (2013) Doing business in Latin America, obtained from http://www.industryweek.com/expansion-management/doing-business-latin-america.

World Atlas (2013) Flight distances; Travel distance calculator, obtained from http://www.worldatlas.com/aatlas/infopage/howfar.htm.

World Bank (2012) Doing business report, obtained from http://www.doingbusiness.org/data/exploretopics/enforcing-contracts/frontier.

World Economic Forum (2011) Global competitiveness report, obtained from http://www.weforum.org/issues/global-competitiveness.

Yahoo! Finance (2012) IBOVESPA index, obtained from http://es.finance.yahoo.com/q?s=%5EBVSP.

8

MARKETING TO LATIN AMERICAN CONSUMERS

OPENING CASE: CAMPERO

An Interview with the President and CEO of Pollo Campero

Pollo Campero is a very popular restaurant chain in Guatemala, Central America and around the world. It was created in 1971 when Dionisio Gutierrez, Sr. took advantage of the opportunity to develop a restaurant company, by leveraging the poultry business that his father, Juan Bautista Gutierrez, had established in the 1960s. As the company grew, in 1982, Juan José Gutierrez, his son, became president and leader of the company. In 1994, Pollo Campero developed a franchise concept and platform that enabled the brand to expand internationally. As such, the company now has restaurants beyond its base of operations in Guatemala with restaurants in El Salvador, USA, Spain, Italy, Ecuador, Honduras, the Middle East, and Indonesia. Juan José Gutierrez, Co-CEO of Corporacion Multi-Inversiones (CMI), the holding company that owns Pollo Campero, shares, in the following interview which took place on March 12, 2012, his experience at the helm of this Latin American multinational powerhouse.

Interviewer:	Mauricio Garita (MG)
Interviewee:	Juan José Gutierrez (JJG)
MG:	**What has been the biggest challenge that Pollo Campero has encountered when entering the Central American market and the South American market?**
JJG:	The biggest challenge that we confronted while expanding into new markets has been the creation of consumer relevant branding for Pollo Campero. Our company has developed and nurtured the preferred and loved Campero taste during the last forty years. During this time, the company has literally grown up with the families of Guatemala and El Salvador, and our guests, in turn, have been loyal to their preferences. As the years have passed, our clients have included us in their special family events and celebrations. We have become part of their family tradition and our brand has been woven into the fabric of their lives.

In contrast, when we enter new markets we do not have the same emotional link with the new guests, which is why our challenge is to position the brand with a relevant strategy for that new country. The branding strategy has to bring to life the unique and delicious flavor that Pollo Campero offers to every guest that experiences our brand in a new market. The Pollo Campero positioning is meant to be unique in each of the competitive markets we are entering.

Once the country strategy is defined, we amplify the brand experience through restaurant design, menu adaptation and merchandising, and country/market specific pricing. The menu includes traditional recipes from each of the countries we are aiming to enter. After this, we take on the daily challenge of differentiating a brand versus the competitive set of concepts and offerings in that market.

MG: **What has been the most important opportunity of the Central and South American markets?**

JJG: The Central and South American markets have much potential because they have a high consumption of chicken and a high affinity to fast food restaurant consumption.

Given the socioeconomic structure, the major potential resides with the middle class income segment. The challenge is to position the brand so that it is relevant and it offers a high-value proposition for those targeted consumers.

MG: **If you could start again the process of expansion, what changes to the Latin American strategy of expansion would you modify?**

JJG: The journey has been a very interesting and rich experience that made us stronger as a company. Looking back I would have changed the adaptation process of the Campero model in each country. The adaptation process would include a more rapid and better understanding of the local consumer, the competitive environment, and the definition of the Pollo Campero brand. In hindsight, this would have facilitated faster and more successful development in every country.

In addition, I believe that it is important to have the right partners for the venture in each new market. Partners that have the necessary skills for operating restaurants, the knowledge of the local supply chain, and the financial capability necessary to develop a brand in each market are most important.

MG: **What advice would you give to those who want to enter Latin America?**

JJG: Latin American markets are very challenging with demanding consumers and strong competitors. My advice will be that before venturing into Latin America one must do the upfront work to understand the local market, the consumer and the industry. After knowing this information, one can develop a clear proposal relevant to the guest and differentiated vs. the competitive set. This will lead to a successful business in the long run.

INTRODUCTION

The opening case in this chapter summarizes some of the primary issues business people should consider when thinking about doing business in Latin America.

Pollo Campero is a large multinational company, which uses market intelligence to monitor and forecast the trends, opportunities, weaknesses, and threats that exist in world and Latin American markets. The interview with CEO Juan Jose Gutierrez brings to light the importance of identifying critical advantages that would be immediately present when penetrating foreign markets (emotional links), as well as the need to adapt to local preferences, and, critically important, sourcing local partners. Such insights from key players on the Latin American business stage, if heeded, are invaluable for the development of practical business plans on how to do business in Latin America.

The issues discussed in this chapter relate to the general marketing environment in Latin America, the importance of market research, of intra-regional differences, the characteristics of Latin American consumers, and the marketing strategy.

This chapter will provide a general overview of the many topics that business people should focus on as they begin to consider the marketing strategies they could deploy in Latin America. It might strike you as a lot of preliminary work to be done to develop a brand strategy for every locale, as the Campero operation did in the course of its expansion path—and it is. However, it is better to be prepared rather than assume that market strategies that are fit for other regions will automatically work in Latin American markets. If you are interested in spotting the best marketing opportunities in Latin America, and identifying the optimal market penetration strategies, it is necessary to actively develop the appropriate, relevant marketing research which is defined as the "function that links an organization to its markets through the gathering of information." The information allows for the identification and definition of market-driven opportunities and problems. The information allows for the generation, refinement, and evaluation of marketing actions" (Hair, Bush, and Ortinau, 2003, p. 676). It is with this information that marketers are able to move forward and adapt their marketing strategies to the marketing environment that exists in the respective Latin American countries.

THE LATIN AMERICAN MARKETING ENVIRONMENT

For decades, Latin American consumers were isolated from the most important consumer markets in the world. This was due to a lack of appreciation of the benefits of free trade, which is discussed elsewhere in this book. With the liberalization of trade and the advent of globalization, import and export activity gave a huge boost to consumer consumption. As Latin American markets opened up for trade with the US and other advanced nations, consumer preferences began to hold sway. Consumption became a major economic force in Latin American countries, as consumers there became more sophisticated over time. This captured the attention of scholars as well as businesses all over the world.

A more detailed understanding of consumer markets in Latin America began to take hold at the end of the 1990s.[1] One of the first lessons to be learned was that, as a developing region, Latin America was subject to constant and dramatic changes. The dislocations and creative destruction that ensue from more efficient markets have had a tremendous impact on Latin American society and its consumptive patterns. Urban centers such as Mexico City, Buenos Aires, Argentina, Rio de Janeiro, Brazil, and Bogota, Colombia, have undergone substantial transformations, not the least of which is growth in size and expansion of business activity. Dramatic changes in how Latin American consumers buy goods and services ensued (i.e. use of technology in their buying activities) and a move away from solely using the central market. This is in part due to the fact that greater access to foreign goods had made Latin American consumers savvier and more exigent.

Greater competition from North American, European, and Asian firms has made Latin American businesses more efficient as well. Under freer trade regimes, the incentives for innovation and cost efficiency are simply that much greater. Success in business, therefore, is more difficult than ever in Latin America. However, it is also true that the potential payoffs to success in doing business in Latin America have increased substantially. Disposable incomes are greater than ever, especially among the burgeoning middle class. Given the constant state of flux encountered in Latin American consumer markets, success there will require companies to be constantly vigilant of not only rival competitors' business strategies, but also emerging consumer trends, as well as flexible and sensitive to consumer desires. Again, this is where market research pays off. As marketers better understand the new dynamics of foreign markets, they will be better equipped to address consumer concerns, desires, and needs (Cavazos-Arroyo and Gonzales Garcia, 2012).

Thanks to long delayed economic growth and prosperity, and the relative boom in the ranks of the middle class, the retail sector in Latin America has grown wide and deep. Just about every village, town and city will have some form of retail structure to provide the consumers of that area/region with the goods and services they need for daily living, and *want* for a better quality of life. Brazil ranks number one in the retail sector in terms of growth. Immediately following Brazil is Uruguay, a country not always on the radar of international investors. Thanks to the growth of the middle class, Peru and Chile are two Andean countries that have survived the recession better than most countries in Latin America. Peru, while still growing, has been able to attract some major retail investors into its formal market. The future prospects, moreover, are excellent, as a need has been identified for Peru to develop more retail space just to keep pace with growing consumer demand (A.T. Kearney, 2011). Consumer demand has registered stronger growth than anticipated. This has attracted the attention of foreign investors. For example, the Chilean mall operator, Plaza SA, has just opened its fourth mall in Peru (Bifani, 2012).

Chile has demonstrated great capabilities and a strong retail structure as well. A market-oriented business infrastructure has been established there that promotes, encourages, recruits, and sustains business development and marketing campaigns among new and established business. Several larger grocery retailers (Jumbos and Liders) are now present in Chile, and large fashion stores like Gap have decided to enter the Chilean market (A.T. Kearney, 2011).

Other countries, such as Mexico and Argentina, which once were considered less attractive, have caught the eye of risk-inclined retail investors. Mexico's large population and its significant middle class have been big drawing cards for large retail investors. This attraction, however, has been muted by the drug cartel violence that has scarred the country. Nonetheless, the fact that the Mexican middle class displays strong attraction to American brands is a powerful enticement to do business there.

Bolstered by state spending, Argentina has managed in recent years to sustain her short-term GDP growth and development. Political mismanagement of the economy aside, Argentina remains a large country filled with opportunities. With its 40.5 million population, and a large middle class, it has great potential for consumer-oriented businesses. Large retailers, such as Wal-Mart and Carrefour, have already taken notice and have demonstrated success in this country. Carrefour, Sodinas, and Payless Shoes have found Colombia to be an attractive destination. Even so, it cannot be denied that memories of the past drug cartel violence continue to plague Colombia's efforts to optimize its attraction of FDI, as some investors are still hesitant about making substantial investments there (A.T. Kearney, 2011).

Geographic considerations take on an important role in marketing in Latin America. The particular geography of disparate regions explains much of the different economic and social systems that have arisen in different parts of the Latin American region. For example, South America has many natural barriers that inhibit both national and regional integration, and therefore growth, trade, and communication. South America has a vast landmass with population concentrations on the outer periphery, and an isolated almost uninhabited interior. An example from Colombia makes the case. To get from Bogota to Medellin takes 30 minutes by air. To get there by land it takes 10–12 hours. The poor state of infrastructure not only retards commerce and communications, it can be life threatening (Cateora, Gilly, and Graham, 2009). These types of geographical constraint will rightly significantly influence the choice of marketing and distribution channels used to get products and services to market.

Despite the developmental challenges and institutional obstacles to optimal trade conditions in Latin America, the region has much improved, and the trend line is positive for the foreseeable future. Overall, on the GRDI scale, Brazil and Chile are on the world's top ten lists for retail development. This does not mean that other countries in Latin America are not good destinations, it only means that, when compared to other world location opportunities, these countries present, now, the best opportunities when looking at economic growth and country risk factors (A.T. Kearney, 2011).

MARKET RESEARCH IN LATIN AMERICA

Earlier in this chapter we discussed the definition of marketing research. In summary it is a systematic collection of market intelligence that provides the information for marketing decision making. Inasmuch as market research is essential for the success of any marketing plan and strategy, it behooves any interested business person to first do comprehensive market research before venturing into the Latin

American business arena. It may sound trite, but market research acquires special importance in Latin America. As discussed elsewhere in this book, most Latin American countries are characterized by what is known as a *high-context culture*.[2] This type of cultural trait can have important business consequences. As a result of its uniquely high-context culture, marketing in Latin American is often based on the notion of relationship marketing of the type touched upon in the opening case of this chapter.[3]

Relationship marketing, of course, aims to establish an emotional connection with customers. The focus is on developing and maintaining a relationship with clients so that they become repeat customers. This process of developing the relationship in Latin America may require making some adaptations to the brand strategy that one might originally have had in mind for market in North America, for instance. Sustaining the long-term relationship with local customers requires the proper tailoring of the brand strategy to the particular Latin American markets being considered. For this to work, the peculiarities and preferences of the particular Latin American consumer must be researched and, ultimately, understood.

Prior success is no predictor of profitability in Latin American markets. This is perhaps best exemplified by the failure of Carrefour in Chile. Despite its past successes at penetrating foreign markets, Carrefour notably did not succeed in this highly complex market. Since it performed below its target market share of 2.7%, it decided to leave and move on to other markets. Home Depot and J.C. Penney also failed in Chile because of intense local competition and the loyalty of the traditional customers found in the communities where these large, multinational companies located (Farfan, 2010). Diligent market research will uncover the prevailing opportunities and obstacles to your business success in Latin America.

If sound market research doesn't underpin your strategy of expansion in Latin America, you will most likely fail. In any market, the need for accurate research is essential in order to make appropriate business decisions, from the types of customers the firm will want, target markets, and product acceptability, to strategies of promotion and growth. The diversity and richness of Latin American markets makes these lessons all the more applicable. Failure to complete marketing research will almost certainly lead to poor decisions and a serious misallocation of resources, as well the failure to identify great opportunities.

Market research generally begins with the basic demographic variables. Table 8.1 shows the important demographic indicators for market research in Latin America: gender and population age structure. Reviewing the table will give you a view of the demographic profile of sixteen major Latin American countries.

Table 8.1 summarizes the breakdown of populations for 16 major countries in Latin America. Analyzing the specific details reveals that most of the potential consumers in this arena are women aged between 15 and 64 years. Of the 16 countries, 13, or 87%, have a population in this age category. This indicates to potential marketers in Latin America that they must focus their marketing campaigns and strategies towards this cohort of people. The information from this will determine what types of goods (i.e. fashions, household goods, cosmetics, and other young and older types

Table 8.1 Latin America, specific country populations as of 2010

Country	Total	Male	Female	0–14	15–64	65+
Argentina	40,666	49%	51%	25%	64%	11%
Bolivia	10,031	50%	50%	36%	59%	5%
Brazil	190,657	49%	51%	26%	68%	7%
Chile	17,135	49%	51%	22%	68%	9%
Colombia	46,300	49%	51%	29%	66%	6%
Costa Rica	4,640	51%	49%	25%	68%	6%
Ecuador	13,775	50%	50%	31%	63%	7%
El Salvador	6,194	47%	53%	32%	61%	7%
Guatemala	14,377	49%	51%	42%	54%	4%
Honduras	7,616	50%	50%	37%	59%	4%
Mexico	108,997	49%	51%	28%	66%	7%
Nicaragua	5,822	49%	51%	35%	61%	5%
Paraguay	6,460	50%	50%	34%	61%	5%
Peru	29,403	50%	50%	30%	64%	6%
Uruguay	3,374	48%	52%	23%	64%	14%
Venezuela	29,044	50%	50%	29%	65%	6%

Source: Authors' calculations based on Euromonitor (2010)

of products) can be marketed to this large female group. Marketers have to think about products, services, and brands that are popular among this large female population. Similarly, the male group is not far behind in its composition, so marketers can also divide their product and promotional positioning towards this group. Both populations have great potential and the longevity of the attraction is substantial. From another viewpoint, we see two countries, Argentina and Uruguay, manifesting a growing elderly population. This also offers marketing opportunities, albeit with different products, different income levels, and for probably a shorter period of time. Smart marketing among these three segments of the market can provide major success for those firms interested in these target markets.

Marketing research in Latin America may extend beyond the conventional methodology, and take on a clearly political dimension that would otherwise be absent in a setting like North America. In Venezuela, for example, President Hugo Chavez has intervened on a variety of occasions to change the direction of business. The socialist political philosophy of the government, that socialism is better than free enterprise, is becoming an obstacle to the production, marketing, and sale of goods and services. This is a serious challenge for business investors who might otherwise be interested in marketing their products in this country. Given the menacing spread of pseudo-socialist governments in countries like Venezuela, Ecuador, Bolivia, Nicaragua, and, increasingly, Argentina, the political philosophy of the governing powers needs to be considered when considering doing business in Latin America.[4] The uncertainty of government intervention is a major issue that marketers have to study and be ready for if they are going to market to these Latin American countries.

REGIONAL MARKETING IN LATIN AMERICA

Regional marketing relates to a variety of marketing functions that are directed at achieving marketing goals in a geographic region of a country or a much larger area that may include several countries. Regional marketing involves the application of basic marketing techniques and tactics to successfully promote and market products and services within a region. Marketers may segment geographic regions because one is richer or poorer than another. The products they sell and the brand strategy they use may appeal to one of these two segments. An example of this in the Latin American setting would be marketing to an urban versus a rural population. Given the considerable social, economic, and cultural differences that exist along the urban–rural divide in Latin America, consideration of this marketing tactic makes sense. Peru is a prime example of this. In Peru, much of the consumer activity is among the rural population. Lima, on the other hand, is the largest urban center. It has many modern amenities that would be seen in an advanced Western country. Marketing strategies designed to penetrate Peruvian urban markets would almost certainly confront serious obstacles in that country's rural settings.

The Latin American Middle-Class Consumer

The reader should know that the term "middle class" has a different connotation in Latin America than in North America or Europe. When official government bodies in Latin America refer to "middle class," they are referring to a section of the population that has extricated itself from poverty, yet does not have all of the characteristics of well-to-do citizens. As indicated elsewhere in this book, people earning between $10 and $50 per day comprise the Latin American middle class. As such, the middle class, in the sense described here, remains susceptible to economic problems and crises, more so than their developed world counterparts (World Bank, 2013).

The purchasing power of the middle class has increased the growth of and demand for goods and services. Figure 8.1 provides projections of increases in per capita GDP out into the future. These data reveal the significant impact that middle class spending and consumption will have on many Latin American economies.

This graph illustrates the relationship in per capita GDP for respective countries. Clearly there is an upward movement among all of the countries. This should be a harbinger for future marketing opportunities for interested marketers.

It is not the general rule that members of the Latin American class hold a college degree. On a broad level, the Latin American middle class enjoys less stable employment, and remains a significant distance from being comfortable in its socioeconomic status. Lack of educational achievement comparable to that achieved by the American middle class makes threats to economic status particularly persistent.

Despite the huge surge in the middle class which has taken place over the last decade, Latin America still has only four countries possessing what can be regarded as a large middle class, as a percentage of the overall population. These are Argentina (52.9%), Costa Rica (51.8%), Mexico (60.1%), and Uruguay (55.8%). In sheer

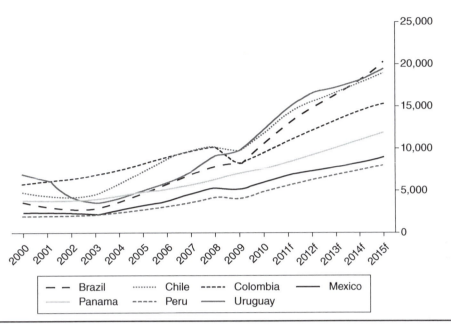

Figure 8.1 Latin America, GDP per capita for selected economies, US dollars

Source: Plenty More Wealth to Come (2011)

numbers, however, the greatest increase in the middle class has taken place in Brazil.[5] Based on recent statistics, 61 million Brazilians can be classified as middle class. In total, the Latin American middle class increased by 56 million from 1999 to 2011 (MercoPress, 2011).

Though the middle class in Latin America is not yet as large as it could be, in population percentage terms, the fact remains that it is growing rapidly, and so is its collective purchasing power. As the move of previously low-income groups to the middle class intensifies, the consumer needs of this emerging group are undergoing important changes. These changes can make the Latin American middle class different from the middle class in developed countries, i.e. Brazil, Peru, and Mexico, as they do not possess the same needs or emotional desires as developed-country consumers. Firms wanting to sell in emerging markets such as Latin America need to develop a value proposition tailored to the needs of this new population (Vassolo, De Castro, and Gomez-Mejia, 2011).

The Latin American middle class deserves the particular attention of would-be business practitioners, as it is playing a critical role in market development. The growth of the middle class in Latin America has had a major effect on the growth of markets and business opportunities, not just because of its growing size, but also on account of its inherent diversity. By all accounts, the Latin American middle class is a heterogeneous group. This market heterogeneity, in conjunction with growing disposable incomes, is what makes the middle class in the region a worthy target for those wishing to do business in Latin America. Brazil and Chile are two countries

Table 8.2 Largest cities in Latin America

City	Country	City population			
Buenos Aires	Argentina	11,655,100		3	1
Sao Paulo	Brazil	10,057,700		2	2
Mexico City	Mexico	8,589,600	11	1	3
Lima	Peru	7,603,500	19	6	4
Bogota	Colombia	6,680,500	22	5	5
Rio de Janeiro	Brazil	6,029,300	25	4	6
Santiago	Chile	5,034,500	27	7	7
Salvador	Brazil	2,539,500	75	14	8
Havana	Cuba	2,328,000	83	21	9
Belo Horizonte	Brazil	2,307,800	86	8	10
Fortaleza	Brazil	2,230,800	90	16	11
Cali	Colombia	2,203,800	91	18	12
Guayaquil	Ecuador	2,196,800	92	20	13
Brasilia	Brazil	2,089,500	99	24	14
Santo Domingo	Dominican Republic	2,061,200	100	19	15
Medellin	Colombia	1,932,400	105	15	16
Maracaibo	Venezuela	1,799,900	115	29	17
Guadalajara	Mexico	1,797,600	116	9	18
Caracas	Venezuela	1,763,100	119	11	19
Ecatepec	Mexico	1,688,600	122	36	20

Source: Butler (2009)

where incomes have been rising, economic development has been flourishing, and people are consuming at an increased rate.

The numbers bear out this argument. The present-day Latin American middle and upper class strata number about 120 million consumers. They spend close to $1.5 billion per year. Most of the members of this class are urban, and approximately 70% of them reside in the region's 20 largest cities. Table 8.2 presents the 20 largest cities in Latin America. It offers an important insight into where the urban population is located.

This group of consumers is comparatively easy to reach via the established retail networks, and even by way of online social media. It is the other 200 million of the middle class that present a more difficult group to connect with. A great many of these people live on the edge of urban centers and find themselves between retail networks sometimes not close to convenient public transportation. Even though cell phones are popular among the members of this class, the typical consumer will have only the basic text and voice capabilities to communicate. This group, moreover, does not universally possess household computers (Americas Market Intelligence, 2012). The percentage of households with computers in Latin America is below 10%. Even at work, most Latin Americans lack internet access.

Table 8.3 Latin American specific consumer expenditures, 2010

Country	Total	Transportation	Communication	Leisure & rec.	Education	Hotel & catering	Misc. goods
Argentina	87,011	29%	9%	20%	3%	17%	22%
Bolivia	5,277	44%	8%	6%	13%	21%	9%
Brazil	579,614	29%	12%	7%	16%	6%	30%
Chile	39,869	17%	16%	7%	14%	15%	32%
Colombia	87,885	23%	10%	10%	10%	24%	22%
Ecuador	18,210	34%	19%	10%	18%	8%	10%
Mexico	274,212	38%	12%	12%	7%	10%	21%
Peru	41,455	21%	7%	5%	17%	20%	30%
Venezuela	97,432	22%	10%	22%	14%	20%	11%

Source: Authors' calculations based on Euromonitor (2010)

The presence of significant obstacles notwithstanding, it is estimated that these 200 million consumers consume $300 billon dollars of food, beverages, home appliances, cell phones, and other products. Commerce in these goods and services represents a huge and growing market that presents great opportunities for ambitious and creative companies that are eager to expand their markets in Latin America (Americas Market Intelligence, 2012).

Table 8.3 provides a summary of what consumer expenditures have been in these selected countries of Latin America in the first decade of the 21st century. Immediately one can see that hotel and catering has the biggest and most consistent pattern of expenditures among all of the countries. Transportation comes in a strong second. This is not surprising since movement of people is a major activity in Latin America. Many of the cities, towns, and villages require transportation to move people to and from their work, as well as in their leisure activities. Much leisure travel takes place in Argentina, Mexico, and Brazil. Argentina's spending on leisure is an important benchmark. It signals a high appetite for luxury goods such as leisure (economic definition); as people get richer, they demand more time off and spend their money on leisure activities. This seems to complement the hotel and catering industry, which is the largest area of expenditure.

Bolivia and Ecuador, by contrast, have poorer populations, so the transportation is generally used for more basic needs. Peru, although it has falling rates of poverty, these remain high nonetheless, which diminishes spending on leisure and recreation.

Poverty in Latin America is one thing, inequality is another.[6] The questionable merits of proposals arguing incessantly for greater equality of incomes notwithstanding, inequality can have consequences for the markets. Economic inequality, for instance, might spur conspicuous consumption by those seeking to show they are a member of at least the middle class, particularly in settings where the poor are further stigmatized by issues of race or ethnicity. This can apply to countries like Peru, Guatemala, and Nicaragua. More generally, this is part of the reason that the Latin

American consumer is typically an aspirational one, i.e. he or she identifies with the dominant culture and purchases accordingly, in order to fortify the sense of belonging. This explains why Grupo Lala, a Mexican dairy company, uses pictures of Aryan-looking families to promote its product in Mexico and Central America, where the majority of consumers are not white.[7]

CLOSE-UP ON PERU

In many ways, Peruvian consumers can be taken as a microcosm of a large part of the consumer class for the Latin American region as a whole. Peruvian consumer behavior has changed dramatically over the past 30 years, capturing the dynamism that has characterized Latin American consumer markets as a whole in this time period. Peruvians are much more attentive now to new products and, particularly, to product quality. Some Peruvians are able and willing to pay higher prices for what were once considered to be luxuries, i.e. convenience and packaging.

Peru has a young, ethnically mixed population, with increasing disposable income. Importantly, more women are entering the workforce, a fact that will change consumptive patterns *permanently*, something marketers would do well to consider. Peruvians are becoming more educated and prosperous, and they, especially women, are making more decisions about the purchase of household goods and products.[8,9] Peruvians buy primarily from small retailers and traditional outlets. Price is a very important factor in bringing consumers into the store in Peru, as elsewhere in Latin America.[10]

The Peruvian case merits particular attention, as what applies here can be applied to other countries in Latin America with similar characteristics, like Bolivia, Ecuador, and Guatemala. Table 8.4 shows the evolution of consumer preferences over time. From the table, one can see the specific products that are important to Peruvian consumers, not just today, but also in the relatively recent past. The fact that more communication capabilities are available has contributed to the knowledge about the products and the desire to consume these products. Even so, satellite television is a luxury in most parts of Peru. If one mentally compares Peru to the US, for instance,

Table 8.4 Peru possession of household durables % of households—historic and future

Categories	1994	1999	2004	2009	2014	2019
Cable TV	0.2	7.3	6.2	10.3	12	13.2
Freezer	3.2	9.8	21.6	32.2	37	40
Microwave oven	0	1.9	22.9	46.9	50.9	51.1
Personal computer	1.8	5.7	11.1	16.9	22.3	27.6
Refrigerator	34.1	35.6	36.4	38.6	41.4	43.1
Satellite TV	0	0	0.1	0.1	0.2	0.2
Telephone	13	24.1	28.4	26.9	26.8	26.8

Source: Euromonitor (2010); Peruvian Consumer Behavior (2010, p. 6)

it may seem that Peru is not keeping up with modern times, but this really reflects the urban–rural dichotomy that characterizes many, if not most, Latin American nations. Peru is in many areas a rural agricultural economy with an infrastructure not yet fully adapted to modernity, especially in the Andes mountains.

The preceding exercise of contrasting rural with urban Peru, i.e. the scarcity of luxury consumer goods in the rural areas, versus the abundance of consumer goods common in a modern society, e.g. refrigerator, cable TV, confirms the validity of market segmentation strategies not just for Peru, but Latin America as a whole. In Peru, as elsewhere in Latin America, there is no "one" Peru, or Bolivia, or Brazil. There are many, and the market penetration strategies designed for securing a foothold in Latin America need to take such factors into account.

MARKETING STRATEGY FOR LATIN AMERICA

Proper marketing research will provide appropriate information about what, where, and when to market in Latin American countries. The selection of the appropriate marketing strategy to deploy in Latin America requires an accurate understanding of market segments and localized consumer behavior. This region of the world has a sizable and growing population characterized by large households, where women are fast becoming the prime decision makers in matters of consumption. In addition, the younger generations are fast emerging as important determinants of consumption, and significant consumers in their own right. For these and other reasons, the potential for novel business opportunities in Latin America in the near and foreseeable future is great.

The temptation to do business in Latin America is great, and with good reason. However, the fact remains that Latin American markets differ from North American ones. The buying patterns of Latin American consumers are certainly influenced by North American consumption modes, but not completely. Not only are Latin American consumption patterns also heavily influenced by local culture, these patterns themselves are also in a state of constant change, both for endogenous as well as exogenous reasons.

As a consumer group, the family or household resembles any other group with problems to solve and, thus, decisions to make (Lindquist and Sirgy 2003). Here the heavy representation of the youth population in the overall demographic structure in countries like Guatemala, Peru, Bolivia, and Brazil should rightfully impact not only on the goods and services to be brought to market, but also the marketing strategy to sell them once there. For instance, the large percentage of young people in countries like Brazil and Peru provide an excellent opportunity for those wishing to sell toys, designer athletic clothing, etc. At the same time, it is typically the mother who influences the decision to purchase these goods. Similarly, women are in charge of elderly care in Latin America, a fact that should be taken into account when marketing adult diapers, medicines for the elderly, health equipment, etc.

Planning a marketing strategy for Latin America requires the consideration of how local attitudes will affect consumer behavior. There are some people who continue to observe the old traditions of yesteryear, while those of the present generation are more connected with the world outside of Latin America and hence want the goods and services that the rest of the world has. People in Brazil who are part of the new middle class will go after the goods they see and desire. Likewise people from Colombia, Peru, and Chile will pursue the goods they see other people consuming. As they learn more about the availability of goods and services, and have the income to purchase, they will consume just like the people of the rest of the world. This will require marketers to design and develop new marketing strategies to meet and satisfy the needs of a larger consumer market.

Two basic approaches may be applied to marketing strategy. On the one hand, a firm's entire marketing strategy might be standardized and used intact in Latin American markets. At the other extreme, all strategic marketing elements can be adapted to meet the exigencies of the foreign market. In reality, a middle-of-the-road approach is most often taken—adapting established marketing practices to local conditions, in a way that stops short of applying a wholly unique marketing strategy for each country of operation. If you are interested in doing business in Latin America, it would pay to heed the lessons learned by other businesses in the course of their expansion efforts (Czinkota and Ronkainen, 2010).

Businesses seeking to expand into Latin American markets might find that they need to contemplate changing not only their marketing strategies, but their products as well. In the different cultures prevailing in Latin America, products will be used in novel ways and under diverse conditions. At a minimum, therefore, marketers will confront a stark decision problem if they decide to do business in Latin America. Either they will go with a standardized product model or adapt their products to the specificities of the Latin American markets. Product adaptation is a difficult decision to make because products are very costly to adapt, as this involves production decisions, not just marketing ones. Yet, sometimes adjustments must be made because the product, in the end, must meet the demands of the Latin American market. Instead of going with a standardized approach, you may choose to adapt your product to Latin American preferences. You may want to do this for various reasons. Once in Latin America, your products may be used differently. It can be the case that specific attributes of a product have less value or meaning in Latin American markets than they did in their markets of origin. All this, obviously, can get very expensive. If your firm finds itself constrained by limited resources, or has narrow goals for expanding into Latin America, product standardization may be the way to go, even if this strategy limits potential market demand.

To succeed in Latin American markets, an understanding is required of the relationship among the physical, social, and cultural environments. Companies doing business in Latin America need to consider these factors when presenting their products. Even big businesses have taken this into account. Companies such as McDonald's have found it necessary to adapt their menus to accommodate the food tastes of the local communities. McDonald's in Mexico, for instance, offers jalapeño peppers as an accompaniment. A simple replication of the US menu would not have been as enticing to Mexican consumers.[11]

Pharmaceutical giant Pfizer has also had to think differently and develop alternative marketing strategies that take into consideration the culture and the regulatory differences of different localities in Latin America (Sibermann, 2012). In addition to cultural preferences and attitudes, it is important to remember that doing business in Latin America means playing by the rules, but different rules. Although Latin America has made great strides in liberalizing trade and facilitating business, many maddening, outdated rules still persist. These affect big and small players alike. Pfizer, for instance, had to adapt its marketing strategy in Latin America on account of the rules in effect in the region. In many Latin American countries, pharmaceutical companies are not allowed to advertise directly to consumers. Additionally, there is limited protection for intellectual property, and even this is not generally respected. Consequently, the consumer has a much easier time getting generic drugs that are produced locally.

As a foreign operator, the rules can apply more to you than local rivals. Local competitors in Latin America will often feel quite comfortable flouting the official rules of doing business in their country, whereas an American might not. In fact, you might find yourself in violation of US law if you disobey local laws and regulations when doing business in Latin America. This is no small point. For instance, many pirated goods are sold in informal markets in Latin America. If the product or service you want to bring to market involves intellectual property, piracy will, obviously, be a clear threat.

INFORMAL MARKETS

Informal markets are large and pervasive in Latin America. Just about everywhere you go you will see itinerant, informal vendors. The informal economy of Latin America is typically composed of very small, micro businesses that are not registered in any way. They are rarely run from business premises, but instead operate in the public venues. In contrast to the regular or formal business arrangement, the informal vendor operates his or her business from homes, street pavements or other informal squatter-like arrangements. In many Latin American cities, towns and villages, the informal vendor(s) are immediately in front of or beside the formal retail market or formal business establishment.

Figure 8.2 offers a glimpse of what an actual informal market looks like.

The pervasiveness of the informal economy is a fact of Latin American business life. Established formal businesses may simply accept the fact that the informal economy is there to stay, and conduct their business in spite of its existence. They may even develop their business and marketing strategies with the informal market in mind. Entrepreneurs looking to exploit new business opportunities in Latin America will also be confronted daily by the existence of the itinerant vendors. Informal vendors may be small, but they can be quite significant, depending on the product or service being sold. Among some product categories, such as food products and artisan goods in countries like Guatemala and Peru, informal vendors can present intense

a.

b.

Figure 8.2 The informal market

competition. Although ubiquitous, informal vendors lack sophistication and service capabilities that a formal business establishment can deliver. And, although price can be a difficult issue, formal enterprises can still compete with the informal marketer, in terms of quality and service, particularly after purchase.

Throughout Latin America, the interface of informal markets with formal markets can represent opportunities as well as threats. In many cases, your travel to a particular Latin American country, such as Bolivia or Ecuador, is not complete until you've actually bought from an informal vendor. So you may want to consider enlisting the aid of informal enterprises if you plan on selling trinkets or light consumer goods to tourists in Latin America, for example. Knowledge of the interface of the informal and formal markets can also help in the development of a marketing strategy that can promote your product or service more successfully.

In many respects the existence of the formal and informal markets has given the Latin American consumer the best of both worlds. It is not uncommon for middle- and even upper-class Latin Americans to shop at modern supermarkets as well as informal markets for their household groceries. For example, a Brazilian housewife might buy baby food at a well-established international supermarket, toothpaste at a local market chain, and vegetables and fruits from transient, informal vendors. The consumptive patterns might vary according not just to convenience, but the importance attached to the product quality and safety, with greatest credibility on this issue attached to foreign firms and the least to the informal vendors.

GEOGRAPHY

Geographical considerations may affect your Latin American marketing strategy. For example, Colombians who live on the coast generally are more casual and accepting of informal products and services. By contrast, Colombians who live in the mountainous interior of the country tend to be more conservative, and thus a more formal marketing approach might be warranted. Knowing that these two types of market exist helps marketers arrange and rearrange their marketing mix strategies to satisfy the customers. Your Latin American marketing strategy should be based on a solid understanding of the geographic location, the market segments, and the traditions and culture of the consumer. For example, in Peru and Bolivia, traditional indigenous cultures are pervasive. Members of these cultures may not be interested in products that the Latino population desires. The marketing mix has to be arranged so as to incorporate the geographic and cultural sensibilities of the local populace, which should not be assumed to be homogenous throughout any given country in Latin America, much less the region itself as a whole.

Of course, aligning the marketing strategy with consumer preferences is the main goal of marketing anywhere, not just in Latin America. However, there is a tendency among Americans to want to export not just marketing strategies, but the simplifying assumptions underpinning these strategies, which may or may not be applicable in

Latin America. What works in the US or Europe, will not necessarily work in Latin America. While fast foods are very popular in US and European societies, such food types are not popular outside the major cities in Latin American countries. Moreover, what works in Mexico might not work in Peru or Argentina. Mexicans like to eat tacos made from a corn tortilla. Peruvian and Argentinian people have ceviche, cuy and empanadas.

The region is varied, and a solid understanding of local peculiarities and regional differences is needed for marketing strategies to work in Latin America. Fortunately, this knowledge can be obtained by using marketing research techniques that drill down into the contemporary details of each market segment. Getting this information will, nonetheless, often be a challenge because of the different cultural attitudes that exist in many parts of Latin America. Research techniques commonly employed in the US and Europe are often regarded as intrusive in Latin America. This particularly applies in the rural communities. When it comes to income queries, for example, Latin Americans will often decline to answer, or will simply lie.

Ignorance of Latin American consumer attitudes, beliefs, and customs can have considerable bottom-line implications. For example, Wal-Mart is one of the world's largest retail operations. Its marketing strategy is best captured by the slogan "Everyday Low Prices." When Wal-Mart expanded to Central America, it bought out some of the largest supermarket chains in Guatemala, El Salvador, and Costa Rica. These brands had developed substantial customer appeal and loyalty over the years, and were known to offer highly popular and effective special discount days. Upon entry, Wal-Mart applied its tried and true marketing strategy, and did away with the sporadic, yet expected, discount days. Consumer reaction was immediate, as was that of the competing local chains. Whereas Wal-Mart did not offer special discounts, other local chains did, and Wal-Mart saw many customers go over to the competition. On a cultural level, many Central American consumers, particularly women in the upper strata of society, approach shopping from a perspective of intrinsic, versus instrumental, value. Every marketing strategy has to include a discussion of the appropriate marketing mix that will address the desires of consumers. The next section focuses on this area of the marketing strategy.

THE MARKETING MIX APPLIED TO LATIN AMERICA

The marketing mix as applied to Latin America is no different than elsewhere; it is still based on the famous "four Ps:" product, price, place, and promotion. However, as we have seen, these factors can take on a different meaning, depending on where one is in Latin America. The product may be modified, prices might differ, the distribution channels might change, and the marketing message (promotion) might be altered to take into account cultural preferences prevalent in a specific locale. The marketing mix is important because it establishes the foundation for marketing strategy.

Product

At the core of the marketing mix is always the product. One of the major challenges of marketing is to sell the entire package including the physical product itself, brand name, warranties, and other aspects that customers assume accompany the product. Particularly in the case of consumer products, marketing managers operating abroad must be alert to the sensitivities to product types that vary according to cultural locations (Geringer *et al.*, 2012). This is particularly relevant for the American wishing to do business in Latin America. For example, selling laptop computers in the altiplano of Bolivia is not realistic from a cultural or an income point of view.

Promotion and Advertising

Promotion is the second element of the marketing mix—the way marketers get their message about a product to the public. In general, the main vehicles whereby the marketer attempts to link the product name, type, and message to customer needs and desires are through personal selling, advertising, and public relations.[12] In this respect, Latin America fits into general trends. Personal selling and advertising are the two most prevalent methods of marketing a product in Latin America (Geringer, 2012).

Marketing in high-context cultures, such as those found in many Latin American nations, generally relies on symbolic and emotional substance as a mechanism to appeal to the customer. Essentially this type of promotion is distinguished according to its level of structure. In a low-structured context, humor and pictorial presentations are used, whereas in a high-structured context, the marketing strategy might rely on the use of expert subscribers (Becker, 2011). The use of a low-structure versus a high-structure promotional strategy will depend on the consumer profile in the target market, as well as the type of product or service being presented.[13]

Low-structure pictorial presentations can be useful if you're selling lunchbox meals aimed at a juvenile market, for instance. High-structure strategies would be the way to go if an independent, expert opinion would prove highly valuable to your promotion strategies; if you sold medicinal products, for instance. The regulatory and cultural configurations of Latin American countries might well impact the choice of high- versus low-structure marketing strategies. The prohibition against advertising pharmaceuticals in certain parts of Latin America, for instance, has already been mentioned. This opens the door for promotional strategies based on expert testimonials.[14] In this regard, the use of brand sponsorships might pay off in Latin America. Some 81% of both Colombian and Venezuelan internet consumers, and 79% of Brazilians are inclined to trust this form of advertising (Burmaster, Lee, and McGiboney, 2009).

As regards pictorial representations in the promotion strategy, one should bear in mind that the saying "packages are created in the factory but brands are created in the mind" (Walter Landor, 2012) applies in Latin America. Latin American consumers view images that create value and meaning in their lives. These images cause them to inquire about and purchase a product (Meyers and Lubliner, 1998). For instance, many established brands in the US have acronyms or logos that may make sense to Americans, but not to Latin Americans. The KFC acronym/logo is known to mean Kentucky Fried Chicken in the United States, where the company operated for decades before shortening its business name, but KFC means nothing in Brazil, Chile, Costa Rica, Guatemala, Honduras, and Peru, where KFC has expanded. Locales in Latin America have both the KFC logo and the words Kentucky Fried Chicken spelled out clearly. Of course, a picture of Col. Sanders figures prominently over both. Given the pricing strategy of KFC, its target market is an upper-middle-class segment that most often can understand English.

An important management decision for achieving good communication about branding and packaging is to hire locally. If you can afford it, employing a local copywriter to support your advertising efforts in each Latin American country would be of tremendous value. The local copywriter will understand how to translate your advertising message into the common local language, thereby increasing the attractiveness of your brand image. Just as importantly, a local hire can tell you which cool-sounding words might actually be insults, depending on the country you plan on doing business in.

Culture affects everything, including our perceptions of what we hear and what we see. People's values vary with their culture, and this affects their perceptions of images, advertising, and packaging. A cultural framework for understanding the subtleties implicated by packaging and advertising strategies should, therefore, be developed (Payne, 2012) before you make the leap into doing business in Latin America.

There are many examples of mistranslated marketing messages transmitted in Latin America. The perhaps most famous example of the Chevy Nova, which translates into Spanish as "doesn't go" might not have been true, but it gets the point across. It helps to have someone who knows that leather (*cuero*) can imply nakedness in some Latin American countries, that the word *pinto* means reddish in some Spanish-speaking countries but penis in other Portuguese-speaking countries, and that *mujer* (Spanish for woman) can be taken to mean "non-virgin" in some circumstances in some Latin American countries.

Promotion of product and services through modern communications technologies (mobile phones, internet, TV, etc.) enables the marketing message to reach a significantly larger customer market base in a cost-effective manner. These new technological methods of contacting the customer have cut across both income and cultural domains. As such, the customer is more informed and more knowledgeable about the products and services that are being offered (Becker, 2011). This has direct relevance for Latin America. As a case in point, it is common for even the poor in Latin America to possess cell phones.

The pervasiveness of modern communications technologies presents both challenges and opportunities to those seeking to do business in Latin America. As more information is presented about foreign goods and services, opportunities to expand sales may multiply. Foreign goods are frequently perceived as being of superior quality throughout Latin America. However, by the same token, more informed customers tend to become more exigent and willing to explore various alternatives to your product or service.

Social networking has excellent potential to become a vehicle for marketing and communication in the Latin American business scene. It is a powerful mechanism for consumers to connect with a range of vendors across a region and across the world. Some of the statistics will highlight the power of social media and marketing in Latin America. As of June, 2011, 114.5 million Latin Americans had at some point been a visitor to social networking sites. Both males and females are very active in social networking in Latin America, but females are more active than males, by a ratio of 53.6% to 46.4%. Brazilian females are the most active participants of all countries. Facebook is the most popular social networking medium (Radwanick, 2011).

Pricing

Although progress has been made over time on the economic development front, and the Latin American middle class is growing both in size and collective purchasing power, disposable income is still low by Western standards. As such, price is and will remain (for the foreseeable future) an important part of most marketing mixes designed for Latin America. However, the price sensibilities of Latin American consumers are not just a function of the relative scarcity of disposable income prevalent in many parts of the region. With the onset of more comprehensive and instantaneous information, and access to ways to compare and assess value of a product, Latin American consumers have become ever more price conscious. In addition, the opening up of Latin American markets means that there will always be an abundant supply of cheap, low-quality, fake brand goods made in China. Selling to price alone in Latin America might well get you in the door, but it can be a disastrous strategy in the long term.

If your goal is to increase profit margins, the focus should be to concentrate more on product/service value rather than price alone. The perceived value proposition will vary among Latin American consumers along income lines. This is true anywhere, of course, but particularly in the case of Latin America, where inequalities and income disparities are often stark. Substantial market research will be required to know not only the income levels but also the patterns of behavior of Latin American consumers, so as to permit the calibration of the pricing strategy (Becker, 2011). Here your market research might get bogged down by the cultural resistance of Latin Americans to share income data. One simple way the authors have found that works around this obstacle is simply to ask consumer respondents the number of cars in their possession, how many rooms they have in their homes, how many of these rooms are lit by electric light bulbs, etc.

Depending on your product and place, your price strategy may need to take into account the cultural proclivity of many Latin Americans to haggle and bargain. A great many deals are consummated using the haggling method to achieve price agreements. Haggling is the rule rather than the exception in the informal markets for produce and artisan crafts, which abound in Latin America. If your plan is to export wall-to-wall carpeting to Ecuador, for instance, you can safely rely on selling through established retailers at the price set at the negotiation table. However, if you plan to sell emblazoned T-shirts through informal distributors and vendors, you can count on constant haggling, before, during, and after the deal is made.

Place: Marketing Channels and Distribution

Place refers to the marketing channels and distribution points used to move goods and services in the market. Although the issue of place is everywhere and always important, its strategic implications vary, depending on the type of product or service being sold, and the type of customer you have. Cell phone airtime in Latin America can be bought from the big telephony giants in prepackaged, standardized plans, or from informal street vendors at the traffic stoplights in the big urban centers. If you want sell shoes or clothes in hard-to-find sizes in Latin American, a reasonable outlet might, on the other hand, be a service like Amazon.com. This strategy could significantly lower your inventory costs and other bricks-and-mortar-type expenses, but you'd have to pay the associated fees to Amazon.com for helping you distribute and sell your wares.

As we move into the second decade of the 21st century we have seen a move by major retail chains to enter the Latin American markets (Wal-Mart is a prime example). Either they are going it alone or they are partnering with country locals to establish their presence in various countries. Most of the major franchise entities like Pizza Hut, McDonald's and Kentucky Fried Chicken are pervasive in most Latin American countries. Local family-owned stores still dominate the main streets and barrios of most Latin American cities, towns, and villages.

Critical to the success of the marketing strategy will be, as always, the sales force. In Latin America, the sales force possesses an inordinate amount of uniquely valuable marketing information, culled from direct experience and observation of what is going on in the streets and in the different outlets. If your interest is in retail sales in Latin America you should be prepared to invest in well-structured training, performance management, and incentive programs for the sales force that will ultimately move your products or services. You should also make the proper arrangement for obtaining timely and regular feedback from the sales force, which can be the source of an important competitive advantage in Latin America. Too often, it is overlooked that the sales force on the ground may hold the essential information about outlets needed to modify strategies for reaching consumers.

THE MOM AND POP STORE

An important part of the business landscape in Latin America is the "mom and pop" retail store. There are literally thousands of mom and pop outlets all over Latin America. These stores are pervasive in just about every country in the region, and could prove to be formidable allies and/or foes. Even with the growth throughout Latin America of huge multinational retail chains like the US-based Wal-Mart or the French company Carrefour, the mom and pops will continue to be the staple of the Latin American business scene long into the future. Persistent, pervasive, and large in number, the mom and pops have attracted a large following of consumer goods companies eager to place their wares in front of consumers. This, in turn, has affected the big chains, as competition for shelf space and consumer attention has intensified.

Mom and pop stores confronting the challenge of competing with large, low-cost, low-price retailers are faced with having to improve their own processes and raise prices, all the while struggling to meet the demands of a shrinking (for them) client base. If you are a smaller company interested in doing business in Latin America, this may prove relevant to you. An outsider capable of sourcing new products and services for sale through alternative distribution channels in Latin America may prove an invaluable, natural ally to these smaller enterprises. As such, the mom and pop stores, taken collectively, may offer an important opportunity for doing business in Latin America, providing unique opportunities for reaching specific locales and local consumers. Even well-established packaged goods companies like Pepsi and Frito-Lay do business with mom and pops. These mom and pop stores have been good for barrios and villages, but also have become very vulnerable to the needs of gangs and criminals. Because they do not have the resources to provide solid security, they can be easily taken advantage of through exploitation or physical violence. This is an issue all mom and pop stores have to be aware of all the time.

The marketing mix may need to be tailored more specifically than just along national lines. Even within smaller countries, for instance, income disparities can pose a serious challenge to the development of a uniform marketing mix. One solution is segmenting, say along income lines. With this approach the suppliers can make decisions on whether to invest or not in expansion into certain neighborhoods or regions within a country.

The issue of market segmentation may determine the nature of the competition your business venture will face in Latin America. The traditional retailers in Latin America provide between 25% and 50% of all the grocery sales. Mom and pops account for 95% of the beer consumed in Colombia, and 80% of the carbonated beverage sales in Mexico. Mom and pop stores persist in Latin America for many reasons; among them are the still low levels of income, which means that many of the target consumers do not own cars. Another factor is the low population density of certain locales, which translates into levels of purchasing less than would be needed to sustain the presence of the large chain outlets (Diaz *et al.*, 2007).

These characteristics, common to many markets in Latin America, may lead to marketing approaches that are different than those one would develop for North American markets. For instance, consumers in the US generally have easy access to private transportation. Given their ease of travel, they are presented with a broader range of product offerings. Most Americans can jump into a car relatively easily and visit a neighborhood or cross-town Wal-Mart or Target to obtain the goods they need. The sporadic bargains and huge line of products is quite different than that which exists in most rural villages in Latin America. This urban–rural dichotomy is of tremendous importance as the rural sector can represent up to 40–50% of the country in Central America, Ecuador, Paraguay, and Bolivia.[15] A properly designed marketing mix that takes into account the pervasiveness of smaller distribution outlets could be the key to success of your business venture in Latin America, as the obstacles are higher, but the competition is less keen.

Up until now, the two main ways of getting goods and services to the Latin American customer in the lower middle class have been the *tienda*, a small, local storefront shopkeeper, and the local community central market. However, modernization has expanded the channel options available to the local customer. Consumers can go to mass-merchandising outlets like Jumbos and Liders in Chile, Wal-Mart in Guatemala, or SAMs in Mexico. These mega department stores carry a greater variety of goods than the consumer could get in the *tienda*. While the *tiendas* and the neighborhood central market can be important for convenience, their force in the community has been significantly diminished because the mass merchandising entities that can offer more standardized, known quality goods, at better prices, in cleaner, safer locations.[16] The modernization effect of mass merchandising entities has given the consumer a broader more comprehensive line of offerings that expands the market significantly (Becker, 2011).

CONCLUSION

Before undertaking the decision to operate in the Latin American environment, there are some key points to consider. Consumers in developing markets are more sophisticated than people in developed countries give them credit for. Technology has provided a huge boost to information exchange and that has informed consumers much more than in past years. Competition can be much stronger than anticipated. The competition, like the consumer, is sophisticated, and much more knowledgeable about consumer tastes and behavior than an outsider would be. Lastly, including local talent in business operations is critically important. The stability and success of the foreign investment requires the inclusion of the local talent; those businesses that are interested in pursuing investment in Latin America must look at the long haul. It takes time and effort, and a lot of patience, to make the investment work (A.T. Kearney, 2011). Given the high and increasing sophistication of both Latin American consumers and business enterprises, the need to associate with local talent may make or break your Latin American business venture.

The fast-growing Latin American middle class presents an array of business opportunities that previously were not available. By and large the potential benefits far outweigh the negative, downside risks of doing business in most Latin American countries.

In this chapter we have presented a glimpse of marketing in Latin America. Specific emphasis has been placed on using marketing research techniques that gather market intelligence to furnish an understanding of what to market, where to market, and when to market. Marketers need to understand that Latin American countries are different to North America, Europe, and Asia. As such, they need to be informed, and prepared to deal with a different marketing environment. The growing middle class, the pervasive informal market, and the multitude of mom and pop stores all create an environment that presents not only challenges but also opportunities. Knowing the proper marketing mix to apply among different countries will go a long way in achieving business success in Latin America.

NOTES

1. Elsewhere in the book we discuss how the exchange of goods, services, and capital was also accompanied by the exchange of ideas on how to conduct business and, more generally, economic, political, and social life. As argued there, this has been a significant force behind the growth of business opportunities in Latin America.

2. A high-context culture is one where "there are extensive information networks among family, friends, associates and even clients. Their relationships are close and personal. They keep well informed about people who are important in their lives" (McDowell, 2003, p. 1).

3. Another issue brought to the fore by the opening case, the sourcing of local partners, is fundamental to relationship marketing in Latin America.

4. This issue is discussed in Chapter 3.

5. The criterion for classifying people in this country as middle class was whether their income and earnings were four times what constituted the poverty line.

6. The issues of poverty and inequality are treated in depth in other chapters of this book.

7. The racial sensitivity of Latin Americans is legion, but remains a taboo subject. It is best not to ever bring this subject up in conversations anywhere in Latin America.

8. On a global level, patterns of consumption are different among men and women. Statistics gathered for OECD countries indicate important gender differences in consumption. To wit, women make more than 80% of household purchasing decisions, they shop more, and are likelier to be moved on price when it comes to cheap basic goods like food, clothing, and items for the household. See http://www.equalclimate.org/en/consumption/.

9. The role of changing demographics and the growing importance of women (and youth!) in global consumptive patterns has been duly noted. Women are the largest growing economic force in the world, and Latin America is no exception. Women's earning power on a global scale is expected to exceed $18 trillion (that's greater than the size of the US economy!) by 2014 (see Voigt, 2009). See also "Women: Saviors of the world economy?" CNN.com International: http://edition.cnn.com/2009/WORLD/asiapcf/10/25/intl.women.global.economy/.

10. International Markets Bureau, Market Analysis Report, June 2010.

11. The strong preference for spicy foods shared by many Mexican consumers is not a trait that is generally found in other Latin American countries, so caution should be taken against inferring general conclusions.

12. The end goal of promotional activities is not only to convince the customer or user of utility and value, but also to appeal to the other members of the distribution channel such as retailers, wholesalers, jobbers, etc.

13. As a case in point, one can take the simple use of money in Guatemala. Official bills in the local currency have different colors, depending on their value. This is due to the fact that many Guatemalans are illiterate and cannot distinguish between numbers. This strategy is obviously not necessary among the literate, more affluent sectors of society.

14. Other examples exist. For example, in Latin America, professional bars are prevalent, for many occupations beyond just the accounting, legal, and medical professions, as is the case in the US, for instance. In Latin America, therefore, expert testimonials might complement local norms of professional courtesy in the selling of professional services, such as consultancies on economic and political matters.

15. http://www.newsecuritybeat.org/2010/10/meeting-the-needs-of-latin-americas-rural-and-urban-populations/.
16. The impact of crime on shopping patterns is particularly important in countries like Venezuela and the Central American countries where street crime and delinquency has soared, making shopping at local, popular on-the-street outlets a game of roulette that risk-averse consumers prefer to avoid.

REFERENCES

Americas Market Intelligence (2012) The next two hundred million: Latin America's emerging middle class, 166 Alhambra Circle, Suite 200 Coral Gables, www.americasmi.com, September, 1–4.

A.T. Kearney (2011) Global retail development index, obtained from http://www.atkearney.com/index.php/Publications/global-retail-development-index.html.

Becker, T. H. (2011) *Doing business in Latin America* (2nd ed.). Westport, CT: Praeger.

Bifani, D. (2012) Chilean companies continue to enter Peru's booming retail market, obtained from http://www.worldpropertychannel.com/latin-america-commercial-news/lima-shopping-malls-mall-aventura-plaza-santa-anita-falabella-ripley-lima-smu-cencosud-at-kearney-global-retail-development-index-peru-retail-report-6116.php, accessed on 10–29–12.

Burmaster, A., Lee, L., and McGiboney, M. (2009) Personal recommendations and consumer opinions posted online are the are the most trusted forms of advertising globally, obtained from http://blog.nielsen.com/nielsenwire/wp-content/uploads/2009/07/pr_global-study_07709.pdf.

Cateora, P., Gilly, M., and Graham, J. (2009) *International marketing* (14th ed.). New York: McGraw-Hill Publishing.

Cavazos-Arroyo, J. and Gonzales Garcia, S. (2012) A cultural perspective. In Penaloza, L., Toulouse, N. and Visconti, L. M. (Eds.), *Marketing management*. New York: Routledge.

Czinkota, M. and Ronkainen, I. A. (2010) *International marketing*. Mason, OH: South-western Publishing.

Euromonitor (2010) *Latin American marketing data and statistics* (5th Ed.). London: Euromonitor International Ltd.

Farfan, B. (2010) US retail industry global store openings planned for 2010, complete list, obtained from http://retailindustry.about.com/od/famousretailers/a/us_retail_chain_global_2010_retail_store_openings.htm (accessed 7/11).

Geringer, M. J., Minor, M. S., and McNett, J. M. (2012) *International business*. New York: McGraw-Hill.

Hair, J. F., Bush, R. P., and Ortinau, D. J. (2003) *Marketing research: Within a changing information environment*. New York: McGraw-Hill.

Landor, W. (2012) Founder of Landor Associates. He had a particular gift for creating designs with broad popular appeal, see http://en.wikipedia.org/wiki/Walter_Landor (accessed 10/20/12).

Largest cities (2003) Rhett Butler, obtained from http://www.mongabay.com/igapo/Latin_America.htm.

Lindquist, J. D. and Sirgy, M. J. (2003) *Shopper, buyer, and consumer behavior: Theory, marketing applications and public policy implications* (2nd ed.). Cincinnati, OH: Atomic Dog Publishing.

McDowell (2003) Native American literature, high context and low context – PCC, obtained from faculty.pcc.edu/~mmcdowel/eng240fall03/eng240highlowcontext.pdf (accessed10/15/12).

MercoPress (2011) Latin America rapidly becoming a middle-class continent, according to ECLAC, obtained fromhttp://en.mercopress.com/2011/04/20/latin-america-rapidly-becoming-a-middle-class-continent-according-to-eclac (accessed 10/31/12).

Meyers, H. M. and Lubliner, M. J. (1998) *The marketer's guide to successful package design*. Lincolnwood, Chicago, IL: NTC Business Books.

Payne, N. (n.d.) International advertising – understanding cultural differences, obtained from http://www.sideroad.com/Cross_Cultural_Communication/international-advertising.html (accessed 10/20/12).

Peruvian Consumer Behavior (2010) Attitudes and perceptions towards food products. International Markets Bureau, Market Analysis Report, June. Agriculture and Agri-Food Canada.

Plenty More Wealth to Come (2011) BMI, central banks, national statistics agencies, Latin America – GDP per capita for selected economies, US$, Mexico commercial banking report Q3. *Business Monitor International Ltd*, 17–23.

Radwanick, S. (2011) The rise of social networking in Latin America. How social media is shaping Latin America's digital landscape. *ComScore*, 1–35.

Sibermann, S. (2012) How Pfizer adapts its sales strategy for Latin America. HBR Blog Network, August. *Harvard Business Review*, 1–2, obtained from http://blogs.hbr.org/cs/2012/08/how_pfizer_adapts_its_sales_strategy_for_latin_america.html (accessed 09/12).

Vassolo, R. S., De Castro, J. O., and Gomez-Mejia, L. R. (2011) Managing in Latin America: Common issues and a research agenda. *Academy of Management Perspectives, 25* (4), 22–36.

Voigt, K. (2009) Women: Saviors of the world economy? CNN.com International, obtained from http://edition.cnn.com/2009/WORLD/asiapcf/10/25/intl.women.global.economy/.

World Bank (2013) Annual report, obtained from http://web.worldbank.org/WBSITE/EXTERNAL/EXTA-BOUTUS/EXTANNREP/EXTANNREP2013/0,,menuPK:9304895~pagePK:64168427~piPK:64168435~theSitePK:9304888,00.html.

9

LEARNING FROM THE PAST, ENGAGING THE FUTURE

Business Lessons in Latin America

SOME FINAL THOUGHTS

The Latin American business environment presents a contradiction of circumstances that can have an impact on investors' decisions for business development in this region of the world. On the one hand there is the continuous unprecedented economic growth connected with many of the Latin American countries. On the other hand, the political and economic decision making among many Latin American countries continues to focus on many of the unproductive policies that created stagnation in the past. Be that as it may, Latin America has left behind the days when its comparative trade advantages rested solely in the agricultural sector. In fact, the region as a whole has moved past not only the agricultural but also the industrial state, to a regional economy more based on services than even industry. That said, the legacy of the import substitution methodology that the Latin American countries chose as an approach to industrialize still leaves a negative imprint on the "doing business climate" for foreign investors. Latin American businessmen are almost universally *mercantilist*. The foreign investor looking to do business in Latin America should make no mistake about it. The Latin American businessman, ever the advocate of free markets, is always and in every place looking to the state for protection from foreign competition at every turn.

That said, the region has moved towards greater economic openness amid an increasingly globalized economy, via free trade pacts, which have slowly but surely introduced liberalizing economic and trade reforms into the economies of the region. This is good news for foreign investors seeking to do business in Latin America. Freer trade policies are increasingly institutionalized into free trade pacts from which the local governments are ever more reticent to back out. Even more important, the peoples of Latin America are increasingly inclined to demand freer trade pacts, because of a greater quantity and quality of goods and services they find available when foreigners come to do business in their countries. Interestingly, blaming foreigners for national defects is still Latin America's favorite pastime. Nonetheless, the Latin American business class still uses the American business class as a referent model. Latin American consumers are among the most ardent fans of American brands. Both factors translate into net positives for Americans and Europeans seeking to do business in Latin America.

Freer trade is on the rise in Latin America. It is the present and the future. This makes the Latin American region an increasingly attractive place to do business, especially as emerging markets take on a more important role in promoting world economic growth. The massive distortions of markets that occurred under state-led development efforts, if not a thing of the past altogether, are waning. Generally, the constant balance of trade and payments crises have been eliminated for now and the present. The exceptions are, as would be naturally expected, the socialist-inclined regimes of Argentina, Venezuela, and countries that follow their state-interventionist lead. For the most part, however, the region has whipped inflation and debt, thanks to the sound advice and implementation of the Washington Consensus. Latin America not only grows faster than the developed world including the United States and Europe, but it does so with lower deficit and debt burdens than the developed world, and with much less inflation than was true thirty years ago.

We must keep in mind the differences in the economic and business outlooks of Latin America and the Caribbean as compared with those of the United States and Europe. The growth outlook in the United States is tepid at best, while the Euro Zone countries are caught up in conditions akin to economic depression and bleak future economic projections. The US and the Euro Zone countries are heavily burdened in deficits and debt, causing significant drags on consumption and investment activity for the near term. The Latin American region, by contrast, has avoided falling into the trap of dependency on deficit spending and debt accumulation, for which reason the future prospects of high GDP growth for the region are considerably better than is the case for both the US and the Euro Zone. Simply put, Latin Americans have whipped debt dependency, whereas the US and the Euro Zone have not. As debt burdens directly imply higher taxes, the business climate in this aspect must be forecast as better in Latin America than in either the US or the Euro Zone. The most current data, then, show that Latin America is better positioned for growth in the coming years than is Europe or the United States.

Politically, Latin America's prospects are less rosy, on a general level. Parting from the premise that liberal, open political and economic orders are better for business, Latin America cannot be considered to be a mature region, politically speaking. Many of the economic reforms that have been introduced have been exemplary in terms of economic and political benefits. Still, the low level of competency found in the Latin American political class, coupled with the stark fear of competition exhibited by the Latin American business class, translates into a general political situation whereby different countries proceed at different speeds on the road toward open, liberal political and economic orders. This can be maddening, as the region often appears to take two steps forward, and one step back. It never leaves behind the possibility of a return to a protectionist, state-interventionist past that was, by all measures, bad for business and, frankly, human development. Cases in point would be those offered by the great strides made in competitiveness and human development in such countries as Costa Rica, Chile, and Uruguay, as opposed to tremendous disappointments offered by Argentina, Venezuela, and to lesser extents Ecuador, Bolivia, and Nicaragua. The Latin American historical tendency to snatch failure from the jaws of victory notwithstanding, the region is most definitely advancing, albeit in fits and starts, and in a geographically and politically differentiated fashion. Taking everything into account, Latin America is more democratic, more market-oriented; more developed today than ever before in its history. As a global player in business development and investment, the future is even brighter.

Institutions matter for business, economic, and human development, and here, too, the verdict is positive, albeit mixed. There is greater convergence among the business classes of Latin America, the United States, and Europe than among their respective political classes, which in Latin America cannot be said to have passed the infantile stage. As has been addressed elsewhere in this book, Latin America scores better on the quality of her private institutions than her public institutions. This is true on a host of matters, on such issues as corporate ethics, efficiency of boards of directors, the strength of auditing and accounting standards, and protection of investor interests. All of this is pertinent to the doing business climate. Of particular interest is the education of the Latin American business person. Latin America scores well on *efficiency enhancers*. This includes such items as the quality of universities and, in particular, the business schools. Staff training is another area where many Latin American countries score well. An American investor seeking to do business in Latin America would find himself quickly in contact with well-trained business persons, a strong critical mass of which speak English. In any context, the verdict must be positive on the existence of a key class that dominates managerial concepts and principles, speaks the international language of business, in conjunction with a consumer class strongly oriented towards all things American and/or European.

In this book, we developed general regional rankings. Although a solid contribution, these regional rankings don't tell the whole story. The global competitiveness context includes the very poor-performing state institutions, which are, excepting the countries linked to the 21st-century Socialism initiative embarked upon by the late president of Venezuela Hugo Chavez, in the process of improving.

One factor that is ever present in Latin America is corruption. It is as Latin American as salsa music. This has obvious implications for the doing business climate. Nevertheless, the upside opportunities to invest outweigh these downside risks. Because of globalization and freer trade, the correct institutional reforms are under way, albeit haltingly and intermittently. Although improvements need to continue, the region has progressed on matters relating to investment freedom, as well as labor and financial freedom. Importantly, the strongest points for the region are its strong scores on fiscal freedom, especially when compared to the developed world, including the

United States and Europe—advanced regions mired in deficit spending, debt, and depression.

It bears repeating that foreign investors seeking to do business in Latin America would be wise to avoid the political risks associated with potential investments in the countries linked to or flirting with the Bolivarian Alliance for the Peoples of Our America (or ALBA) initiative. As we have noted elsewhere, the countries to avoid outright would be Venezuela and Cuba, of course, and the ones to watch closely and consider only under strict scrutiny would be Ecuador, Bolivia, and Nicaragua. Even Argentina has to be put on a watch list, given the power grabs of the Kirchner government, which tellingly includes moves against central bank independence, a surefire route to the inflationary days of macroeconomic instability of her past.

Bright spots appear on the Latin American political horizon and should be taken into account by the investor seeking to do business in Latin America. The private sector in Latin America is competitive, in spite of an underperforming political sector. As the quality of human capital grows in the private sector, positive externalities should transfer to the political sector, as national and foreign businesses demand less corruption and better public services, beginning with public security.

Overall, the economic climate is conducive to doing business in Latin America. Inflation is whipped in key countries, and even erstwhile anti-US countries like Ecuador are dollarized. Bloated government and unsustainable public debt are no longer characteristic of the political regime in Latin America. Frankly, Latin America still has progress to make on the human development front. Poverty still afflicts more than a quarter of the population in Latin America, also one of the most unequal regions of the world. Inequality would not be a problem in and of itself, except that it lends credence to populist politicians who would threaten to undermine the great progress Latin America has made in its macroeconomic environment, as well as in its business and investment climate.

The most important reminder when engaging in business in Latin America is to remember that each country is different from the others. Failing to accept this premise has led companies to deviate from the main objective. This premise is important even if you are dealing with countries from the same region or the same negotiation block.

The difference in every country can be analyzed from three different aspects: economic, political, and social/cultural. The economic analysis is a priority when engaging in business ventures in Latin America. Analyzing GDP, inflation, fiscal reforms, and the tax burden are some of the important aspects an investor should consider.

The political circumstances are important when dealing with negotiations, investments, and expansions. Political issues in Latin America are often changing so an important piece of advice is to track the political structures and philosophies in the country where the investment is targeted, and analyze how could these factors affect decision making.

Without question, business people who study, analyze, and understand the history, culture, and business climate of Latin America will be better prepared to meet the challenges and opportunities that are pervasive in this region of the world.

APPENDIX

ARGENTINA OVERVIEW

Government

Government: Federal presidential constitutional republic
President: Cristina Fernandez
Political party: Partido Justicialista

Top Exports and Imports

Argentina exported 83,949.5 US dollars in 2011. The principal products that Argentina exports are: cakes and oilseed meals, soy, soybean oil, vehicles, corn, trucks, petroleum products, wheat, and gold. These products are 52.1% of the totality of the exports.

Economy

With a population of more than 41.5 million inhabitants and a GDP of more than 495 billion US dollars (2013), Argentina is one of the five largest economies in South America. With so much going for her, Argentina is a constant under-achiever, a country rich in human and economic capital, but with a public sector seemingly bent on degrading the country's best economic advantages.

In recent years, President Cristina Fernandez has promised a focus on promoting economic development with "social inclusion," which unfortunately is too often Latin American code for clientelistic policies that attack business interests for the sake of political interests of the government in power. The Fernandez government has taken to attacking the independence of the central bank, and intimidating economists who report other than the dubious official figures. So unreliable have official statistics become that the IMF has refused to accept Argentina's economic statistics as valid for international accounting purposes.

Still, Argentina is a powerhouse. Argentina has for the near term gotten away with deviating from sound economic policies on account of her size, and other political developments in South America, which have been somewhat favorable to irresponsible left-wing political regimes. In the international sphere, Argentina enjoys decent relations with most of the countries in the region, especially Brazil and Venezuela. Argentina plays a leadership role in promulgating the region's policy position, representing, jointly with Brazil and Mexico, Latin America at the G-20.

Not all is a net negative in Argentina, of course. In matters of education and health, Argentina has a solid reputation for advancing public health and education. The country invests roughly 9–10% of its GDP in health services, and 6% of its GDP in education (and culture). Argentina implements a Universal Child Allowance to the benefit of almost 4 million children and teenagers, more than 9% of the population.

As relates to commerce and industry, Argentina's main commodity exports are wheat, soy pellets, and meal, as well as soybeans, meat, crude oil, and gasoline, with the country benefitting greatly from the power of Chinese demand fueled by the Asiatic country's monstrous growth over the years. Argentina has in recent years experienced strong short-run growth. The sectors reflecting strongest growth have been in the power and textile industries, as well as the automobile industries. Over the last decade since the first recession of the 21st century (ending 2003 roughly), wine exports exploded over 300%, enabling Argentina to reach the elite top five wine producers in the world.

The strong macroeconomic growth Argentina has reflected in recent years has enabled the government of President Cristina Fernandez to cut poverty and unemployment rates to those levels observed prior to the 2001–2002 economic crisis. After some eight years of GDP growth, and downward trending signals, the challenges of the government are to maintain growth and stability in the long term. Notably, growth began to slow in 2012, for the first time since the world recession of 2009.

The World Bank has identified three key areas for Argentina, which are sustainable growth with equity, social inclusion, and, importantly, improved governance. The areas for improvement aim to sustain medium-term economic growth and poverty mitigation. Measures involved include infrastructure upgrades, improvements in competitiveness, quality, and agriculture/livestock production, as well as consolidating health improvements. It is noteworthy that an international organization such as the World Bank takes special interest in improving the effectiveness and accountability of the corrupt public sector, with the aim of improving performance management in the public sector as well as its accountability, with the end goal being a wholesale improvement in the level of trust in public institutions.

World Bank data tell us the following about Argentina, as of 2011. The Argentine economy is 65% services, 26% industry and 9% agriculture. Exports of goods and services are estimated at 22% of GDP, whereas imports come in at 20%. Merchandise trade is estimated to total over 35.5% of GDP. There is good connectivity in the country as there are 135 mobile cellular subscriptions per 100 people, and 47.7 internet users per 100 people. Argentina's terms of trade have improved significantly, some 27% in 2010 over 2000.[1]

International Monetary Fund data tell us the following about Argentina. Argentina grew at 3.06% in 2013, half her average annual rate reflected in the 2007–2012 time period. Growth is expected to rebound slightly to a 3.79% annual average for the 2013–2017 time period. By 2017, the GDP per capita in current dollar terms is expected to approach $12,731. The debt to GDP ratio is expected to hover around 41.5%. The country's trade balance is expected to remain stable at just under -1.14% of GDP.[2]

In matters of the Global Competitiveness Index, Argentina ranks poorly: 94th out of 144 countries. In Doing Business, Argentina ranks 124th, out of a larger sample of 185 countries. It is not easy to start a business in Argentina, as evidenced by her abysmal ranking of 154 in that category. Paying Taxes is another area of burden, with a ranking of 149, and Trade Across Borders, 139. Still, Argentina scores well on its ranking of Human Development, 45 out of 186 countries analyzed by the United Nations. Argentina also scores well on the gender front, with a ranking of 32 out of 135 nations taken into account by the Global Gender Gap highlighted by the World Economic Forum. On the matter of Economic Liberty, Argentina receives a grade of 46.7 out of 100, as reported by the Heritage Foundation. On the Corruption Perceptions Index elaborated by Transparency International, Argentina gets a ranking of 102 out of the 183 countries analyzed.

Table A.1 Business climate indicators, Argentina[3]

Indicators: Argentina	
Global Competitiveness Index, World Economic Forum, ranking 1–144	94
GCI Subindex A Basic requirements	96
GCI Subindex B Efficiency enhancers	86
GCI Subindex C Innovation and sophistication factors	88
Doing Business, World Bank, ranking 1–185	124
DB Starting a Business	154
DB Dealing with Construction Permits	171
DB Getting Electricity	74
DB Registering Property	135
DB Getting Credit	70
DB Protecting Investors	117
DB Paying Taxes	149
DB Trading Across Borders	139
DB Enforcing Contracts	48
DB Resolving Insolvency	94
Human Development Index, United Nations, ranking 1–186	45
Global Gender Gap, World Economic Forum, ranking 1–135	32
Travel and Tourism Competitiveness, World Economic Forum, ranking 1–140	60
Democracy Index, Economist Intelligence Unit, ranking 1–167	52
Freedom Status, Freedom House	Free
Index of Globalization, KOF (0 to 100)	58.94
Index of Economic Liberty, Heritage Foundation (0 to 100)	47
Corruption Perception Index, Transparency International, ranking 1–183	102

Source: Authors' calculations based on various indicators

Table A.2 Data profile, Argentina

	2000	2010	2011
Economy			
GDP (current US$) (billions)	284.20	368.71	445.99
Agriculture, value added (% of GDP)	5	10	9
Industry, value added (% of GDP)	28	31	26
Services, etc., value added (% of GDP)	67	59	65
Exports of goods and services (% of GDP)	11	22	22
Imports of goods and services (% of GDP)	12	18	20
Gross capital formation (% of GDP)	16	22	23
States and markets			
Time required to start a business (days)	—	26	26
Market capitalization of listed companies (% of GDP)	58.4	17.3	9.8
Military expenditure (% of GDP)	1.1	0.9	0.7
Mobile cellular subscriptions (per 100 people)	18	133	135
Internet users (per 100 people)	7.0	40.0	47.7
Roads, paved (% of total roads)	29	—	—
High-technology exports (% of manufactured exports)	9	7	—
Global links			
Merchandise trade (% of GDP)	18.1	33.8	35.5
Net barter terms of trade index (2000 = 100)	100	127	—
External debt stocks, total (DOD, current US$) (millions)	140,914	127,849	—
Total debt service (% of exports of goods, services and income)	69.4	16.7	—
Net migration (thousands)	−50	−200	—
Workers' remittances and compensation of employees, received (current US$) (millions)	86	641	—
Foreign direct investment, net inflows (BoP, current US$) (millions)	10,418	7,055	7,243
Net official development assistance and official and received (current US$) (millions)	52	121	—

Source: Authors' calculations based on various indicators

Table A.3 International Monetary Fund projections, Argentina[4]

Country	Subject Descriptor	2013	2007–2012	2013–2017
Argentina	Gross domestic product, constant prices, % change	3.06	6.15	3.79
	Gross domestic product, current prices, billions, USD	$495.07	$474.81	$552.51
	Gross domestic product per capita, current prices, USD	$11,932	$11,573	$12,731
	Gross domestic product based on purchasing-power-parity (PPP) per capita GDP, Int'l dollar	$18,800	$18,205	$22,521

(Continued)

Table A.3 (Continued)

Country	Subject Descriptor	2013	2007–2012	2013–2017
	Gross domestic product based on purchasing-power-parity (PPP) share of world total, %	0.90	0.85	0.89
	Inflation, end of period consumer prices, % change	9.85	8.95	9.85
	Volume of imports of goods and services, % change	9.19	10.94	7.08
	Volume of imports of goods, % change	9.28	10.91	7.10
	Volume of exports of goods and services, % change	7.51	3.30	5.63
	Volume of exports of goods, % change	7.51	3.30	5.64
	Population, millions	41.49	41.03	43.40
	General government revenue, % GDP	38.38	35.27	38.60
	General government total expenditure, % GDP	40.87	37.85	40.53
	General government net lending/borrowing, % GDP	−2.49	−2.58	−1.94
	General government gross debt, % GDP	42.80	53.94	41.50
	Current account balance, billions, USD	−$0.36	$1.26	−$10.71
	Current account balance, % GDP	−0.07	1.29	−1.14

Source: Authors' calculations based on various indicators

BELIZE OVERVIEW

Government

Government: Unitary parliamentary constitutional monarchy
Monarch: Elizabeth II
Governor-General: Sir Colville Young
Prime Minister: Dean Barrow

Top Exports and Imports

Belize exported 282.1 thousands of US dollars in 2010. The principal products that Belize exports are: crude oil, fruit juices, bananas, sugar, crustaceans, beans, fruits, fish, wood boards, and molasses. These products are 95.5% of the totality of the exports.

Economy

Belize has a population of some 35 million inhabitants and a GDP of approximately $1.59 billion, in current dollar terms. In per capita terms, Belize has a GDP of $4,495 in current dollar terms. Inflation is modest, reported at 2.5% per year. Government expenditures run about 29% of GDP, whereas revenues are only 27% per year. Belize

Table A.4 Business climate indicators, Belize[5]

Indicators: Belize	
Global Competitiveness Index, World Economic Forum, ranking 1–144	N/A
GCI Subindex A Basic requirements	N/A
GCI Subindex B Efficiency enhancers	N/A
GCI Subindex C Innovation and sophistication factors	N/A
Doing Business, World Bank, ranking 1–185	105
DB Starting a Business	158
DB Dealing with Construction Permits	21
DB Getting Electricity	58
DB Registering Property	136
DB Getting Credit	129
DB Protecting Investors	128
DB Paying Taxes	45
DB Trading Across Borders	102
DB Enforcing Contracts	169
DB Resolving Insolvency	30
Human Development Index, United Nations, ranking 1–186	96
Global Gender Gap, World Economic Forum, ranking 1–135	62
Travel and Tourism Competitiveness, World Economic Forum, ranking 1–140	N/A
Democracy Index, Economist Intelligence Unit, ranking 1–167	N/A
Freedom Status, Freedom House	Free
Index of Globalization, KOF (0 to 100)	48.25
Index of Economic Liberty, Heritage Foundation (0 to 100)	57
Corruption Perception Index, Transparency International, ranking 1–183	N/A

Source: Authors' calculations based on various indicators

has a debt problem, with a public debt representing some 80% of GDP, which is projected to remain high at about 76.7% of GDP on average in the 2013–2017 time frame. Belize runs a deficit in her current account of 4.37% of GDP, which is expected to hover around −4.73% in the 2013–2017 time frame. The outlook for growth in imports and exports in both Goods and Goods and Services for the 2013–2017 time frame is slightly negative. Inflation is expected to remain stable at 2.5% per annum on average for the 2013–2017 time frame.[6]

Belize ranks 105 out of 185 countries in terms of Doing Business, and 158 for Starting a Business, 136 for Registering Property, and a dismal 169 for Enforcing Contracts. The country scores 57.3 out of 100 on Economic Liberty, as measured by the Heritage Foundation, but just 48.25 on the Index of Globalization, reflecting a somewhat poor orientation toward free trade across borders.[7]

Table A.5 World Bank data profile, Belize[8]

	2000	2010	2011
Economy			
GDP (current US$) (billions)	0.83	1.40	1.45
GDP growth (annual %)	13.0	2.9	1.9
Inflation, GDP deflator (annual %)	0.4	0.7	1.5
Agriculture, value added (% of GDP)	17	—	—
Industry, value added (% of GDP)	21	—	—
Services, etc., value added (% of GDP)	62	—	—
Exports of goods and services (% of GDP)	53	58	66
Imports of goods and services (% of GDP)	74	58	65
Gross capital formation (% of GDP)	32	—	—
Revenue, excluding grants (% of GDP)	20.4	—	—
Cash surplus/deficit (% of GDP)	−5.7	—	—
States and markets			
Time required to start a business (days)	—	44	44
Market capitalization of listed companies (% of GDP)	—	—	—
Military expenditure (% of GDP)	0.9	1.1	1.1
Mobile cellular subscriptions (per 100 people)	7	62	70
Internet users (per 100 people)	6.0	14.0	—
Roads, paved (% of total roads)	17	—	—
High-technology exports (% of manufactured exports)	0	—	—
Global links			
Merchandise trade (% of GDP)	89.2	71.8	83.3
Net barter terms of trade index (2000 = 100)	100	101	104
External debt stocks, total (DOD, current US$) (millions)	630	1,307	1,278
Total debt service (% of exports of goods, services and primary income)	17.5	15.3	13.9
Net migration (thousands)	−2	−1	—
Personal remittances, received (current US$) (millions)	26	78	76
Foreign direct investment, net inflows (BoP, current US$) (millions)	23	96	95
Net official development assistance and official aid received (current US$) (millions)	15	25	30

Source: World Bank, World Development Indicators, online database

Table A.6 International Monetary Fund projections, Belize[9]

Country	Subject Descriptor	2013	2007–2012	2013–2017
Belize	Gross domestic product, constant prices, % change	2.50	1.97	2.50
	Gross domestic product, current prices, billions, USD	$1.59	$1.52	$1.94
	Gross domestic product per capita, current prices, USD	$4,495	$4,386	$5,014

Country	Subject Descriptor	2013	2007–2012	2013–2017
	Gross domestic product based on purchasing-power-parity (PPP) per capita GDP, Int'l dollar	$8,492	$8,358	$9,202
	Gross domestic product based on purchasing-power-parity (PPP) share of world total, %	0.00	0.00	0.00
	Inflation, end of period consumer prices, % change	2.50	2.08	2.50
	Volume of imports of goods and services, % change	−1.56	1.62	−1.16
	Volume of imports of goods, % change	−1.85	2.32	−1.45
	Volume of exports of goods and services, % change	−3.97	0.85	−0.52
	Volume of exports of goods, % change	−7.00	4.83	−2.16
	Population, millions	0.35	0.35	0.39
	General government revenue, % GDP	27.10	27.97	26.65
	General government total expenditure, % GDP	29.26	29.06	28.94
	General government net lending/borrowing, % GDP	−2.16	−1.09	−2.28
	General government gross debt, % GDP	79.61	82.95	76.72
	Current account balance, billions, USD	−$0.07	−$0.04	−$0.11
	Current account balance, % GDP	−4.37	−4.73	−4.73

Source: International Monetary Fund

BOLIVIA OVERVIEW

Government

Government: Unitary presidential constitutional republic
President: Evo Morales
Vice president: Alvaro Garcia Linera
Political party: Partido Movimiento al Socialismo

Top Exports and Imports

Bolivia exported 9181.6 thousands of dollars in 2011. The principal products that Bolivia exports are: gas, minerals, pewter, cakes and oilseed meals, silver, soybean oil, crude oil, and gold. These products are 87% of the totality of the exports.

Economy

The Bolivian economy produces an estimated $29 billion per year, but has a population of some 11.05 million, which translates into a per capita GDP of just $2,602, in current dollar terms. The good news is that the economy grew at 5% in 2013, and is expected to maintain this pace in the 2013–2017 periods. In the near term, import volumes are expected to grow, on average, at about 4.57% per year, and exports some 4.14% per annum. Bolivia maintains a trade surplus of 1% of GDP, which is expected to remain in slightly positive territory in the 2013–2017 period. In Bolivia, government revenues are strong, roughly 35.65% of GDP. This has allowed the government to invest in projects aimed at lowering the poverty rates, with some success.[10]

In terms of Political Liberty, the Democracy Index ranking for Bolivia is 84th out of 167 countries, which corresponds to Freedom House classifying Bolivia as a Partly Free country. On the matter of Economic Liberty, the Heritage Foundation scores Bolivia 47.9 out of 100, and on the Index of Globalization, Bolivia obtains a score of 53.79, surely bolstered by its international sales of raw materials.

Because of the drawbacks of its political system, Bolivia has a mediocre ranking in terms of Global Competitiveness: 104. In the GCI Sub index B (Efficiency Enhancers) Bolivia ranks a paltry 122. In Doing Business overall, Bolivia ranks 155th out of 185 countries. In Starting a Business, Bolivia ranks near the bottom of the whole world sample of 185 countries, with a ranking of 174. In Paying Taxes, the situation is even worse, with the country ranking 180 out of 185. On the Human Development front, Bolivia ranks 108 out of 186 countries. It is hard to see how the country will develop at the rate that it needs to in order to improve its ranking with such a dismal ranking on the Doing Business front. Bolivia ranks 105 out of 183 nations on the Corruption Perceptions Index elaborated by Transparency International, signaling strong defects in the area of political institutions.[11]

Table A.7 Business climate indicators, Bolivia[12]

Indicators: Bolivia	
Global Competitiveness Index, World Economic Forum, ranking 1–144	104
GCI Subindex A Basic requirements	94
GCI Subindex B Efficiency enhancers	122
GCI Subindex C Innovation and sophistication factors	100
Doing Business, World Bank, ranking 1–185	155
DB Starting a Business	174
DB Dealing with Construction Permits	114
DB Getting Electricity	126
DB Registering Property	139
DB Getting Credit	129
DB Protecting Investors	139
DB Paying Taxes	180
DB Trading Across Borders	125
DB Enforcing Contracts	136
DB Resolving Insolvency	68
Human Development Index, United Nations, ranking 1–186	108
Global Gender Gap, World Economic Forum, ranking 1–135	30
Travel and Tourism Competitiveness, World Economic Forum, ranking 1–140	117
Democracy Index, Economist Intelligence Unit, ranking 1–167	85
Freedom Status, Freedom House	Partly Free
Index of Globalization, KOF (0 to 100)	53.79
Index of Economic Liberty, Heritage Foundation (0 to 100)	48
Corruption Perception Index, Transparency International, ranking 1–183	105

Source: Authors' calculations based on various indicators

Table A.8 International Monetary Fund projections, Bolivia[13]

Country	Subject Descriptor	2013	2007–2012	2013–2017
Bolivia	Gross domestic product, constant prices, % change	5.00	4.86	5.00
	Gross domestic product, current prices, billions, USD	$28.74	$26.75	$36.96
	Gross domestic product per capita, current prices, USD	$2,602	$2,469	$3,098
	Gross domestic product based on purchasing-power-parity (PPP) per capita GDP, Int'l dollar	$5,236	$5,017	$6,319
	Gross domestic product based on purchasing-power-parity (PPP) share of world total, %	0.07	0.06	0.07
	Inflation, end of period consumer prices, % change	4.54	7.70	4.15
	Volume of imports of goods and services, % change	4.08	15.35	4.57
	Volume of imports of goods, % change	4.08	15.35	4.57
	Volume of exports of goods and services, % change	3.86	6.23	4.14
	Volume of exports of goods, % change	3.86	6.23	4.14
	Population, millions	11.05	10.84	11.93
	General government revenue, % GDP	35.65	35.85	35.60
	General government total expenditure, % GDP	35.48	34.05	35.16
	General government net lending/borrowing, % GDP	0.17	1.80	0.44
	General government gross debt, % GDP	33.66	37.61	31.58
	Current account balance, billions, USD	$0.30	$0.48	−$0.01
	Current account balance, % GDP	1.06	6.08	0.50

Source: International Monetary Fund

BRAZIL OVERVIEW

Government

Government: Federal presidential constitutional republic
President: Dilma Rousseff
Vice president: Michel Temer

Economy

Brazil will host the World Cup in 2014, and also the Olympic games in 2016. While this is expected to bring in enormous amounts of money, public unrest has erupted around Brazil, because of public discontent over corruption and waste, and public investments directed at sports events rather than the needs of the middle class and the poor.

Brazil is the world's seventh-largest economy, producing some $2,504 billion in 2013. That is expected to grow to $3,254 by 2017. With a population of nearly 200 million people, the per capita GDP for Brazil is $12,643, in current dollar terms, which is expected to grow to nearly $16,000 by 2017. The economy is expected to grow at an estimated 3.95% in 2013, and maintain an average annual rate of growth of 4.12% in the 2013–2017 period. The volume of imports is expected to grow at an average annual rate of 6.48% in the 2013–2017 period, compared to 7.66% for exports. General gross debt is expected to hover around 60% of GDP, and inflation to be contained under 5% per annum. The current account deficit is expected to grow negatively, from −2.8% of GDP in 2013, to an average annual rate of −3.21% of GDP in the near term.[14]

In terms of Global Competitiveness, Brazil ranks well: 48th out of 144. This is due to the fact that Brazil, on account of her size, has reached a critical mass of savvy business persons and market-oriented technical economists. This explains why her scores on Business Sophistication and Innovation are so strong, with a ranking of 39 out of 144. In matters of Doing Business, Brazil doesn't do as well, with a ranking of 130 out of 185. Starting a Business, Dealing with Construction Permits, and Resolving Insolvency are particularly poor showings for Brazil, with rankings of 121, 131, and 143, respectively. Paying Taxes is another area where Brazil fares poorly, with a ranking of 156. On the Human Development front, Brazil has made strong gains, to obtain a ranking of 84 out of 186 countries, obviously with much room for improvement. Brazil ranks fairly well on the Democracy Index, with a ranking of 45 out of 167 countries, for a classification as a Free country by Freedom House. However, economic liberty could still improve in Brazil, with the country scoring 57.7 out of 100 on the Index of Economic Liberty presented by the Heritage Foundation, and 59.36 on the Index of Globalization. Brazil ranks only 69th out of 183, leaving it with much room for improvement, and incentives to do so in order to boost economic performance.[15]

Table A.9 Business climate indicators, Brazil[16]

Indicators: Brazil	
Global Competitiveness Index, World Economic Forum, ranking 1–144	48
GCI Subindex A Basic requirements	73
GCI Subindex B Efficiency enhancers	38
GCI Subindex C Innovation and sophistication factors	39
Doing Business, World Bank, ranking 1–185	130
DB Starting a Business	121
DB Dealing with Construction Permits	131
DB Getting Electricity	60
DB Registering Property	109
DB Getting Credit	104
DB Protecting Investors	82
DB Paying Taxes	156
DB Trading Across Borders	123
DB Enforcing Contracts	116

Indicators: Brazil

DB Resolving Insolvency	143
Human Development Index, United Nations, ranking 1–186	85
Global Gender Gap, World Economic Forum, ranking 1–135	62
Travel and Tourism Competitiveness, World Economic Forum, ranking 1–140	52
Democracy Index, Economist Intelligence Unit, ranking 1–167	44
Freedom Status, Freedom House	Free
Index of Globalization, KOF (0 to 100)	59.36
Index of Economic Liberty, Heritage Foundation (0 to 100)	57.7
Corruption Perception Index, Transparency International, ranking 1–183	69

Source: Authors' calculations based on various indicators

Table A.10 International Monetary Fund projections, Brazil[17]

Country	Subject Descriptor	2013	2007–2012	2013–2017
Brazil	Gross domestic product, constant prices, % change	3.95	3.78	4.12
	Gross domestic product, current prices, billions, USD	$2,504	$2,425	$3,254
	Gross domestic product per capita, current prices, USD	$12,643	$12,340	$15,919
	Gross domestic product based on purchasing-power-parity (PPP) per capita GDP, Int'l dollar	$12,584	$12,038	$15,388
	Gross domestic product based on purchasing-power-parity (PPP) share of world total, %	2.87	2.86	2.86
	Inflation, end of period consumer prices, % change	5.10	5.34	4.62
	Volume of imports of goods and services, % change	5.30	11.99	6.48
	Volume of imports of goods, % change	5.30	11.99	6.48
	Volume of exports of goods and services, % change	6.64	1.11	7.66
	Volume of exports of goods, % change	6.64	1.11	7.66
	Population, millions	198.04	196.53	204.43
	General government revenue, % GDP	35.28	34.79	35.44
	General government total expenditure, % GDP	36.85	37.18	37.25
	General government net lending/borrowing, % GDP	−1.58	−2.39	−1.81
	General government gross debt, % GDP	61.17	64.97	57.28
	Current account balance, billions, USD	−$70.07	−$62.34	−$108.08
	Current account balance, % GDP	−2.80	−1.66	−3.21

Source: International Monetary Fund

CHILE OVERVIEW

Government

Government: Unitary presidential constitutional republic
President: Sebastian Piñera
Political party: Partido Independiente

Top Exports and Imports

Chile exported 80,765.6 thousands of dollars in 2011. The principal products that Chile exports are: copper, minerals, fish, wood pulp, wine, gold, and grapes. These products are 70.5% of the totality of the exports.

Economy

Chile is one of Latin America's most dynamic and yet consistent economies. Her GDP per capita growth is over 3% per annum. Thanks to her great progress, achieved by staying true to market-oriented principles and the precepts of political and economic liberty, Chile became in 2010 the first Latin American country to join the OECD, effectively recognizing that it had entered the ranks of the developed countries. Chile did this by following strict inflation targets, and maintains both a flexible exchange rate and strong fiscal discipline. Chile strives to achieve recognition as a country bent on achieving global competitiveness and promoting investment that will bring quality jobs.

Chile is easily the rock star in Latin America as far as political and economic developments go. In economic terms, Chile is easily the most market- and business-friendly economy in the region. With a population of just over 17.5 million in 2013, Chile produced nearly $292 billion, for a GDP per capita in current dollar terms of $16,630. Inflation hovers around and is expected to remain near 3% per year. In terms of volume, both exports and imports grow in the 4% range. Fiscal balance is maintained, with strong state revenues closing in at around 23% of GDP. Chile runs a current account deficit of about -3% of GDP.[18]

In terms of Global Competitiveness, Chile obtains a general ranking of 33 out of 144, with strong showings in all three sub-categories of Basic Requirements, Efficiency Enhancers, and Business Sophistication and Innovation. On Doing Business, Chile ranks even better in relative terms: 37th out of 185. Starting a Business is relatively easy in Chile (rank 32), as is Paying Taxes (36), and Protecting Investors (32). On the Human Development front, Chile ranks 44th out of 186 nations evaluated by the United Nations. Chile is certainly the Latin American country that best understands the value of liberty, obtaining a strong 79 out of 100 possible score on the matter of Economic Liberty, as measured by the Index of Economic Liberty produced by the Heritage Foundation, and 73.31 on the Index of Globalization. Chile ranks 35th out of167 on the Democracy Index, for a classification as a Free Country by Freedom House. Chilean political institutions are relatively free of corruption, as indicated by its rank of 20 on the Corruptions Perceptions Index published by Transparency International.[19]

Table A.11 Business climate indicators, Chile[20]

Indicators: Chile	
Global Competitiveness Index, World Economic Forum, ranking 1–44	33
GCI Subindex A Basic requirements	28
GCI Subindex B Efficiency enhancers	32
GCI Subindex C Innovation and sophistication factors	45
Doing Business, World Bank, ranking 1–185	37
DB Starting a Business	32
DB Dealing with Construction Permits	84
DB Getting Electricity	40
DB Registering Property	55
DB Getting Credit	53
DB Protecting Investors	32
DB Paying Taxes	36
DB Trading Across Borders	48
DB Enforcing Contracts	70
DB Resolving Insolvency	98
Human Development Index, United Nations, ranking 1–186	40
Global Gender Gap, World Economic Forum, ranking 1–135	87
Travel and Tourism Competitiveness, World Economic Forum, ranking 1–140	57
Democracy Index, Economist Intelligence Unit, ranking 1–167	36
Freedom Status, Freedom House	Free
Index of Globalization, KOF (0 to 100)	73.31
Index of Economic Liberty, Heritage Foundation (0 to 100)	79
Corruption Perception Index, Transparency International, ranking 1–183	20

Source: authors' calculations based on various indicators

Table A.12 International Monetary Fund projections, Chile[21]

Country	Subject Descriptor	2013	2007–2012	2013–2017
Chile	Gross domestic product, constant prices, % change	4.45	4.06	4.57
	Gross domestic product, current prices, billions, USD	$291.97	$268.28	$385.82
	Gross domestic product per capita, current prices, USD	$16,630	$15,416	$21,271
	Gross domestic product based on purchasing-power-parity (PPP) per capita GDP, Int'l dollar	$19,256	$18,354	$23,924
	Gross domestic product based on purchasing-power-parity (PPP) share of world total, %	0.39	0.37	0.39
	Inflation, end of period consumer prices, % change	3.00	3.89	3.00

(Continued)

Table A.12 (Continued)

Country	Subject Descriptor	2013	2007–2012	2013–2017
	Volume of imports of goods and services, % change	4.22	9.05	4.59
	Volume of imports of goods, % change	4.43	11.10	4.63
	Volume of exports of goods and services, % change	4.25	1.98	4.33
	Volume of exports of goods, % change	4.25	1.56	4.33
	Population, millions	17.56	17.40	18.14
	General government revenue, % GDP	23.00	24.21	22.33
	General government total expenditure, % GDP	23.62	22.75	22.58
	General government net lending/borrowing, % GDP	−0.62	1.46	−0.25
	General government gross debt, % GDP	12.25	7.66	12.90
	Current account balance, billions, USD	−$8.76	−$8.58	−$10.24
	Current account balance, % GDP	−3.00	−0.01	−2.79

Source: International Monetary Fund

COLOMBIA OVERVIEW

Government

Government: Unitary presidential constitutional republic
President: Juan Manuel Santos
Vice president: Angelino Garzón
Political party: Primero Colombia

Top Exports and Imports

Colombia exported 56,173.2 thousands of dollars in 2011. The principal products that Colombia exports are: crude oil, charcoal, gold, coffee, flowers, polymerization products, ferroalloys, bananas, and petroleum products. These products account for 79.7% of the totality of exports.

Economy

Colombia is a rising economic star in Latin America. With a 2013 GDP of more than $387 billion and a population of more than 47 million, Colombia enjoys a GDP per capita of $8216 in current dollar terms. Inflation is steady at 3% per year in 2013, and expected to remain so in the near term. In volume, imports are expected to grow in the 4% range per annum over the 2013–2017 period, compared to a 5% average annual range for export volumes. Government debt is contained at roughly 31% of GDP, as is the fiscal deficit at -1.16% of GDP in 2013. Colombia has a trade deficit amounting to -2.89% of GDP for 2013, which is expected to shrink to -2.54% of GDP on yearly average, for the 2013–2017 term.[22]

In terms of Global Competitiveness, Colombia ranks 69th out of 144 countries, and 66 in Business and Sophistication Factors. Surprisingly, on the Doing Business front, Colombia is doing exceedingly well, ranking 45th out of 185 countries. On average, it is easier to start a business in Colombia, when compared to the rest of the Latin American countries taken as a whole. Getting Electricity is an area of low rank for Colombia, 134th out of 185 countries, as is Enforcing Contracts (rank 154), signaling strong defects in the legal system. On the Human Development front, taken in the Latin American context, Colombia does fairly well, with a ranking of 87 out of 186 countries. Colombia only ranks 94 out of 183 countries, leaving much room for improvement. On the matter of political liberty, Colombia obtains a ranking on the Democracy Index of the Economist Intelligence Unit of 55 out of 167 nations, for a classification as a Partly Free country by Freedom House. On the matter of the Index of Economic Liberty, elaborated by the Heritage Foundation, Colombia scores much better, with a score of 69.6 out of 100, and a score of 56.32 on the Index of Globalization. Colombia is a trending economic powerhouse, which has seen the benefits of restoring law and order in the face of left-wing terrorism, and is being duly rewarded by market forces for this fact.[23]

Table A.13 Business climate indicators, Colombia[24]

Indicators: Colombia	
Global Competitiveness Index, World Economic Forum, ranking 1–44	69
GCI Subindex A Basic requirements	77
GCI Subindex B Efficiency enhancers	63
GCI Subindex C Innovation and sophistication factors	66
Doing Business, World Bank, ranking 1–185	45
DB Starting a Business	61
DB Dealing with Construction Permits	27
DB Getting Electricity	134
DB Registering Property	52
DB Getting Credit	70
DB Protecting Investors	6
DB Paying Taxes	99
DB Trading Across Borders	91
DB Enforcing Contracts	154
DB Resolving Insolvency	21
Human Development Index, United Nations, ranking 1–186	91
Global Gender Gap, World Economic Forum, ranking 1–135	63
Travel and Tourism Competitiveness, World Economic Forum, ranking 1–140	77
Democracy Index, Economist Intelligence Unit, ranking 1–167	57
Freedom Status, Freedom House	Partly Free
Index of Globalization, KOF (0 to 100)	56.32
Index of Economic Liberty, Heritage Foundation (0 to 100)	69
Corruption Perception Index, Transparency International, ranking 1–183	94

Source: Authors' calculations based on various indicators

Table A.14 International Monetary Fund projections, Colombia[25]

Country	Subject Descriptor	2013	2007–2012	2013–2017
Colombia	Gross domestic product, constant prices, % change	4.41	4.38	4.47
	Gross domestic product, current prices, billions, USD	$387.40	$365.40	$482.16
	Gross domestic product per capita, current prices, USD	$8,216	$7,842	$9,755
	Gross domestic product based on purchasing-power-parity (PPP) per capita GDP, Int'l dollar	$11,219	$10,729	$13,676
	Gross domestic product based on purchasing-power-parity (PPP) share of world total, %	0.61	0.59	0.61
	Inflation, end of period consumer prices, % change	3.05	4.16	3.01
	Volume of imports of goods and services, % change	4.89	11.08	4.56
	Volume of imports of goods, % change	4.89	11.08	4.56
	Volume of exports of goods and services, % change	8.82	7.47	5.52
	Volume of exports of goods, % change	8.82	7.47	5.52
	Population, millions	47.15	46.60	49.43
	General government revenue, % GDP	28.23	26.88	27.47
	General government total expenditure, % GDP	29.38	28.43	28.62
	General government net lending/borrowing, % GDP	−1.16	−1.55	−1.15
	General government gross debt, % GDP	30.92	33.74	29.18
	Current account balance, billions, USD	−$11.19	−$10.66	−$11.34
	Current account balance, % GDP	−2.89	−2.81	−2.54

Source: International Monetary Fund

COSTA RICA OVERVIEW

Government
Government: Unitary presidential constitutional republic
President: Laura Chinchilla
Vice president: Alfio Piva
Political party: Partido Liberación Nacional

Top Exports and Imports
Costa Rica exported 10,217.4 thousands of dollars in 2011. The principal products that Costa Rica exports are: electronic valves and tubes, medicine instruments, bananas, tropical fruits, coffee, medicines, electric mechanisms, and orthopedic devices. These products represent 57.8% of the totality of the exports.

Economy

If Chile is the rock star of Latin America, Costa Rica is the rising star of Central America. With a population of 4.72 million people, Costa Rica produced in 2013 some $49.21 in GDP, measured in current dollar terms. That is expected to grow to more than $64 billion by 2017. The Costa Rican economy grew at 4.3% in 2013, and is expected to continue at just over that figure for the 2013–2017 time period. In current dollar terms, GDP per capita stands at $10,431, which is expected to grow to more than $13,083 by 2017. Thanks to strong economic growth, Costa Rica has a trade deficit of -5.28% of GDP. General government gross debt is contained at roughly 35% of GDP, but that figure is expected to rise to nearly 41% of GDP by 2017. Costa Rica posted a large fiscal deficit of -5.13% of GDP, with revenues of 14.38% of GDP exceeded by government spending of 19.5% of GDP. Inflation was at 5% in 2013, but is expected to hover around 4.4% per annum in the near term.[26]

Costa Rica scores relatively well on matters of Global Competitiveness, with a rank of 57 out of 144. On Basic Requirements, she scores a 67, and 60 on Efficiency Enhancers. Costa Rica scores an impressive rank of 35th out of 144 on Innovation and Business Sophistication Factors. On Doing Business, Costa Rica still has not improved as much as she should have, with a ranking of 110 out of 185. While Getting Electricity and Registering Property are strong points, Protecting Investors gets a poor rank of 169, and Paying Taxes also, with a rank of 125. On matters of Human Development, Costa Rica scores even better than in overall competitiveness, with a rank of 69 out of 186 countries. Costa Rica is one of the few Latin American countries to leave behind the Iberian legacy of machismo, i.e. gender discrimination against women. Costa Rica scores 29 on the Global Gender Gap, out of 135 countries. In strong measure due to its excellent progress on the gender equity front, Costa Rica ranks 20th out of 167 on the Democracy Index, for a classification as a Free country by Freedom House. Costa Rica scores 67 out of 100 on the Index of Economic Liberty, and 63.09 on the Index of Globalization, indicating a country that is cognizant of the benefits of globalization and free trade.[27]

Table A.15 Business climate indicators, Costa Rica[28]

Indicators: Costa Rica	
Global Competitiveness Index, World Economic Forum, ranking 1–144	1
GCI Subindex A Basic requirements	67
GCI Subindex B Efficiency enhancers	60
GCI Subindex C Innovation and sophistication factors	35
Doing Business, World Bank, ranking 1–185	110
DB Starting a Business	128
DB Dealing with Construction Permits	128
DB Getting Electricity	45
DB Registering Property	46

(Continued)

Table A.15 (Continued)

Indicators: Costa Rica	
DB Getting Credit	83
DB Protecting Investors	169
DB Paying Taxes	125
DB Trading Across Borders	51
DB Enforcing Contracts	128
DB Resolving Insolvency	128
Human Development Index, United Nations, ranking 1–186	62
Global Gender Gap, World Economic Forum, ranking 1–135	29
Travel and Tourism Competitiveness, World Economic Forum, ranking 1–140	44
Democracy Index, Economist Intelligence Unit, ranking 1–167	22
Freedom Status, Freedom House	Free
Index of Globalization, KOF (0 to 100)	63.09
Index of Economic Liberty, Heritage Foundation (0 to 100)	67
Corruption Perception Index, Transparency International, ranking 1–183	48

Source: Authors' calculations based on various indicators

Table A.16 International Monetary Fund projections, Costa Rica[29]

Country	Subject Descriptor	2013	2007–2012	2013–2017
Costa Rica	Gross domestic product, constant prices, % change	4.30	3.88	4.44
	Gross domestic product, current prices, billions, USD	$49.21	$44.88	$64.49
	Gross domestic product per capita, current prices, USD	$10,431	$9,619	$13,083
	Gross domestic product based on purchasing-power-parity (PPP) per capita GDP, Int'l dollar	$13,128	$12,559	$16,051
	Gross domestic product based on purchasing-power-parity (PPP) share of world total, %	0.07	0.07	0.07
	Inflation, end of period consumer prices, % change	5.00	7.39	4.40
	Volume of imports of goods and services, % change	5.14	5.86	4.01
	Volume of imports of goods, % change	6.38	4.66	6.39
	Volume of exports of goods and services, % change	3.08	3.27	2.41
	Volume of exports of goods, % change	5.68	2.93	6.35
	Population, millions	4.72	4.67	4.93
	General government revenue, % GDP	14.38	14.53	14.52
	General government total expenditure, % GDP	19.50	17.57	20.42
	General government net lending/borrowing, % GDP	−5.13	−3.04	−5.91
	General government gross debt, % GDP	34.90	28.71	40.71
	Current account balance, billions, USD	−$2.60	−$2.45	−$3.54
	Current account balance, % GDP	−5.28	−5.31	−5.41

Source: International Monetary Fund

DOMINICAN REPUBLIC OVERVIEW

Government

Government: Unitary representative democratic republic
President: Danilo Medina
Vice president: Margarita Cedeño de Fernández

Economy

The Dominican Republic boasts a population of some 10.42 million, which produces a GDP of nearly $62 billion as of 2013. This translates into a GDP per capita in current dollar terms of nearly $6,000 per year. The volume of imports of goods and services is expected to grow at an average annual rate of 5.33%, compared to the volume of exports and services, which is expected to grow at an average annual yearly rate of 7.37% in the 2013–2017 period. The Dominican Republic runs a large fiscal deficit of -3.34% of GDP, which is expected to average nearly -3.91% of GDP in the 2013–2017 time period. Public debt stands at 31.69% of GDP in 2013, and on average will stand at about roughly two percentage points higher in the near term. Inflation is moderate at 5% in 2013, and is expected to remain so, at about 4.3% per annum, on average, in the near term.[30]

The Dominican Republic lags in terms of Global Competitiveness, with a rank of 105th out of 144 countries. She scores poorly in her rankings on Basic Requirements, Efficiency Enhancers, and Sophistication and Innovation Factors. In Doing Business, she ranks 116th out of 185 countries. Getting Electricity and Registering Property are problem areas, as is Resolving Insolvency. On the Human Development front, the Dominican Republic ranks 98, which is better than other neighbors in the Central American region, excepting Costa Rica and Panama. On the Democracy Index, in a ranking of 167 countries, the Dominican Republic obtains a ranking of 70, which is in the top half of the countries of the world. Her Freedom Status as per Freedom House is Free. The Dominican Republic scores 59.7 on the Index of Economic Liberty. The country has challenges in the matter of public corruption, as shown by the ranking of 118 out of 183 countries on the Corruption Perceptions Index published by Transparency International.[31]

Table A.17 Business climate indicators, Dominican Republic[32]

Indicators: Dominican Republic	
Global Competitiveness Index, World Economic Forum, ranking 1–144	105
GCI Subindex A Basic requirements	111
GCI Subindex B Efficiency enhancers	93
GCI Subindex C Innovation and sophistication factors	105
Doing Business, World Bank, ranking 1–185	116
DB Starting a Business	137

(Continued)

Table A.17 (Continued)

Indicators: Dominican Republic	
DB Dealing with Construction Permits	108
DB Getting Electricity	122
DB Registering Property	110
DB Getting Credit	83
DB Protecting Investors	100
DB Paying Taxes	98
DB Trading Across Borders	46
DB Enforcing Contracts	84
DB Resolving Insolvency	156
Human Development Index, United Nations, ranking 1–186	96
Global Gender Gap, World Economic Forum, ranking 1–135	89
Travel and Tourism Competitiveness, World Economic Forum, ranking 1–140	72
Democracy Index, Economist Intelligence Unit, ranking 1–167	60
Freedom Status, Freedom House	Free
Index of Globalization, KOF (0 to 100)	55.07
Index of Economic Liberty, Heritage Foundation (0 to 100)	59.7
Corruption Perception Index, Transparency International, ranking 1–183	118

Source: Authors' calculations based on various indicators

Table A.18 International Monetary Fund projections, Dominican Republic[33]

Country	Subject Descriptor	2013	2007–2012	2013–2017
Dominican Republic	Gross domestic product, constant prices, % change	4.50	5.58	4.90
	Gross domestic product, current prices, billions, USD	$61.97	$59.13	$81.18
	Gross domestic product per capita, current prices, USD	$5,946	$5,776	$7,251
	Gross domestic product based on purchasing-power-parity (PPP) per capita GDP, Int'l dollar	$10,033	$9,645	$12,173
	Gross domestic product based on purchasing-power-parity (PPP) share of world total, %	0.12	0.11	0.12
	Inflation, end of period consumer prices, % change	5.00	6.28	4.30
	Volume of imports of goods and services, % change	5.74	3.82	5.33
	Volume of imports of goods, % change	7.06	2.54	6.65
	Volume of exports of goods and services, % change	12.50	2.55	7.37
	Volume of exports of goods, % change	17.61	3.68	9.00
	Population, millions	10.42	10.24	11.20
	General government revenue, % GDP	13.56	14.70	13.56
	General government total expenditure, % GDP	16.90	17.41	17.47

Country	Subject Descriptor	2013	2007–2012	2013–2017
	General government net lending/borrowing, % GDP	−3.34	−2.71	−3.91
	General government gross debt, % GDP	31.69	27.70	33.83
	Current account balance, billions, USD	−$4.51	−$4.41	−$4.71
	Current account balance, % GDP	−7.28	−7.39	−6.41

Source: International Monetary Fund

ECUADOR OVERVIEW

Government

Government: Unitary presidential constitutional republic
President: Rafael Correa
Political party: Alianza Pais

Top Exports and Imports

Ecuador exported 22,322.1 thousands of dollars in the 2011. The principal products that Ecuador exports are: crude oil, bananas, crustaceans, fish, flowers, cacao, and oil. These products are 85.4% of the totality of exports.

Economy

Ecuador boasts a population in 2013 of 15.47 million inhabitants, which together produced a GDP in current dollar terms of $76.4 billion, which is expected to rise to nearly $97 billion by 2017. In GDP per capita terms, the average Ecuadorian citizen earns about $4,939 in current dollars, which is expected to grow to $5,903 by 2017. Inflation is contained in the 4% range, and is expected to drop to the 3% range on an annual average basis for the 2013–2017 term. The volume of imports of goods and services is expected to grow at an average annual rate of 2.99%, compared to 2.76% for exports of goods and services. Ecuador enjoys a trade surplus of over 3% of GDP in 2013, but that is expected to decline to just under 0.3% of GDP on an average annual rate for the 2013–2017 time period. Ecuador maintains fiscal discipline, with both government revenues and spending coming in at over 40% of GDP. The government of Ecuador will increase public spending in the ostensible pursuit of the reduction of poverty and social inclusion. For all her anti-Yankee rhetoric, Ecuador adopted the US dollar as the official currency, to overcome problems of political instability.[34]

On matters of Global Competitiveness, Ecuador obtains a fair ranking of 86 out of 144. The country scores even better on Basic Requirements, but lags in Efficiency Enhancers. On Doing Business, Ecuador has fallen behind, with a very poor ranking of 139. Starting a Business in Ecuador is particularly difficult, as her ranking of 169 would bear out. Getting Electricity and Protecting Investors are strong negative areas for Ecuador, as is Trading Across Borders. On Human Development, Ecuador has made progress, with a ranking of 83 out of 186 countries. Ecuador's rank on the Democracy Index is a poor 89 out of 167, for a classification of Partly Free by Freedom House. On the Index of Globalization, Ecuador scores 54.16, and on the Index of Economic Liberty overall, it scores 46.9.[35]

Table A.19 Business climate indicators, Ecuador[36]

Indicators: Ecuador	
Global Competitiveness Index, World Economic Forum, ranking 1–144	86
GCI Subindex A Basic requirements	75
GCI Subindex B Efficiency enhancers	100
GCI Subindex C Innovation and sophistication factors	93
Doing Business, World Bank, ranking 1–185	139
DB Starting a Business	169
DB Dealing with Construction Permits	104
DB Getting Electricity	146
DB Registering Property	101
DB Getting Credit	83
DB Protecting Investors	139
DB Paying Taxes	84
DB Trading Across Borders	128
DB Enforcing Contracts	99
DB Resolving Insolvency	137
Human Development Index, United Nations, ranking 1–186	89
Global Gender Gap, World Economic Forum, ranking 1–135	33
Travel and Tourism Competitiveness, World Economic Forum, ranking 1–140	87
Democracy Index, Economist Intelligence Unit, ranking 1–167	87
Freedom Status, Freedom House	Partly Free
Index of Globalization, KOF (0 to 100)	54.16
Index of Economic Liberty, Heritage Foundation (0 to 100)	46.9
Corruption Perception Index, Transparency International, ranking 1–183	118

Source: Authors' calculations based on various indicators

Table A.20 International Monetary Fund projections, Ecuador[37]

Country	Subject Descriptor	2013	2007–2012	2013–2017
Ecuador	Gross domestic product, constant prices, % change	4.12	4.18	3.67
	Gross domestic product, current prices, billions, USD	$76.40	$70.84	$96.91
	Gross domestic product per capita, current prices, USD	$4,939	$4,648	$5,903
	Gross domestic product based on purchasing-power-parity (PPP) per capita GDP, Int'l dollar	$9,191	$8,841	$10,681
	Gross domestic product based on purchasing-power-parity (PPP) share of world total, %	0.16	0.16	0.16
	Inflation, end of period consumer prices, % change	4.47	4.97	3.37
	Volume of imports of goods and services, % change	2.50	4.01	2.99

Country	Subject Descriptor	2013	2007–2012	2013–2017
	Volume of imports of goods, % change	2.82	6.69	0.29
	Volume of exports of goods and services, % change	13.46	3.07	2.76
	Volume of exports of goods, % change	13.25	0.73	1.49
	Population, millions	15.47	15.24	16.42
	General government revenue, % GDP	43.31	35.04	40.34
	General government total expenditure, % GDP	42.77	36.13	41.21
	General government net lending/borrowing, % GDP	0.54	−1.08	−0.88
	General government gross debt, % GDP	18.79	19.39	19.07
	Current account balance, billions, USD	$2.32	−$0.24	−$2.52
	Current account balance, % GDP	3.04	0.69	−0.36

Source: International Monetary Fund

EL SALVADOR OVERVIEW

Government

Government: presidential constitutional republic
President: Mauricio Funes
Vice president: Salvador Cerén
Political party: Partido Frente Martí para la Liberación Nacional

Top Exports and Imports

El Salvador exported 4107.6 thousands of dollars in 2011. The principal products that El Salvador exports are: coffee, underwear, clothes, tights, petroleum products, sugar, paper, medicines, and gold. These products are 49.5% of the totality of its exports.

Economy

El Salvador is a small country of some six million people. Its GDP stands at over $25 billion in 2013, for a GDP per capita of $4,210 in current terms. The GDP growth rate posted at 2% per year in 2013, and is expected to tick upwards slightly for an average annual growth rate of 2.5 in 2013. The volume of imports of goods and services is expected to grow at an average annual rate in the 5% range, compared to the 4% range for imports of goods and services in the same period. El Salvador runs both a fiscal and trade deficit, at −2.93% and −4.26% of GDP, respectively. Neither deficit is expected to come into balance in the short term.[38]

El Salvador obtains a ranking of 101 out of 144 on the Global Competitiveness Index. In Doing Business, she obtains a ranking of 113 out of 185 countries. On matters of Starting a Business, Dealing with Construction Permits, Getting Electricity, Protecting Investors, and Paying Taxes, El Salvador leaves much room for improvement. The country, however, ranks much better in Trading Across Borders. On the Human Development front, El Salvador ranks better than neighbors Honduras and Guatemala, with a ranking of 105 out of 186 countries. On a bright note, El Salvador ranks well, 61 out of 167, on the Democracy Index, for a classification as Free by Freedom House. On a range of 0 to 100, El Salvador scores 66.7 on Index of Economic Liberty, and obtains a score of 63.71 on KOF's Index of Globalization, showing the country is open to trade.[39]

Table A.21 Business climate indicators, El Salvador[40]

Indicators: El Salvador	
Global Competitiveness Index, World Economic Forum, ranking 1–144	101
GCI Subindex A Basic requirements	99
GCI Subindex B Basic Efficiency enhancers	103
GCI Subindex C Innovation and sophistication factors	107
Doing Business, World Bank, ranking 1–185	113
DB Starting a Business	139
DB Dealing with Construction Permits	146
DB Getting Electricity	131
DB Registering Property	56
DB Getting Credit	53
DB Protecting Investors	169
DB Paying Taxes	153
DB Trading Across Borders	80
DB Enforcing Contracts	71
DB Resolving Insolvency	89
Human Development Index, United Nations, ranking 1–186	107
Global Gender Gap, World Economic Forum, ranking 1–135	94
Travel and Tourism Competitiveness, World Economic Forum, ranking 1–140	96
Democracy Index, Economist Intelligence Unit, ranking 1–167	61
Freedom Status, Freedom House	Free
Index of Globalization, KOF (0 to 100)	63.71
Index of Economic Liberty, Heritage Foundation (0 to 100)	66.7
Corruption Perception Index, Transparency International, ranking 1–183	83

Source: Authors' calculations based on various indicators

Table A.22 International Monetary Fund projections, El Salvador[41]

Country	Subject Descriptor	2013	2007–2012	2013–2017
El Salvador	Gross domestic product, constant prices, % change	2.00	1.05	2.50
	Gross domestic product, current prices, billions, USD	$25.20	$23.99	$31.46
	Gross domestic product per capita, current prices, USD	$4,210	$4,034	$5,112
	Gross domestic product based on purchasing-power-parity (PPP) per capita GDP, Int'l dollar	$7,939	$7,734	$9,186

Country	Subject Descriptor	2013	2007–2012	2013–2017
	Gross domestic product based on purchasing-power-parity (PPP) share of world total, %	0.06	0.06	0.05
	Inflation, end of period consumer prices, % change	2.80	3.42	2.80
	Volume of imports of goods and services, % change	4.70	0.66	5.20
	Volume of imports of goods, % change	4.79	0.85	5.38
	Volume of exports of goods and services, % change	5.17	3.52	4.66
	Volume of exports of goods, % change	5.46	4.24	4.87
	Population, millions	5.99	5.95	6.15
	General government revenue, % GDP	18.66	17.15	19.04
	General government total expenditure, % GDP	21.59	20.84	21.57
	General government net lending/borrowing, % GDP	−2.93	−3.69	−2.53
	General government gross debt, % GDP	51.68	46.37	49.90
	Current account balance, billions, USD	−$1.07	−$1.19	−$0.95
	Current account balance, % GDP	−4.26	−4.69	−3.50

Source: International Monetary Fund

GUATEMALA OVERVIEW

Government

Government: Unitary presidential constitutional republic
President: Otto Perez Molina
Vice president: Roxana Baldetti
Political party: Partido Patriota

Top Exports and Imports

Guatemala exported 7,055.2 thousands of dollars in 2011. The principal products that Guatemala exports are: coffee, sugar, bananas, crude oil, cardamom, palm oil, medicines, cosmetics, and rubber. These products are 55% of the totality of its exports.

Economy

Guatemala has a population of some 15.48 million people in 2013, and produced a GDP of just over $53 billion, for a GDP per capita of $3,435 in current terms. The economy grows at a 3.2% per annum clip, a pace that it is expected to keep for the near terms. By 2017, it is expected that Guatemala will be producing a GDP of more than $67 billion, but that GDP per capita will still only rise to $3,935 per year. Thanks to a well-functioning, independent central bank, Guatemala is expected to keep inflation down to moderate levels, around 4% per annum, for the near term. The volume of both imports and exports of goods and services is expected to grow at an average annual rate in the range of 4% for the 2013–2017 time period. Guatemala runs a moderate fiscal deficit of around -2.1% of GDP, and a trade deficit of around -3.64% of GDP. Government revenues stand close to 12% of GDP, whereas expenditures are closer to 15% of GDP. Public debt hovers around 25% of GDP; although it seems successive governments are bent on increasing that figure.[42]

Guatemala is a medium-ranked country on the matter of Global Competitiveness, with a ranking of 83 out of 144 countries. On Basic Requirements, Guatemala ranks 88, and 81 on Efficiency Enhancers. Guatemala scores relatively well, ranking 70, on Business Sophistication and Innovation Factors, indicating that the country possesses a competent, innovative managerial class. This is reflected in its ranking for Doing Business, 93 out of 185 countries—a relatively decent ranking in spite of the dismal ranking of 172 for Starting a Business. Poor rankings in the areas of Protecting Investors, Paying Taxes, and Trading Across Borders impact negatively on the Doing Business climate in Guatemala. On the Human Development front, Guatemala ranks quite poorly, 131 out of 186 countries, as she does in the Global Gender Gap, 116 out of 135 countries. Guatemala is classified as Partly Free by Freedom House, and obtains a ranking of 82 out of 167 countries on the Democracy Index. On the Index of Economic Liberty, Guatemala obtains a score of 60 out of 100, and 60.86 on the Index of Globalization. Guatemala suffers from corrupt political institutions, as evidenced by the poor ranking of 113 out of 183 nations on the Corruptions Perceptions Index.[43]

Table A.23 Business climate indicators, Guatemala[44]

Indicators: Guatemala	
Global Competitiveness Index, World Economic Forum, ranking 1–144	83
GCI Subindex A Basic requirements	88
GCI Subindex B Basic Efficiency enhancers	81
GCI Subindex C Innovation and sophistication factors	70
Doing Business, World Bank, ranking 1–185	93
DB Starting a Business	172
DB Dealing with Construction Permits	94
DB Getting Electricity	34
DB Registering Property	20
DB Getting Credit	12
DB Protecting Investors	158
DB Paying Taxes	124
DB Trading Across Borders	117
DB Enforcing Contracts	96
DB Resolving Insolvency	109
Human Development Index, United Nations, ranking 1–186	133

Indicators: Guatemala

Global Gender Gap, World Economic Forum, ranking 1–135	116
Travel and Tourism Competitiveness, World Economic Forum, ranking 1–140	86
Democracy Index, Economist Intelligence Unit, ranking 1–167	81
Freedom Status, Freedom House	Partly Free
Index of Globalization, KOF (0 to 100)	60.86
Index of Economic Liberty, Heritage Foundation (0 to 100)	60
Corruption Perception Index, Transparency International, ranking 1–183	113

Source: Authors' calculations based on various indicators

Table A.24 International Monetary Fund projections, Guatemala[45]

Country	Subject Descriptor	2013	2007–2012	2013–2017
Guatemala	Gross domestic product, constant prices, % change	3.20	3.33	3.38
	Gross domestic product, current prices, billions, USD	$53.19	$50.30	$67.25
	Gross domestic product per capita, current prices, USD	$3,435	$3,330	$3,935
	Gross domestic product based on purchasing-power-parity (PPP) per capita GDP, Int'l dollar	$5,297	$5,192	$5,887
	Gross domestic product based on purchasing-power-parity (PPP) share of world total, %	0.09	0.10	0.09
	Inflation, end of period consumer prices, % change	4.00	5.59	4.00
	Volume of imports of goods and services, % change	4.55	2.32	4.70
	Volume of imports of goods, % change	6.02	1.48	5.11
	Volume of exports of goods and services, % change	3.78	3.78	4.11
	Volume of exports of goods, % change	5.06	2.68	4.49
	Population, millions	15.48	15.11	17.09
	General government revenue, % GDP	12.62	11.78	13.29
	General government total expenditure, % GDP	14.72	14.24	15.09
	General government net lending/borrowing, % GDP	−2.10	−2.46	−1.80
	General government gross debt, % GDP	25.40	22.91	25.78
	Current account balance, billions, USD	−$1.94	−$1.76	−$2.44
	Current account balance, % GDP	−3.64	−2.94	−3.62

Source: International Monetary Fund

GUYANA OVERVIEW

Government

Government: Unitary semi-presidential republic
President: Donald Ramotar
Prime Minister: Sam Hinds

Economy

Guyana is a tiny country, just off the northern coast of South America. With a population of 0.78 million people, it produces a GDP of just over $3 billion per year, and has a GDP per capita of $3,865 in current terms. GDP per capita is expected to grow to more than $5,053 per year in current dollar terms, thanks to a forecast average annual growth rate of GDP of 4.87%. Due in part to strong growth, inflation will come in at just under 6% per annum in 2013, and is expected to hover just below 5% on an average annual basis in the near term. Whereas the volume of imports of goods and services is expected to grow in the 5% per year range, on average, for the 2013–2017 term, exports of goods and services will come in at the 5% range. Guyana will post a fiscal deficit of -3.12% in 2013, which is expected to grow on an average annual basis to -3.29% in the near term. Public debt is high, at about 60% of GDP. Guyana runs a heavy trade deficit, -17.61% of GDP, which is expected, on an average annual basis, to grow even more into negative territory in the near term.[46]

Guyana ranks 114 out of 185 on the Doing Business index. Getting Electricity, Registering Property, and Getting Credit are areas of poor showing, as are Paying Taxes and Resolving Insolvency. On the Human Development front, Guyana scores poorly, with a ranking of 117 out of 186 countries. Surprisingly, Guyana does very well on the Global Gender Gap, ranking 42 out of 135 countries. Guyana is classified as a Fully Free country by Freedom House, and obtains a score of 53.8 on the Index of Globalization by KOF, and 53.19 on the Index of Economic Liberty.[47]

Table A.25 Business climate indicators, Guyana[48]

Indicators: Guyana	
Global Competitiveness Index, World Economic Forum, ranking 1–44	N/A
GCI Subindex A Basic requirements	N/A
GCI Subindex B Efficiency enhancers	N/A
GCI Subindex C Innovation and sophistication factors	N/A
Doing Business, World Bank, ranking 1–185	114
DB Starting a Business	89
DB Dealing with Construction Permits	29
DB Getting Electricity	148
DB Registering Property	114
DB Getting Credit	167
DB Protecting Investors	82

Indicators: Guyana

DB Paying Taxes	118
DB Trading Across Borders	84
DB Enforcing Contracts	75
DB Resolving Insolvency	138
Human Development Index, United Nations, ranking 1–186	118
Global Gender Gap, World Economic Forum, ranking 1–135	42
Travel and Tourism Competitiveness, World Economic Forum, ranking 1–140	98
Democracy Index, Economist Intelligence Unit, ranking 1–167	N/A
Freedom Status, Freedom House	Free
Index of Globalization, KOF (0 to 100)	53.19
Index of Economic Liberty, Heritage Foundation (0 to 100)	53.8
Corruption Perception Index, Transparency International, ranking 1–183	133

Source: Authors' calculations based on various indicators

Table A.26 International Monetary Fund projections, Guyana[49]

Country	Subject Descriptor	2013	2007–2012	2013–2017
Guyana	Gross domestic product, constant prices, % change	5.50	4.30	4.87
	Gross domestic product, current prices, billions, USD	$3.01	$2.79	$3.98
	Gross domestic product per capita, current prices, USD	$3,865	$3,596	$5,053
	Gross domestic product based on purchasing-power-parity (PPP) per capita GDP, Int'l dollar	$8,474	$7,950	$10,789
	Gross domestic product based on purchasing-power-parity (PPP) share of world total, %	0.01	0.01	0.01
	Inflation, end of period consumer prices, % change	5.98	6.07	4.96
	Volume of imports of goods and services, % change	11.48	7.12	6.69
	Volume of imports of goods, % change	11.76	7.94	6.51
	Volume of exports of goods and services, % change	6.17	4.98	5.42
	Volume of exports of goods, % change	4.55	2.24	5.89
	Population, millions	0.78	0.78	0.79
	General government revenue, % GDP	28.80	28.13	28.70
	General government total expenditure, % GDP	31.92	31.75	31.99
	General government net lending/borrowing, % GDP	−3.12	−3.62	−3.29
	General government gross debt, % GDP	60.00	62.89	57.77
	Current account balance, billions, USD	−$0.53	−$0.39	−$0.49
	Current account balance, %GDP	−17.61	−11.82	−18.95

Source: International Monetary Fund

HAITI OVERVIEW

Government

Government: Unitary semi-presidential republic
President: Michel Martelly
Prime Minister: Laurent Lamothe

Economy

Haiti has a population of 10.32 million inhabitants, who produce a paltry $8.53 billion, accounting for a GDP per capita of $827, in current terms. The good news is that GDP grew at 6.5% in 2013, and is expected to hold at an annual average of just under 6% in the 2013–2017 period. Inflation is expected to hold steady at 5% in 2013, and come in at an average annual rate of 4% in the near term. The volume of imports of goods and services is expected to reflect an average annual growth rate of 4.31%, whereas exports of goods and services are expected to reflect an average annual growth rate of 11.86% in the 2013–2017 time period. Haiti posts state revenues of nearly 27% of GDP, but spends nearly 32% of GDP, reflecting a fiscal deficit of -4.74% of GDP in 2013. This trend is expected to continue throughout the near term. Haiti will post a trade deficit of -5.31% of GDP in 2013, and the trade deficit will average -4.66% of GDP in the 2013–2017 time period.[50]

Haiti scores 48.1 on the Index of Economic Liberty and 36.55 on the Index of Globalization, both figures indicating the country is not open to trade. This poor showing bears out the rest of the indicators for Haiti, which give it the classification as the basket case of Latin America. On matters of Global Competitiveness, Haiti ranks 142 out of 144 countries in the world sample, with poor rankings in Basic Requirements, Efficiency Enhancers, and Business Sophistication and Innovation. To make matters worse, Haiti's Doing Business climate is abhorrent, ranking 174 out of 185, with Starting a Business getting a ranking of 183. Registering Property, Getting Credit, Protecting Investors, and Paying Taxes are all areas of very poor ranking for Haiti. Trading Across Borders is yet another area with a quite poor showing by Haiti. On the Democracy Index, Haiti is ranked 114 out of 167, for a Partly Free classification by Freedom House. Public institutions are corrupt in Haiti, as is borne out in the ranking of 165 out of 183 on the Corruptions Perceptions Index. All of this explains why Haiti is ranked 158 out of 186 on the Human Development Index.[51]

Table A.27 Business climate indicators, Haiti[52]

Indicators: Haiti	
Global Competitiveness Index, World Economic Forum, ranking 1–144	142
GCI Subindex A Basic requirements	140
GCI Subindex B Efficiency enhancers	143
GCI Subindex C Innovation and sophistication factors	143
Doing Business, World Bank, ranking 1–185	174
DB Starting a Business	183

Indicators: Haiti

DB Dealing with Construction Permits	136
DB Getting Electricity	71
DB Registering Property	130
DB Getting Credit	159
DB Protecting Investors	169
DB Paying Taxes	123
DB Trading Across Borders	149
DB Enforcing Contracts	97
DB Resolving Insolvency	160
Human Development Index, United Nations, ranking 1–186	161
Global Gender Gap, World Economic Forum, ranking 1–135	N/A
Travel and Tourism Competitiveness, World Economic Forum, ranking 1–140	N/A
Democracy Index, Economist Intelligence Unit, ranking 1–167	116
Freedom Status, Freedom House	Partly Free
Index of Globalization, KOF (0 to 100)	36.55
Index of Economic Liberty, Heritage Foundation (0 to 100)	48.1
Corruption Perception Index, Transparency International, ranking 1–183	165

Source: Authors' calculations based on various indicators

Table A.28 International Monetary Fund projections, Haiti[53]

Country	Subject Descriptor	2013	2007–2012	2013–2017
Guyana	Gross domestic product, constant prices, % change	6.50	1.96	5.94
	Gross domestic product, current prices, billions, USD	$8.53	$7.90	$12.00
	Gross domestic product per capita, current prices, USD	$827	$777	$1,099
	Gross domestic product based on purchasing-power-parity (PPP) per capita GDP, Int'l dollar	$1,374	$1,292	$1,744
	Gross domestic product based on purchasing-power-parity (PPP) share of world total, %	0.02	0.02	0.02
	Inflation, end of period consumer prices, % change	5.00	7.35	4.00
	Volume of imports of goods and services, % change	10.39	8.23	4.31
	Volume of imports of goods, % change	13.55	7.88	5.07
	Volume of exports of goods and services, % change	19.60	5.70	11.86
	Volume of exports of goods, % change	23.06	5.97	13.02
	Population, millions	10.32	10.16	10.92
	General government revenue, % GDP	26.96	22.49	25.09
	General government total expenditure, % GDP	31.70	24.52	29.85
	General government net lending/borrowing, % GDP	−4.74	−2.03	−4.76
	General government gross debt, % GDP	20.07	24.31	25.69
	Current account balance, billions, USD	−$0.45	−$0.34	−$0.48
	Current account balance, % GDP	−5.31	−3.45	−4.66

Source: International Monetary Fund

HONDURAS OVERVIEW

Government

Government: constitutional republic
President: Porfirio Lobo Sosa
Vice president: Maria Antonieta de Bográn
Political party: Partido Nacional

Top Exports and Imports

Honduras exported 3896.8 thousands of dollars in 2011. The principal products that Honduras exports are: coffee, bananas, crustaceans, gold, palm oil, cigars, soaps, fish, and fresh fruits. These products are 69.3% of the totality of exports.

Economy

Honduras is country of some 8.37 million inhabitants, who together produce a GDP of nearly $19 billion, for a GDP per capita of just $2,246 per year in current dollar terms. Total GDP is expected to increase to $25.15 billion by 2017, and GDP per capita to an estimated $2,766, due in part to an average annual GDP growth rate of 3.76 forecast for the 2013–2017 period. Government revenues represent roughly 24% of GDP, but spending some 27% of GDP, which resulted in a fiscal deficit of -3.16% of GDP in 2013. Honduras is expected to continue running fiscal deficits on the average of -2.5% of GDP in the near term, with average annual inflation rates of over 6% also. Honduras also posted a large negative trade balance in 2013, −9.57% of GDP, which is expected to average -8.21% of GDP in the 2013–2017 time period. In volume terms, both imports and exports of goods and services are expected to grow at an average annual rate of 6% for the near term.[54]

Honduras posts a ranking of 90 out of 144 on the Global Competitiveness Index, with even poorer rankings in Basic Requirements and Efficiency Enhancers. In Doing Business, Honduras ranks 125 out of 185 countries, with strong negative rankings in Starting a Business, Protecting Investors, Enforcing Contracts and Paying Taxes. Honduras's ranking on Human Development is 121, and 74 out of 135 on the Global Gender Gap. Honduras ranks 84 on the Democracy Index, out of 167, and obtains a Partly Free status from Freedom House. On the Index of Globalization, Honduras scores 61.44, and 58.4 out of 100 on the Index of Economic Liberty. Honduras struggles with public corruption, as shown by her ranking of 133 out of 183 countries on the Corruption Perceptions Index.[55]

Table A.29 Business climate indicators, Honduras[56]

Indicators: Honduras	
Global Competitiveness Index, World Economic Forum, ranking 1–144	90
GCI Subindex A Basic requirements	101
GCI Subindex B Efficiency enhancers	102
GCI Subindex C Innovation and sophistication factors	91
Doing Business, World Bank, ranking 1–185	125
DB Starting a Business	155
DB Dealing with Construction Permits	65

Indicators: Honduras

DB Getting Electricity	117
DB Registering Property	92
DB Getting Credit	12
DB Protecting Investors	169
DB Paying Taxes	139
DB Trading Across Borders	90
DB Enforcing Contracts	179
DB Resolving Insolvency	133
Human Development Index, United Nations, ranking 1–186	120
Global Gender Gap, World Economic Forum, ranking 1–135	74
Travel and Tourism Competitiveness, World Economic Forum, ranking 1–140	88
Democracy Index, Economist Intelligence Unit, ranking 1–167	85
Freedom Status, Freedom House	Partly Free
Index of Globalization, KOF (0 to 100)	61.44
Index of Economic Liberty, Heritage Foundation (0 to 100)	58.4
Corruption Perception Index, Transparency International, ranking 1–183	133

Source: Authors' calculations based on various indicators

Table A.30 International Monetary Fund projections, Honduras[57]

Country	Subject Descriptor	2013	2007–2012	2013–2017
Honduras	Gross domestic product, constant prices, % change	3.56	3.07	3.76
	Gross domestic product, current prices, billions, USD	$18.81	$18.18	$25.15
	Gross domestic product per capita, current prices, USD	$2,246	$2,217	$2,766
	Gross domestic product based on purchasing-power-parity (PPP) per capita GDP, Int'l dollar	$4,722	$4,593	$5,415
	Gross domestic product based on purchasing-power-parity (PPP) share of world total, %	0.05	0.05	0.05
	Inflation, end of period consumer prices, % change	6.48	6.88	6.22
	Volume of imports of goods and services, % change	8.04	−1.79	6.79
	Volume of imports of goods, % change	8.04	−1.79	6.79
	Volume of exports of goods and services, % change	8.58	6.19	6.68
	Volume of exports of goods, % change	8.58	6.19	6.68
	Population, millions	8.37	8.20	9.09
	General government revenue, % GDP	24.02	24.63	23.34
	General government total expenditure, % GDP	27.18	27.48	25.84
	General government net lending/borrowing, % GDP	−3.16	−2.85	−2.50
	General government gross debt, % GDP	32.25	24.83	31.68
	Current account balance, billions, USD	−$1.80	−$1.79	−$1.71
	Current account balance, %GDP	−9.57	−8.80	−8.21

Source: International Monetary Fund

JAMAICA OVERVIEW

Government
Government: Parliamentary democracy under constitutional
Monarch: Elizabeth II
Governor-General: Patrick Allen
Prime Minister: Portia Simpson-Miller

Top Exports and Imports
Jamaica exported 1408.4 thousands of dollars in 2011. The principal products that Jamaica exports are: aluminum hydroxide, petroleum products, alcoholic beverages, alcohol, sugar, beer, tubers, coffee, gold, and crustaceans. These products are 75.6% of the totality of exports.

Economy
Jamaica has a population of some 2.77 million people, which produce a GDP of nearly $16 billion, for a GDP per capita of almost $6,000 per year in current terms. Growth is projected to be slow in the coming near term, 2013–2017; Jamaica is expected to grow at an average annual rate of just 1.25%, which explains why GDP per capita is expected to reach only $6,169 in 2017. Inflation will post high in 2013, nearly 8% per annum, and will drop down to an average annual rate of 6.4% for the 2013–2017 time period. Jamaica runs a high fiscal deficit, over -5% of GDP in 2013, which is expected to grow even more negative to an average annual fiscal deficit of -6.38% of GDP in the near term. Jamaica confronts a massive debt problem, with public debt a staggering 140% of GDP. Similarly, the trade deficit was -11.12% of GDP in 2013, and is expected to average -9% of GDP on a yearly basis in the near term. The volume of imports of goods and services is expected to post an average annual rate of increase of 8.58% in the 2013–2017 time period, compared to 9.33% for exports of goods and services.[58]

Jamaica scores relatively well on the Doing Business front, with an overall ranking of 90 out of 185. Jamaica obtains one of the best rankings in the world in the area of Starting a Business, with a ranking of 21; a similarly noteworthy showing is reflected in the ranking of 32 on Resolving Insolvency. Jamaica needs to improve on Getting Electricity, Registering Property, Getting Credit, Paying Taxes, Trading Across Borders, and Enforcing Contracts. However, Jamaica's rank of 80 on Protecting Investors is better than her general rank of 90, a good indicator for foreign investors wishing to do business in Jamaica. Jamaica ranks well on the Democracy Index, 44 out of 167 countries, for a classification as a Free country by Freedom House. Jamaica scores 66.8 out of 100 on the Index of Economic Liberty and 61.34 on the Index of Globalization. Jamaica's nascent adherence to liberty translates into an improved ranking of 83 out of 183 countries on the Corruption Perceptions Index.[59]

Table A.31 Business climate indicators, Jamaica[60]

Indicators: Jamaica	
Global Competitiveness Index, World Economic Forum, ranking 1–144	N/A
GCI Subindex A Basic requirements	N/A
GCI Subindex B Efficiency enhancers	N/A
GCI Subindex C Innovation and sophistication factors	N/A
Doing Business, World Bank, ranking 1–185	90
DB Starting a Business	21
DB Dealing with Construction Permits	50
DB Getting Electricity	123
DB Registering Property	105
DB Getting Credit	104
DB Protecting Investors	82
DB Paying Taxes	163
DB Trading Across Borders	106
DB Enforcing Contracts	129
DB Resolving Insolvency	32
Human Development Index, United Nations, ranking 1–186	85
Global Gender Gap, World Economic Forum, ranking 1–135	51
Travel and Tourism Competitiveness, World Economic Forum, ranking 1–140	65
Democracy Index, Economist Intelligence Unit, ranking 1–167	39
Freedom Status, Freedom House	Free
Index of Globalization, KOF (0 to 100)	61.34
Index of Economic Liberty, Heritage Foundation (0 to 100)	66.8
Corruption Perception Index, Transparency International, ranking 1–183	83

Source: Authors' calculations based on various indicators

Table A.32 International Monetary Fund projections, Jamaica[61]

Country	Subject Descriptor	2013	2007–2012	2013–2017
Jamaica	Gross domestic product, constant prices, % change	1.05	−0.37	1.25
	Gross domestic product, current prices, billions, USD	$15.79	$15.26	$17.36
	Gross domestic product per capita, current prices, USD	$5,696	$5,526	$6,169
	Gross domestic product based on purchasing-power-parity (PPP) per capita GDP, Int'l dollar	$9,303	$9,119	$10,347
	Gross domestic product based on purchasing-power-parity (PPP) share of world total, %	0.03	0.03	0.03

(Continued)

Table A.32 (Continued)

Country	Subject Descriptor	2013	2007–2012	2013–2017
	Inflation, end of period consumer prices, % change	7.96	11.48	6.40
	Volume of imports of goods and services, % change	10.41	1.79	8.58
	Volume of imports of goods, % change	11.31	2.33	8.52
	Volume of exports of goods and services, % change	8.70	0.06	9.33
	Volume of exports of goods, % change	8.47	−2.85	11.98
	Population, millions	2.77	2.76	2.81
	General government revenue, % GDP	25.27	26.66	25.46
	General government total expenditure, % GDP	30.72	33.45	31.84
	General government net lending/borrowing, % GDP	−5.44	−6.79	−6.38
	General government gross debt, % GDP	140.19	134.74	141.02
	Current account balance, billions, USD	−$1.76	−$1.79	−$1.19
	Current account balance, % GDP	−11.12	−13.10	−9.00

Source: International Monetary Fund

MEXICO OVERVIEW

Government

Government: Federal presidential constitutional republic
President: Enrique Peña Nieto

Top Exports and Imports

Mexico exported 349,459.3 thousands of dollars in 2011. The principal products that Mexico exports are: crude oil, vehicles, television, statistical machines, trucks, gold, cables, and engines. These products represent 51.4% of the totality of exports.

Economy

Mexico is a giant in Latin America, with a population of more than 116 million in 2013, who produce a GDP of $1.21 trillion in current dollar terms. This is expected to grow to nearly $1.5 trillion by 2017. Mexico's per capita GDP is $10,431 in 2013, in current dollars. GDP is expected to growing in the 3.36% range on an average yearly basis in the 2013–2017 term, with inflation for the period projected to be just over 3% on an average annual basis. In volume terms, the imports and exports of goods and services are expected to reflect growth in the 7% range, on an average annual basis for the 2013–2017 time period. Fiscal deficits are expected to continue in the -2% of GDP range, and trade deficits in the -1% of GDP range for the near term. Public debt is expected to hold at about 43% of GDP.[62]

Mexico is a powerhouse in Latin America. It is gaining ground in the realm of Global Competitiveness, with a ranking of 53 out of 144, with roughly similar strong showings in Basic Requirements, Efficiency Enhancers, and Business Sophistication and Innovation Factors. Mexico ranks even better in Doing Business, with a ranking of 48 out of 185 countries, and a ranking of 36 for starting a Business and also Dealing with Construction Permits. Notably, Mexico ranks 26th on Resolving Insolvency, an excellent ranking. Getting Electricity, Registering Property, and Paying Taxes are still areas for improvement. Mexico obtains a ranking of 57 out of 186 nations on the Human Development Index, reflecting the strong progress it has made due to sustained economic growth and political reforms undertaken after the debt crisis. Mexico scores a respectable 67 out of 100 on the Index of Economic Liberty, and 59.96 on the Index of Globalization. Mexico ranks 51 out 167 nations on the Democracy Index, but obtains only a status of Partly Free from Freedom House, due in part to its prosecution of the highly violent war on drugs. Mexico suffers from public corruption, as her poor ranking on the Corruptions Perceptions Index would indicate.[63]

Table A.33 Business climate indicators, Mexico[64]

Indicators: Mexico	
Global Competitiveness Index, World Economic Forum, ranking 1–144	53
GCI Subindex A Basic requirements	63
GCI Subindex B Efficiency enhancers	53
GCI Subindex C Innovation and sophistication factors	49
Doing Business, World Bank, ranking 1–185	48
DB Starting a Business	36
DB Dealing with Construction Permits	36
DB Getting Electricity	130
DB Registering Property	141
DB Getting Credit	40
DB Protecting Investors	49
DB Paying Taxes	107
DB Trading Across Borders	61
DB Enforcing Contracts	76
DB Resolving Insolvency	26
Human Development Index, United Nations, ranking 1–186	61
Global Gender Gap, World Economic Forum, ranking 1–135	84
Travel and Tourism Competitiveness, World Economic Forum, ranking 1–140	43
Democracy Index, Economist Intelligence Unit, ranking 1–167	51
Freedom Status, Freedom House	Partly Free
Index of Globalization, KOF (0 to 100)	59.96
Index of Economic Liberty, Heritage Foundation (0 to 100)	67
Corruption Perception Index, Transparency International, ranking 1–183	105

Source: Authors' calculations based on various indicators

Table A.34 International Monetary Fund projections, Mexico[65]

Country	Subject Descriptor	2013	2007–2012	2013–2017
Mexico	Gross domestic product, constant prices, % change	3.45	1.95	3.36
	Gross domestic product, current prices, billions, USD	$1,210.23	$1,162.89	$1,490.48
	Gross domestic product per capita, current prices, USD	$10,431	$10,123	$12,343
	Gross domestic product based on purchasing-power-parity (PPP) per capita GDP, Int'l dollar	$15,881	$15,300	$18,661
	Gross domestic product based on purchasing-power-parity (PPP) share of world total, %	2.12	2.15	2.09
	Inflation, end of period consumer prices, % change	3.27	4.34	3.06
	Volume of imports of goods and services, % change	5.08	3.86	7.17
	Volume of imports of goods, % change	7.02	3.90	7.02
	Volume of exports of goods and services, % change	5.95	4.34	7.53
	Volume of exports of goods, % change	6.14	3.12	6.85
	Population, millions	116.02	114.87	120.73
	General government revenue, % GDP	23.14	22.41	22.96
	General government total expenditure, % GDP	25.25	25.26	24.99
	General government net lending/borrowing, % GDP	−2.11	−2.85	−2.04
	General government gross debt, % GDP	43.16	42.48	43.07
	Current account balance, billions, USD	−$13.73	−$10.96	−$17.11
	Current account balance, % GDP	−1.14	−0.93	−1.10

Source: International Monetary Fund

NICARAGUA OVERVIEW

Government
Government: Unitary presidential constitutional republic
President: Daniel Ortega
Political party: Frente Sandinista de Liberación Nacional

Top Exports and Imports
Nicaragua exported 2,280.7 thousands of dollars in 2011. The principal products that Nicaragua exports are: coffee, beef, gold, crustaceans, sugar, peanut, cheese, milk, cream, and beans. These products account for 76.4% of the totality of its exports.

Economy

With a population of more than six million inhabitants, Nicaragua manages to produce a GDP estimated at $8.41 billion in 2013. This is expected to grow to $10.55 billion by 2017. GDP per capita, however, is a paltry $1,387 for 2013, and will grow to only $1,643 per annum in dollar terms by 2017, indicating that the forecast average annual growth rate of 4% for 2013–2017 will be insufficient for the country's needs. Tellingly, inflation is projected to average 6.94% in the 2013–2017 term. Nicaragua maintains fiscal discipline as far as fiscal deficits go, and public debt has been brought down to 58% of GDP, from an average annual percentage of GDP of more than 76% in the 2007–2012 period. Government revenues and spending hover around the 33–34% of GDP range. Nicaragua runs an astronomical trade deficit, -18% of GDP, which is expected to average -16.12% of GDP in the 2013–2017 term.[66]

Nicaragua ranks 108 on the Global Competitiveness Index, behind neighbors like Guatemala, Costa Rica, and Panama, with particularly poor showing on Efficiency Enhancers, and Business Sophistication and Innovation Factors. On Doing Business, Nicaragua ranks 119 out of 185. Particular areas of concern for the Nicaraguan Doing Business climate are Starting a Business, Dealing with Construction Permits, Getting Electricity, Registering Property, Getting Credit, Protecting Investors, and especially Paying Taxes (ranking 158). These are the reasons why Nicaragua scores only 129 out of 186 nations on the Human Development Index. Where Nicaragua outperforms the entire region is on the Global Gender Gap, with a super ranking of 9, meaning the rights of women are more respected in Nicaragua than in any other country in Latin America. On the Democracy Index, Nicaragua ranks 92 out of 167 nations measured by the Economist Intelligence Unit, for a Partly Free classification by Freedom House. Nicaragua obtains on the Index of Economic Liberty a score of 56.6 out of 100, and a score of 55.11 out of 100 on the Index of Globalization. Run by a socialist government, it is no surprise that Nicaragua obtains an abysmal ranking of 130 out of 183 nations on the Corruption Perceptions Index.[67]

Table A.35 Business climate indicators, Nicaragua[68]

Indicators: Nicaragua	
Global Competitiveness Index, World Economic Forum, ranking 1–144	108
GCI Subindex A Basic requirements	104
GCI Subindex B Efficiency enhancers	119
GCI Subindex C Innovation and sophistication factors	116
Doing Business, World Bank, ranking 1–185	119
DB Starting a Business	131
DB Dealing with Construction Permits	154
DB Getting Electricity	129
DB Registering Property	123
DB Getting Credit	104

(Continued)

Table A.35 (Continued)

Indicators: Nicaragua	
DB Protecting Investors	100
DB Paying Taxes	158
DB Trading Across Borders	81
DB Enforcing Contracts	55
DB Resolving Insolvency	80
Human Development Index, United Nations, ranking 1–186	129
Global Gender Gap, World Economic Forum, ranking 1–135	9
Travel and Tourism Competitiveness, World Economic Forum, ranking 1–140	100
Democracy Index, Economist Intelligence Unit, ranking 1–167	92
Freedom Status, Freedom House	Partly Free
Index of Globalization, KOF (0 to 100)	55.11
Index of Economic Liberty, Heritage Foundation (0 to 100)	56.6
Corruption Perception Index, Transparency International, ranking 1–183	130

Source: Authors' calculations based on various indicators

Table A.36 International Monetary Fund projections, Nicaragua[69]

Country	Subject Descriptor	2013	2007–2012	2013–2017
Nicaragua	Gross domestic product, constant prices, % change	4.00	2.96	4.00
	Gross domestic product, current prices, billions, USD	$8.41	$7.83	$10.55
	Gross domestic product per capita, current prices, USD	$1,387	$1,313	$1,643
	Gross domestic product based on purchasing-power-parity (PPP) per capita GDP, Int'l dollar	$3,459	$3,336	$4,095
	Gross domestic product based on purchasing-power-parity (PPP) share of world total, %	0.02	0.02	0.02
	Inflation, end of period consumer prices, % change	7.55	9.46	6.94
	Volume of imports of goods and services, % change	6.46	7.39	5.85
	Volume of imports of goods, % change	3.00	9.07	5.04
	Volume of exports of goods and services, % change	8.87	9.83	7.96
	Volume of exports of goods, % change	8.03	11.42	7.85
	Population, millions	6.06	5.96	6.42
	General government revenue, % GDP	33.71	33.30	33.74
	General government total expenditure, % GDP	34.59	33.78	34.58
	General government net lending/borrowing, % GDP	−0.88	−0.49	−0.84
	General government gross debt, % GDP	58.25	76.18	51.30
	Current account balance, billions, USD	−$1.52	−$1.61	−$1.48
	Current account balance, % GDP	−18.08	−17.78	−16.12

Source: International Monetary Fund

PANAMA OVERVIEW

Government

Government: Unitary presidential constitutional republic
President: Ricardo Martinelli
Vice President: Juan Carlos Varela
Political Party: Cambio Democrático

Top Exports and Imports

Panama exported 610 thousands of dollars in 2009. The principal products that Panama exports are: fish, fresh fruits, bananas, crustaceans, tropical fruits, gold, medicines, coffee, scrap metal, and meat meal. These products are 78.7% of the totality of exports.

Economy

Thanks to American vision and determination to build the Panama Canal, Panama is the powerhouse of Central America. With a population of just 3.72 million inhabitants, Panama produces a GDP of more than $38.01 billion. This represents a GDP per capita of $10,216 in current terms. GDP per capita will increase to more than $13,213 by 2017, thanks to a projected average annual GDP growth rate of 6.51% in the 2013–2017 time period. Inflation is expected to be between 4% and 5% in that same time period. The volume of imports of goods and services is expected to see an average annual growth rate of 5.38% in the 2013–2017 period, compared to 7.24% for the volume of exports of goods and services. Panama runs large trade deficits, an estimated -11.83% of GDP in 2013, and is expected to average -10.8% of GDP in the 2013–2017 term. Fiscal deficits are expected to average -1.81% of GDP over the next five years, but public debt is expected to hold steady at an average annual share of GDP of 32% in the 2013–2017 term.[70]

Panama is a highly competitive nation, with a ranking of 40 on the Global Competitiveness Index, with strong rankings on Basic Requirements, Efficiency Enhancers (ranking of 50 each), and Business Sophistication and Innovation (48). Panama obtains a solid ranking of 61 out of 185 on the Doing Business front, with an excellent ranking of 23 on Starting a Business, 16 on Getting Electricity, and 9 for Trading Across Borders. Registering Property, Paying Taxes, Enforcing Contracts, and Resolving Insolvency are lagging areas. Panama obtains a solid ranking of 40 out of 135 on the Global Gender Gap, and 58 out of 186 on the Human Development Index. Panama's ranking on the Democracy Index is 47 out of 167, for a Fully Free classification by Freedom House. On the Index of Economic Liberty, Panama scores 62.5, and 68.24 on the Index of Globalization. Panama has progress to make on the public corruption front, as evidenced by her ranking of 83 out of 183 countries on the Corruption Perceptions Index.[71]

Table A.37 Business climate indicators, Panama[72]

Indicators: Panama	
Global Competitiveness Index, World Economic Forum, ranking 1–144	40
GCI Subindex A Basic requirements	50
GCI Subindex B Efficiency enhancers	50
GCI Subindex C Innovation and sophistication factors	48
Doing Business, World Bank, ranking 1–185	61
DB Starting a Business	23
DB Dealing with Construction Permits	73
DB Getting Electricity	16
DB Registering Property	107
DB Getting Credit	53
DB Protecting Investors	82
DB Paying Taxes	172
DB Trading Across Borders	9
DB Enforcing Contracts	125
DB Resolving Insolvency	110
Human Development Index, United Nations, ranking 1–186	59
Global Gender Gap, World Economic Forum, ranking 1–135	40
Travel and Tourism Competitiveness, World Economic Forum, ranking 1–140	56
Democracy Index, Economist Intelligence Unit, ranking 1–167	46
Freedom Status, Freedom House	Free
Index of Globalization, KOF (0 to 100)	68.24
Index of Economic Liberty, Heritage Foundation (0 to 100)	62.5
Corruption Perception Index, Transparency International, ranking 1–183	83

Source: Authors' calculations based on various indicators

Table A.38 International Monetary Fund projections, Panama

Country	Subject Descriptor	2013	2007–2012	2013–2017
Panama	Gross domestic product, constant prices, % change	7.46	8.79	6.51
	Gross domestic product, current prices, billions, USD	$38.01	$34.82	$52.80
	Gross domestic product per capita, current prices, USD	$10,216	$9,527	$13,213
	Gross domestic product based on purchasing-power-parity (PPP) per capita GDP, Int'l dollar	$16,329	$15,266	$20,799
	Gross domestic product based on purchasing-power-parity (PPP) share of world total, %	0.07	0.06	0.07
	Inflation, end of period consumer prices, % change	5.50	5.41	4.40
	Volume of imports of goods and services, % change	10.28	16.09	5.38
	Volume of imports of goods, % change	10.28	16.09	5.38
	Volume of exports of goods and services, % change	6.65	7.95	7.24
	Volume of exports of goods, % change	1.85	14.99	4.11

Country	Subject Descriptor	2013	2007–2012	2013–2017
	Population, millions	3.72	3.66	4.00
	General government revenue, % GDP	24.03	24.92	24.38
	General government total expenditure, % GDP	26.62	25.60	26.19
	General government net lending/borrowing, % GDP	−2.59	−0.68	−1.81
	General government gross debt, % GDP	35.93	42.06	32.01
	Current account balance, billions, USD	−$4.50	−$4.21	−$5.03
	Current account balance, % GDP	−11.83	−9.20	−10.80

Source: International Monetary Fund

PARAGUAY OVERVIEW

Government
Government: Unitary presidential constitutional republic
President: Federico Franco
Vice President: Oscar Denis

Top Exports and Imports
Paraguay exported 5,517.3 thousands of dollars in 2011. The principal products that Paraguay exports are: soy, beef, cakes and oilseed meals, corn, wheat, leather, sugar, and nuts. These products represent 82.2% of the totality of its exports.

Economy
Paraguay is a country of 6.79 million people, which produces a GDP of over $31 billion in current terms. That accounts for a GDP per capita of $4,574 in current dollars, which is expected to grow to $5,698 per year by 2017, thanks to a projected average annual rate of GDP growth of nearly 6% in the 2013–2017 time period. The volume of both imports and exports of goods and services is expected to average in the range of 8% for the next five years. Government revenues are projected to keep pace with government spending, both estimated to average roughly just under 21% of GDP in the 2013–2017 term. Public debt is kept in check, representing just 11.96% of GDP in 2013, and averaging 10.75% of GDP in the 2013–2017 period. Inflation is expected to come in at an average annual rate of 4.58% in the same time frame.[74]

Paraguay holds a ranking of 116 out 144 on the Global Competitiveness Index. Paraguay doesn't rank particularly well in Basic Requirements (106), Efficiency Enhancers (110), or Business Sophistication and Innovation Factors (123). Her ranking on Doing Business is 103 out of 185. Doing Business, Starting a Business, Paying Taxes, Trading Across Borders, Enforcing Contracts, and Resolving Insolvency are problem areas, but the country ranks well on Getting Electricity, and relatively well on Protecting Investors. On the Human Development Index, Paraguay does not rank well, just 107th out of 185 countries. Paraguay ranks 62 out of 167 on the Democracy Index, for a classification of Partly Free by Freedom House. On the Index of Economic Liberty, Paraguay obtains a score of 61.1 out of 100, and 57.53 out of 100 on the Index of Globalization.[75]

Table A.39 Business climate indicators, Paraguay[76]

Indicators: Paraguay	
Global Competitiveness Index, World Economic Forum, ranking 1–144	116
GCI Subindex A Basic requirements	106
GCI Subindex B Efficiency enhancers	110
GCI Subindex C Innovation and sophistication factors	123
Doing Business, World Bank, ranking 1–185	103
DB Starting a Business	111
DB Dealing with Construction Permits	71
DB Getting Electricity	26
DB Registering Property	67
DB Getting Credit	83
DB Protecting Investors	70
DB Paying Taxes	141
DB Trading Across Borders	155
DB Enforcing Contracts	106
DB Resolving Insolvency	144
Human Development Index, United Nations, ranking 1–186	111
Global Gender Gap, World Economic Forum, ranking 1–135	83
Travel and Tourism Competitiveness, World Economic Forum, ranking 1–140	123
Democracy Index, Economist Intelligence Unit, ranking 1–167	70
Freedom Status, Freedom House	Partly Free
Index of Globalization, KOF (0 to 100)	57.53
Index of Economic Liberty, Heritage Foundation (0 to 100)	61.1
Corruption Perception Index, Transparency International, ranking 1–183	150

Source: Authors' calculations based on various indicators

Table A.40 International Monetary Fund projections, Paraguay[77]

Country	Subject Descriptor	2013	2007–2012	2013–2017
Paraguay	Gross domestic product, constant prices, % change	11.00	3.96	5.94
	Gross domestic product, current prices, billions, USD	$31.07	$26.09	$41.90
	Gross domestic product per capita, current prices, USD	$4,574	$3,917	$5,698
	Gross domestic product based on purchasing-power-parity (PPP) per capita GDP, Int'l dollar	$6,736	$6,108	$8,011
	Gross domestic product based on purchasing-power-parity (PPP) share of world total, %	0.05	0.05	0.05
	Inflation, end of period consumer prices, % change	5.00	5.41	4.58
	Volume of imports of goods and services, % change	17.47	9.82	8.01

Country	Subject Descriptor	2013	2007–2012	2013–2017
	Volume of imports of goods, % change	17.47	9.82	8.01
	Volume of exports of goods and services, % change	22.40	1.36	8.27
	Volume of exports of goods, % change	22.40	1.36	8.27
	Population, millions	6.79	6.66	7.35
	General government revenue, % GDP	20.91	19.81	20.70
	General government total expenditure, % GDP	22.13	19.00	20.65
	General government net lending/borrowing, % GDP	−1.22	0.81	0.05
	General government gross debt, % GDP	11.96	15.24	10.75
	Current account balance, billions, USD	−$0.14	−$0.30	−$0.56
	Current account balance, %GDP	−0.44	−0.87	−1.18

Source: International Monetary Fund

PERU OVERVIEW

Government
Government: Unitary presidential constitutional republic
President: Ollanta Humala
Vice President: Marisol Espinoza

Top Exports and Imports
Peru exported 44,686.4 thousands of dollars in 2011. The principal products that Peru exports are: gold, pewter, petroleum products, minerals, meat meal, coffee, gas, zinc, and iron. These products are 70.9% of the totality of exports.

Economy
Peru is a country with a population of nearly 31 million people, which in 2013 produced a GDP of nearly $212 billion. This translates into a GDP per capita of $6,850. This is expected to grow to $8,705 by 2017 thanks to an average annual GDP growth rate forecast at 5.97% for the 2013–2017 term. The volume of imports of goods and services is expected to grow in the 2013–2017 time period at an average annual rate of 7.38%, compared to 9.44% for the volume of exports of goods and services in the same time period. Inflation is expected to remain steady at 2% per year, on average. Peru practices fiscal discipline, maintaining a budget surplus of 1.45% of GDP in 2013, which is expected to average 1.22% in the near term. Peru's current account deficit of −2.96% of GDP in 2013, is expected to average -2.68% of GDP in the 2013–17 term. Public debt is kept in check, reporting in at 18.35% of GDP in 2013, with forecast declines in the near term.[78]

Peru is the "comeback kid" of Latin America. Achieving a Global Competitiveness ranking of 61, Peru also ranks relatively well in Basic Requirements (69) and Efficiency Enhancers (57), although Business Sophistication and Innovation Factors lag behind with a ranking of 94. Peru has made strong strides to achieve an impressive ranking of 43 on the Doing Business front, with strong showings in key areas such as Starting a Business (60), Registering Property (19), Getting Credit (23), Protecting Investors (13), and Trading Across Borders (60). As in most Latin American nations, Paying Taxes is a lagging area, as is Enforcing Contracts (115) and Resolving Insolvency (106). Peru ranks 80 out of 186 on Human Development Index, but has made incredible advancements thanks to her steadfast adoption of business-friendly policies. Peru ranks well on the Democracy Index, 56, for a classification as Free by Freedom House. The Heritage Foundation gives Peru a score of 68.2 out of 100 on the Index of Economic Liberty, while on the Index of Globalization it scores 64.53.[79]

Table A.41 Business climate indicators, Peru[80]

Indicators: Peru	
Global Competitiveness Index, World Economic Forum, ranking 1–144	61
GCI Subindex A Basic requirements	69
GCI Subindex B Efficiency enhancers	57
GCI Subindex C Innovation and sophistication factors	94
Doing Business, World Bank, ranking 1–185	43
DB Starting a Business	60
DB Dealing with Construction Permits	86
DB Getting Electricity	77
DB Registering Property	19
DB Getting Credit	23
DB Protecting Investors	13
DB Paying Taxes	85
DB Trading Across Borders	60
DB Enforcing Contracts	115
DB Resolving Insolvency	106
Human Development Index, United Nations, ranking 1–186	77
Global Gender Gap, World Economic Forum, ranking 1–135	78
Travel and Tourism Competitiveness, World Economic Forum, ranking 1–140	69
Democracy Index, Economist Intelligence Unit, ranking 1–167	61
Freedom Status, Freedom House	Free
Index of Globalization, KOF (0 to 100)	64.53
Index of Economic Liberty, Heritage Foundation (0 to 100)	68.2
Corruption Perception Index, Transparency International, ranking 1–183	83

Source: Authors' calculations based on various indicators

Table A.42 International Monetary Fund projections, Peru[81]

Country	Subject Descriptor	2013	2007–2012	2013–2017
Peru	Gross domestic product, constant prices, % change	5.80	6.89	5.97
	Gross domestic product, current prices, billions, USD	$211.98	$200.29	$286.45

Country	Subject Descriptor	2013	2007–2012	2013–2017
	Gross domestic product per capita, current prices, USD	$6,850	$6,573	$8,705
	Gross domestic product based on purchasing-power-parity (PPP) per capita GDP, Int'l dollar	$11,275	$10,679	$14,362
	Gross domestic product based on purchasing-power-parity (PPP) share of world total, %	0.40	0.36	0.42
	Inflation, end of period consumer prices, % change	2.00	3.44	2.00
	Volume of imports of goods and services, % change	6.26	10.98	7.38
	Volume of imports of goods, % change	6.26	10.98	7.38
	Volume of exports of goods and services, % change	8.68	3.10	9.44
	Volume of exports of goods, % change	8.68	3.10	9.44
	Population, millions	30.95	30.47	32.91
	General government revenue, % GDP	21.37	20.57	21.54
	General government total expenditure, % GDP	19.93	19.35	20.31
	General government net lending/borrowing, % GDP	1.45	1.22	1.22
	General government gross debt, % GDP	18.35	24.82	17.20
	Current account balance, billions, USD	−$6.27	−$6.08	−$6.96
	Current account balance, % GDP	−2.96	−1.78	−2.68

Source: International Monetary Fund

SURINAME OVERVIEW

Government

Government: Unitary presidential constitutional republic
President: Dési Bouterse
Vice President: Robert Ameerali

Economy

Suriname is a multicultural country, comprising five different ethnic groups. It has a population of 0.55 million people, and produces a GDP of $5.69 billion. Suriname's bread and butter are trade and transport activities tied to its financial services. Its GDP and population figures amount to a GDP per capita of $10,294. The volume of exports of goods and services is expected to grow at an average annual rate of 4.59% in the coming years, whereas the volume of imports of goods and services is expected to grow at only a 1.51% average annual growth rate in the 2013–2017 term. Inflation is expected to remain in the 4% range in the same time period. Suriname maintains fiscal balance, and surpluses are projected for the near term. In addition, Suriname's trade deficit, which will stand at −2.05% of GDP in 2013, will converge to nearly zero, based on average annual figures for the 2013–2017 time period. Public revenues and spending are expected to hold at 24% of GDP, and general government gross debt to hold steady, below current figures of 18.09% of GDP for 2013.[82]

Suriname ranks a woeful 164 on Doing Business, with particularly poor showings in Registering Property (171), Getting Credit (159), Protecting Investors (183), and Enforcing Contracts and Resolving Insolvency (180). Surprisingly, Paying Taxes is an area where Suriname ranks well: 49th out of 185. On the Human Development Index, Suriname ranks 104 out of 186 countries, and 106 out of 135 on the Global Gender Gap. Nevertheless, it does relatively well on the Democracy Index, ranking 54th of 167 countries, for a Fully Free classification by Freedom House. Suriname scores 47.78 on the Index of Globalization and 52 out of 100 on the Index of Economic Liberty.[83]

Table A.43 Business climate indicators, Suriname[84]

Indicators: Suriname	
Global Competitiveness Index, World Economic Forum, ranking 1–144	N/A
GCI Subindex A Basic requirements	N/A
GCI Subindex B Efficiency enhancers	N/A
GCI Subindex C Innovation and sophistication factors	N/A
Doing Business, World Bank, ranking 1–185	164
DB Starting a Business	178
DB Dealing with Construction Permits	92
DB Getting Electricity	39
DB Registering Property	171
DB Getting Credit	159
DB Protecting Investors	183
DB Paying Taxes	49
DB Trading Across Borders	97
DB Enforcing Contracts	180
DB Resolving Insolvency	158
Human Development Index, United Nations, ranking 1–186	105
Global Gender Gap, World Economic Forum, ranking 1–135	106
Travel and Tourism Competitiveness, World Economic Forum, ranking 1–140	N/A
Democracy Index, Economist Intelligence Unit, ranking 1–167	56
Freedom Status, Freedom House	Free
Index of Globalization, KOF (0 to 100)	47.78
Index of Economic Liberty, Heritage Foundation (0 to 100)	52
Corruption Perception Index, Transparency International, ranking 1–183	88

Source: Authors' calculations based on various indicators

Table A.44 International Monetary Fund projections, Suriname[85]

Snapshot and Forecast: Suriname	2013	2007–2012	2013–2017
Gross domestic product, constant prices, % change	4.48	4.09	4.81
Gross domestic product, current prices, billions, USD	$5.69	$5.09	$8.06
Gross domestic product per capita, current prices, USD	$10,294	$9,339	$13,822
Gross domestic product based on purchasing-power-parity (PPP) per capita GDP, Int'l dollar	$12,804	$12,255	$15,755
Gross domestic product based on purchasing-power-parity (PPP) share of world total, %	0.008	0.008	0.008
Inflation, end of period consumer prices, % change	4.95	8.47	4.21
Volume of imports of goods and services, % change	4.09	10.48	1.51
Volume of imports of goods, % change	4.95	10.34	0.70
Volume of exports of goods and services, % change	−0.10	9.31	4.59
Volume of exports of goods, % change	1.90	0.24	2.03
Population, millions	0.55	0.55	0.58
General government revenue, % GDP	24.06	24.71	24.58
General government total expenditure, % GDP	24.07	24.77	23.43
General government net lending/borrowing, % GDP	−0.01	−0.06	1.15
General government gross debt, % GDP	18.09	17.46	16.73
Current account balance, billions, USD	−$0.12	−$0.01	−$0.25
Current account balance, % GDP	−2.05	4.34	−0.41

Source: International Monetary Fund

URUGUAY OVERVIEW

Government

Government: Unitary presidential constitutional republic
President: Jose Mujica
Vice President: Danilo Astori
Political Party: Frente Amplio

Top Exports and Imports

Uruguay exported 6,740.6 thousands of dollars in 2011. The principal products that Uruguay exports are: beef, soy, rice, wheat, wood, milk, cream, leather, cheese, and fish. These products account for 54.2% of the totality of its exports.

Economy

Uruguay is a country of some 3.39 million inhabitants, with a GDP of $57.32, which translates into a GDP per capita, in current terms, of $15,897 per year. GDP is expected to grow at an average annual rate of 4%, bringing GDP per capita up to $20,799 by 2017. Uruguay maintains fiscal discipline, posting a manageable fiscal deficit of -1.43% of GDP in 2013, which is expected to average -1.19% of GDP in the 2013–2017 time period. Similarly, the trade deficit, reported at -1.92% of GDP in 2013, is expected to average -1.87% of GDP in the near term. Public revenues and spending are expected to hover around the area of 33% to 35% of GDP for the near future. Public debt is expected to drop from the 45.39% of GDP reported in 2013 to an average yearly share of GDP of 40.65% in the 2013–2017 time period. Inflation is a worry in Uruguay, reaching 7.28% in 2013, and expected to average 6.36% in the coming years, 2013–2017.[86]

Uruguay ranks relatively well on Global Competitiveness, with a ranking of 74 out of 144 countries, doing particularly well on Basic Requirements (43), and remaining steady on Efficiency Enhancers (73), and Business Sophistication and Innovation (78). On Doing Business, Uruguay ranks 89 out of 185 countries, for a middling ranking, but does quite well on Starting a Business, with a rank of 39, Getting Electricity (20), and Resolving Insolvency (54). Areas of significant lag are Dealing with Construction Permits (158), Registering Property (164), and Paying Taxes (140). Uruguay does relatively well on Human Development, ranking 58. On the Global Gender Gap, Paraguay ranks 76 out of 135 countries, but ranks very well on the Democracy Index, with a ranking of 18, earning her a Fully Free status from Freedom House. The Heritage Foundation gave a score of 69.7 on the Index of Economic Liberty to Uruguay, which also garnered a score of 65.71 on the Index of Globalization. Uruguay is a country to keep an eye on, particularly because with a rank of 20 out of 163 on the Corruption Perceptions Index, she has strongly demonstrated understanding of an element that a good many Latin American countries do not seem to understand: that the quality of institutions matters to the conduct of doing business.[87]

Table A.45 Business climate indicators, Uruguay[88]

Indicators: Uruguay	
Global Competitiveness Index, World Economic Forum, ranking 1–144	74
GCI Subindex A Basic requirements	43
GCI Subindex B Efficiency enhancers	73
GCI Subindex C Innovation and sophistication factors	78
Doing Business, World Bank, ranking 1–185	89
DB Starting a Business	39
DB Dealing with Construction Permits	158
DB Getting Electricity	20
DB Registering Property	164
DB Getting Credit	70
DB Protecting Investors	100
DB Paying Taxes	140
DB Trading Across Borders	104
DB Enforcing Contracts	102
DB Resolving Insolvency	54

Indicators: Uruguay

Human Development Index, United Nations, ranking 1–186	51
Global Gender Gap, World Economic Forum, ranking 1–135	76
Travel and Tourism Competitiveness, World Economic Forum, ranking 1–140	58
Democracy Index, Economist Intelligence Unit, ranking 1–167	18
Freedom Status, Freedom House	Free
Index of Globalization, KOF (0 to 100)	65.71
Index of Economic Liberty, Heritage Foundation (0 to 100)	69.7
Corruption Perception Index, Transparency International, ranking 1–183	20

Source: Authors' calculations based on various indicators

Table A.46 International Monetary Fund projections, Uruguay[89]

Country	Subject Descriptor	2013	2007–2012	2013–2017
Uruguay	Gross domestic product, constant prices, % change	4.00	5.71	4.00
	Gross domestic product, current prices, billions, USD	$57.32	$49.72	$71.55
	Gross domestic product per capita, current prices, USD	$16,897	$14,707	$20,799
	Gross domestic product based on purchasing-power-parity (PPP) per capita GDP, Int'l dollar	$16,635	$15,840	$20,577
	Gross domestic product based on purchasing-power-parity (PPP) share of world total, %	0.07	0.06	0.06
	Inflation, end of period consumer prices, % change	7.28	7.86	6.36
	Volume of imports of goods and services, % change	6.64	8.41	7.29
	Volume of imports of goods, % change	5.89	9.84	6.80
	Volume of exports of goods and services, % change	6.44	7.48	5.32
	Volume of exports of goods, % change	8.04	8.10	6.85
	Population, millions	3.39	3.38	3.44
	General government revenue, % GDP	33.35	31.41	33.82
	General government total expenditure, % GDP	34.78	32.58	35.01
	General government net lending/borrowing, % GDP	−1.43	−1.17	−1.19
	General government gross debt, % GDP	45.39	59.09	40.65
	Current account balance, billions, USD	−$1.10	−$1.47	−$1.37
	Current account balance, % GDP	−1.92	−2.72	−1.87

Source: International Monetary Fund

VENEZUELA OVERVIEW

Government

Government: Federal presidential constitutional republic
President: Nicolás Maduro
Vice President: Jorge Arreaza
Political Party: Partido Socialista Unido

Top Exports and Imports

Venezuela exported 89,774.1 thousands of dollars in 2011. The principal products that Venezuela exports are: crude oil, petroleum products, oils, gas, iron, ships, boats, and aluminum. These products are 99.1% of the totality of exports.

Economy

Venezuela is the lost cause of Latin America. A large country of 30.97 million people, with a GDP of nearly $350 billion, it boasts a GDP per capita of $11,290. This figure is actually expected to decrease to $11,173 by 2017, as GDP is calculated to grow at an average annual rate of only 2.98% in the 2013–2017 term. For the 2013–2017 time period, the volume of imports of goods and services is expected to decline at an average annual rate of −5.53%, while the volume of imports of goods and services is expected to decline at an average annual rate of −2.13% in the same time frame. Government revenues stand close to 34.2% of GDP in 2013, but government spending nears 39.64% of GDP. This translates to a fiscal deficit of −5.44% of GDP, which itself correlates to a general government gross debt of more than 56% of GDP. Venezuela is projected to have fiscal deficits, on average, of −5.68% of GDP in the 2013–2017 time period. As a result, public debt is expected to explode to more than 68% of GDP, on average, in the near term 2013–2017. Inflation soared to more than 29% in 2013, and is expected to remain close to 28%, on a yearly average basis, in the 2013–2017 time period.[90]

Venezuela is woefully uncompetitive, ranking 126 out of 144 on the Global Competitiveness Index, with poor showings in Basic Requirements (126), Efficiency Enhancers (135), and Business Sophistication and Innovation (135). On Doing Business, Venezuela ranks even worse: 180 out of 185 countries. Venezuela ranks poorly on each of the basic categories involved in the elaboration of the Doing Business Index. Starting a Business ranks 152, Getting Electricity, 160. The reader should take note that, on Protecting Investors, Venezuela ranks among the bottom five countries in the whole world, with a ranking of 181 out of 185. On the matter of Paying Taxes, Venezuela ranks dead last in the world: 185. Thanks to oil wealth, Venezuela ranks much better on Human Development: 73 out of 186 nations. Also, it must be said that Venezuela's rank of 48 out of 135 on the Global Gender Gap is not an altogether poor showing. Still, Venezuela ranks 95 out of 167 countries on the Democracy Index, giving her a Partly Free status according to Freedom House. Venezuela scores 36.1 on the Index of Economic Liberty, and 50.9 on the Index of Globalization, reflecting the country's relative isolation from the outside world. Venezuela is among the most corrupt, least transparent regimes in the world, as shown by its ranking of 165 on the Corruption Perceptions Index.[91]

Table A.47 Business climate indicators, Venezuela[92]

Indicators: Venezuela	
Global Competitiveness Index, World Economic Forum, ranking 1–144	126
GCI Subindex A Basic requirements	126
GCI Subindex B Efficiency enhancers	117
GCI Subindex C Innovation and sophistication factors	135
Doing Business, World Bank, ranking 1–185	180
DB Starting a Business	152
DB Dealing with Construction Permits	109
DB Getting Electricity	160
DB Registering Property	90
DB Getting Credit	159
DB Protecting Investors	181
DB Paying Taxes	185
DB Trading Across Borders	166
DB Enforcing Contracts	80
DB Resolving Insolvency	163
Human Development Index, United Nations, ranking 1–186	71
Global Gender Gap, World Economic Forum, ranking 1–135	48
Travel and Tourism Competitiveness, World Economic Forum, ranking 1–140	106
Democracy Index, Economist Intelligence Unit, ranking 1–167	95
Freedom Status, Freedom House	Partly Free
Index of Globalization, KOF (0 to 100)	50.9
Index of Economic Liberty, Heritage Foundation (0 to 100)	36.1
Corruption Perception Index, Transparency International, ranking 1–183	165

Source: Authors' calculations based on various indicators

Table A.48 International Monetary Fund projections, Venezuela[93]

Country	Subject Descriptor	2013	2007–2012	2013–2017
Venezuela	Gross domestic product, constant prices, % change	3.26	3.21	2.98
	Gross domestic product, current prices, billions, USD	$349.66	$337.98	$374.56
	Gross domestic product per capita, current prices, USD	$11,290	$11,132	$11,173
	Gross domestic product based on purchasing-power-parity (PPP) per capita GDP, Int'l dollar	$13,584	$13,242	$15,092
	Gross domestic product based on purchasing-power-parity (PPP) share of world total, %	0.48	0.49	0.47

(Continued)

Table A.48 (Continued)

Country	Subject Descriptor	2013	2007–2012	2013–2017
	Inflation, end of period consumer prices, % change	29.20	25.86	27.94
	Volume of imports of goods and services, % change	−2.14	7.10	−5.53
	Volume of imports of goods, % change	0.33	4.40	−6.68
	Volume of exports of goods and services, % change	−2.11	−3.21	−2.13
	Volume of exports of goods, % change	−2.24	−3.29	−2.30
	Population, millions	30.97	30.36	33.52
	General government revenue, % GDP	34.20	32.00	31.65
	General government total expenditure, % GDP	39.64	37.37	37.34
	General government net lending/borrowing, % GDP	−5.44	−5.37	−5.68
	General government gross debt, % GDP	56.45	38.04	68.05
	Current account balance, billions, USD	$19.49	$22.55	$10.29
	Current account balance, % GDP	5.58	7.22	3.96

Source: International Monetary Fund

NOTES

1. Authors' analysis based on World Bank data. World Bank, World Development Indicators: www.worldbank.org (accessed May 2013).
2. Authors' analysis based on International Monetary Fund data. International Monetary Fund, World Economic Outlook: www.imf.org (accessed May 2013).
3. Authors' calculations based on various indicators. Ease of Doing Business Index, 2013. World Bank. http://www.doingbusiness.org/rankings (accessed May 2013). Human Development Index, 2013. United Nations. http://hdr.undp.org/en/statistics/hdi/ (accessed May 2013). Global Competitiveness Index, 2012–2013. World Economic Forum. www.weforum.org (accessed May 2013). Travel and Tourism Competitiveness Index. World Economic Forum. www.weforum.org (accessed May 2013). Global Gender Gap. World Economic Forum. www.weforum.org (accessed May 2013). Index of Democracy, 2012. Economist Intelligence Unit. http://www.eiu.com/Handlers/WhitepaperHandler.ashx?fi=Democracy-Index-2012.pdf&mode=wp&campaignid=DemocracyIndex12 (accessed May 2013). KOF Index of Globalization. http://globalization.kof.ethz.ch/ (accessed May 2013). Freedom in the World. Freedom House. http://www.freedomhouse.org/ (accessed May 2013). Index of Economic Liberty. Heritage Foundation. www.heritage.org (accessed May 2013). Corruptions Perceptions Index. Transparency International. http://www.transparency.org/research/cpi/overview (accessed May 2013). Global Competitiveness Index, 2012–2013. World Economic Forum. www.weforum.org (accessed May 2013).
4. Authors' analysis based on data from the International Monetary Fund. World Economic Outlook, online database: www.imf.org (accessed May 2013).
5. Authors' calculations based on various indicators. Ease of Doing Business Index, 2013. World Bank. http://www.doingbusiness.org/rankings (accessed May 2013). Human Development Index, 2013. United Nations. http://hdr.undp.org/en/statistics/hdi/ (accessed May 2013). Global Competitiveness Index, 2012–2013. World Economic Forum. www.weforum.org (accessed May 2013). Travel and Tourism Competitiveness Index. World Economic Forum. www.weforum.org (accessed May 2013). Global Gender Gap. World Economic Forum. www.weforum.org (accessed May 2013). Index of

Democracy, 2012. Economist Intelligence Unit. http://www.eiu.com/Handlers/WhitepaperHandler.ashx?fi=Democracy-Index-2012.pdf&mode=wp&campaignid=DemocracyIndex12 (accessed May 2013). KOF Index of Globalization. http://globalization.kof.ethz.ch/ (accessed May 2013). Freedom in the World. Freedom House. http://www.freedomhouse.org/ (accessed May 2013). Index of Economic Liberty. Heritage Foundation. www.heritage.org (accessed May 2013). Corruptions Perceptions Index. Transparency International. http://www.transparency.org/research/cpi/overview (accessed May 2013). Global Competitiveness Index, 2012–2013. World Economic Forum. www.weforum.org (accessed May 2013).

6. Authors' analysis based on data from the International Monetary Fund. World Economic Outlook, online database. www.imf.org (accessed May 2013).

7. Authors' calculations based on various indicators. Ease of Doing Business Index, 2013. World Bank. http://www.doingbusiness.org/rankings (accessed May 2013). Human Development Index, 2013. United Nations. http://hdr.undp.org/en/statistics/hdi/ (accessed May 2013). Global Competitiveness Index, 2012–2013. World Economic Forum. www.weforum.org (accessed May 2013). Travel and Tourism Competitiveness Index. World Economic Forum. www.weforum.org (accessed May 2013). Global Gender Gap. World Economic Forum. www.weforum.org (accessed May 2013). Index of Democracy, 2012. Economist Intelligence Unit. http://www.eiu.com/Handlers/WhitepaperHandler.ashx?fi=Democracy-Index-2012.pdf&mode=wp&campaignid=DemocracyIndex12 (accessed May 2013). KOF Index of Globalization. http://globalization.kof.ethz.ch/ (accessed May 2013). Freedom in the World. Freedom House. http://www.freedomhouse.org/ (accessed May 2013). Index of Economic Liberty. Heritage Foundation. www.heritage.org (accessed May 2013). Corruptions Perceptions Index. Transparency International. http://www.transparency.org/research/cpi/overview (accessed May 2013). Global Competitiveness Index, 2012–2013. World Economic Forum. www.weforum.org (accessed May 2013).

8. Authors' calculations based on World Bank data. World Bank. World Development Indicators. Online Database. www.worldbank.org (accessed May 2013

9. Authors' analysis based on data from the International Monetary Fund. World Economic Outlook, online database. www.imf.org (accessed May 2013).

10. Ibid.

11. Authors' calculations based on various indicators. Ease of Doing Business Index, 2013. World Bank. http://www.doingbusiness.org/rankings (accessed May 2013). Human Development Index, 2013. United Nations. http://hdr.undp.org/en/statistics/hdi/ (accessed May 2013). Global Competitiveness Index, 2012–2013. World Economic Forum. www.weforum.org (accessed May 2013). Travel and Tourism Competitiveness Index. World Economic Forum. www.weforum.org (accessed May 2013). Global Gender Gap. World Economic Forum. www.weforum.org (accessed May 2013). Index of Democracy, 2012. Economist Intelligence Unit. http://www.eiu.com/Handlers/WhitepaperHandler.ashx?fi=Democracy-Index-2012.pdf&mode=wp&campaignid=DemocracyIndex12 (accessed May 2013). KOF Index of Globalization. http://globalization.kof.ethz.ch/ (accessed May 2013). Freedom in the World. Freedom House. http://www.freedomhouse.org/ (accessed May 2013). Index of Economic Liberty. Heritage Foundation. www.heritage.org (accessed May 2013). Corruptions Perceptions Index. Transparency International. http://www.transparency.org/research/cpi/overview (accessed May 2013). Global Competitiveness Index, 2012–2013. World Economic Forum. www.weforum.org (accessed May 2013).

12. Ibid.

13. Authors' analysis based on data from the International Monetary Fund. World Economic Outlook, online database. www.imf.org (accessed May 2013).

14. Authors' analysis based on data from the International Monetary Fund. World Economic Outlook, online database. www.imf.org (accessed May 2013).

15. Authors' calculations based on various indicators. Ease of Doing Business Index, 2013. World Bank. http://www.doingbusiness.org/rankings (accessed May 2013). Human Development Index, 2013. United Nations. http://hdr.undp.org/en/statistics/hdi/ (accessed May 2013). Global Competitiveness Index, 2012–2013. World Economic Forum. www.weforum.org (accessed May 2013). Travel and Tourism Competitiveness Index. World Economic Forum. www.weforum.org (accessed May 2013). Global Gender Gap. World Economic Forum. www.weforum.org (accessed May 2013). Index of Democracy, 2012. Economist Intelligence Unit. http://www.eiu.com/Handlers/WhitepaperHandler.ashx?fi=Democracy-Index-2012.pdf

&mode=wp&campaignid=DemocracyIndex12 (accessed May 2013). KOF Index of Globalization. http://globalization.kof.ethz.ch/ (accessed May 2013). Freedom in the World. Freedom House. http://www.freedomhouse.org/ (accessed May 2013). Index of Economic Liberty. Heritage Foundation. www.heritage.org (accessed May 2013). Corruptions Perceptions Index. Transparency International. http://www.transparency.org/research/cpi/overview (accessed May 2013). Global Competitiveness Index, 2012–2013. World Economic Forum. www.weforum.org (accessed May 2013).

16. Ibid.

17. Authors' analysis based on data from the International Monetary Fund. World Economic Outlook, online database. www.imf.org (accessed May 2013).

18. Ibid.

19. Authors' calculations based on various indicators. Ease of Doing Business Index, 2013. World Bank. http://www.doingbusiness.org/rankings (accessed May 2013). Human Development Index, 2013. United Nations. http://hdr.undp.org/en/statistics/hdi/ (accessed May 2013). Global Competitiveness Index, 2012–2013. World Economic Forum. www.weforum.org (accessed May 2013). Travel and Tourism Competitiveness Index. World Economic Forum. www.weforum.org (accessed May 2013). Global Gender Gap. World Economic Forum. www.weforum.org (accessed May 2013). Index of Democracy, 2012. Economist Intelligence Unit. http://www.eiu.com/Handlers/WhitepaperHandler.ashx?fi=Democracy-Index-2012.pdf&mode=wp&campaignid=DemocracyIndex12 (accessed May 2013). KOF Index of Globalization. http://globalization.kof.ethz.ch/ (accessed May 2013). Freedom in the World. Freedom House. http://www.freedomhouse.org/ (accessed May 2013). Index of Economic Liberty. Heritage Foundation. www.heritage.org (accessed May 2013). Corruptions Perceptions Index. Transparency International. http://www.transparency.org/research/cpi/overview (accessed May 2013). Global Competitiveness Index, 2012–2013. World Economic Forum. www.weforum.org (accessed May 2013).

20. Ibid.

21. Authors' analysis based on data from the International Monetary Fund. World Economic Outlook, online database. www.imf.org (accessed May 2013).

22. Ibid.

23. Authors' calculations based on various indicators. Ease of Doing Business Index, 2013. World Bank. http://www.doingbusiness.org/rankings (accessed May 2013). Human Development Index, 2013. United Nations. http://hdr.undp.org/en/statistics/hdi/ (accessed May 2013). Global Competitiveness Index, 2012–2013. World Economic Forum. www.weforum.org (accessed May 2013). Travel and Tourism Competitiveness Index. World Economic Forum. www.weforum.org (accessed May 2013). Global Gender Gap. World Economic Forum. www.weforum.org (accessed May 2013). Index of Democracy, 2012. Economist Intelligence Unit. http://www.eiu.com/Handlers/WhitepaperHandler.ashx?fi=Democracy-Index-2012.pdf&mode=wp&campaignid=DemocracyIndex12 (accessed May 2013). KOF Index of Globalization. http://globalization.kof.ethz.ch/ (accessed May 2013). Freedom in the World. Freedom House. http://www.freedomhouse.org/ (accessed May 2013). Index of Economic Liberty. Heritage Foundation. www.heritage.org (accessed May 2013). Corruptions Perceptions Index. Transparency International. http://www.transparency.org/research/cpi/overview (accessed May 2013). Global Competitiveness Index, 2012–2013. World Economic Forum. www.weforum.org (accessed May 2013).

24. Ibid.

25. Authors' analysis based on data from the International Monetary Fund. World Economic Outlook, online database. www.imf.org (accessed May 2013).

26. Ibid.

27. Authors' calculations based on various indicators. Ease of Doing Business Index, 2013. World Bank. http://www.doingbusiness.org/rankings (accessed May 2013). Human Development Index, 2013. United Nations. http://hdr.undp.org/en/statistics/hdi/ (accessed May 2013). Global Competitiveness Index, 2012–2013. World Economic Forum. www.weforum.org (accessed May 2013). Travel and Tourism Competitiveness Index. World Economic Forum. www.weforum.org (accessed May 2013). Global Gender Gap. World Economic Forum. www.weforum.org (accessed May 2013). Index of Democracy, 2012. Economist Intelligence Unit. http://www.eiu.com/Handlers/WhitepaperHandler.ashx?fi=Democracy-Index-2012.pdf&mode=wp&campaignid=DemocracyIndex12 (accessed May

2013). KOF Index of Globalization. http://globalization.kof.ethz.ch/ (accessed May 2013). Freedom in the World. Freedom House. http://www.freedomhouse.org/ (accessed May 2013). Index of Economic Liberty. Heritage Foundation. www.heritage.org (accessed May 2013). Corruptions Perceptions Index. Transparency International. http://www.transparency.org/research/cpi/overview (accessed May 2013). Global Competitiveness Index, 2012–2013. World Economic Forum. www.weforum.org (accessed May 2013).

28. Ibid.
29. Authors' analysis based on data from the International Monetary Fund. World Economic Outlook, online database. www.imf.org (accessed May 2013).
30. Ibid.
31. Authors' calculations based on various indicators. Ease of Doing Business Index, 2013. World Bank. http://www.doingbusiness.org/rankings (accessed May 2013). Human Development Index, 2013. United Nations. http://hdr.undp.org/en/statistics/hdi/ (accessed May 2013). Global Competitiveness Index, 2012–2013. World Economic Forum. www.weforum.org (accessed May 2013). Travel and Tourism Competitiveness Index. World Economic Forum. www.weforum.org (accessed May 2013). Global Gender Gap. World Economic Forum. www.weforum.org (accessed May 2013). Index of Democracy, 2012. Economist Intelligence Unit. http://www.eiu.com/Handlers/WhitepaperHandler. ashx?fi=Democracy-Index-2012.pdf&mode=wp&campaignid=DemocracyIndex12 (accessed May 2013). KOF Index of Globalization. http://globalization.kof.ethz.ch/ (accessed May 2013). Freedom in the World. Freedom House. http://www.freedomhouse.org/ (accessed May 2013). Index of Economic Liberty. Heritage Foundation. www.heritage.org (accessed May 2013). Corruptions Perceptions Index. Transparency International. http://www.transparency.org/research/cpi/overview (accessed May 2013). Global Competitiveness Index, 2012–2013. World Economic Forum. www.weforum.org (accessed May 2013).
32. Ibid.
33. Authors' analysis based on data from the International Monetary Fund. World Economic Outlook, online database. www.imf.org (accessed May 2013).
34. Ibid.
35. Authors' calculations based on various indicators. Ease of Doing Business Index, 2013. World Bank. http://www.doingbusiness.org/rankings (accessed May 2013). Human Development Index, 2013. United Nations. http://hdr.undp.org/en/statistics/hdi/ (accessed May 2013). Global Competitiveness Index, 2012–2013. World Economic Forum. www.weforum.org (accessed May 2013). Travel and Tourism Competitiveness Index. World Economic Forum. www.weforum.org (accessed May 2013). Global Gender Gap. World Economic Forum. www.weforum.org (accessed May 2013). Index of Democracy, 2012. Economist Intelligence Unit. http://www.eiu.com/Handlers/WhitepaperHandler. ashx?fi=Democracy-Index-2012.pdf&mode=wp&campaignid=DemocracyIndex12 (accessed May 2013). KOF Index of Globalization. http://globalization.kof.ethz.ch/ (accessed May 2013). Freedom in the World. Freedom House. http://www.freedomhouse.org/ (accessed May 2013). Index of Economic Liberty. Heritage Foundation. www.heritage.org (accessed May 2013). Corruptions Perceptions Index. Transparency International. http://www.transparency.org/research/cpi/overview (accessed May 2013). Global Competitiveness Index, 2012–2013. World Economic Forum. www.weforum.org (accessed May 2013).
36. Ibid.
37. Authors' analysis based on data from the International Monetary Fund. World Economic Outlook, online database. www.imf.org (accessed May 2013).
38. Ibid.
39. Authors' calculations based on various indicators. Ease of Doing Business Index, 2013. World Bank. http://www.doingbusiness.org/rankings (accessed May 2013). Human Development Index, 2013. United Nations. http://hdr.undp.org/en/statistics/hdi/ (accessed May 2013). Global Competitiveness Index, 2012–2013. World Economic Forum. www.weforum.org (accessed May 2013). Travel and Tourism Competitiveness Index. World Economic Forum. www.weforum.org (accessed May 2013). Global Gender Gap. World Economic Forum. www.weforum.org (accessed May 2013). Index of

Democracy, 2012. Economist Intelligence Unit. http://www.eiu.com/Handlers/WhitepaperHandler. ashx?fi=Democracy-Index-2012.pdf&mode=wp&campaignid=DemocracyIndex12 (accessed May 2013). KOF Index of Globalization. http://globalization.kof.ethz.ch/ (accessed May 2013). Freedom in the World. Freedom House. http://www.freedomhouse.org/ (accessed May 2013). Index of Economic Liberty. Heritage Foundation. www.heritage.org (accessed May 2013). Corruptions Perceptions Index. Transparency International. http://www.transparency.org/research/cpi/overview (accessed May 2013). Global Competitiveness Index, 2012–2013. World Economic Forum. www.weforum.org (accessed May 2013).

40. Ibid.
41. Authors' analysis based on data from the International Monetary Fund. World Economic Outlook, online database. www.imf.org (accessed May 2013).
42. Ibid.
43. Authors' calculations based on various indicators. Ease of Doing Business Index, 2013. World Bank. http://www.doingbusiness.org/rankings (accessed May 2013). Human Development Index, 2013. United Nations. http://hdr.undp.org/en/statistics/hdi/ (accessed May 2013). Global Competitiveness Index, 2012–2013. World Economic Forum. www.weforum.org (accessed May 2013). Travel and Tourism Competitiveness Index. World Economic Forum. www.weforum.org (accessed May 2013). Global Gender Gap. World Economic Forum. www.weforum.org (accessed May 2013). Index of Democracy, 2012. Economist Intelligence Unit. http://www.eiu.com/Handlers/WhitepaperHandler. ashx?fi=Democracy-Index-2012.pdf&mode=wp&campaignid=DemocracyIndex12 (accessed May 2013). KOF Index of Globalization. http://globalization.kof.ethz.ch/ (accessed May 2013). Freedom in the World. Freedom House. http://www.freedomhouse.org/ (accessed May 2013). Index of Economic Liberty. Heritage Foundation. www.heritage.org (accessed May 2013). Corruptions Perceptions Index. Transparency International. http://www.transparency.org/research/cpi/overview (accessed May 2013). Global Competitiveness Index, 2012–2013. World Economic Forum. www.weforum.org (accessed May 2013).
44. Ibid.
45. Authors' analysis based on data from the International Monetary Fund. World Economic Outlook, online database. www.imf.org (accessed May 2013).
46. Ibid.
47. Authors' calculations based on various indicators. Ease of Doing Business Index, 2013. World Bank. http://www.doingbusiness.org/rankings (accessed May 2013). Human Development Index, 2013. United Nations. http://hdr.undp.org/en/statistics/hdi/ (accessed May 2013). Global Competitiveness Index, 2012–2013. World Economic Forum. www.weforum.org (accessed May 2013). Travel and Tourism Competitiveness Index. World Economic Forum. www.weforum.org (accessed May 2013). Global Gender Gap. World Economic Forum. www.weforum.org (accessed May 2013). Index of Democracy, 2012. Economist Intelligence Unit. http://www.eiu.com/Handlers/WhitepaperHandler. ashx?fi=Democracy-Index-2012.pdf&mode=wp&campaignid=DemocracyIndex12 (accessed May 2013). KOF Index of Globalization. http://globalization.kof.ethz.ch/ (accessed May 2013). Freedom in the World. Freedom House. http://www.freedomhouse.org/ (accessed May 2013). Index of Economic Liberty. Heritage Foundation. www.heritage.org (accessed May 2013). Corruptions Perceptions Index. Transparency International. http://www.transparency.org/research/cpi/overview (accessed May 2013). Global Competitiveness Index, 2012–2013. World Economic Forum. www.weforum.org (accessed May 2013).
48. Ibid.
49. Authors' analysis based on data from the International Monetary Fund. World Economic Outlook, online database. www.imf.org (accessed May 2013).
50. Ibid.
51. Authors' calculations based on various indicators. Ease of Doing Business Index, 2013. World Bank. http:// www.doingbusiness.org/rankings (accessed May 2013). Human Development Index, 2013. United Nations. http://hdr.undp.org/en/statistics/hdi/ (accessed May 2013). Global Competitiveness Index, 2012–2013.

World Economic Forum. www.weforum.org (accessed May 2013). Travel and Tourism Competitiveness Index. World Economic Forum. www.weforum.org (accessed May 2013). Global Gender Gap. World Economic Forum. www.weforum.org (accessed May 2013). Index of Democracy, 2012. Economist Intelligence Unit. http://www.eiu.com/Handlers/WhitepaperHandler.ashx?fi=Democracy-Index-2012.pdf &mode=wp&campaignid=DemocracyIndex12 (accessed May 2013). KOF Index of Globalization. http:// globalization.kof.ethz.ch/ (accessed May 2013). Freedom in the World. Freedom House. http://www. freedomhouse.org/ (accessed May 2013). Index of Economic Liberty. Heritage Foundation. www.heritage. org (accessed May 2013). Corruptions Perceptions Index. Transparency International. http://www.trans- parency.org/research/cpi/overview (accessed May 2013). Global Competitiveness Index, 2012–2013. World Economic Forum. www.weforum.org (accessed May 2013).

52. Ibid.
53. Authors' analysis based on data from the International Monetary Fund. World Economic Outlook, online database. www.imf.org (accessed May 2013).
54. Ibid.
55. Authors' calculations based on various indicators. Ease of Doing Business Index, 2013. World Bank. http:// www.doingbusiness.org/rankings (accessed May 2013). Human Development Index, 2013. United Nations. http://hdr.undp.org/en/statistics/hdi/ (accessed May 2013). Global Competitiveness Index, 2012–2013. World Economic Forum. www.weforum.org (accessed May 2013). Travel and Tourism Competitiveness Index. World Economic Forum. www.weforum.org (accessed May 2013). Global Gender Gap. World Economic Forum. www.weforum.org (accessed May 2013). Index of Democracy, 2012. Economist Intelligence Unit. http://www.eiu.com/Handlers/WhitepaperHandler.ashx?fi=Democracy-Index-2012.pdf &mode=wp&campaignid=DemocracyIndex12 (accessed May 2013). KOF Index of Globalization. http:// globalization.kof.ethz.ch/ (accessed May 2013). Freedom in the World. Freedom House. http://www. freedomhouse.org/ (accessed May 2013). Index of Economic Liberty. Heritage Foundation. www.heritage. org (accessed May 2013). Corruptions Perceptions Index. Transparency International. http://www.trans- parency.org/research/cpi/overview (accessed May 2013). Global Competitiveness Index, 2012–2013. World Economic Forum. www.weforum.org (accessed May 2013).

56. Ibid.
57. Authors' analysis based on data from the International Monetary Fund. World Economic Outlook, online database. www.imf.org (accessed May 2013).
58. Ibid.
59. Authors' calculations based on various indicators. Ease of Doing Business Index, 2013. World Bank. http://www.doingbusiness.org/rankings (accessed May 2013). Human Development Index, 2013. United Nations. http://hdr.undp.org/en/statistics/hdi/ (accessed May 2013). Global Competitiveness Index, 2012–2013. World Economic Forum. www.weforum.org (accessed May 2013). Travel and Tourism Competitiveness Index. World Economic Forum. www.weforum.org (accessed May 2013). Global Gender Gap. World Economic Forum. www.weforum.org (accessed May 2013). Index of Democracy, 2012. Economist Intelligence Unit. http://www.eiu.com/Handlers/WhitepaperHandler.ashx?fi=Democracy- Index-2012.pdf&mode=wp&campaignid=DemocracyIndex12 (accessed May 2013). KOF Index of Globalization. http://globalization.kof.ethz.ch/ (accessed May 2013). Freedom in the World. Freedom House. http://www.freedomhouse.org/ (accessed May 2013). Index of Economic Liberty. Heritage Foundation.

60. Ibid.
61. Authors' analysis based on data from the International Monetary Fund. World Economic Outlook, online database. www.imf.org (accessed May 2013).
62. Ibid.
63. Authors' calculations based on various indicators. Ease of Doing Business Index, 2013. World Bank. http://www.doingbusiness.org/rankings (accessed May 2013). Human Development Index, 2013. United Nations. http://hdr.undp.org/en/statistics/hdi/ (accessed May 2013). Global Competitiveness Index, 2012–2013. World Economic Forum. www.weforum.org (accessed May 2013). Travel and Tourism Competitiveness Index. World Economic Forum. www.weforum.org (accessed May 2013). Global Gender

Gap. World Economic Forum. www.weforum.org (accessed May 2013). Index of Democracy, 2012. Economist Intelligence Unit. http://www.eiu.com/Handlers/WhitepaperHandler.ashx?fi=Democracy-Index-2012.pdf&mode=wp&campaignid=DemocracyIndex12 (accessed May 2013). KOF Index of Globalization. http://globalization.kof.ethz.ch/ (accessed May 2013). Freedom in the World. Freedom House. http://www.freedomhouse.org/ (accessed May 2013). Index of Economic Liberty. Heritage Foundation.

64. Ibid.
65. Authors' analysis based on data from the International Monetary Fund. World Economic Outlook, online database. www.imf.org (accessed May 2013).
66. Ibid.
67. Authors' calculations based on various indicators. Ease of Doing Business Index, 2013. World Bank. http://www.doingbusiness.org/rankings (accessed May 2013). Human Development Index, 2013. United Nations. http://hdr.undp.org/en/statistics/hdi/ (accessed May 2013). Global Competitiveness Index, 2012–2013. World Economic Forum. www.weforum.org (accessed May 2013). Travel and Tourism Competitiveness Index. World Economic Forum. www.weforum.org (accessed May 2013). Global Gender Gap. World Economic Forum. www.weforum.org (accessed May 2013). Index of Democracy, 2012. Economist Intelligence Unit. http://www.eiu.com/Handlers/WhitepaperHandler.ashx?fi=Democracy-Index-2012.pdf&mode=wp&campaignid=DemocracyIndex12 (accessed May 2013). KOF Index of Globalization. http://globalization.kof.ethz.ch/ (accessed May 2013). Freedom in the World. Freedom House. http://www.freedomhouse.org/ (accessed May 2013). Index of Economic Liberty. Heritage Foundation.
68. Ibid.
69. Authors' analysis based on data from the International Monetary Fund. World Economic Outlook, online database. www.imf.org (accessed May 2013).
70. Ibid.
71. Authors' calculations based on various indicators. Ease of Doing Business Index, 2013. World Bank. http://www.doingbusiness.org/rankings (accessed May 2013). Human Development Index, 2013. United Nations. http://hdr.undp.org/en/statistics/hdi/ (accessed May 2013). Global Competitiveness Index, 2012–2013. World Economic Forum. www.weforum.org (accessed May 2013). Travel and Tourism Competitiveness Index. World Economic Forum. www.weforum.org (accessed May 2013). Global Gender Gap. World Economic Forum. www.weforum.org (accessed May 2013). Index of Democracy, 2012. Economist Intelligence Unit. http://www.eiu.com/Handlers/WhitepaperHandler.ashx?fi=Democracy-Index-2012.pdf&mode=wp&campaignid=DemocracyIndex12 (accessed May 2013). KOF Index of Globalization. http://globalization.kof.ethz.ch/ (accessed May 2013). Freedom in the World. Freedom House. http://www.freedomhouse.org/ (accessed May 2013). Index of Economic Liberty. Heritage Foundation.
72. Ibid.
73. Authors' analysis based on data from the International Monetary Fund. World Economic Outlook, online database. www.imf.org (accessed May 2013).
74. Ibid.
75. Authors' calculations based on various indicators. Ease of Doing Business Index, 2013. World Bank. http://www.doingbusiness.org/rankings (accessed May 2013). Human Development Index, 2013. United Nations. http://hdr.undp.org/en/statistics/hdi/ (accessed May 2013). Global Competitiveness Index, 2012–2013. World Economic Forum. www.weforum.org (accessed May 2013). Travel and Tourism Competitiveness Index. World Economic Forum. www.weforum.org (accessed May 2013). Global Gender Gap. World Economic Forum. www.weforum.org (accessed May 2013). Index of Democracy, 2012. Economist Intelligence Unit. http://www.eiu.com/Handlers/WhitepaperHandler.ashx?fi=Democracy-Index-2012.pdf&mode=wp&campaignid=DemocracyIndex12 (accessed May 2013). KOF Index of Globalization. http://globalization.kof.ethz.ch/ (accessed May 2013). Freedom in the World. Freedom House. http://www.freedomhouse.org/ (accessed May 2013). Index of Economic Liberty. Heritage Foundation.
76. Ibid.

77. Authors' analysis based on data from the International Monetary Fund. World Economic Outlook, online database. www.imf.org (accessed May 2013).

78. Ibid.

79. Authors' calculations based on various indicators. Ease of Doing Business Index, 2013. World Bank. http://www.doingbusiness.org/rankings (accessed May 2013). Human Development Index, 2013. United Nations. http://hdr.undp.org/en/statistics/hdi/ (accessed May 2013). Global Competitiveness Index, 2012–2013. World Economic Forum. www.weforum.org (accessed May 2013). Travel and Tourism Competitiveness Index. World Economic Forum. www.weforum.org (accessed May 2013). Global Gender Gap. World Economic Forum. www.weforum.org (accessed May 2013). Index of Democracy, 2012. Economist Intelligence Unit. http://www.eiu.com/Handlers/WhitepaperHandler.ashx?fi=Democracy-Index-2012.pdf&mode=wp&campaignid=DemocracyIndex12 (accessed May 2013). KOF Index of Globalization. http://globalization.kof.ethz.ch/ (accessed May 2013). Freedom in the World. Freedom House. http://www.freedomhouse.org/ (accessed May 2013). Index of Economic Liberty. Heritage Foundation.

80. Ibid.

81. Authors' analysis based on data from the International Monetary Fund. World Economic Outlook, online database. www.imf.org (accessed May 2013).

82. Ibid.

83. Authors' calculations based on various indicators. Ease of Doing Business Index, 2013. World Bank. http://www.doingbusiness.org/rankings (accessed May 2013). Human Development Index, 2013. United Nations. http://hdr.undp.org/en/statistics/hdi/ (accessed May 2013). Global Competitiveness Index, 2012–2013. World Economic Forum. www.weforum.org (accessed May 2013). Travel and Tourism Competitiveness Index. World Economic Forum. www.weforum.org (accessed May 2013). Global Gender Gap. World Economic Forum. www.weforum.org (accessed May 2013). Index of Democracy, 2012. Economist Intelligence Unit. http://www.eiu.com/Handlers/WhitepaperHandler.ashx?fi=Democracy-Index-2012.pdf&mode=wp&campaignid=DemocracyIndex12 (accessed May 2013). KOF Index of Globalization. http://globalization.kof.ethz.ch/ (accessed May 2013). Freedom in the World. Freedom House. http://www.freedomhouse.org/ (accessed May 2013). Index of Economic Liberty. Heritage Foundation.

84. Ibid.

85. Authors' analysis based on data from the International Monetary Fund. World Economic Outlook, online database. www.imf.org (accessed May 2013).

86. Ibid.

87. Authors' calculations based on various indicators. Ease of Doing Business Index, 2013. World Bank. http://www.doingbusiness.org/rankings (accessed May 2013). Human Development Index, 2013. United Nations. http://hdr.undp.org/en/statistics/hdi/ (accessed May 2013). Global Competitiveness Index, 2012–2013. World Economic Forum. www.weforum.org (accessed May 2013). Travel and Tourism Competitiveness Index. World Economic Forum. www.weforum.org (accessed May 2013). Global Gender Gap. World Economic Forum. www.weforum.org (accessed May 2013). Index of Democracy, 2012. Economist Intelligence Unit. http://www.eiu.com/Handlers/WhitepaperHandler.ashx?fi=Democracy-Index-2012.pdf&mode=wp&campaignid=DemocracyIndex12 (accessed May 2013). KOF Index of Globalization. http://globalization.kof.ethz.ch/ (accessed May 2013). Freedom in the World. Freedom House. http://www.freedomhouse.org/ (accessed May 2013). Index of Economic Liberty. Heritage Foundation.

88. Ibid.

89. Authors' analysis based on data from the International Monetary Fund. World Economic Outlook, online database. www.imf.org (accessed May 2013).

90. Ibid.

91. Authors' calculations based on various indicators. Ease of Doing Business Index, 2013. World Bank. http://www.doingbusiness.org/rankings (accessed May 2013). Human Development Index, 2013. United Nations. http://hdr.undp.org/en/statistics/hdi/ (accessed May 2013). Global Competitiveness Index, 2012–2013. World Economic Forum. www.weforum.org (accessed May 2013). Travel and Tourism

Competitiveness Index. World Economic Forum. www.weforum.org (accessed May 2013). Global Gender Gap. World Economic Forum. www.weforum.org (accessed May 2013). Index of Democracy, 2012. Economist Intelligence Unit. http://www.eiu.com/Handlers/WhitepaperHandler.ashx?fi=Democracy-Index-2012.pdf&mode=wp&campaignid=DemocracyIndex12 (accessed May 2013). KOF Index of Globalization. http://globalization.kof.ethz.ch/ (accessed May 2013). Freedom in the World. Freedom House. http://www.freedomhouse.org/ (accessed May 2013). Index of Economic Liberty. Heritage Foundation.

92. Ibid.

93. Authors' analysis based on data from the International Monetary Fund. World Economic Outlook, online database. www.imf.org (accessed May 2013).

RESOURCES

Adekane, J. (2011) Marketing Latin America revealed, http://www.eliteproductsourcing.com/wholesale/marketing-latin-america-revealed/ (accessed 7/27/11).

Agarwal, S. and Ramaswami, S. (1992) Choice of foreign entry mode: Impact of ownership, location and internalization factors. *Journal of International Business Studies*, 23, (1), 1–27.

All Business (2011) Mergers: A definition. *All Business Magazine*. D&B Company business glossary, http://www.allbusiness.com/glossaries/merger/4944560-1.html.

Banco Mundial (2012) *Doing business 2013: Regulaciones inteligentes para las pequeñas y medianas empresas* (10a. edición). Washington: Estados Unidos.

Cecolim, A. and Hestbaek, P. (2012) Logistics 2012: A special intermodal South America Report: Latin trade special supplement. Integrating supply chain is key step for Latin American companies seeking lower costs, reduced transit time and improved customs services.

Chowla, P. (2011) Ha llegado la hora de un nuevo consenso. Bretton Woods Project.

CNBC (2013) Sao Paulo Bovespa index, http://data.cnbc.com/quotes/.BVSP-BR/tab/2.

Comparing Cultures Systematically Describing Cultural Differences, http://www.sagepub.com/upm-data/23125_Chapter_3.pdf. Adapted from Hofstede, G. (1991) *Culture and organizations: Software of the mind*. London.

Cultural Dimension of Doing Business in Latin America (n.d.) http://blog.davincimeetingrooms.com/2013/02/28/you-can-do-business-in-latin-america/.

Deep, R. and Parek, H. (2005) Logistics supply chain challenges and opportunities. *American Shipper*.

Diaz, A., Lacayo, J., and Salcedo, L.A. (2007) Selling to mom and pops, stores in Latin America. *McKinsey Quarterly*, Special Edition, 71–81.

ECLAC (2009) Physical infrastructure and regional integration, http://www.cepal.org/usi/noticias/bolfall/9/42049/FAL-280-WEB-ENG.pdf.

Economist Intelligence Unit (n.d.) http://www.eiu.com/Handlers/WhitepaperHandler.ashx?fi=Democracy-Index-2012.pdf&mode=wp&campaignid=DemocracyIndex12.

Economist Intelligence Unit (2012) Democracy index 2012: Democracy at a standstill, obtained from www.eiu.com.

Euromonitor (2010) Latin America enjoys mobile telephone boom. Euromonitor global market research, http://www.euromonitor.com/.

European Travel Commission New Media Trend Watch (n.d.) http://www.newmediatrendwatch.com/regional-overview/104-latin-america (accessed 7/27/11).

FAL (Facilitation of Transport and Trade in Latin America and the Caribbean) (2009) The economic infrastructure gap in Latin America and the Caribbean. *Bulletin, 293* (1), www.cepal.org/transporte.

Feffer, R. (2011) http://www.bootsnall.com/articles/11–04/traditional-markets-in-latin-america-a-guide-for-first-time-shoppers.html, 7 April.

Ferreiro, J., Gómez, C., Rodríguez, C., and Correa, E. (2007) Liberalización financiera en América Latina: efectos sobre los mercados financieros locales. Universidad del País Vasco. Universidad Autónoma Nacional de México.

Freedom House (2013) Freedom in the world, http://www.freedomhouse.org/.

Heritage Foundation (2013) Index of economic liberty, www.heritage.org.

IDB (2010) Microfinance in Latin America, http://www.themix.org/sites/default/files/2010%20Micro finance%20Americas%20-%20The%20Top%20100%20-%20EN.pdf.

IDB (2012) The benefits of logistics investments: Opportunities for Latin America and the Caribbean, http://people.hofstra.edu/jean-paul_rodrigue/downloads/JP_Rodrigue_The_Benefits_of_Logistics_Investments_Final.pdf.

IMAP (2010) Retail industry global report 2010. IMAP reports for 2010, http://www.imap.com/imap/media/resources/IMAPRetailReport8_23CB9AA9C6EBB.pdf.

IMF.org (2010) www.imf.org.

InfoTechnology (2012) Entrevista con Andrés Moreno, http://www.infotechnology.com/entreprenerds/Moreno-de-OpenEnglish-El-inversor-estadounidense-se-fija-en-el-potencial-regional-de-un-proyecto-20121218-0002.html.

International Monetary Fund (n.d.) World economic outlook, online database, obtained from http://www.imf.org/external/pubs/ft/weo/2013/01/weodata/weoselgr.aspx.

Jácome, L. (2006) Metas de inflación en América Latina: Lecciones para Guatemala. Jornadas Económicas, Banco de Guatemala.

KOF (n.d.) Index of globalization, http://globalization.kof.ethz.ch/.

Latin American Monitor (2011) The shape of growth in 2011. *Business Monitor International*, www.latinamericanmonitor.com.

Li, H. (2011) Marketing to Latin America: It's all about image, http://www.ibtimes.com/articles/123445/20110316/marketing-to-latin-america-brand-image.htm (accessed 7/27/11).

Map of Latin America (n.d.) http://www.volunteerlatinamerica.com/map/index.html.

McKinsey (2010) Understanding Latin America's supply chain risks, http://mkqpreview1.qdweb.net/PDF-Download.aspx?ar=1958.

Myers, H. M. and Lubliner, M. J. (1998) *The marketer's guide to successful package design*. Lincolnwood, Chicago, IL: NTC Business.

Nielsen, L. (2012) Importance of communication in the business world. *Global Advertising and Culture*, http://smallbusiness.chron.com/importance-communication-business-world-2877.html.

OECD (2011) Latin American Economic Outlook 2011. Centre de Development OECD, http://www.latame-conomy.org/en/.

OECD/Economic Commission for Latin America and the Caribbean (2013) *Perspectivas económicas de América Latina 2013: Políticas de pymes para el cambio estructural*, OECD Publishing, doi: 10.1787/leo-2013-es.

One World Nation (2012) Countries of the world by area, http://www.nationsonline.org/oneworld/countries_by_area.htm/ (accessed 11/3/12).

Organización de Cooperación y Desarrollo Económico, Comisión Económica para América Latina y El Caribe (2012) Perspectivas Económicas de América Latina 2013: Políticas de PYMES para el cambio estructural.

Paluck, N. (2011) Doing business with Web 2.0 in Latin America: Position yourself as an expert, http://www.livinginperu.com/business-1240-marketing-doing-business-with-web-2-0-latin-america-position-yourself-as-an-expert (accessed 7/27/11).

Penaloza, L., Toulouse, N., and Visconti, L.M. (Eds.) (2012) *Management: A cultural perspective.* New York: Routledge.

Piccone, T. J. (2010) Perilous times for Latin America. In Griffiths, R. J. (Ed.), *Annual Editions: 2010-2013.* New York: McGraw-Hill, 170–171.

Programa de las Naciones Unidas para el Desarrollo (2013) Informe sobre desarrollo humano 2013 *El ascenso del sur: Progreso humano en un mundo diverso.*

Samli, C. A. (2011) *Infrastructuring: The key to achieving economic development, productivity and quality of life.* New York: Springer.

Santos, M. & Ramirez, L. (2012) Investigation on MD campaign. Presented at Universidad del Itsmo, Guatemala, as part of the conference in the course of marketing strategies.

SELA (2011) Physical infrastructure for integration in Latin America and the Caribbean. *Sistemaeconomico Latinomericano y del Caribe,* June.

TeleGeography (2011) Global Comms insight, http://www.telegeography.com/research-services/global comms-insight/index.html.

Transparency International (2013) Corruptions perceptions index 2012, obtained from http://www.transparency.org/research/cpi/overview.

US Commercial Service (2010) Mining industry overview and exporting opportunities in Latin America. Trade Winds Forum for the Americas, http://www.globalvirginia.com/Information%20Documents/Latin_America_ Mining_Guide.pdf.

UN Comtrade (2011) UN Comtrade statistics division, http://comtrade.un.org/db/.

United Nations (2013) Human development index, obtained from http://hdr.undp.org/en/statistics/hdi/.

World Bank (2013) Ease of doing business index 2013, online database, obtained from http://www.doing business.org/rankings.

World Economic Forum (2011) Global gender gap, obtained from www.weforum.org.

World Economic Forum (2011) Travel and tourism competitiveness report 2011, Geneva, obtained from www.weforum.org.

World Economic Forum (2013) Global competitiveness index, 2012–2013, www.weforum.org.

World Religions (n.d.) http://www.google.com/imgres?imgurl=http://www.proprofs.com/quiz-school/upload/yuiupload/377981806.jpg&imgrefurl=http://www.proprofs.com/quiz-school/story.php%3Ftitle%3Dworld-religions-test&usg=__6iT4BnPGDcqz5aaGeIIBOWbMjhY=&h=640&w=865&sz=107&hl=en&start=6&sig2=aY3AXVezmHtNv_-KnPi6EA&zoom=1&tbnid=mzqvGAq-PY0CEM:&tbnh=107&tbnw=145&ei=wlTlUfuiGs7h4AO7_IDYDA&itbs=1&sa=X&ved=0CDIQrQMwBQ.

World Bank (2011) GDP per capita data, http://data.worldbank.org/.

INDEX